Real-life entrepreneurs succeed by challenging dominant business models. Progress in entrepreneurship research should match this logic. This book offers many disruptive yet actionable ideas that entrepreneurship scholars can use to challenge dominant assumptions and to publish interesting entrepreneurship research.

Carlo Salvato, Professor, Bocconi University, Italy

Challenging Entrepreneurship Research is intentionally a mind-expanding book. It not only embraces and extends the consensus (or mainstream) lines of thought in entrepreneurship's mainstream, but also brings in the dissensus, non-mainstream, lines of thought. Together, the book is a thoughtful dialectic. I found myself constantly jumping back and forth in the book connecting and contrasting the ideas of the different authors, invariably returning new insights and thoughts about the process of entrepreneurship research in which we all share.

Jerome Katz, Professor, Saint Louis University, USA

Entrepreneurship research has undoubtedly come a long way over the past two decades both conceptually and empirically and now is an opportune time to take stock and question the direction of travel. This stimulating volume provides a number of insightful contributions that help point the way forward. Researchers increasingly need to engage with practice and policy, not only to ensure the relevance of entrepreneurship research but also to identify interesting research questions and this is an important message reinforced in this volume. As the contributions make clear, such engagement involves consideration of the dark side of entrepreneurship as a complement to the overwhelmingly positive perspectives that have previously dominated the agenda.

Mike Wright, Professor, Imperial College London, UK

Well-timed, this volume represents a much-needed contribution to a growing research literature that has taken as its task to present challenging entrepreneurship research that also challenges entrepreneurship research. This is an important contribution to a more reflexive, indeed entrepreneurial entrepreneurship research.

Daniel Hjorth, Professor, Copenhagen Business School, Denmark

Because entrepreneurship has grown and become legitimate there is a danger that scholars will "play it safe" and not pursue sufficiently interesting research. Challenging Entrepreneurship Research helps us to question our assumptions and broaden our thinking by offering chapters from different perspectives provoking thoughts about how to move the field forward.

Dean A. Shepherd, David H. Jacobs Chair in Strategic Entrepreneurship, Indiana University, USA

T0291199

Challenging Entrepreneurship Research

The growth of entrepreneurship research has been accompanied by an increased convergence and institutionalization of the field. In many ways this is of course positive, but it also represents how the field has become "mainstream" with the concomitant risk that individual scholars become embedded in a culture and incentive system that emphasizes and rewards incremental research questions, while reducing the incentives for scholars to conduct challenging research.

This book challenges this status quo from accepted theories, methodologies and paradigmatic assumptions, to the relevance (or lack of) for contemporary practice and the impact of key journals on scholars' directions in entrepreneurship research.

An invited selection of the younger generation of scholars within the field of entrepreneurship research adopt a critical and constructive posture on what has been achieved in entrepreneurship research, the main assumptions which underlie it, but also open up new paths for creative entrepreneurship research in the future. This is a must-read for all scholars, educators and advanced students in entrepreneurship research.

Hans Landström is Professor in Entrepreneurship at Lund University, Sweden.

Annaleena Parhankangas is Assistant Professor at the University of Illinois at Chicago, USA.

Alain Fayolle is Professor of Entrepreneurship, the founder and director of the Entrepreneurship Research Centre at EM Lyon Business School, France.

Philippe Riot is Head of the Strategy, Organizations and Entrepreneurship Department of EMLYON Business School, France.

Routledge Rethinking Entrepreneurship Research

Edited by Alain Fayolle and Philippe Riot

The current focus on entrepreneurship as a purely market-based phenomenon and an unquestionably desirable economic and profitable activity leads to undervaluing and under researching important issues in relation to power, ideology or phenomenology. New postures, new theoretical lenses and new approaches are needed to study entrepreneurship as a contextualized and socially embedded phenomenon. The objective of this series therefore is to adopt a critical and constructive posture towards the theories, methods, epistemologies, assumptions and beliefs which dominate mainstream thinking. It aims to provide a forum for scholarship which questions the prevailing assumptions and beliefs currently dominating entrepreneurship research and invites contributions from a wide range of different communities of scholars, which focus on novelty, diversity and critique.

Rethinking Entrepreneurship
Debating research orientations
Edited by Alain Fayolle and Philippe Riot

Family Entrepreneurship
Rethinking the research agenda
Kathleen Randerson, Cristina Bettinelli, Alain Fayolle and Giovanna Dossena

Challenging Entrepreneurship Research
Edited by Hans Landström, Annaleena Parhankangas, Alain Fayolle and Philippe Riot

Challenging Entrepreneurship Research

Edited by
Hans Landström,
Annaleena Parhankangas, Alain Fayolle
and Philippe Riot

LONDON AND NEW YORK

First published 2016
by Routledge

2 Park Square, Milton Park, Abingdon, Oxfordshire OX14 4RN
52 Vanderbilt Avenue, New York, NY 10017

Routledge is an imprint of the Taylor & Francis Group, an informa business

First issued in paperback 2019

British Library Cataloguing in Publication Data
A catalogue record for this book is available from the British Library

Library of Congress Cataloging in Publication Data
   Challenging entrepreneurship research / edited by Hans Landström,
Annaleena Parhankangas, Alain Fayolle and Philippe Riot.
   pages cm. -- (Routledge rethinking entrepreneurship research)
   Includes bibliographical references and index.
   ISBN 978-1-138-92231-0 (hardback) -- ISBN 978-1-315-68591-5 (ebook)
   1. Entrepreneurship--Research. 2. Entrepreneurship--Study and teaching. I.
Landström, Hans, editor.
   HB615.C5186 2016
   338'.04072--dc23
   2015028243

ISBN: 978-1-138-92231-0 (hbk)
ISBN: 978-0-367-87306-6 (pbk)

Typeset in Bembo
by Taylor & Francis Books

Contents

List of illustrations

Figures

Tables

Boxes

List of contributors

Gry Agnete Alsos is Professor in Entrepreneurship and Innovation at Bodø Graduate School of Business, University of Nordland, Norway, where she currently also acts as Associate Dean of Research. She conducts research within areas such as business start-up processes, portfolio entrepreneurship, rural entrepreneurship, gender perspectives to entrepreneurship and innovation, as well as entrepreneurship and innovation policies. She is particularly interested in how different types of entrepreneurs develop their ventures and how they acquire and utilize knowledge and other resources in these processes.

Ester Barinaga is Professor (mso) in Social Entrepreneurship at the Department of Management, Politics and Philosophy at the Copenhagen Business School, Denmark. She has published articles in, among others, *Geoforum*, *Human Relations*, *Ethnicities*, and *Journal of Social Entrepreneurship*. Her latest books are *Social Entrepreneurship: Cases and Concepts* (2014) and *Betongen berättar: Handbok för muralaktivister* (2015). Her current work focuses on concepts, tools, and strategies that may help us better design organizations and initiatives aimed at social change in general, and the dissolution of the immigrant condition in particular.

Henrik Berglund is Associate Professor at the Department of Technology Management and Economics at Chalmers University of Technology, Sweden. His research interests include management of technological change, entrepreneurship as method, venture capital, economics of entrepreneurship, and qualitative methodology. Current research projects include a phenomenological investigation of how early stage venture capitalists view start-up patenting, and an action-research project focusing on prescriptive methods of entrepreneurship with special emphasis on the lean start-up approach.

Fabienne Bornard has been developing entrepreneurship education in the Inseec Business School (former ESC Chambery), France, since 2000, after 10 years of experiences in the creation and development of small businesses. She got a Ph.D. in Entrepreneurship in Savoy University, France, in 2007, on the subject of the social representation of the company by its creator and its influences on the entrepreneurial process. She teaches entrepreneurship, strategy and innovation and creativity. Her research interests are the entrepreneur's cognition and entrepreneurial education.

Alex Coad is Senior Research Fellow at SPRU (Science Policy Research Unit) at the University of Sussex, UK. Alex is also an Associate Editor at *Research Policy*. His research interests include firm growth, entrepreneurship and innovation. From June 2015 onwards, Alex starts as Economic Analyst at the European Commission (JRC-IPTS, Sevilla).

Caroline Essers is Assistant Professor in Strategic Human Resource Management at the Radboud University Nijmegen, Faculty of Management, the Netherlands. Caroline's research focuses at the social dynamics of entrepreneurship, such as the identity constructions of (female migrant) entrepreneurs and their networking. She uses diverse perspectives in her research on entrepreneurship, such as intersectionality, postcolonial feminist theory and social constructivist approaches like the narrative/life-story approach. Her work has been published in *Organization Studies, Organization, Human Relations, Gender, Work and Organization, British Journal of Management, Entrepreneurship and Regional Development*, and *International Journal of Entrepreneurial Behaviour and Research*. She is an Associate Editor for *Gender, Work and Organization*.

Matthias Fink is Head of the IFI Institute for Innovation Management at the JKU Linz, Austria and Professor in Innovation and Entrepreneurship at the IIMP, ARU Cambridge, UK. Matthias holds a Ph.D. and a postdoctoral qualification from WU Vienna. In research, Matthias' focus is on entrepreneurship as a driver of innovation and change in regional contexts, entrepreneurial finance and ethical issues in business research. His research has been published in journals such as *Journal of Business Venturing, Entrepreneurship Theory and Practice, British Journal of Management, Journal of Banking and Finance, Technological Forecasting and Social Change* as well as *Regional Studies*.

Denise Fletcher is Professor of Entrepreneurship and Innovation at the University of Luxembourg where she is Academic Director of the Management Group and Study Director for the Masters in Entrepreneurship and Innovation program. Prior to this she held a Senior Lecturer role at the University of Sheffield, UK, becoming a Reader in Entrepreneurship and Family Business in 2011. Utilizing theories from relational sociology, Denise's academic work centers on explaining how time, context, action and interaction cohere in the production of entrepreneurial forms of work in owner-managed, spousal, sibling, team-based or family enterprises. She has published widely in the small business and entrepreneurship journals and is also involved in running a small business with her partner.

Chrystelle Gaujard is Lecturer at a French engineering school, HEI. She started her career as a junior consultant for an innovation and strategy consulting firm. Her doctoral work focused on the start-up organization and management. Since 2009, she is responsible for the students and professional entrepreneurship programs. She is also involved in the ADICODE device (Atelier de l'Innovation et du Codesign), designing and running creative sessions for innovation projects. Her research work focuses on entrepreneurship and innovation education in the research lab LEM (Lille Economie Management).

Isabella Hatak is Associate Professor at the IFI Institute for Innovation Management at the JKU Linz and at the Institute for Small Business Management and Entrepreneurship at the WU Vienna, Austria. She holds a Ph.D. and a postdoctoral qualification from the WU Vienna and an MSc in coaching and organizational development. Isabella is a visiting fellow to the Institute for International Management Practice at ARU Cambridge. Her interdisciplinary work was published in journals such as *Journal of Business Ethics, Family Business Review, Journal of Managerial Psychology* and *Technological Forecasting and Social Change*.

Steffen Korsgaard is Associate Professor at Aarhus University, Denmark and Adjunct Associate Professor at University of Oslo, Norway. His main research interests include entrepreneurship theory and the social and spatial context of entrepreneurial processes. He is a member of the iCARE research group at Aarhus University, where he is involved in research and development of entrepreneurship education. His research has been published in journals such as *Entrepreneurship Theory and Practice, International Small Business Journal* and *Entrepreneurship and Regional Development*.

Richard Lang is a Marie Curie Research Fellow at the School of Social Policy at University of Birmingham, UK and an Assistant Professor at the IFI Institute for Innovation Management at JKU Linz, Austria. After his Ph.D. studies at WU Vienna and KU Leuven, Belgium, he received an APART-fellowship of the Austrian Academy of Sciences and was a William Plowden Research Fellow at the University of Birmingham. His research interests include social capital and networks, social/community entrepreneurship, cooperative and community-led housing, and urban/regional development. He published in journals such as *Voluntas, Technological Forecasting and Social Change* and *European Planning Studies*.

Daniela Maresch is Assistant Professor at the IFI Institute for Innovation Management at the JKU Linz, Austria. She holds a Ph.D. from WU Vienna and WWU Münster, Germany, as well as an LL.M. (WU) in Business Law. Besides her career in academia, Daniela worked in financial reporting for a major Austrian utility and in corporate law for a renowned Viennese law firm. Her research is at the intersection of innovation, finance and business law: trust in bank lending, social aspects of disruptive technologies and IP protection in business angel investments. She recently published in *Journal of Financial Research*.

Paul Nightingale is Professor and Deputy Director of SPRU, the Science Policy Research Unit, at the University of Sussex, UK. He is Editor of

Research Policy and formerly Editor of *Industrial and Corporate Change*. His work covers the analysis and governance of technical change, and he has repeatedly been published in entrepreneurship.

Noreen O'Shea obtained her Ph.D. from the University of Sussex, UK, in 2009. She has been an Associate Professor and Researcher in Entrepreneurship at Novancia Business School, Paris, since then, where she teaches on the Master and MSc programs. She currently coordinates the entrepreneurship track in the Master program. Her research topics include the construction of professional identity and the role of tacit knowledge in entrepreneurial contexts. She also studies developments in policy-making, particularly for women entrepreneurs.

Luke Pittaway is the Copeland Professor of Entrepreneurship and Director of the Center for Entrepreneurship at Ohio University (Athens, OH), USA. He was formerly the William A. Freeman Distinguished Chair in Free Enterprise and the Director of the Center for Entrepreneurial Learning and Leadership at Georgia Southern University where he managed programs in entrepreneurship until May 2013. Dr. Pittaway's research focuses on entrepreneurship education and learning and he has a range of other interests including: entrepreneurial behavior; networking; entrepreneurial failure; business growth; and, corporate venturing.

Paul Selden completed his Ph.D. degree in 2008 at The Nottingham Trent University, UK. The focus of his doctoral thesis was a cognitive constructivist approach to the temporality of creative entrepreneurial decision-making processes. Since then he has continued to pursue an interest in the entrepreneurial experience of time into the areas of practical narrative, the relational causality of action-context relationships, the creation of entrepreneurial opportunities, the nature of context, entrepreneurship as an artificial science, entrepreneurship as a complex emergent system, as well as entrepreneurship theory development and modes of explanation.

Philippe Silberzahn is Associate Professor at EMLYON Business School, France, and Research Fellow at Ecole Polytechnique. His research interests lie at the intersection of strategy and entrepreneurship. He studies how businesses deal with radical uncertainty. He explores the role and actions of entrepreneurs in the process of market creation, and how large organizations manage strategic surprises and disruptions. He has published articles and books on these topics. He has over twenty years of prior industry experience as an entrepreneur and CEO. He holds an MSc in Computer Science, an MS in Management from the Sorbonne University, an MBA from the London Business School, and a Ph.D. from Ecole Polytechnique.

Deirdre Tedmanson is Program Director for Social Sciences in the School of Psychology, Social Work and Social Policy at the University of South Australia, a member of its Centre for Social Change and a Research Scholar with the

Centre for Aboriginal Economic Policy Research at the Australian National University. Deirdre's research focuses on participatory action research with Aboriginal organizations and communities on policy and service issues including mental health and social emotional well-being; gender and cultural aspects of social enterprise; and Indigenous entrepreneurship. She has published widely including in *Organization, Gender, Work and Organization, the Management Learning Journal, Journal of Management Inquiry* and *International Journal of Entrepreneurial Behaviour and Research.*

Olivier Toutain is Associate Professor in Entrepreneurship and Managing Director of the incubator at Burgundy School of Business, Dijon, France. Before making an academic career he has a long professional experience as managing director of a business support agency in France and as an entrepreneur within the consulting industry. His research interests include entrepreneurship, entrepreneurship education and entrepreneurial processes, and he has published his research at different conferences and in publications such as *Entreprendre & Innover* and *L'Expansion Entrepreneuriat*. He is also an expert in entrepreneurship education at OECD.

Richard Tunstall is Lecturer in Enterprise at the Centre of Enterprise and Entrepreneurship Studies, University of Leeds, UK, and Visiting Scholar at Aarhus University, Denmark. He is Chair of the Entrepreneurship Studies Network Special Interest Group, Vice-President (UK) of the European Council of Small Business and Associate Editor of the International Journal of Entrepreneurial Behaviour and Research. Following a Bachelors in English Literature and Masters in Entrepreneurial Studies, his Ph.D. took a social constructionist approach to exploring social processes in internal corporate venturing. He has published peer-reviewed papers in the areas of corporate entrepreneurship, entrepreneurship education and rural entrepreneurship.

Karl Wennberg is Professor in Management at the Stockholm School of Economics and Deputy Director at Institute of Analytical Sociology, Linköping University, Sweden. He sits on the Editorial Boards of *Academy of Management Journal, Journal of Business Venturing, Strategic Entrepreneurship Journal* and *Entrepreneurship Theory and Practice*, and *International Small Business Journal*. His work focuses broadly on entrepreneurship, organizational change, and the macro-level implications of organizational dynamics.

Caroline Verzat graduated from ESSEC Business School in France. She also holds a Ph.D. in Sociology of Organization (University of Paris IX-Dauphine). She started her professional career as an organizational consultant. Then she managed the innovation department at Ecole Centrale de Lille. In 2009 she joined Novancia as Professor in Entrepreneurship. She graduated from the HDR (Habilitation à Diriger des Recherches) on entrepreneurial mind-set education in 2012 at Grenoble University. She joined the research lab REGARDS at Reims University where she is Associate Researcher. Her research interests focus on entrepreneurship education and coaching.

1 Institutionalization of entrepreneurship as a scholarly field

Consequences and challenges

Hans Landström, Annaleena Parhankangas, Alain Fayolle and Philippe Riot

1.1 The aims of the book

In order to create a dynamic and viable field of research it is fundamental that scholars in entrepreneurship are able to formulate interesting research questions and conduct interesting research. If they fail in these respects, the research field will become less attractive and over time few scholars will take any notice of it. Therefore, 'interestingness' is necessary for the survival and growth of entrepreneurship as a research field (Frank and Landström 2016).

Interestingness could be regarded as something personal and subjective. But it is not only a matter of idiosyncratic opinions – there are collectively held assessments regarding, for example, topics that are perceived as interesting and theories and methodologies that are popular (Alvesson and Sandberg 2013). Obviously, what is regarded as interesting depends on the audience, and in entrepreneurship research we can identify many potential audiences from a set of fellow researchers, students, entrepreneurs, investors, media, policy-makers, etc. In order to be interesting, entrepreneurship researchers need to attract at least one of these audiences – the wider the audience finding the research interesting the more impact it will have (Shugan 2003).

When asking scholars what they regard as interesting, a lot of different answers will be given. For example, a study can raise an important issue in society, use an innovative method and design, or provide findings that are applicable in practice (Bartunek, Rynes and Ireland 2006; Das and Long 2010; Alvesson and Sandberg 2013). However, in his seminal work in 1971, Davis argued that interesting research must be something more – our studies need to challenge some, but not all, of our assumptions about a phenomenon.

In recent decades entrepreneurship as an academic field has grown significantly – all over the world academic departments and centres offer courses and education programmes on entrepreneurship, in addition to conducting research on entrepreneurship and/or related issues. This development has contributed to the increased quality of entrepreneurship research, and entrepreneurship has matured as a research field, moved toward 'normal science' and received greater legitimacy, i.e., become institutionalized in the academic arena. Due to this institutionalization, current research within the field often fails to challenge our taken-for-granted assumptions about entrepreneurship and entrepreneurs.

Although recent progress cannot be disputed, we believe that the time has come for a substantive rethink of our research – a rethink that will require challenging some of the assumptions that we have in entrepreneurship research. Such rethinking can be done within the framework of mainstream entrepreneurship research as well as from more critical-paradigmatic and ideological perspectives.

In this book we hope to initiate a debate among entrepreneurship scholars about the future direction of entrepreneurship as a scholarly field. We will try to provoke such a debate and present a series of chapters that in different ways – from within and from outside the mainstream field – will try to challenge some of the assumptions and accepted research practices in entrepreneurship research. We believe that this debate is particularly timely and will serve the field well. For example, entrepreneurship scholars have recently begun to challenge prevailing assumptions about theory and methodological practices (Zahra and Wright 2011, Special Issue in *Entrepreneurship and Regional Development* 2013; Shepherd 2015).

1.2 Development of entrepreneurship as a research field

History can always be described in different ways, depending on the focus of the analysis and the way we interpret history. In this introductory section, we will present our view of the evolution of entrepreneurship as a research field and show the institutionalization process of entrepreneurship research in academia. In our interpretation of history we will use a model developed by Hambrick and Chen (2008), in which they argue that emerging research fields seem to follow an institutionalization process, including three overlapping phases: (1) differentiation of the field from existing fields, (2) resource mobilization to ensure a critical mass of scholars and secure control of the resources needed, and (3) legitimacy building in the eyes of the academic establishment.

1.2.1 Early contributions to entrepreneurship research

During most of the nineteenth and twentieth centuries, entrepreneurship could be regarded as a fairly marginal topic in some mainstream disciplines such as economics, economic history, sociology and psychology (Landström and Benner 2010; Landström 2014). The development of our knowledge could mainly be attributed to individual scholars, of whom Schumpeter is probably the best known economist with an interest in entrepreneurship (Schumpeter 1912, 1934), but we should also mention Knight (1921) and representatives of the Austrian School of Economics, for example, Kirzner (1973). In the 1940s, a number of scholars (e.g. Landes, Gerschenkron and Redlich) anchored in economic history, began to take an interest in entrepreneurship, and later, scholars from psychology and sociology entered the field, of whom McClelland (1961) is probably the most famous.

This marginalization of entrepreneurship in mainstream disciplines may be partly explained by a limited interest in entrepreneurship and small businesses in society. Economic development and dynamics were assumed to be based on mass production and large companies were seen as superior in terms of efficiency. The marginalization may also be explained by changes within some mainstream disciplines, for example, economics became increasingly formalized and mathematically oriented, which made it difficult to include the entrepreneur in models.

1.2.2 Entrepreneurship as a research field

In the 1970s and 1980s, entrepreneurship gradually started the journey towards becoming a field in its own right. This was an era of 'academic entrepreneurs' characterized by an enthusiastic but small and fragmented research community, whose members accomplished many pioneering achievements both in terms of (a) new knowledge, and (b) different initiatives, for example, conferences, journals and professional organizations (Aldrich 2012; Landström 2005). These early achievements contributed to the successful differentiation of the field from other disciplines, making it more visible not only to researchers but also, and more importantly, to policy-makers and politicians, providing it with 'external' legitimacy.

The 1990s was a decade characterized by strong resource mobilization including extensive growth of the research community and the building of a strong infrastructure – new publication opportunities, social networks (conferences and professional organizations) and more sources of funding – what Aldrich (2012) called 'institutional entrepreneurship' involving collective action by many scholars, groups and associations. However, the research became highly fragmented – it was a 'melting pot' for scholars from various fields, thus a range of new research issues emerged and different methodological approaches and concepts/theories were imported from other fields.

In the 2000s we can identify a trend towards increased convergence and institutionalization of the field. In order to become a legitimate academic research field, entrepreneurship research has started to focus on a reasonable and coherent set of research questions and conform to the norms and standards of well-established fields by adopting a 'normal science' approach. Over time there has been a stronger focus on robustness in entrepreneurship studies, reflected in the use of larger samples, pre-tested variables, sophisticated statistical analyses, etc. The legitimacy of the field has shifted from external actors (such as policy-makers, media, etc.) to an academic legitimacy. To some extent entrepreneurship has become 'mainstream' – thousands of scholars around the world regard themselves as entrepreneurship scholars and teachers, while in many countries entrepreneurship is considered an integral part of the academic system.

Predicting the future is always difficult (and maybe even impossible), but following the trends in entrepreneurship research that we have seen over the last couple of years, we expect that the institutionalization process will continue. We can identify a trend towards an increased diffusion of entrepreneurship research, for example, in different contexts (e.g. a growing interest in entrepreneurship research in China and the rest of Asia), in different disciplines (e.g. economic geography, economic history and economics), and a differentiation of entrepreneurship as a phenomenon (e.g. social entrepreneurship and public entrepreneurship). But we can also identify a trend indicating that entrepreneurship research is becoming more and more influential with a greater impact on mainstream disciplines, represented by the increased penetration of entrepreneurship research into top management, strategy and organization behaviour journals. On the other hand, we can identify a growing unease with current mainstream entrepreneurship research on the part of scholars representing more critical and often alternative paradigmatic perspectives.

This brief summary demonstrates that over the years much progress has been made and we know a lot more about entrepreneurship today than we did 30 or 40 years ago (Landström 2005), and there has also been a large amount of interesting research:

- The field has produced much high-quality research that has provided us with a great deal of knowledge about entrepreneurship and small business, as well as inspiring others in their own research, teaching and practice (Davidsson 2013).
- The social structure of the field is characterized by an intense co-production of research from international collaboration and many networks of scholars with similar interests (Landström 2005).
- A strong infrastructure in terms of journals, conferences, teaching opportunities, PhD courses, role models, etc. (Aldrich 2012).

We will also argue that over the years, entrepreneurship has been regarded as an interesting field of research and the field has grown significantly (more or less independently of the measures used), for which there might be several reasons:

- Entrepreneurship is inherently interesting. For example, it is a phenomenon that focuses on novelty and change, that looks at the unknown and is based on nonlinear thinking.
- Entrepreneurship has been the subject of political and policy interest – a 'tool' for solving all kinds of societal and economic problems.
- Entrepreneurship has been regarded as interesting by scholars from different fields – a large number of scholars have rushed into this emerging and promising field of research.

1.2.3 Conclusion: increased institutionalization of the field

The conclusion that we can make from this historical retrospect is that entrepreneurship has become more and more institutionalized and received greater academic legitimacy. This institutionalization has been accompanied by an 'international isomorphism' (Aldrich 2000) that has created a global 'uniformity' of entrepreneurship research. Historically and culturally entrepreneurship is anchored in an Anglo-Saxon research paradigm. The US is regarded as the leading country for entrepreneurship research and as such, is a 'role model' for entrepreneurship research around the world. In addition, over recent decades we can identify a strong trend towards what we will call a 'business school syndrome'. In many countries universities have shifted from elite institutions to general public organizations for the purpose of serving as an engine of economic growth in society – moving towards marketization and managerialism, including stronger performance indicators to judge quality, i.e., university rankings and individual citation rates (Harley, Muller-Camen and Collin 2004).

These trends point to a stronger institutionalization of entrepreneurship research, which carries a risk that individual scholars will become embedded in a culture and incentive system that places greater emphasis on the more incremental research issues, thus reducing the incentive to conduct challenging, long-term and 'interesting' research. Studies will contribute less and less, merely creating nuances of what we already know. Robust studies are of course important, but we also need to stimulate entrepreneurship scholars, especially PhD candidates, to formulate challenging and interesting research questions and conduct interesting research. Thus, it is important that we start to challenge the underlying assumptions that we have in entrepreneurship research and start to rethink our research – building a new research agenda for the future. We hope that this book will contribute to the discussion.

1.3 Subjects, methods and theories: three key issues for research

One of our main concerns about entrepreneurship as a scholarly field is that we believe many of the assumptions within the field are rooted in the evolution of entrepreneurship research. In many cases these assumptions emerged in the early days and have persisted for a long period of time. In this respect we can talk about 'imprintings', i.e., the research develops characteristics that reflect prominent features of the environment that will persist over time despite significant environmental changes, and 'path dependencies' that represent a more steady accumulation of incremental changes that gain more and more predominance over time (Marquis and Tilcsik 2013). In our view, entrepreneurship research is in many ways based on assumptions that are rooted – imprinted and path dependent – in the early stages, which could be regarded as a 'sensitive period' of entrepreneurship research.

Following the arguments of Davis (1971), in order to become interesting we need to challenge the assumptions that have emerged since the early days of entrepreneurship research. Thus, in order to make entrepreneurship research more interesting in the future, we must take a closer look at the assumptions on which our research is anchored. Our assumptions will influence: (1) the subjects of our research, (2) the way in which we research entrepreneurship, i.e., our methods and methodological approaches, and (3) the theories and concepts that we use and develop within entrepreneurship research.

1.3.1 Imprinted research subjects in the 1970s and 1980s

We will argue that there are some 'imprinted' assumptions in entrepreneurship and in the subjects we study that were already assimilated in the early period of entrepreneurship research – in the 1970s and 1980s in the US (with a delay of 10 years in Europe), and the emergence of what today could be called the 'knowledge economy' – and ever since, these assumptions have been fairly persistent in our research on entrepreneurship.

In the 1970s and 1980s, entrepreneurship 'took off' as a response to the new societal challenges that emerged at that point in time, for example, technological breakthroughs (e.g. DNA and microprocessors), the introduction of institutional reforms (such as tax laws, deregulation of financial institutions, Bayh-Dole Act, etc.), the twin oil crises (1973 and 1979) that triggered uncertainty with regards to large corporations and the ability of large systems to provide new jobs, as well as to create new innovations and dynamics in society, a globalization of the world economy, a change of mentality when 'small is beautiful' became a catchword, and not least, political driving forces represented by Thatcher in the UK and Reagan in the US. All of the above made entrepreneurship an important element of the policy agenda in many countries.

During this 'sensitive period' some assumptions emerged that have been very persistent in entrepreneurship research, and we will elaborate on a few that have been imprinted in our research for a long time.

First, entrepreneurship as a research field is heavily rooted in a neoliberal capitalistic political ideology. It emerged during the 1970s and 1980s, influenced by the neo-liberal capitalistic political ideology of Thatcherism and Reaganism, which gives associations to concepts such as freedom, liberalism, market dominance and free individual choice. Thus, entrepreneurship has a political and ideological meaning. Looking at entrepreneurship research we can conclude that much of it seems to (1) focus on financial and economic value creation, (2) that it is often regarded as something positive and good for society – entrepreneurship creates new industries and jobs, and (3) that our knowledge about entrepreneurship has a US (or Anglo-Saxon) bias. We can of course challenge these assumptions with questions such as: What knowledge will emerge if we start from other power structures in society? What about entrepreneurship in other spheres of society and in other contexts? Is entrepreneurship truly a vehicle for economic and social mobility?

Second, we will argue that many of our research topics today are rooted in the challenges of yesterday (and not of today or tomorrow). Many of the research issues that have occupied entrepreneurship scholars for a long period of time relate to the challenges in the economy during the sensitive period of entrepreneurship research. Over time, we have seen a great deal of research on, for example, economic performance and growth, traditional masculine industries related to innovation and technology-based ventures, financial issues and venture capital, and individual-opportunity nexus. The obvious questions are: Are entrepreneurship scholars studying the main challenges in society today (e.g. in relation to the economic crisis, climate change, water constraints, social problems and integration, etc.) or are we studying old questions? In what way are entrepreneurship scholars visible in the main societal debate today?

1.3.2 Path dependencies in research methodologies

In a similar way, there are strong path dependencies when it comes to how we conduct our research – in the methodological approaches and in the methods that we use.

Empirical research is obvious in new fields: Before we can theorize the phenomenon we require a detailed empirical understanding of it (Eisenhardt 1989). Such understanding also strengthens the validity and power of the concepts and theories developed (Ghoshal 2005). However, when it comes to the way we conduct our research (methodological approaches and methods), we know from the internationalization of research (Edquist and Hommen 2009; Schott 1993) that countries regarded as 'leading' within a field will constitute a role model for others to follow. In this respect, entrepreneurship research is no exception, and ever since its 'take-off' in the 1970s and 1980s it has been rooted in a US research hegemony, with some path dependencies in the methodology.

In line with such argumentation, entrepreneurship is heavily anchored in a functionalist paradigmatic approach (Burrell and Morgan 1979; Grant and Perren 2002), indicating a focus on regularities, explanations, generalizations and knowledge accumulation. As a consequence, other paradigmatic approaches have been largely neglected, which might hamper our understanding of entrepreneurship and phenomena related to entrepreneurship. In addition, entrepreneurship is a rather mono-methodological field (Davidsson and Wiklund 2001; Edelman, Manolova and Brush 2009) dominated by (a) micro-level analysis (individual and firm levels of analysis), and (b) focus on rigour and sophistication, quantitative studies, large databases, archival data, pre-tested variables and advanced statistical analysis, but also (c) a fairly uncritical development of new knowledge in that we seldom find confirmatory and replicative studies or critical debates about the knowledge within the field.

If we assume that entrepreneurship is something unique characterized by high diversity, non-linear behaviour and sometimes non-rational thinking, where 'luck' may have a significant impact on the outcome – thus, a phenomenon that cannot be adequately explained by calculating the 'average' – we can question whether the methodologies and methods that we employ in contemporary entrepreneurship research really have the potential to capture its specifics.

1.3.3 Conceptual issues: theories and practice, dealing with rigour and relevance

Since the emergence of entrepreneurship in the 1970s and 1980s, there has been a strong belief that entrepreneurship knowledge will support policy and business practice by helping to solve societal problems and assisting entrepreneurs to ensure the success of their ventures. Relevance was in focus!

However, entrepreneurship research has become more and more institutionalized, which tends to favour rigour at the cost of relevance, while at the same time rigour promotes the institutionalization of the research field (Frank and Landström 2016). Thus, in this respect we have seen a 'new sensitive period' in entrepreneurship research where legitimacy is increasingly anchored in academia and to a lesser extent among external stakeholders such as practitioners and policy-makers. The research has also become more (a) influenced by high-ranked scientific journals and the norms that they impose, (b) influenced by research questions that are more 'gap-driven' – searching for gaps in existing knowledge, and (c) driven by the aim of being published in high-ranked journals, that is, inward looking with a tendency to lose contact with real-world issues. Rigour is in focus!

This change in the basis for legitimacy (from external stakeholder to academia) has created rigour-relevance frustration among many entrepreneurship scholars, thus triggering a debate about the gap between scientific rigour and practical relevance within entrepreneurship research. We can challenge this focus on rigour by asking the following questions: How can we make our research more 'relevant' and 'actionable'? How can we conduct research that is both rigorous and relevant?

1.4 Challenging the assumptions and accepted research practices in entrepreneurship research

We have argued that in order to create an interesting field in the future, we need to challenge some of the assumptions in entrepreneurship research, which is the intention of this book. We will describe the background and contents below.

1.4.1 The book project

The starting point of the book has different roots. In June 2013, EM Lyon organized the Babson Annual Conference in Lyon (France). On this occasion, a workshop entitled 'Enacting Entrepreneurship Out of the Box' was organized and based on the workshop it was decided to publish a book, 'Rethinking Entrepreneurship: Debating Research Orientations' in a new book series, 'Routledge Rethinking Entrepreneurship Research'.

In this second volume of the series we would try to challenge prevailing assumptions and research practices in entrepreneurship research. Experienced researchers mostly wrote the chapters in the first book. For the second book we have chosen to invite young scholars who all show the potential for a brilliant academic career to participate in the project and write a chapter in which they challenge some of the assumptions in entrepreneurship research.

Over a period of two years we completed three rounds of review work. A milestone in the project was the organization of a Professional Development

Workshop (PDW) at the 2014 Academy of Management Meeting in Philadelphia, at which a couple of chapters in the book were presented and discussed. The interest in the workshop was extensive and we had a lively discussion about the future of entrepreneurship research.

The outcome was that this book contains contributions that in different ways challenge some of our assumptions in entrepreneurship research – from the subjects that we research to our methodologies and theoretical approaches. As such, the book seeks to highlight some of the 'blind spots' shared by entrepreneurship scholars and open new avenues for further research. We hope that this book will serve as an impetus for lively discussion that will ultimately make entrepreneurship more diverse, inclusive, relevant and interesting for scholars, entrepreneurs and policy-makers.

1.4.2 Contributions in the book

The institutionalization of entrepreneurship as a research field has increasingly stimulated 'gap-spotting' behaviour and research has tended to become preoccupied by certain lines of thinking, leading to scholars feeling restricted and the evolution of the field becoming rather narrow. Therefore, in order to create a stimulating and interesting field it is important to challenge current assumptions and research practices. According to the argumentation in Chapter 7 by Denise Fletcher and Paul Seldon (see also Alvesson and Deetz 2000), we can challenge our assumptions about research in different ways. We have divided the contributions in the book into two parts. The first (Chapters 2 to 6) comprises contributions that challenge our assumptions anchored 'within' mainstream entrepreneurship research structuring of knowledge (what Alvesson and Deetz call 'consensus discourse'). The second part of the book (Chapters 7 to 11) contains contributions that challenge current entrepreneurship research based on a 'disruption' of mainstream research (or 'dissensus discourse') in the sense of a more critical ideology and paradigmatic approach that questions and challenges mainstream research.

We believe that the mix of 'consensus' and 'dissensus' contributions in the book will promote a more lively and fruitful discussion about the future of the field, as well as create different views on the 'interestingness' of the field. If only consensus-based discussions and critics can be heard, there is a risk that no real dynamics will occur, while if only dissensus-based criticism is expressed, there is a risk of mainstream scholars regarding the discussion as inappropriate and unhelpful.

Part I: contributions with a consensus-discourse focus

Part I of the book includes contributions that challenge some of the assumptions in entrepreneurship research from a 'consensus' perspective: the need to include more 'passion' in our research; create 'differences'; challenge the individual-opportunity nexus view of entrepreneurship that has dominated the discussion in entrepreneurship research since Shane and Venkataraman's seminal work in 2000; and challenge the policy assumptions in entrepreneurship research.

In Chapter 2, entitled 'Entrepreneurship research with passion: a note on the aesthetics of basic research', Matthias Fink and his colleagues argue that although entrepreneurship research has made a great deal of positive progress, it has been accompanied by increased institutionalization. The institutionalization process limits the leeway of individual scholars to focus on what they believe is interesting research and reduces their passion for unique and novel ideas. Thus, it hampers interesting research on entrepreneurship.

In this chapter, the authors borrow from the philosophy of aesthetics in order to understand why scholars' passion provides a key to creating interesting research and use two of their own studies to illustrate their argumentation. The lessons from the chapter can be summarized as follows:

- We need greater passion in entrepreneurship research! Studies conducted by passionate researchers are more 'beautiful' and also regarded as more interesting by their audience. Thus passion fosters 'beautiful' and interesting research.
- Within the more institutionalized context that we find in entrepreneurship research, academic leaders must allow greater space for intellectual freedom, reduce the competitive pressure and create more intense collaboration within and between research groups. Scholars need to 'fall in love' again with their research projects and free themselves from extrinsic motivation such as citations and rankings.

In the next chapter (Chapter 3) entitled 'Pragmatic entrepreneurs and institutionalized scholars? On the path-dependent nature of entrepreneurship scholarship', Henrik Berglund and Karl Wennberg start with the question: The essence of entrepreneurship is being different. If this is the case, why does so much of entrepreneurship research seem to be so very similar? They argue that the increased maturation and institutionalization of entrepreneurship as a scholarly field have led to greater influence from established research fields such as strategic management and organization theory, and as a consequence, an increased 'taking-for-grantedness' of research questions, unit of analysis and research designs. Thus, much entrepreneurship research becomes fairly narrow in focus and echoes mainstream disciplines.

Taking inspiration from real-world entrepreneurs and the philosophical tradition of pragmatism, the authors provide some suggestions for entrepreneurship research:

- Entrepreneurship scholars need to pay more attention to the fundamental nature of entrepreneurship and practising entrepreneurs.
- Entrepreneurs are pragmatic individuals and in the same way as real-world entrepreneurs, entrepreneurship scholars need to adopt a 'down to earth', actionable and pluralistic view of entrepreneurship.

- This pragmatic view of entrepreneurship calls for epistemological inspiration from pragmatic philosophy, theoretical inspiration from disciplines other than strategic management and organization theory, as well as methodological inspiration from a wide range of traditions.

Ever since Shane and Venkataraman presented their article 'The promise of entrepreneurship as a field of research' in the year 2000, the individual-opportunity nexus view of entrepreneurship has dominated the discussion in entrepreneurship research, while the works of Israel Kirzner and the Austrian School of Economics have strongly influenced theoretical as well as empirical works on entrepreneurship. Taking the Austrian economic tradition and Shane and Venkataraman's application of the theory as a starting point, the next two chapters challenge some of the assumptions made in these approaches. In the first one (Chapter 4), Steffen Korsgaard grapples with the Kirznerian heritage in the light of the financial crisis of 2008 and onwards. The financial crisis highlighted some economic, social and environmental consequences that challenged several of the assumptions and values embedded in the opportunistic exploitation mindset incorporated in the Kirznerian heritage. In his chapter, Korsgaard discusses three anomalies in the works by Kirzner: the socialized nature of entrepreneurship; the role of context in entrepreneurial processes; and the relationship between entrepreneurship and the environment.

On the basis of these anomalies, Korsgaard elaborates in detail on the Austrian economic tradition and explores how we could resolve these anomalies, while still retaining useful aspects of the Kirznerian heritage. Korsgaard argues for the following solutions to the three anomalies:

- A functional definition of entrepreneurship remains useful as it allows us to capture entrepreneurial phenomena irrespective of organizational forms and driving forces, but we need to re-interpret how this functional definition works and the outcomes it produces.

Therefore, we have to consider the following aspects:

a   We have to consider the function of entrepreneurship in terms of value creation more broadly than on a one-dimensional aspect such as 'economic value creation', and develop multidimensional conceptions of value and growth.

b   Kirzner's work is rooted in the concept of 'risk', but 'uncertainty' becomes central when the image of opportunity discovery is challenged – risk may tend to ignore the fundamental volatility in recent market trends – and uncertainty needs to play a more central role, together with a stronger focus on the issue of 'resources', in the conceptualization of the entrepreneurship function.

In the second one (Chapter 5), based on Shane and Venkataraman's seminal work in 2000, Gry Agnete Alsos elaborates on and challenges the individual-opportunity nexus view of entrepreneurship. The individual-opportunity nexus view focuses less on the characteristics of the individual entrepreneur and places greater emphasis on the combination of individuals and opportunities, thus enabling entrepreneurial processes to take place not only in the creation of new organizations but also in existing organizations. However, although the individual-opportunity nexus view has created much interesting knowledge about the entrepreneurial process, Alsos argues that it still focuses too strongly on the single individual and discrete opportunity. Instead, we must be aware that many ventures are started by teams and we need to understand the context in which these new ventures are embedded, particularly when it comes to the role of the entrepreneur's family. In addition, insights from various research fields indicate that we cannot always talk about single discrete opportunities, but opportunities that are related and/or interconnected to each other and to the existing activities. The main argument in the chapter is that through the simplification of focusing on the single entrepreneur and single opportunity, much of the complexity of entrepreneurial processes remains hidden.

In the chapter, Alsos' starting point is a critique of the single individual and single opportunity view within current research on the individual-opportunity nexus, after which she presents some suggestions for future entrepreneurship research:

- Opportunity identification, development and exploitation should be seen as a social process involving several interconnected individuals and opportunities that are path-dependent.
- Use of theoretical and conceptual frameworks that capture the complexity and multi-level nature of the individual-opportunity nexus, for example, a stronger integration of a portfolio entrepreneurial household framework – a framework that takes into consideration the involvement of several individuals and their interactions in the opportunity exploration and exploitation processes and helps to understand the path-dependent nature of opportunities and their interconnectedness.

We end this part of the book by challenging the almost universally accepted view of entrepreneurship as something 'positive' that has a significant impact on the economy. However, as argued by Paul Nightingale and Alex Coad in Chapter 6: 'Challenging assumptions and bias in entrepreneurship research', the evidence for this positive view of entrepreneurship is at best inconclusive, and the belief is heavily influenced by ideological and methodological biases that when combined, can create a strong demand for a Kuhnian paradigm with an extremely positive bias. This paradigm is stabilized by both an external demand from political ideologies and policy-makers as well as an internal supply influenced by publication (and funding) biases, poor research designs and methodological problems. However, as research designs and methodologies have improved over time, a more nuanced understanding of entrepreneurship that recognizes the limits and eventual 'negative' impact of entrepreneurial activities has emerged.

From this chapter we learn that the economic impact of entrepreneurial firms is usually rather poor and their relative performance seems to be negative when it comes to, for example, wage levels, patents, new products, labour productivity, etc. However, there seems to be a skewed distribution of impacts, between the high impact 'gazelle' firms at one end and the long tail of more typical poorly performing firms – 'muppets' – at the other. The chapter also creates a new way of understanding public policy:

- Poorly performing firms typically reflect limitations within their internal management and in the external environment that restrict their growth, rather than the function of the financial markets.
- Policy measures that encourage market entry may be dysfunctional – more policy interventions could simply increase the number of poorly performing start-ups. Instead, policy should focus on high-potential firms, improve the quality of existing poorly performing firms and encourage innovative driven growth.

Part II: contributions with a dissensus–discourse focus

Part II of the book contains chapters that in different ways challenge our assumptions and research practices from a 'dissensus' perspective. In contrast to mainstream entrepreneurship research, the authors argue for alternative paradigmatic and ideological premises including: a review of critical perspectives in entrepreneurship research; a methodological focus on 'engaged scholarship'; an argumentation for a variety of philosophical paradigms in understanding entrepreneurship; a challenge of the masculine and western-oriented dominance in entrepreneurship research; and finally, a focus on our pedagogical assumptions and practices in entrepreneurship.

Denise Fletcher and Paul Seldon begin Part II of the book with 'A critical review of critical perspectives in entrepreneurship research' (Chapter 7), in which they discuss and reflect on studies of critical inquiries in entrepreneurship research. The chapter is based on a literature review of 42 works published between 2000 and 2014 that had the terms 'critical' and 'entrepreneurship' in the title. The authors found a broad range of critical approaches in entrepreneurship research, from critical reviews of particular topics to critical inquiries that challenge the philosophical foundations of current research and studies that are explicitly critical of entrepreneurship based on a Critical Theory, Postmodern or Post-Structuralist research tradition.

In addition, to encourage more substantive studies using critically inspired research strategies, Fletcher and Seldon make the following suggestions:

- There is a need for more dialogue about, awareness of and receptivity towards more critical approaches in order to ensure that entrepreneurship remains a vibrant and dynamic research field.

- In order to avoid the risk of 'critical scholars' becoming caught in their own epistemological bind, there is a need to review critical inquiries in entrepreneurship research.

In the next chapter (Chapter 8), entitled 'Engaged scholarship: taking responsibility for the politics of method mediation', Ester Barinaga argues for a stronger scholarship of engagement in entrepreneurship research. At the heart of her argumentation is the relationship between the world we aim to study and the reality that we describe in our research. The methods we use mediate between the world and our descriptions of it (method mediation), and in our scientific practice we simplify that world as well as produce the reality, which is never a neutral process. Thus, research becomes a continuous process of simplifying the world and crafting reality, with strong political consequences – what realities should we contribute to strengthening and/or weakening?

In her chapter, Barinaga suggests an alternative methodological approach in which entrepreneurship scholars engage more strongly in the communities in which they study – 'scholarship engagement' – thus building a different relationship between reality and our descriptions of reality. Such engaged scholarship is based on (1) situated knowledge (positioned in a specific place within a stream of action and in a particular body), (2) reflections on the scholar's own role in the phenomenon that he/she describes, and as a consequence, and (3) engaged scholarship becomes intentionally political. At the end of the chapter, Barinaga elaborates on a couple of questions that scholars need to address in order to challenge existing theories and methodologies, as well as develop more engaged scholarship.

Barinaga challenged our use of methodology in entrepreneurship research. In the next chapter (Chapter 9) entitled 'Is there still a Heffalump in the room? Examining paradigms in historical entrepreneurship research', the focus is on the philosophical paradigms and theories that we use in our research. The authors Luke Pittaway and Richard Tunstall use Burrell and Morgan's (1979) paradigms of social sciences to explore the underlying paradigmatic assumptions in psychology and social psychology research on entrepreneurship from the 1960s to the 1990s. Based on their analysis they present a couple of common 'traps' that entrepreneurship researchers fall into when applying philosophical assumptions: (1) an overriding desire to create a scientific discipline (based on a 'normative science' approach) rather than a social scientific discipline that takes aspects such as randomness, luck, chaos and desires into account, (2) a common underestimation of contextual, social and institutional factors, and (3) an assumption that entrepreneurs are 'special' individuals without considering social aspects (e.g. families and the social context) or entrepreneurship as an aspect of everyday life, the characteristics of which are relatively 'mundane'.

Pittaway and Tunstall conclude their chapter by arguing for a more explicit reflection on our philosophical paradigms that we use in entrepreneurship research:

- As expressed by Pittaway and Tunstall (p. 196): 'While we may stand on the shoulders of giants, we may also unthinkingly build on their assumptions'.

Therefore, when developing and applying theories, entrepreneurship researchers need to more explicitly reflect on the underlying guiding paradigmatic assumptions.

- Pittaway and Tunstall call for increased diversity in the underlying paradigmatic assumptions in entrepreneurship research, and not least they argue for a growth in 'interpretive' and 'critical' approaches.

In Chapter 10, Deirdre Tedmanson and Caroline Essers challenge the generalized masculine and western orientation in entrepreneurship research, but also the ways in which contemporary political discourse in the Netherlands tend to construct Muslims. In their chapter 'Challenging constructions of entrepreneurial identities' they highlight the identity narratives of Turkish Muslim businesswomen in the Netherlands that exhibit quite different ways of interpreting and responding to their marginalization and how they shape their entrepreneurial identity.

In their chapter, Tedmanson and Essers construct a reflexive and nuanced view of entrepreneurship, from which we learn that:

- The 'hybrid identity' – not only Muslim, but also female, Turkish and entrepreneur – is an important and unique response of Muslim businesswomen in contemporary Dutch society.
- It is important for a society to promote and acknowledge a climate in which the heterogeneity of different identities can be accepted and in which value can be created.

Finally, we turn to a pedagogical focus in entrepreneurship. In Chapter 11, Caroline Verzat and her colleagues discuss different pedagogical approaches in entrepreneurship education. Over the years many critical voices have been raised with regard to entrepreneurship education and there seems to be a gap between what is actually taught in our courses and programmes and the reality that entrepreneurs experience in their daily lives. Taking their starting point in Sarasvathy's effectuation reasoning (Sarasvathy 2001; Sarasvathy and Venkataraman 2011), Verzat and her colleagues propose the use of effectual learning models based on a socio-constructivist approach, as well as the adoption of an effectual design and action-oriented process when designing new entrepreneurship programmes and courses. In the chapter, the authors explore four education programmes to illustrate an innovative approach in entrepreneurship education.

The chapter by Verzat and colleagues provides many lessons in how to design entrepreneurship programmes and courses. The main challenge is to be effectual by staying as close as possible to the entrepreneurial way of doing, acting and thinking. From the chapter we learn that:

- The authors encourage the use of effectual logic when designing entrepreneurship studies and programmes that will enable the isomorphic experience of entrepreneurial reality as it evolves, that is, closely related to an action-research epistemology.

In this respect, the authors suggest that we:

a   Change the relationship between researchers, educators and would-be entrepreneurs in order to create a 'co-learning' process.
b   Regard the entrepreneurial education as a unique ecosystem. All stakeholders in the education co-produce a sustainable entrepreneurial ecosystem.
c   To create conditions for learning the processes it is necessary to ensure diversity of participants, promote experiential and collaborative learning processes, as well as how to cope with failure, social complexity and power relations, by adopting a critical constructive posture and using a comprehensive language.

References

Aldrich, H.E. (2000) 'Learning together: National differences in entrepreneurship research'. In Sexton, D.L. and Landström, H. (eds) *The Blackwell Handbook of Entrepreneurship*. Oxford: Blackwell Publishers, pp. 5–25.

Aldrich, H.E. (2012) 'The emergence of entrepreneurship as an academic field: A personal essay on institutional entrepreneurship', *Research Policy*, 41, pp. 1240–1248.

Alvesson, M. and Deetz, S. (2000) *Doing Critical Management Research*. London: Sage.

Alvesson, M. and Sandberg, J. (2013) *Constructing Research Questions. Doing Interesting Research*. Thousand Oaks, CA: Sage.

Bartunek, J.M., Rynes, S.L. and Ireland, R.D. (2006) 'What makes management research interesting, and why does it matter?', *Academy of Management Journal*, 49(1), pp. 9–15.

Burrell, G. and Morgan, G. (1979) *Sociological Paradigms and Organisational Analysis*. London: Heinemann.

Das, H. and Long, B.S. (2010) 'What makes management research interesting?', *Journal of Management Issues*, 22(1), pp. 127–144.

Davidsson, P. (2013) 'Some reflection on research "schools" and geographies', *Entrepreneurship and Regional Development*, 25(1–2), pp. 100–110.

Davidsson, P. and Wiklund, J. (2001) 'Levels of analysis in entrepreneurship research: Current research practice and suggestions for the future', *Entrepreneurship Theory and Practice*, 24(4), pp. 81–99.

Davis, M.S. (1971) 'That is interesting! Towards a phenomenology of sociology and a sociology of phenomenology', *Philosophy of the Social Sciences*, 1(2), pp. 309–344.

Edelman, L.F., Manolova, T.S. and Brush, C.G. (2009) *Still blinded by the cites: Has there been progress in entrepreneurship research?* Paper at the Academy of Management Annual Meeting, Chicago, August.

Edquist, C. and Hommen, L. (2009) *Small Country Innovation System*. Cheltenham: Edward Elgar.

Eisenhardt, K. (1989) 'Building theories from case studies', *Academy of Management Review*, 29, pp. 333–349.

Entrepreneurship and Regional Development (2013) Special Issue, 1–2.

Frank, H. and Landström, H. (2016) 'What makes entrepreneurship research interesting? Strategies to overcome the rigor-relevance gap', *Entrepreneurship and Regional Development*, 28(1–2), pp. 51–75.

Ghosal, S. (2005) 'Scholarship that endures'. In Ketchen, D.J. and Bergh, D.D. (eds) *Research Methodology in Strategy and Management*. New York: Elsevier, pp. 1–10.

Grant, P. and Perren, L. (2002) 'Small business and entrepreneurship research. Meta-theories paradigms and prejudices', *International Small Business Journal*, 20(2), pp. 185–211.

Hambrick, D. and Chen, M.-J. (2008) 'New academic fields as admittance-seeking social movements: The case of Strategic Management', *Academy of Management Review*, 33, pp. 32–54.

Harley, S., Muller-Camen, M. and Collin, A. (2004) 'From academic communities to managed organisations', *Journal of Vocational Behavior*, 64, pp. 329–345.

Kirzner, I.M. (1973) *Competition and Entrepreneurship*. Chicago, IL: Chicago University Press.

Knight, F.H. (1921) *Risk, Uncertainty and Profit*. New York: Houghton Mifflin.

Landströn, H. (2005) *Pioneers in Entrepreneurship and Small Business Research*. New York: Springer.

Landström, H. (2014) 'Entrepreneurship research and its historical background'. In Baker, T. and Welter, F. (eds) *The Routledge Companion to Entrepreneurship*. London: Routledge, pp. 21–40.

Landström, H. and Benner, M. (2010) 'Entrepreneurship research: A history of scholarly migration'. In Landström, H. and Lohrke, F. (eds) *Historical Foundations of Entrepreneurship Research*. Cheltenham: Edward Elgar, pp. 15–45.

Marquis, C. and Tilcsik, A. (2013) 'Imprinting: Towards a multilevel theory', *Academy of Management Annals*, 7(1), pp. 195–245.

McClelland, D.C. (1961) *The Achieving Society*. Princeton, NJ: Van Nostrand.

Sarasvathy, S.D. (2001) 'Causation and effectuation: Toward a theoretical shift from economic inevitability to entrepreneurial contingency', *Academy of Management Review*, 26(2), pp. 243–263.

Sarasvathy, S.D. and Venkataraman, S. (2011) 'Entrepreneurship as method: Open questions for an entrepreneurial future', *Entrepreneurship Theory and Practice*, 35(1), pp. 113–135.

Schott, T. (1993) 'World science: Globalization of institutions and participation', *Science, Technology and Human Values*, 18(2), pp. 196–208.

Schumpeter, J.A. (1912) *Theorie der Wirtschaftlichen Entwicklung*. Leipzig: Dunker and Humblot.

Schumpeter, J.A. (1934) *The Theory of Economic Development*. Cambridge, MA: Harvard University Press.

Shepherd, D. (2015) 'Editorial: Party on! A call for entrepreneurship research that is more interactive, activity based, cognitively hot, compassionate and prosocial', *Journal of Business Venturing*, 30, pp. 489–507.

Shugan, S.M. (2003) 'Defining interesting research problems', *Marketing Science*, 22(1), pp. 1–15.

Zahra, S.A. and Wright, M. (2011) 'Entrepreneurship's next act', *Academy of Management Perspectives*, 25(4), pp. 67–83.

Part I
Consensus challenges

2 Entrepreneurship research with passion

A note on the aesthetics of basic research

Matthias Fink, Daniela Maresch, Isabella Hatak and Richard Lang

2.1 Introduction

The successful development of entrepreneurship as a field of research was accompanied by a process of institutionalization (Aldrich 2012) that is reflected in the establishment of numerous entrepreneurship-specific scientific journals, associations, research institutions, policies as well as interest and lobbying groups (Klandt 2004; Lück and Böhmer 1994; Shane and Venkataraman 2000). While progressing the institutionalization of entrepreneurship research has led to better access to resources and enhanced productivity, the emerging rules, norms and maxims may limit the leeway of the individual researchers to focus their research on what they are interested in. Thus, the process of institutionalization also brings about the threat of creating frustration and squelching scholars' passion for unique and novel ideas. This may ultimately hamper interesting entrepreneurship research. The resulting paradox can be summarized as follows: The tremendous success of entrepreneurship research as an academic discipline seems to hamper interesting research in this field. Our findings in a recently published survey among entrepreneurship scholars underpin the relevance of this threat.

Motivated by the high level of frustration with research that we detected among our peers, in this chapter, we strive to shed light into this paradox. We argue that the philosophy of art and beauty (i.e., *aesthetics* according to Lyas 1997) helps us to understand why researchers' passion provides a key to interesting research even in maturing disciplines such as entrepreneurship. More specifically, the beauty of a research topic or method may trigger the flow of energy for the researcher to deal with it regardless of the consequences (i.e., *passion* according to Bataille 2001) and, at the same time, attract the attention of the audience and make it want to learn more about it (i.e., it is *interesting* according to the Merriam-Webster Online Dictionary). We illustrate our reasoning with a discussion of two studies in entrepreneurship that we recently published in highly ranked journals. We assess the authors' passion and the resulting study's beauty drawing on diverse concepts of aesthetics. Additionally, we provide some indication for how interesting these two studies are for the scientific community.

We find that the study with more passionate researchers is beautiful under all applied concepts of aesthetics and report higher interest in the research community measured by number of Researchgate downloads and Google Scholar citations. In contrast, the study where some of the researchers were less passionate about the researched topic appears to be less beautiful under some of the aesthetic criteria. Interestingly, this study attracts less attention in the scientific community, reflected in lower numbers of downloads and citations. Thus, the preliminary evidence seems to support the claim that researchers' passion for their own research fosters beautiful and, thus, interesting entrepreneurship research.

The argument developed in this chapter has far-reaching implications for the future development of entrepreneurship research. The insights call for passionate entrepreneurship researchers. This requires creating spaces of intellectual freedom within research institutions. While on the macro-level competition between research groups enhances productivity, reduced competitive pressure and intensive cooperation within the research groups seems to be crucial for passionate researchers to unfold their innovativeness and creativity.

In the remainder of this chapter we establish the concepts of institutionalization, passion and interest (Section 2.2) and employ diverse criteria of aesthetics to link them to each other in a discussion of two sample studies (Section 2.3). In Section 2.4 we present the conclusions and implications.

2.2 Institutionalization, passionate scholars and interesting research

Without question, the development of entrepreneurship as a field of research can be seen as a success story. During the last decades, not only have the relevant academic structures expanded drastically (Klandt 2004; Lück and Böhmer 1994), but also the public discourse has been strongly influenced by the thought of entrepreneurship and innovation (Shane and Venkataraman 2000). Entrepreneurship researchers are impressively productive. Each year a large number of papers are published in numerous scientific journals and edited volumes and an at least equally high number of presentations are held at international conferences and workshops (Hisrich and Drnovsek 2002; Low 2001; MacMillan 1993).

Considerable amounts of resources from the public as well as the private sector have been invested in this new discipline. As a result, practitioners and policy-makers are now intensifying their call for relevant insights in return (Ashforth 2005). Entrepreneurship research has reached a state of maturity, where we need to ask for a critical reflection that goes beyond the usual critical discussion of published individual findings (Sarasvathy 2004; Steyaert 2005; Welter 2011).

One critical aspect of entrepreneurship research that is relevant for our argument is that it has been undergoing a process of institutionalization (Aldrich 2012). According to Scott (1995), during institutional processes regulative, normative and cognitive institutions evolve (Garud, Hardy and Maguire 2007;

Scott 1995, 2010), which can be described as follows: 'the regulative … guides action through coercion and threat of formal sanction; the normative … guides action through norms of acceptability, morality and ethics; and the cognitive guides action through the very categories and frames by which actors know and interpret their world' (Garud *et al.* 2007, p. 958). Sociological institutionalists argue that in order to understand practices, the meanings individuals attribute to these practices need to be understood (Meyer and Rowan 1977). Institutions constitute the social identity of the entrepreneurship community and the single researchers (Jepperson 1991). Along the guidelines of the institutions, meanings of researchers' practices are collectively constructed through social interactions within the community (Scott 1995), which thereby create common understandings of its identity, actions and relationships (Berger and Luckmann 1967; Lang, Kibler and Fink 2013). Thus, shared meanings and institutions are subject to social change (Scott 2010).

Accordingly, in the process of institutionalization of the field of entrepreneurship research, not only the practices of the legitimacy of specific research behaviour within scientific community, but also the practices of single researchers have been transformed. Regulative frameworks such as codes of conduct have been imposed for researchers (Martin 2013). Norms establish within the scientific community (Treviño and McCabe 1994) leading to stronger mutual social control among peers (McCabe, Trevino and Butterfield 2001; Titus, Wells and Rhoades 2008). Within the institutionalized setting individuals are guided by rules and norms in their framing and interpretation of the world. Increased institutionalization of a field of research implies a reduction of the individual researchers' freedom in their research practices. Thus, besides all the positive effects on the academic field, the process of institutionalization also brings about a threat: the reduction in the entrepreneurship scholars' leeway in their research practice might squelch their passion for entrepreneurship research (Shane 2003).

For management studies, Heath and Sitkin (2001) identified this adverse effect of the institutionalization of an academic field. They describe how academics become indifferent regarding their research and start to crowd out of innovative thinking and novel ideas into endless variations of tired themes that are in line with common wisdom and, thus, easier to publish. Similarly, Ashforth (2005, p. 400) provocatively describes the loss of scholars' passion in the process of institutionalization as follows: 'We become vanilla pudding: comfort food, yes, but ultimately with little bland, with a lot of empty calories.'

Unfortunately, there is empirical indication that this threat is relevant for entrepreneurship research as illustrated by the critical reflection presented in our contribution to an earlier issue of this book series (Fink *et al.* 2016). In this survey, we draw on the results of an anonymous and personalised online survey conducted among 323 entrepreneurship researchers from German-speaking countries in 2009. Almost three-quarters of the respondents (74.6 per cent) agree with the statement that the results of entrepreneurship research are hardly noticed and hardly applicable outside the relevant scientific community. Seventy point eight per cent of entrepreneurship researchers share the opinion that the researchers working in this field only produce for themselves. More than half (55.6 per cent) of the interviewed entrepreneurship scholars indicate that for being successful in their field of research meeting methodical demands is far more important than pursuing research that is of interest for others. In a nutshell, this survey shows a largely individual utility-driven understanding of research that leads to a dramatic level of frustration especially among entrepreneurship researchers in early to mid-career stages, thus highlighting the need for a reintroduction of interest in the topic as the prime engine for conducting passionate entrepreneurship research. All in all, according to the survey results, entrepreneurship researchers perceive their work as rather unconnected, method-driven and largely useless – thus, as not very interesting after all.

At the same time, the surveyed entrepreneurship researchers are highly motivated and productive. Given the pessimistic self-evaluation of their output, their impressive drive and work ethos cannot be rooted in genuine interest in and passion for their own research. Indeed, the activities of the entrepreneurship researchers seem to be based on motivation. This is in line with the observation that entrepreneurship researchers are under pressure to publish in highly rated journals (Davis, Riske-Morris and Diaz 2007) in order to have a successful career in academia (Moffatt 2011; Van Yperen, Hamstra and van der Klauw 2011). Studies on research productivity have focused on resources and funding, on demographic antecedents of the researchers and on the characteristics of the research institutions (Abramo and D'Angelo 2011; Fabel, Hein and Hofmeister 2008), but largely ignored the motivational background of the researchers.

However, shedding light on the motivational background of entrepreneurship researchers seems to be decisive for resolving the dilemma formulated above. Especially, it is important to delineate between motivation and passion. Passion is the flow of energy to deal with a matter regardless of its consequences (Bataille 2001). Motivation is fundamentally different from passion in that the latter is based on intrinsic desire whereas the former is based on extrinsic mechanisms of reward and sanction (Westwood 2006). However, the reward could always be greater and, thus, behaviour that is only based on motivation is often frustrating in the long run (Linstead and Brewis 2007). Frustration, in turn, kills researchers' passion and, with it, kills their energy to turn to exciting and challenging research. In contrast passionate researchers will, in their research, have the energy to deal with the most challenging topics, methods and settings, which potentially leads to ground-breaking findings. Compared to mass produced studies by extrinsically motivated researchers that only provide incremental contributions to scientific progress, such ambitious, innovative research is more likely to be of interest also for others.

Scholars' passion for their profession has been identified as an important driver for innovative and ground-breaking research that is interesting to the scientific community and practice (Ashforth 2005; Neumann 2006; Weber 1998). However, the claim that the researchers' passion for their own research provides a possible key to interesting entrepreneurship research needs yet to be justified more substantially. To close this gap, we will revert to theoretical considerations from aesthetics in the next section to establish a link between the passion of the creator of an object (artwork, or in our case scientific publications) and the object's properties that make it interesting to others. We take the reader on a ramble that briefly discusses selected aspects of aesthetics against the backdrop of entrepreneurship research. To make our reasoning more illustrative, we use two of our recently published studies in entrepreneurship research as examples.

2.3 Aesthetics as a link between researchers' passion and audience's interest

In this section we first present the key aspects of the two sample studies which are then, in a second step, assessed regarding the passion of the involved researchers and, finally, regarding the level of interest they attract.

2.3.1 Two sample studies

Theoretical consideration from aesthetics can be rather abstract and puzzling. Thus, to illustrate the arguments put forth in the remainder of this text, we use two of our own entrepreneurship studies that have both been published online in *Entrepreneurship Theory and Practice* during 2013. Choosing our own studies as examples is not a sign of egocentricity. Rather, it was inevitable, since we need to report on the passion of the researchers involved – information that is not accessible for publications by others.

The first study (Kautonen, van Gelderen and Fink 2015) demonstrates the relevance and robustness of the 'theory of planned behaviour' in the prediction of business start-up intentions and subsequent behaviour. It employs structural equation modelling (SEM) to analyse longitudinal survey data (N=969) collected among the adult population in Finland in 2011 and 2012. The article discusses conceptual and methodological issues related to studying the intention-behaviour relationship and outlines avenues for future research.

The results of the study show that the individuals' attitude, subjective norms and perceived behavioural control regarding entrepreneurship jointly explain 59 per cent of the variation in intention. In turn, entrepreneurial intention and perceived behavioural control explain 31 per cent of the variation in subsequent start-up behaviour. The key contribution of this study is that a theory which has been applied in numerous studies of entrepreneurial intentions and only assumes subsequent action, can now be applied with demonstrated validity of the intention-action link. The study was neither contract research, nor externally funded in any other way.

The second study (Lundström *et al.* 2014) documents a methodology used in Sweden that enabled researchers, for the first time, to quantify tax spending on small and medium enterprise policy and entrepreneurship policy. The resulting expenditure patterns were then compared with the policy focus expressed by experts. Important areas were found to suffer from a mismatch of identified spending and reported priority, implying a gap between actual expenditure and political rhetoric. To demonstrate the feasibility of the approach also in other contexts the methodology is then successfully extended beyond Sweden to include Poland, Austria and the Flanders region of Belgium. The key contribution of this study is that it quantifies taxpayers' engagement in entrepreneurship policies in different countries. This study was contract research from public funding bodies in each of the participating countries.

2.3.2 Assessment of the level of passion

Before we start our ramble, we need to evaluate the level of passion the researchers had for the topic they study. We revert to the three dimensions of the passion scale proposed by Carbonneau *et al.* (2008): (1) time devoted to a task, (2) importance ascribed to the task, and (3) positive emotional attachment to the task. In the case of research, drawing on the first dimension of the passion scale, one way to assess the researchers' level of passion is to consider the effort they have put in collecting, analysing and publishing the data. From this perspective, both studies can be rated as elaborate and time-consuming. For the first study, researchers ran two rounds of large-scale data collection to build up a longitudinal dataset in two countries. The second study was based on tracking cash through the complex structure of (state-funded) agencies that offered support to entrepreneurs and small businesses. This data collection was carried out in four geographical contexts. Without a group of researchers who are ready to invest considerable effort, such a study would not be possible. However, for the second study, the effort was compensated financially, while for the first one it was not. Thus, from this perspective, in the first study researchers were solely driven by their passion for the research, while in the second study they were partly driven by the motivation to gain a financial reward.

Alternatively, the level of the researchers' passion for a topic can be assessed by considering the importance of this study in the researchers' portfolio – if a study is a one-shot activity driven by a publication opportunity or if it is embedded in a broader stream of research, which is driven by a consistent research agenda (i.e., research programme). By looking at the publication lists of the researchers involved it becomes apparent that with respect to the first study all researchers have been working in this very field and even on this specific research question for some years. For all of them this publication is the next logical building block in a broader and long term-oriented research programme. In contrast, the team of authors of the second study only comprised a few researchers who have been working on this research question for a considerable time span and who conduct follow-up research on this topic. The other authors jumped in as the multi-national project offered an attractive opportunity to publish. Thus, from this perspective, the level of researchers' passion for the topic of the first study can clearly be rated as high, whereas it is heterogeneous among the team members of the second study.

Additionally, the level of passion for a study that is conducted in a team can be assessed in terms of the response time the individual authors need to respond to their co-authors' requests. The response time expresses the priority of a study or paper in a scholar's research portfolio. Looking at the e-mail correspondence on the two studies shows that the response times were considerably shorter for the first study.

Finally, we can assess the passion of the researchers involved in the two sample studies by relying on the authors' self-reports of their emotional attachment to the topic. This approach reveals that the researchers had considerably more passion for the first study than for the second. Given the different roles the two studies play in their individual research agendas, the different level of emotional involvement is not surprising.

Overall, the researchers have put enormous efforts into both studies. However, the work on study one was the highest priority for all authors as it was part of a long-term agenda that had been driven by passion for the topic, while the input in study two was more instrumental from some of the authors. With this difference of passion of the researchers in mind, we will now turn to the assessment of whether the two sample studies are interesting. For that we use the aesthetic criteria proposed in major concepts from the theory of art.

2.3.3 Assessment of the level of interest

Aesthetics is the philosophy of art, beauty and taste with a wide range of competing concepts (Hofstadter and Kuhns 1976; Taliaferro 2011). In the following we will not try to present a comprehensive overview of these concepts, but pick five that appear to be most promising for our purpose. We will not discuss these five concepts in detail, but only elaborate on those aspects that are relevant for assessing the level of interest of the two sample studies. Especially, we focus on the aesthetic criteria put forth by the different philosophers to delineate beautiful/attractive/interesting matters from the rest.

The first stop of our ramble (see Table 2.1) takes us back to the fourth to third century BC, when Plato proposed 'skilled craft as an imitation of reality (ideal forms)' as an objective aesthetic criterion. A rather crude application of this concept to entrepreneurship research highlights the importance of the researchers' skills in providing an as good as possible imitation of reality. The idea of ideal forms representing reality in classical Greek tragedy proposed by Plato, may find its rough parallel within the idea of statistical representativity in quantitative research. It requires the skilled craft of mastering the sophisticated methods of quantitative social science in order to communicate to the audience close to reality, and thus interesting, insights about reality.

Let's turn to the two sample studies in order to illustrate this reasoning. Both studies are methodically on a very high level. Both studies employed sophisticated methods of data collection and especially study one employs state-of-the-art methods of quantitative data analysis. While study one is explicative, study two is descriptive in large parts. In study one the researchers use their skills to

Table 2.1 Summary of the ramble

			Study 1	Study 2
Level of passion for the topic surveyed			*Highly passionate researchers*	*Less passionate researchers*
Philosopher	*Aesthetic criteria*	*O/S*		
Plato (fourth to third century BC)	Skilled craft as an imitation of reality	O	Sophisticated methods of data collection and analysis enables statistical reconstruction of real-world causal relationship that is generalizable beyond the sampled cases → *More interesting for readers*	Major effort and refined methods in data collection enable a fine grained description of reality in the researched cases → *Less interesting for readers*
Aristotle (fourth century BC)	Emotions/ thoughts triggered by imitation may lead to catharsis and may educate the audience	O	Realizing the small share of intenders who actually start-up a company may make readers revisit their body of knowledge → *Interesting for readers*	Seeing the mis-match of the official communications and the real amount of tax money spent on entrepreneurship and small business policy might increase the reader's interest in this topic → *Interesting for readers*
Kant (eighteenth century)	Subjective disinterested pleasure	S	The study is not directly useful for the reader, but it is a pleasure to read for those appreciating the-orizing and methods → *Interesting for specific readers*	The study is not directly useful for the reader, but it is a pleasure to read for those appreciat-ing facts and figures → *Interesting for specific readers*
Freud (nineteenth to twentieth century)	Sublimation, i.e., a gratification that substitutes for the actual satisfaction of a desire	S	In spite of having intentions none of the authors has yet started a substantial business. Doing research, that shows that we are not alone in this, feels good. The findings also help the non-entrepreneurs among the readers to sublimate. → *Interesting for specific readers*	This research helped the authors to compensate for the frustration of not having control over the way tax money is spent by showing that it is, in large parts, spent wrong. This effect is shared with some of the readers. → *Interesting for specific readers*

			Study 1	*Study 2*
Goodman *(twentieth century)*	Create worlds that seem right in relation to our needs and habits (similar to viability)	S	The statistical model provides a viable reconstruction of the subjects' behaviour → *Interesting for readers*	This publication focuses on providing a description of facts → *Not interesting for readers*
Indicators for readers' interest				
Views on ResearchGate (April 2015)			198	34
Google Scholar Citations (April 2015)			15	3

Notes: O=objective criterion; S=subjective criterion.

imitate a real-world phenomenon (causal relationship) based on data collected from randomly sampled subjects, whereas in study two the data collected are facts and figures and are not put in a causal relationship to each other. Thus, study one reveals a principle that is more general than the description of facts in study two. While both studies strive to imitate reality using skilled craft, study one provides a more general insight than study two. Thus, applying Plato's aesthetic criterion of 'skilled craft as an imitation of reality' to our two sample studies leaves study one to appear more interesting than study two.

We stay in ancient Greece and move on from Plato to one of his students, Aristotle, who had a less pessimistic view on art. While Plato argued that the imitation of reality will never be perfect and is even misleading for the audience, Aristotle stressed the educative value of the emotions and thoughts of the audience triggered by experiencing the imitations (*carthasis*) that highlighted specific features of reality. In Aristotle's concept the core aesthetic criteria are the emotions and thoughts triggered by imitations of reality. This criterion gets close to the concept put forth by Landström (2013) who argues that it is the challenging of state-of-the-art and widely agreed wisdoms and methods that makes research interesting.

Looking at our two sample studies we find that both studies present results which are surprising, even for those who have been working on these very subjects for years. Study one highlights the relevance of the gap between entrepreneurial intentions and actions and, thus, not only questions empirical studies only looking at intentions but also the costly initiatives to enhance entrepreneurial intentions. Study two reveals a surprisingly high sum of tax spending on initiatives targeted at the promotion of entrepreneurship and small business. In both cases it was the unique database that made it possible to take a different perspective in the analysis. The first study could rely on a longitudinal sample collected from a regionally stratified random sample of the general population in two countries, allowing for analysing if entrepreneurial intentions were turned into action on the level of the individual case. In study two we tracked the cash through the financing unit all the way down to the entrepreneur or small business. This is innovative since most previous studies have either aggregated the spending or the subsidies received and most of them have relied on the label that the spending unit gave the money. However, we found that only a small share of the tax spending on entrepreneurship and small business policies were labelled as such, and were rather labelled as measures of regional development policies, social policies or culture initiatives. Thus, the new way of doing the research has led to surprising findings in both studies that trigger emotions and thoughts among the readers. Thus, applying Aristotle's aesthetic criterion of 'imitations of reality that trigger emotions and thoughts among the audience' to our two sample studies, leaves both studies appearing equally interesting.

Making a big jump in time our ramble takes us to the eighteenth century, when Kant developed the concept of 'subjective disinterested pleasure' as the core aesthetic criterion. In this concept, artwork pleases recipients without satisfying any need or purpose. His example would be a rose that neither fulfils any need nor serves any purpose for the observer, but it is a pleasure to look at. Reading good entrepreneurship research might also induce pleasure even if the contents communicated are neither of purpose for the readers, nor satisfy any of their needs. We argue that it is more often the fellow researchers rather than the practitioners who read academic publications on entrepreneurship, even though the findings presented should be more relevant to practitioners.

Applying Kant's aesthetic criterion of 'subjective disinterested pleasure' to our two sample studies, shows that both are equally interesting, but for different audiences. What is a pleasure to read for one might not be a pleasure for others. Kant claims the aesthetic judgement to be subjective in that it is rooted in the individual's reasoning only, but at the same time to be general in that the individual expects others to share his view.

The next stop of our ramble is a short visit to Vienna at the turn of the nineteenth to the twentieth century. Acknowledging that in modern society one cannot satisfy all natural desires, Freud proposed the concept of sublimation. He defines sublimation as a gratification that substitutes for the actual satisfaction of a desire. In this concept, artwork as well as research can represent such a gratification.

Looking at our two sample studies from this perspective of aesthetics, again, reveals decisive differences between the two publications. In spite of having intentions none of the authors of the first study has yet started a substantial business. Doing research which shows that we are not alone with this, feels good. However, the findings unfold this effect not only for us, but they also help the non-entrepreneurs among the readers to sublimate the desire to be active as an entrepreneur. In contrast, the second study helped the authors to compensate for the frustration of not having direct control over the way tax money is spent by showing that it is, in large parts, spent wrong. This effect is shared with some of the readers. Thus, applying Freud's concept of sublimation to our two sample studies, leaves both studies appear equally interesting, but to different readers depending on their individual desires.

The last stop of our ramble is modern aesthetics. Among others, it was especially Goodman who proposed that good artwork 'creates world that seem right in relation to our needs and habits'. This concept is somewhat close to the idea that Maturana (1980) communicates in their analogy of empirical research as navigating a submarine. In fact, through our methods we only gain an indirect understanding of our world, similar to the captain of the submarine who has to rely on the values displayed on the submarine's instruments when navigating in the dark of the deep sea. From these values, the captain does not gain a perception of the outside world, but rather she or he derives a construction of the invisible world that makes navigation possible. Collected data are the values displayed on the instruments, and the models derived from the analysis are our constructions. As the captain's construction of the world outside the submarine helps him/her to navigate, similarly, our models help entrepreneurs to succeed. In this thinking, empirical studies do not claim to present the truth, that is, a representation of the reality, but rather strive to develop viable models that will constantly need to be empirically challenged and refined.

Against the backdrop of Goodman's aesthetic criterion of the creation of a world that seems right in relation to our needs and habits, sample study one is by far more interesting than study two. The empirically supported model of how entrepreneurial intentions translate into action ticks the boxes defined by Goodman exactly: to the best of our knowledge it seems right. However, future studies will challenge and refine it and most likely exchange it for an even more viable alternative. In contrast, the second study does not develop a model or any other creation of the world and thus does not meet the criterion proposed by Goodman.

All in all, it seems that the study with more passionate researchers can be considered interesting for readers under all applied aesthetic criteria, while the study where some of the researchers were less passionate about the researched topic, rates lower in interest for others under some of the aesthetic criteria such as Plato's or Goodman's.

2.4 Conclusion

In this chapter, we argue that the successful institutionalization of entrepreneurship as a field of research brings about the threat to limit the leeway for research activities, creates frustration and squelches passion among researchers. We draw on the criteria of aesthetics to establish a link between the passion of the creator/author of an artwork/scientific publication and its properties that make it interesting to others. To illustrate our reasoning, we briefly discuss two of our recently published studies in entrepreneurship research, in which the authors had different levels of passion for the studies' topics. Against the backdrop of these aesthetic criteria, we first gather evidence if the two studies are interesting for the academic community.

While the presented discussion is far from being a rigorous deduction, it, however, seems to support the claim that researchers' passion for their own research fosters interesting entrepreneurship research. We find that the study with more passionate researchers is interesting for readers under all applied concepts of aesthetics. In contrast, the study where some of the researchers were less passionate about the researched topic appears to be less or even not interesting under some of the aesthetic criteria. More specifically, the study which was more important to the researchers, on which the researchers devoted more time and to which the researchers were more emotionally attached, also meets more of the aesthetics criteria. At the same time, the study with the more passionate researchers has also attracted more interest from the research community in terms of downloads and citation rates. A comparison of the number of people who viewed the two sample studies on ResearchGate (www. researchgate.net) points in the same direction: study one was viewed 198 times, while study two was only viewed 34 times by April 2015. The same picture arises when looking at the Google Scholar citations until April 2015, with study one being cited 15 times and study two only being cited three times.

This evidence supports our argumentation that, in order to generate interesting entrepreneurship research, more passionate researchers, who invest time on topics that are important to them and that they are emotionally attached to, are needed. With such passion entrepreneurship researchers can break new ground and come up with findings that educate us, provide pleasure to us and help us to orientate in our life-worlds, thus publishing findings that are interesting to us. In the current institutional environment of entrepreneurship research, such innovative entrepreneurship research, however, has to break through the barriers of widely accepted wisdom. Thus, compared to the reproduction of countless variations of the same research, ground-breaking entrepreneurship research requires additional energy. In this chapter, we have shown that one source that may energize entrepreneurship researchers to walk that extra mile towards interesting research is passion.

Obviously, it is not as long a shot as it may seem to apply the theoretical considerations of what is an interesting artwork to scientific studies and publications. However, this chapter suffers from the typical limitations of applying concepts from one discipline to the very different context of another discipline. Notwithstanding the rather crude way we have put together the theoretical building blocks without accounting for incommensurability arising from paradigms and technical language, we think we have produced a paper that is at least interesting to some. For sure, it may serve as a starting point for discussion.

The argument developed here also has practical implications for the future development of entrepreneurship research. The insights call for entrepreneurship researchers who free themselves from their extrinsic motivation such as idols, rankings and social status and fall in love again with their research subject. In Frey's (2003, p. 210) words, young scholars have to free themselves from 'intellectual prostitution'. In contrast to Ashforth (2005), who concludes from his detection of fading passion among researchers that more control and sanction are needed in academia, we argue in line with Weber (1998) that passionate researchers who conduct interesting research only develop in settings of reduced competitive pressure and more cooperation, which is based on open communication and trust among researchers. This call is also in line with Ashforth (2005, p. 403), who sees each young scholar entering academia as a potential change agent and who stresses that a 'few judicious system changes would go a long way toward liberating rather than squelching [young scholars'] passion'.

Linking back the findings to sociological institutionalism provides a more fine-grained roadmap for facilitating interesting entrepreneurship research. The interplay between Scott's (1995) three pillars of institutions suggests two possible interventions into the development of entrepreneurship as a field of research. First, the regulative and normative pillar set the boundaries for the researchers' framing and interpretation of the world on the cognitive level. Thus, with careful design of the regulations prevailing in the research setting and a trust-based community with supportive norms, space can be created for the individual researcher which is necessary for the development of cognitive categories and structures allowing innovative entrepreneurship research. This also implics responsible leadership that, on the micro level of the research group, protects the individual researcher from direct competitive pressure but, on the macro level, ensures research output that is competitive with the output of other research groups. Interestingly, buffering the competitive pressure and creating space for the free development of individual researchers is at the same time a prerequisite for the second possible intervention into the development of entrepreneurship as a field of research. Even though Scott (1995) views institutions as social structures that have attained a high degree of resilience, the individual researchers can act as change agents. As members of the scientific community, individual researchers co-construct rules and norms. In order to tap the potential of this second option for intervention, placement strategies need to strive for selecting the most passionate and, thus, effective candidates instead of the most efficient and, thus, productive ones. While, in this chapter, we have conceptualized the phenomenon of passion on the individual level, through the interdependencies between the institutional pillars the social interaction with passionate researchers might also energize the normative and regulation pillar to move from motivation-focused to passion-focused research practice.

Interestingly, firm development offers a rich analogy: economically successful firms also often lose their innovativeness. However, this is only true if the entrepreneur sees entrepreneurship as a means to achieve other ends like driving sports cars or gaining social status. In contrast, if the entrepreneur is passionate about running and developing the business itself, innovation is not a means any more, but an end and economic success does not hamper, but facilitates innovation, because it provides the necessary resources (Bowen, Rostami and Steel 2010). For established firms, to avoid tapping into the maturity trap, entrepreneurship research suggests corporate venturing. Such measures include the creation of creative space for members of the organization in order to free them from rules and norms that otherwise restrict their creativity within the organization.

This approach is close to the first possible intervention into the development of entrepreneurship as a field of research suggested above. Corporate venturing also suggests that firms which have grown out of the start-up phase, integrate entrepreneurial individuals in the organization in order to break-up crusted structures and routines. This approach is close to the second measure suggested for the further development of the field of entrepreneurship research. Thus, this analogy also reinforces our claim: there will be no interesting entrepreneurship research without passionate researchers. We as the members of this research community have to do our best to facilitate passion among our peers.

References

Abramo, G. and D'Angelo, C. (2011) 'National scale research performance assessment at the individual level', *Scientometrics*, 86(2), pp. 347–364.

Aldrich, H.E. (2012) 'The emergence of entrepreneurship as an academic field: A personal essay on institutional entrepreneurship', *Research Policy*, 41(7), pp. 1240–1248.

Ashforth, B.E. (2005) 'Becoming vanilla pudding. How we undermine our passion for research', *Journal of Management Inquiry*, 14(4), pp. 400–403.

Berger, P. and Luckmann, T. (1967) *The Social Construction of Reality. A Treatise in the Sociology of Knowledge.* New York: Anchor Books.

Bowen, F.E., Rostami, M. and Steel, P. (2010) 'Timing is everything: A meta-analysis of the relationships between organizational performance and innovation', *Journal of Business Research*, 63(11), pp. 1179–1185.

Carbonneau, N., Vallerand, R.J., Fernet, C. and Guay, F. (2008) 'The role of passion for teaching in intrapersonal and interpersonal outcomes', *Journal of Educational Psychology*, 100(4), pp. 977–987.

Davis, M.S., Riske-Morris, M. and Diaz, S.R. (2007) 'Causal factors implicated in research misconduct: Evidence from ORI case files', *Science and Engineering Ethics*, 13(4), pp. 395–414.

Fabel, O., Hein, M. and Hofmeister, R. (2008) 'Research productivity in business economics: An investigation of Austrian, German, and Swiss universities', *German Economic Review*, 9(4), pp. 506–531.

Fink, M., Hatak, I., Lang, R. and Maresh, D. (2016) 'Entrepreneurship research without passion'. In Fayolle, A. and Riot, P. (eds) *Rethinking Entrepreneurship.* London: Routledge, Chapter 11.

Frey, B.S. (2003) 'Publishing as prostitution? Choosing between one's own ideas and academic success', *Public Choice*, 116(1–2), pp. 205–223.

Garud, R., Hardy, C. and Maguire, S. (2007) 'Institutional entrepreneurship as embedded agency: An introduction to the Special Issue', *Organization Studies*, 28(7), pp. 957–969.

Goodman, N. (1977) 'When is Art?'. In Perkins, D. and Leondar, B. (eds) *The Arts and Cognition.* Baltimore, MD: Johns Hopkins University Press, pp. 11–19.

Heath, C. and Sitkin, S.B. (2001) 'Big-B versus big-O: What is organizational about organizational behaviour?', *Journal of Organizational Behavior*, 22(1), pp. 43–58.

Hisrich, R. and Drnovsek, M. (2002) 'Entrepreneurship and small business research – a European perspective', *Journal of Small Business and Enterprise Development*, 9(2), pp. 172–222.

Hofstadter, A. and Kuhns, R. (1976) *Philosophies of Art and Beauty, Selected Readings in Aesthetics from Plato to Heidegger.* Chicago, IL: University of Chicago Press.

Jepperson, R. (1991) 'Institutions, institutional effects, and institutionalism'. In Powell, W.W. and Di Maggio, P.J. (eds) *The New Institutionalism in Organizational Analysis.* Chicago, IL: University of Chicago Press, pp. 143–163.

Kautonen, T., van Gelderen, M. and Fink, M. (2015) 'Robustness of the theory of planned behaviour in predicting entrepreneurial intentions and actions', *Entrepreneurship Theory and Practice*, 39(3), pp. 655–674.

Klandt, H. (2004) 'Entrepreneurship education and research in German-speaking Europe', *Academy of Management Learning and Education*, 3(3), pp. 293–301.

Landström, H. (2013) *What makes scholars 'interesting' in entrepreneurship research? Learning from the past.* Paper at the Babson 2013 Pre-Conference 'Thinking Entrepreneurship Out of the Box', EM Lyon Business School, France, June.

Lang, R., Kibler, E. and Fink, M. (2013) 'Understanding place-based entrepreneurship in rural central Europe – a comparative institutional analysis', *International Small Business Journal*, 32(2), pp. 204–227.

Linstead, S. and Brewis, J. (2007) 'Passion, knowledge and motivation: Ontologies of desire', *Organization*, 14(3), pp. 351–371.

Lück, W. and Böhmer, A. (1994) 'Entrepreneurship als wissenschaftliche Disziplin in den USA', *Zeitschrift für betriebswirtschaftliche Forschung*, 46(5), pp. 403–421.

Lundström, A., Vikström, P., Fink, M., Meulemann, M., Głodek, P., Storey, D. and Kroksgård, A. (2014) 'International comparisons of the costs and coverage of SME and entrepreneurship policy: Sweden, Poland, Austria, UK and the Flanders Region of Belgium', *Entrepreneurship Theory and Practice*, 38(4), pp. 941–957.

Lyas, C. (1997) *Aesthetics.* Montreal: McGill-Queens Press.

MacMillan, I.C. (1993) 'The emerging forum for entrepreneurship scholars', *Journal of Business Venturing*, 8(5), pp. 377–382.

Martin, B.R. (2013) 'Whither research integrity? Plagiarism, self-plagiarism and coercive citation in an age of research assessment', *Research Policy*, 42(5), pp. 1005–1014.

Maturana, H.R. and Varela, F.J. (1980) *Autopoiesis and Cognition: The Realization of Living.* Dordrecht: Reidel.

McCabe, D.L., Trevino, L.K. and Butterfield, K.D. (2001) 'Cheating in academic institutions: A decade of research', *Ethics and Behavior*, 11(3), pp. 219–232.

McCloskey, M.A. (1987) *Kant's Aesthetic.* London: Macmillan.

Meyer, J.W. and Rowan, B. (1977) 'Institutionalized organizations – formal-structure as myth and ceremony', *American Journal of Sociology*, 83(2), pp. 340–363.

Moffatt, B. (2011) 'Responsible authorship: Why researchers must forgo honorary authorship', *Accountability in Research*, 18(2), pp. 76–90.

Neumann, A. (2006) 'Professing passion: Emotion in the scholarship of professors at research universities', *American Educational Research Journal*, 43(3), pp. 381–424.

Sarasvathy, S.D. (2004) 'The questions we ask and the questions we care about: Reformulating some problems in entrepreneurship research', *Journal of Business Venturing*, 19(5), pp. 707–717.

Scott, W.R. (1995) *Institutions and Organizations.* Thousand Oaks, CA: Sage.

Scott, W.R. (2010) 'Reflections: The past and future of research on institutions and institutional change', *Journal of Change Management*, 10(1), pp. 5–21.

Shane, S. and Venkataraman, S. (2000) 'The promise of entrepreneurship as a field of research', *Academy of Management Review*, 25(1), pp. 217–226.

Shane, S. (2003) *A General Theory of Entrepreneurship: The Individual-Opportunity Nexus.* Cheltenham: Edward Elgar.

Steyaert, C. (2005) 'Entrepreneurship: In between what? On the "frontier" as a discourse of entrepreneurship research', *International Journal of Entrepreneurship and Small Business*, 2(1), pp. 2–16.

Taliaferro, C. (2011) *Aesthetics*. London: Oneworld.

Titus, S.L., Wells, J.A. and Rhoades, L.J. (2008) 'Repairing research integrity', *Nature*, 453(7198), pp. 980–982

Treviño, L.K. and McCabe, D.L. (1994) 'Meta-learning about business ethics: Building honorable business school communities', *Journal of Business Ethics*, 13(6), pp. 405–416.

Van Yperen, N.W., Hamstra, M.R.W. and van der Klauw, M. (2011) 'To win, or not to lose, at any cost: The impact of achievement goals on cheating', *British Journal of Management*, 22(2), pp. 5–15.

Weber, J. (1998) 'Maintaining the "research high road" with passion', *Business and Society*, 37(1), pp. 92–93.

Welter, F. (2011) 'Contextualizing entrepreneurship – conceptual challenges and ways forward', *Entrepreneurship Theory and Practice*, 35(1), pp. 165–184.

3 Pragmatic entrepreneurs and institutionalized scholars?

On the path-dependent nature of entrepreneurship scholarship

Henrik Berglund and Karl Wennberg

3.1 Introduction

In his early review of the scientific discourse on entrepreneurship, Marc Casson (1982) concluded that 'The essence of entrepreneurship is being different'. If this is the case, why does so much of entrepreneurship research seem to us to be so very similar? This is the question we seek to explore in this chapter.

Recent research surveys by Aldrich (2012), Landström, Harirchi and Åström (2012) and others suggest that one reason why entrepreneurship research could be perceived as becoming more homogeneous is the maturation and institutionalization of entrepreneurship as a research field. While this maturity may have led to an increase in quantity as well as improved methodological sophistication, we contend that it may also have led to an increased 'taking-for-grantedness' of certain research questions and methodological dogmas (Powell and DiMaggio 1983).

In this chapter we critically discuss a number of common research questions, units of analysis, and research designs in mainstream entrepreneurship journals. An important point of departure for this discussion is what we see as influences from the established research areas of strategy and organization theory, and we argue that this may have led to an increasing institutionalization of entrepreneurship research both in terms of the research questions asked and the tools used to answer them. We discuss the discrepancy that we believe exists between the methodological imperatives promoted by this trend and what we believe to be the fundamental nature of entrepreneurship, outlining some challenges and potential ways forward for entrepreneurship researchers interested in generating new types of answers to under-researched issues in the field. We conclude the chapter by suggesting that an alternative way forward is to embrace the philosophical tradition of pragmatism as providing a way to combine realistic meta-theoretical foundations with methodological guidelines that may enhance the likelihood of producing theory-driven research that yields findings also of practical relevance.

3.2 How is scholarship institutionalized?

Institutionalization, the taken-for-grantedness of rules, procedures and ways of organizing production and social interaction, is one of the most well-researched areas of organization science (Meyer and Rowan 1977). However, with few exceptions, entrepreneurship scholars tend to use the tools of institutional analysis to investigate industries, firms and entrepreneurs rather than their own community of scholarship. Two important exceptions are the recent literature reviews by Landström *et al.* (2012) and Aldrich (2012) who outline the historical development of the field of entrepreneurship, showing how entrepreneurship research has become both increasingly cumulative and institutionalized. We will not discuss the potential pros and cons with this institutionalization beyond noting that it has been successful in attracting many new scholars to an increasingly global academic field.

As some authors have argued (e.g. Aldrich 2012; Baker and Pollock 2007), a potential driver of the institutionalization of entrepreneurship research is the borrowing of research questions and tools from strategic management and organization theory. Many entrepreneurship scholars have their training in these areas, and to a lesser extent in the disciplines of economics, sociology or psychology (Busenitz *et al.* 2003). Since entrepreneurship research is primarily conducted at business schools, perspectives from strategic management and organization theory tend to dominate the academic discourse (Baker and Pollock 2007). While everyone may not agree with this description, it resonates with our experiences after 10–15 years of entrepreneurship scholarship, including experiences from publishing in both US-based and European-based academic journals, participating in discussions at major conferences such as the RENT Conference, the Babson Entrepreneurship Research Conference and the Academy of Management Conferences. Important traces of this influence can be seen in the entrepreneurship field's increasing adoption of perspectives, theories, value-laded assumptions and methodological canons common in strategic management and organization theory. For example, many have lamented but few have addressed the lack of process-oriented studies in entrepreneurship, despite the obvious insight that many aspects of entrepreneurship can better be understood as a process rather than a choice, a single event or a fixed unit of analysis such as an individual or a new firm (Van de Ven and Engleman 2004).

To briefly describe how scholarship may become institutionalized in the field of entrepreneurship research, we will here outline the related issues of: (1) institutionalization of research questions, (2) institutionalization of units of analysis, and (3) institutionalization of research designs. We then move on to our main point, which is to discuss alternative approaches to identifying research questions, choosing a unit of analysis and designing studies. The approach we suggest is inspired by the philosophical tradition of pragmatism, which we see as an interesting way to combine relevant meta-theoretical foundations with methodological guidelines relevant for the entrepreneurship field.

3.2.1 Institutionalization of research questions

In an essay reflecting on the disjunction between the questions we as a field ask and the questions we perhaps ought to care about, Saras Sarasvathy (2004a) suggested that we have spent too much time 'pursuing the holy grail of firm performance as a measurable consequence of entrepreneurial characteristics' (Sarasvathy 2004a, p. 716) instead of seeking more nuanced and creative ways to actually foster entrepreneurship in individuals and economies. Indeed, much entrepreneurship research seeks to distinguish between more or less entrepreneurial individuals and firms, for example, in the psychological studies of entrepreneurs or the studies on the entrepreneurial orientation of firms (Rauch and Frese 2007; Rauch *et al.* 2009), or follows research in strategic management and organization theory to look at success factors or ways of organizing in young firms (Duchesneau and Gartner 1990; Gartner and Carter 2003). To illustrate this claim, we downloaded and read the last two years of papers (September 2012 to September 2014) in one top-ranked entrepreneurship journal, *Journal of Business Venturing*. We found that among the 75 published empirical studies, 13 (17 per cent) dealt with predictors of 'entry' (new venture creation, self-employment, etc.) and 36 (48 per cent) with 'performance' (financial success, growth, new product development, survival, etc.). Only 26 empirical articles (35 per cent) studied phenomena not directly related to entrepreneurial entry or success. Why, still, the predominant focus on 'who becomes an entrepreneur?' and 'what predicts success?' in entrepreneurship research?

In terms of research questions, many have argued that entrepreneurship research needs to move beyond questions related to new venture creation, self-employment and firm growth (Davidsson 2003; Sarasvathy 2004a; Shane and Venkataraman 2000). In addition to being fairly well researched to date, these questions are also attended to by other scholarly domains such as sociology, economics, psychology, strategic management and organization studies. In her essay, Sarasvathy (2004a) suggests that the field would benefit from focusing less on the 'boundary sciences' *per se*, for example, the psychology of individuals, the resources of firms, or the characteristics of the firm environment, and instead spend time understanding what happens on the interfaces between them, for example, the ways in which entrepreneurs engage their environment as part of the entrepreneurial process. If entrepreneurship is to be seen as a legitimate independent area of scholarship we see it as important to develop new questions and to encourage a self-reflexive academic debate in the entrepreneurship scholarly community.

In addition to staying close to actual entrepreneurial processes, one way of finding interesting and relevant questions may be to consider how more mature fields, including organization theory and strategy, have identified new and often counterintuitive research questions and in effect deinstitutionalized themselves. We believe that an increased focus on new and often counterintuitive research questions could be very fruitful for theory development in the entrepreneurship field, compared to simply adopting common theoretical frameworks and methods from neighbouring fields and applying them in an entrepreneurship setting. Weick (1990) suggested several heuristics for identifying research questions, often by more deeply interrogating real-world phenomena, such as 'noticing an anomaly', 'challenging dominating levels of analysis', 'creating language that may enrich explanation', 'noticing simple activities and exploiting them as metaphors', or to more generally 'pursuing possible counterintuitive explanations'. Similarly, Davis (1971), in his classic article 'That's Interesting!', suggests a number of heuristics for developing interesting research questions, that is, research questions that break with taken-for-granted assumptions in various ways. One such heuristic is to assume that 'What seems to be a general phenomenon is in reality a local phenomenon'. Davies exemplifies with Malinowski's anthropological research which indicated the Oedipal complex and its resolution, which had been taken as a universal, was in fact not common to all societies. In entrepreneurship research, investigations of venture capital practices have found that cultural and institutional differences have large effects on the roles VCs assume and the activities they perform (Berglund 2011), with some suggesting that the value of principal-agency theory, for understanding relations in the venture capital industry, is culturally bounded (Wright, Pruthi and Lockett 2005). This point illustrates how formulating new research questions may often imply a reconsideration of basic phenomena and the actors involved.

3.2.2 Institutionalization of unit of analysis

Unlike social science fields such as strategic management and organization studies in which basic units of analyses remain relatively stable over time, change and emergence are generally acknowledged to be fundamental characteristics of entrepreneurship. This means that business ideas, individuals, groups, business models, etc. are not stable throughout the process of creating new organizations and business ventures (Katz and Gartner 1988). Stated differently, central units of analysis tend to change or even transform from one form (e.g. idea or individual) into another (e.g. product, team, or firm) during the process (McMullen and Dimov 2013). To assume that opportunities, stakeholders, ventures and other central units of analysis remain stable over the duration of an entrepreneurial process may lead us to ignore essential aspects of entrepreneurial processes. Reflecting on these complications, McMullen and Dimov (2013) define entrepreneurship as 'the sequential encounter and institution of information – *through actions and interactions* – that becomes embedded in the final product' (McMullen and Dimov 2013, p. 1493, emphases added). It is worth mentioning that McMullen and Dimov argue that entrepreneurship entails 'the institutionalization of information' as encountered by entrepreneurial actors, that is, how entrepreneurs repeatedly make use of new information from their actions and interactions. From this perspective, there is both a process by which such information is interpreted and becomes embedded in some product that is under development, and a potential end state of the process in terms of what the product turns out to be.

Such a definition puts emphasis on the process of emergence and formation of products, organizations and markets; the 'pre-historical' phase that occurs before they stabilize and become tractable to uniform criteria for definition and sampling (cf. Sarasvathy 1998). While the notion of an uncertain and ambiguous pre-history has received some attention from the fields of organization theory and strategic management, it is not central. Instead, it is discussed in terms of events that are admittedly important, but that occur 'before' the proper stable units of analysis have emerged (Fiol and Romanelli 2011; Helfat and Lieberman 2002). The field of entrepreneurship, on the other hand, focuses squarely on these early formative stages where uncertainty, emergence and transformation are essential, rather than incidental. Keeping this distinction in mind, we should be careful not to forcibly fit emergent and changing phenomena into the static units of analysis used in other fields. Instead, it is important to develop conceptual and methodological tools that fit with the properties of the phenomena at hand (Berglund 2015). Entrepreneurship researchers have merely begun to grapple with these issues and in doing so, the influence of theories and constructs from more traditional fields of management may be constraining.

An illustrative case in point is the notion of entrepreneurial opportunities, which has emerged as a central unit of analysis in the entrepreneurship field. Being borrowed from economic theory, opportunities are commonly regarded as ontologically real phenomena that are not known by everyone due to information asymmetries. The opportunity then helps to guide the entrepreneurial process, which is said to consist of discovery, evaluation and exploitation (Shane and Venkataraman 2000). This understanding of opportunities clearly does not sit well with a definition of entrepreneurship that rests on uncertainty, emergence and transformation. Consequently, several authors have suggested that opportunities should not be conceptualized as ontologically real entities. Instead, opportunities should be seen as subjectively imagined by the entrepreneur (Klein 2008) where the main function of such imagined opportunities is to inspire and guide the entrepreneurial process (Berglund 2007). Borrowing a term from the sociology of science, opportunities are not ontologically real, but rather have an 'unfolding ontology', which means that while they can have material instantiations (e.g. in a business plan), they are defined by their potentiality, their incompleteness of being, their ability to unfold and develop, and their capacity to stimulate creative action (Knorr Cetina 2001; cf. Miettinen and Virkkunen 2005). This reconceptualization of opportunities as something that exists and unfolds on the intersection between the entrepreneur and the surrounding environment resonates with Sarasvathy's (2004a) idea that entrepreneurship is about unfolding, transformational processes of design. It also illustrates the importance of defining concepts and designing research projects in ways that are sensitive to the character of the phenomenon at hand.

3.2.3 Institutionalization of research designs

Another type of institutionalization concerns the way research is done. Given the nature of the phenomenon and the insights and discussions provided by entrepreneurship scholars, one could expect a more comprehensive methodological toolbox. Although there is a good number of both inductive and deductive studies in entrepreneurship, the type of designs adopted in these two types of research approaches by and large follow the mainstream traditions in organization theory and strategic management (Van de Ven and Engleman 2004). One reason for this could be training, with few entrepreneurship scholars being trained in, for example, psychology, philosophy or experimental studies.

This situation would of course not be a problem if the phenomena studied were similar to what is being studied in the fields where researchers are trained. However, as mentioned above, a core argument 'for' entrepreneurship as a specific field of inquiry is that entrepreneurship is distinct in terms of the uncertain, emergent and potentially transformative nature of entrepreneurial processes (McMullen and Dimov 2013; Venkataraman *et al.* 1990). In entrepreneurship, time and process thus present distinct methodological challenges compared to the traditional design of process studies in organization theory and strategic management, which focus on a set of activities conducted between particular start and end points where the researcher follows a presumably stable type of entity (e.g. a firm, a project or an individual), approximated by certain attributes, that are then related to particular outcomes of interest (Langley *et al.* 2013). This obviously makes sense when one samples entities that are relatively stable. However, as Van de Ven (2007) discusses in some detail, there is a quite stark distinction between studying the process of stable entities over time and studying entities that are highly fluid or stochastic in nature (such as a business idea or an emerging firm). When entities are fluid and cannot be readily sampled in uniform ways, studying these as a process means that research designs need to capture them as sequences of events or activities allowing for description of how particular things change over time. While some scholars have used longitudinal designs to empirically study entrepreneurship as a process that unfolds over time (Gartner *et al.* 2004; Samuelsson and Davidsson 2009), the methods of analysing such processes are still by and large confined to case studies and regression analyses of historical data. It is questionable whether the overwhelming focus on case studies and regression analyses of historical data (cross-sectional or longitudinal) is due to these really being 'the best tools for the job' to study the processes claimed by theorists as central to the development of entrepreneurship research (Davidsson and Tonelli 2013).

Aldrich (2009) reviewed all articles published in the *Administrative Science Quarterly* (a top-ranked journal where some of the most impactful entrepreneurship research has been published) between 2000 and 2007. In reviewing the 128 empirical articles published during these 8 years, he found that less than 35 per cent of all studies actually describe the context of study in terms of nation, region and time period studied. Without actually mentioning the country, time period or region studied, much of the important context of empirical studies is omitted, and hence our ability to compare and contrast across studies diminished. Further and perhaps more relevant for the generalizability and contextualization of entrepreneurship theory, Aldrich notes that a whopping 88 per cent of all single-country studies were based on data from the United States. Consequently, also in choosing areas of study, moving beyond the taken-for-granted focus on studies in developed economies, perhaps predominantly new ventures in high-technology industries, remains a challenge to entrepreneurship research. While Silicon Valley still represents a beacon of entrepreneurship that many take inspiration from, it is highly questionable whether the preponderance of studies taking place in such settings is fruitful for gaining new knowledge and developing theoretical insights to benefit the field at large (cf. Berglund 2011).

In addition to choosing an area of study, the methods utilized bear close resemblance to those predominant in strategy and organization research in mostly being based on various types of regression analyses or comparative case studies. In this regard, we are interested in discussing why other methods are not used in entrepreneurship research, such as sequence analysis – the comparison of sequences of events in order to find similarities and identifiable patterns (Abbott 1990; Lichtenstein *et al.* 2007), or 'fussy sets' – an increasingly popular mixture of qualitative and quantitative approaches (Fiss 2011). Why still so few experimental designs, despite re-occurring calls for such designs to be used in entrepreneurship studies (Patel and Fiet 2010)? Why still so few historical studies?

Even if entities are fluid and difficult to sample, recent advances in longitudinal research tools allow for such design to be crafted and studied as sequences of events or activities that change over time (Johnson *et al.* 2014). It seems to us that also in the usage of research methods, the prevailing tradition of variance-based regression analysis dominating most of strategic management and organization studies is increasingly becoming institutionalized and diffused also in entrepreneurship research through PhD training and in the publishing processes. The development of rigor is of course good, but not at the expense of confining methods utilized to a narrow set of standardized methodologies.

Taking a cue from the discussion above, one interesting source of inspiration when thinking about suitable research tools to answer the broad and complex questions suggested as unique to entrepreneurship scholarship (Aldrich 1999; Davidsson 2004; Shane and Venkataraman 2000; Zahra and Wright 2011) can be found in the philosophical tradition of pragmatism (Sarasvathy 2009).

3.3 Pragmatism: what makes entrepreneurs and entrepreneurship research different?

As described in the above, becoming institutionalized means that the scope of questions asked and the range of perspectives and methods utilized tends to be taken-for-granted. While it is prudent for all fields of research to continually question fundamental assumptions and remain open to new insights and perspectives, it can also be quite productive to focus on a narrow set of questions and methods (Kuhn 2012). We contend that much of entrepreneurship research is indeed quite narrowly focused, and in a way that echoes mainstream research in strategic management and organization theory (Baker and Pollock 2007). This can be interpreted in two ways. Either entrepreneurship is not a distinctive field of research characterized by unique questions and in need of carefully developed methods, but merely a contextual domain where scholars from other disciplines choose to make their inquiries (Sorenson and Stuart 2008). Or, the other interpretation takes seriously the idea that entrepreneurship scholarship is indeed a distinctive field of research that can and should provide answers to problems not attended to by the more established social sciences. We have arrived at the latter interpretation, mainly by asking ourselves whether we as a field pose questions that help us better understand entrepreneurial processes and their effects on society, and whether we ask questions that matter to entrepreneurs. Our conclusion is that we must pay more attention to the fundamental nature of entrepreneurship and, relatedly, to the research questions we ask, the units of analysis we employ and the way we design our studies.

From studies, teaching and consultation, most researchers have frequent contacts with practising entrepreneurs. In our own experience, entrepreneurs are often open, tolerant and curious about researchers' experiences and views, but most are not very reflexive when it comes to their own theories and methods. Entrepreneurs are pragmatic types. They want to build and change things, and often draw upon a multitude of skills, experiences and repertoires of themselves and of other stakeholders in doing so. However, in the last decade a growing number of experienced entrepreneurs have sought to turn their practical experiences and tacit knowledge into theories and models, often in the form of prescriptive methods that offer advice on how to efficiently develop new businesses under uncertain conditions (e.g. Blank and Dorf 2012; Furr and Ahlstrom 2011; Ries 2011; Savoia 2011). Practitioner theories, such as customer development and the lean startup, are also increasingly being used in teaching and employed in the design of incubators and accelerators around the world. However, they have not been subject to much scholarly scrutiny. There is clearly a growing disconnect between the theories developed and tested by entrepreneurship scholars and the more practically oriented writings that offer highly actionable as well as readily testable prescriptions. Would it, for instance, not be of interest to both entrepreneurs and scholars to test the generality and validity of the prescriptions suggested in the 'lean startup' literature? To compare the espoused theories and the theories in use of ostensibly lean entrepreneurs? To evaluate the effects of programs based on lean startup principles? There are of course a number of research efforts that do reflect on the nature of entrepreneurship and the appropriate units of analysis, and that investigate entrepreneurship in ways that are closely attuned to the details of actual entrepreneurial processes (e.g. Baker and Nelson 2005; Sarasvathy 2009). Whether these practitioners and academics call what they do lean startup (Ries 2011), customer development (Blank and Dorf 2012), effectuation (Sarasvathy 2008) or bricolage (Baker and Nelson 2005), they all share a very down to earth and pragmatic view of entrepreneurship.

This pragmatism of entrepreneurs is perhaps the most obvious, arguably a very interesting, and unfortunately a very under-researched aspect of entrepreneurship. The reason may be because it concerns mundane everyday practices and simple 'how to's' of entrepreneurship.[1] As a philosophical tradition, pragmatism was primarily developed by Charles Sanders Peirce (1935), William

James (1890/2011), and John Dewey (1916/2012). Their central idea was that thinking and theorizing is not primarily about accurately representing objective reality, but rather about helping mankind progress by developing knowledge that lets us achieve things and more generally helps us deal with problems and challenges as they arise. This was a big idea that had far-reaching implications for traditional philosophical questions such as the nature of truth and the validity of theories. Truth was seen as contingent rather than universal, and theories were seen as tools rather than more or less correct answers (James). And since the use value of a tool depends on the task at hand, the validity of theories, and by implication the nature of truth, was seen as contingent rather than universal.

It also has clear implications for entrepreneurship researchers. We see such a pragmatist tradition similar in spirit to many practitioner theories as well as to effectuation, bricolage and other practically oriented entrepreneurship research programs (cf. Johannisson 2011; Kraaijenbrink 2012). Therefore, it is ironic that the pragmatist emphasis on action over 'correct representation', stands in such stark contrast to much prevailing work in entrepreneurship research that seeks to arrive at the 'actual meaning' of concepts, such as what 'opportunities' are, how hazardous 'newness' is to new venture survival, or what it means to have an 'entrepreneurial orientation'. A more pragmatist approach to entrepreneurship research would instead take a cue from practising entrepreneurs, who typically could care less about 'truth' in their efforts to move their ventures forward. Pragmatist entrepreneurship researchers might want to approach the notion of opportunities in different ways for different purposes (Berglund 2007). Or similarly, how entrepreneurs can actively manage external stakeholders' impressions of venture newness or maturity to achieve specific goals (Lounsbury and Glynn 2001). The pragmatic assertion that a theory's validity and appropriateness must be established in relation to purposes and situational contingencies also resonates with the basic idea that entrepreneurship concerns emergent and transformative processes characterized by chance and change. In light of these considerations, pragmatist scholars should also be wary of attempts to close down conceptual debates in the name of theoretical coherence (cf. Berglund 2015), or to base theories on empirical evidence that fails to sufficiently account for important situational differences, such as between innovative and more imitative forms of entrepreneurship, or between different industries and regions.

3.4 Implications for entrepreneurial scholarship

If we are to take the pragmatism of real-world entrepreneurs seriously, entrepreneurship scholars need to cultivate a pluralistic view of studying entrepreneurship and dispense with methodological and theoretical dogmas. Rather than thinking about entrepreneurship solely as a context of study (Sorenson and Stuart 2008), pragmatic entrepreneurship scholars would emphasize practical use-value as an important validity criterion, and seek logical proximity between research questions, methods, analyses and conclusions, over external validity or theoretical grandeur. Sociologist Robert Merton's focus on the 'how did this phenomenon come about?', instead of grand theoretical schemes or simple cause-effect relationships, could serve as an inspiration here. Merton propagated a focus on social mechanisms and theories suitable for answering such questions, what he referred to as 'theories of the middle range' (Merton 1968). A somewhat related and decidedly pragmatic source of inspiration is provided by Herbert Simon (1981) who envisioned a 'sciences of the artificial', suitable for professional fields such as management and entrepreneurship, that is distinct from both the natural and social sciences in its focus on processes of design and emergence that highlight the theoretical and empirical importance of the contingent (not the necessary) and the possible (not the existing) (cf. Sarasvathy 2009).

Clearly, neither we nor Merton or Simon suggest that the scholarly community should altogether dispense with attempts to identify cause-effect relations, or ignore the insights made during decades of study in favour of a nihilistic 'anything goes' approach to scholarship. However, the contextual and processual nature of most entrepreneurship phenomena, combined with the inherent uncertainty and ambiguity of entrepreneurial processes, suggests that stable cause-effect attributes among stable entities will be difficult to identify and generalize. So even if causal claims make for attractive publication opportunities, we should remember that the ultimate test of our research's value is not text and publications *per se*, but our ability to say something useful that other researchers, and by extension practitioners, can discuss, criticize, refine, and in the end apply as a guide to their own thinking and acting. In pursuing this goal, we can be inspired not only by Simon, Merton and others, but also by the pragmatism of practising entrepreneurs as we think about ways of posing research questions, identifying appropriate and interesting (versus well-researched) units of analysis, and using a wide enough theoretical and methodological toolbox to investigate the research question at hand.

In this chapter we have also noted that as a consequence of the institutionalization of entrepreneurship research into a field largely dominated by traditions from organization theory and strategic management, the firm (and sometimes the individual) remains a central unit of analysis, despite strong and repeated calls for researchers to focus on processes and to broaden the units of analysis to also include ideas, groups, ventures and regions. As mentioned, processes of entrepreneurship often take place before more stable entities, like individuals and firms, have been established (Sarasvathy 1998) and more often than not the final business developed is the emergent result of various types of exchanges between multiple stakeholders. An entrepreneurial idea – or business opportunity – is thus realized only when it becomes a tangible concept that can be understood by others and distributed to them. This begs some questions. First, if entrepreneurship by and large takes place in social exchanges over time, entrepreneurship research may want to put further attention on the actual exchanges taking place. Economics, sociology and anthropology have long discussed the character of exchange from various perspectives, and there should be ample opportunities to draw upon such ideas and develop them further in the entrepreneurship domain (Graeber 2011; Podolny 1994). Second, if entrepreneurship concerns phenomena that are emergent in nature, and/or in a state of flux, researchers may want to reconsider the units of analysis in their studies. Also here, we suggest researchers look at Murray Davis' (1971) work. Another of his heuristics for generating new ideas among scholars is to assume that what seems to be a stable and unchanging phenomenon is in reality an unstable and changing phenomenon, for example, Marx saying that the economic organization of a society, which was thought highly stable, was in fact subject to radical change in short periods of time.

When it comes to concept and theory development within the field of entrepreneurship itself, it may conversely be of value to avoid the premature establishment of general and abstract definitions. One example mentioned earlier is the concept of 'entrepreneurial opportunities', where a voluminous theoretical literature debates the existence and nature of opportunities, but where empirical research remains scarce (Barreto 2012; McMullen, Plummer and Acs 2007; Mole and Mole 2010; Sarason, Dean and Dillard 2006; Sarasvathy *et al.* 2005; Shane and Venkataraman 2000). Here, experimental studies (Baron and Ensley 2006) or phenomenological studies investigating how opportunities are experienced and enacted by entrepreneurs may reveal a more pluralistic picture fruitful for further theorizing. In one such study, one of us concluded that:

> A suitable way of conceiving opportunities is therefore not as either existing or created per se, but as a bundle of more or less clear opportunity perceptions and opportunity projections that become relevant in a variety of situations and for a number of different reasons. It is in this multifaceted role that opportunities are truly relevant, since acting as if opportunities are both existing and created provides the cognitive and practical drivers that guide entrepreneurial actions.
>
> (Berglund 2007, pp. 269–270)

By emphasizing how various conceptions of entrepreneurial opportunities were used by entrepreneurs to achieve particular ends, this study illustrates a pragmatic approach to theory development. In doing so, it also highlights the significant value of reconsidering the ontological and epistemological foundations that are often taken for granted in many strands of entrepreneurship research.

In this chapter we have argued that the institutionalization of much of entrepreneurship scholarship into a narrowly confined corridor of questions, methods and theories originating in strategy and organization studies could lead to a type of 'mental straightjacket' limiting the development of entrepreneurship as a field. Some scholars have called for a grounding of investigations in 'the mud of common human experience' (Sarasvathy 2004b, p. 289), arguing that 'the everyday is the scene where social change and individual creativity take place as a slow result of constant activity' (Steyaert 2004, p. 10). Many have also undertaken such investigations, often through discourse analysis (Ahl 2004) such as investigations of metaphors and talks about entrepreneurship

(Cliff, Langton and Aldrich 2005) and even more pragmatically by investigating how entrepreneurs construct narratives to convince stakeholders to support their ventures (Lounsbury and Glynn 2001; Martens, Jennings and Jennings 2007). However, attention has been scarce towards the 'simple activities' of entrepreneurs or to 'pursue possible counterintuitive explanations' of phenomena that we observe. If entrepreneurship research would heed this call, we believe that epistemological inspiration from pragmatic philosophy, theoretical inspiration from disciplines beyond strategy and organization studies, and methodological inspiration from a wider range of traditions may prove valuable.

In addition to being open to new research areas and research questions, it is important for entrepreneurship scholars to reflect on the proper unit of analysis. In their well-cited theory article, Davidsson and Wiklund (2001) urged researchers to challenge dominating levels of analysis and also consider the difference between individual-level, group-level and firm-level predictors and outcomes, something that has been slow to catch on (e.g. Autio, Pathak and Wennberg 2013; Ruef 2010; Yang and Aldrich 2014). Social science explanations often work at distinctively different levels of analysis than the phenomenon they explain (Stinchcombe 1991; Weick 1979).

3.5 Conclusions

In his Pulitzer prize-winning book chronicling the development of pragmatism, Louis Menand summarized the central beliefs shared by its founding fathers:

> They all believed that ideas are not 'out there' waiting to be discovered, but are tools – like forks and knives and microchips – that people devise to cope with the world in which they find themselves. They believed that ideas are produced not by individuals, but by groups of individuals – that ideas are social. They believed that ideas do not develop according to some inner logic of their own, but are entirely dependent, like germs, on their human carriers and the environment. And they believe that since ideas are provisional responses to particular and unreproducible circumstances, their survival depends not on their immutability but on their adaptability.
>
> (Menand 2001, pp. xi–xii)

Entrepreneurs are commonly depicted as actors pragmatic in determining what knowledge is useful to their venture development efforts. While we must not forget that the pursuit of academic knowledge is an altogether different activity, it is still our firm belief that we as entrepreneurship scholars would benefit both from acknowledging the pragmatism of entrepreneurs and from embracing a bit of this same attitude in our own work as researchers, by developing theories that are instrumental and action-oriented, that acknowledge the context dependence of entrepreneurship, and that respect and reflect the experiences of the pragmatic entrepreneurs we study.

Note

1 An exception is Saras Sarasvathy's work on effectuation, which is explicitly rooted in the pragmatist tradition (cf. Sarasvathy 2009, p. 183).

References

Abbott, A. (1990) 'A primer on sequence methods', *Organization Science*, 1(4), pp. 375–392.

Ahl, H. (2004) *The Scientific Reproduction of Gender Inequality: A Discourse Analysis of Research Texts on Women's Entrepreneurship*. Copenhagen: Copenhagen University Press.

Aldrich, H. (1999) *Organizations Evolving*. London: Sage.

Aldrich, H.E. (2009) 'Lost in space, out of time: How and why we should study organizations comparatively'. In King, B., Felin, T. and Whetten, D. (eds) *Studying Differences between Organizations: Comparative Approaches to Organizational Research*. Research in the Sociology of Organizations, Vol. 26, Bingley: Emerald Group, pp. 21–44.

Aldrich, H.E. (2012) 'The emergence of entrepreneurship as an academic field: A personal essay on institutional entrepreneurship', *Research Policy*, 41, pp. 1240–1248.

Autio, E., Pathak, S. and Wennberg, K. (2013) 'Consequences of cultural practices for entrepreneurial behaviors', *Journal of International Business Studies*, 44(4), pp. 334–362.

Baker, T. and Nelson, R. (2005) 'Creating something from nothing: Resource construction through entrepreneurial bricolage', *Administrative Science Quarterly*, 50(3), pp. 329–366.

Baker, T. and Pollock, T.G. (2007) 'Making the marriage work: The benefits of strategy's takeover of entrepreneurship for strategic organization', *Strategic Organization*, 5(3), pp. 297–312.

Baron, R.A. and Ensley, M.D. (2006) 'Opportunity recognition as the detection of meaningful patterns: Evidence from comparisons of novice and experienced entrepreneurs', *Management Science*, 52(9), pp. 1331–1344.

Barreto, I. (2012) 'Solving the entrepreneurial puzzle: The role of entrepreneurial interpretation in opportunity formation and related processes', *Journal of Management Studies*, 49(2), pp. 356–380.

Berglund, H. (2007) 'Opportunities as existing and created: A study of entrepreneurs in the Swedish mobile internet industry', *Journal of Enterprising Culture*, 15(3), pp. 243–273.

Berglund, H. (2011) 'Early stage VC investing: Comparing California and Scandinavia', *Venture Capital: An International Journal of Entrepreneurial Finance*, 13(2), pp. 119–145.

Berglund, H. (2015) 'Between cognition and discourse: Phenomenology and the study of entrepreneurship', *International Journal of Entrepreneurial Behaviour and Research, Special Issue: Embracing Qualitative Research Philosophies and Methods*, 21(3), pp. 472–488.

Blank, S. and Dorf, B. (2012) *The Startup Owner's Manual: The Step-by-Step Guide for Building a Great Company*. Pescadero, CA: K&S Ranch, Incorporated.

Busenitz, L.W., West, I., Page, G., Shepherd, D., Nelson, T., Chandler, G.N. and Zacharakis, A. (2003) 'Entrepreneurship research in emergence: Past trends and future directions', *Journal of Management*, 29(3), pp. 285–308.

Casson, M. (1982) *The Entrepreneur: An Economic Theory*. Oxford: Martin Robertson.

Cliff, J.E., Langton, N. and Aldrich, H.E. (2005) 'Walking the talk? Gendered rhetoric vs. action in small firms', *Organization Studies*, 26(1), pp. 63–91.

Davidsson, P. (2003) 'The domain of entrepreneurship research: Some suggestions'. In Katz, J. and Shepherd, D. (eds) *Advances in Entrepreneurship, Firm Emergence and Growth*. Vol. 6, Oxford: Elsevier/JAI Press, pp. 315–372.

Davidsson, P. (2004) *Researching Entrepreneurship*. New York: Springer.

Davidsson, P. and Tonelli, M. (2013) *Killing our darling: Why we need to let go of the entrepreneurial opportunity construct*. Paper from the Australia Centre for Entrepreneurship, Brisbane.

Davidsson, P. and Wiklund, J. (2001) 'Levels of analysis in entrepreneurship research: Current practice and suggestions for the future', *Entrepreneurship Theory and Practice*, 25(4), pp. 81–99.

Davis, M.S. (1971) 'That's interesting', *Philosophy of the Social Sciences*, 1(2), pp. 309–344.

Dewey, J. (2012) *How We Think*. Mineola, NY: Courier Dover Publications.

DiMaggio, P.J. and Powell, W.W. (1983) 'The iron cage revisited: Institutional isomorphism and collective rationality in organizational fields', *American Sociological Review*, 48(2), pp. 147–160.

Duchesneau, D.A. and Gartner, W.B. (1990) 'A profile of new venture success and failure in an emerging industry', *Journal of Business Venturing*, 5(5), pp. 297–312.

Fiol, C.M. and Romanelli, E. (2011) 'Before identity: The emergence of new organizational forms', *Organization Science*, 23(3), pp. 597–611.

Fiss, P.C. (2011) 'Building better causal theories: A fuzzy set approach to typologies in organization research', *Academy of Management Journal*, 54(2), pp. 393–420.

Furr, N. and Ahlstrom, P. (2011) *Nail it Then Scale it*. Open Library: NISI Institute.

Gartner, W., Shaver, K., Carter, N. and Reynolds, P. (2004) *Handbook of Entrepreneurial Dynamics: The Process of Organizational Creation*. Thousand Oaks, CA: Sage.

Gartner, W.B. and Carter, N.M. (2003) 'Entrepreneurial behavior and firm organizing processes'. In Acs, Z.J. and Audretsch, D.B. (eds) *Handbook of Entrepreneurship Research*. New York: Springer, pp. 195–221.

Graeber, D. (2011) *Debt: The First 5,000 Years*. London: Melville House.

Helfat, C. and Lieberman, M. (2002) 'The birth of capabilities: Market entry and the importance of pre-history', *Industrial and Corporate Change*, 11(4), pp. 725–760.

James, W. (1890/2011) *The Principles of Psychology*. Boston, MA: Digireads.com Publishing.

Johannisson, B. (2011) 'Towards a practice theory of entrepreneuring', *Small Business Economics*, 36(2), pp. 135–150.

Johnson, A.R., van de Schoot, R., Delmar, F. and Crano, W.D. (2014) 'Social influence interpretation of interpersonal processes and team performance over time using Bayesian model selection', *Journal of Management*.

Katz, J. and Gartner, W.B. (1988) 'Properties of emerging organizations', *Academy of Management Review*, 13(3), pp. 429–441.

Klein, P.G. (2008) 'Opportunity discovery, entrepreneurial action, and economic organization', *Strategic Entrepreneurship Journal*, 2(3), pp. 175–190.

Knorr Cetina, K. (2001) 'Objectual practice'. In Schatzki, T.R., Knorr Cetina, K. and von Savigny, E. (eds) *The Practice Turn in Contemporary Theory*. Routledge, pp. 175–188.

Kraaijenbrink, J. (2012) 'The nature of the entrepreneurial process: Causation, effectuation, and pragmatism', *New Technology-Based Firms in the New Millennium*, 9, pp. 187–199.

Kuhn, T.S. (2012) *The Structure of Scientific Revolutions*. Chicago, IL: University of Chicago Press.

Landström, H., Harirchi, G. and Åström, F. (2012) 'Entrepreneurship: Exploring the knowledge base', *Research Policy*, 42, pp. 1154–1181.

Langley, A., Smallman, C., Tsoukas, H. and Van de Ven, A. (2013) 'Process studies of change in organization and management', *Academy of Management Journal*, 56(1), pp. 1–13.

Lichtenstein, B.B., Carter, N.M., Dooley, K.J. and Gartner, W.B. (2007) 'Complexity dynamics of nascent entrepreneurship', *Journal of Business Venturing*, 22(2), pp. 236–261.

Locke, K. and Golden-Biddle, K. (1997) 'Constructing opportunities for contribution: Structuring intertextual coherence and "problematizing" in organizational studies', *Academy of Management Journal*, 40(5), pp. 1023–1062.

Lounsbury, M. and Glynn, M.A. (2001) 'Cultural entrepreneurship: Stories, legitimacy, and the acquisition of resources', *Strategic Management Journal*, 22, pp. 545–564.

Martens, M.L., Jennings, J.E. and Jennings, P.D. (2007) 'Do the stories they tell get them the money they need? The role of entrepreneurial narratives in resource acquisition', *Academy of Management Journal*, 50(5), pp. 1107–1132.

McMullen, J., Plummer, L. and Acs, Z. (2007) 'What is an entrepreneurial opportunity?', *Small Business Economics*, 28(4), pp. 273–283.

McMullen, J.S. and Dimov, D. (2013) 'Time and the entrepreneurial journey: The problems and promise of studying entrepreneurship as a process', *Journal of Management Studies*, 50(8), pp. 1481–1512.

Menand, L. (2001) *The Metaphysical Club*. London: Macmillan.

Merton, R. (1968) *Social Theory and Social Structure*. New York: Free Press.

Meyer, J.W. and Rowan, B. (1977) 'Institutionalized organizations: Formal structure as myth and ceremony', *American Journal of Sociology*, 83(2), p. 340.

Miettinen, R. and Virkkunen, J. (2005) 'Epistemic objects, artefacts and organizational change', *Organization*, 12(3), pp. 437–456.

Mole, K.F. and Mole, M. (2010) 'Entrepreneurship as the structuration of individual and opportunity: A response using a critical realist perspective: Comment on Sarason, Dean and Dillard', *Journal of Business Venturing*, 25(2), pp. 230–237.

Patel, P.C. and Fiet, J.O. (2010) 'Enhancing the internal validity of entrepreneurship experiments by assessing treatment effects at multiple levels across multiple trials', *Journal of Economic Behavior and Organization*, 76(1), pp. 127–140.

Peirce, C.S. (1935) *Collected Papers*. Cambridge, MA: Harvard University Press.

Podolny, J.M. (1994) 'Market uncertainty and the social character of economic exchange', *Administrative Science Quarterly*, 39, pp. 458–483.

Rauch, A. and Frese, M. (2007) 'Let's put the person back into entrepreneurship research: A meta-analysis on the relationship between business owners' personality traits, business creation, and success', *European Journal of Work and Organizational Psychology*, 16(4), pp. 353–385.

Rauch, A., Wiklund, J., Lumpkin, G.T. and Frese, M. (2009) 'Entrepreneurial orientation and business performance: An assessment of past research and suggestions for the future', *Entrepreneurship Theory and Practice*, 33(3), pp. 761–787.

Ries, E. (2011) *The Lean Startup: How Today's Entrepreneurs Use Continuous Innovation to Create Radically Successful Businesses*. New York: Random House Digital.

Ruef, M. (2010) *The Entrepreneurial Group*. Princeton, NJ: Princeton University Press.

Samuelsson, M. and Davidsson, P. (2009) 'Does venture opportunity variation matter? Investigating systematic process differences between innovative and imitative new ventures', *Small Business Economics*, 33(2), pp. 229–255.

Sarason, Y., Dean, T. and Dillard, J.F. (2006) 'Entrepreneurship as the nexus of individual and opportunity: A structuration view', *Journal of Business Venturing*, 21(3), pp. 286–305.

Sarasvathy, S.D. (1998) *How do firms come to be? Towards a theory of the prefirm*. Doctoral Dissertation, Pittsburgh, PA: Carnegie Mellon University.

Sarasvathy, S.D. (2004a) 'The questions we ask and the questions we care about: Reformulating some problems in entrepreneurship research', *Journal of Business Venturing*, 19(5), pp. 707–717.

Sarasvathy, S.D. (2004b) 'Constructing corridors to economic primitives: Entrepreneurial opportunities as demand-side artifacts'. In Butler, J. (ed.) *Opportunity Identification and Entrepreneurial Behavior*. Greenwich, CN: Information Age Publishing, pp. 291–312.

Sarasvathy, S.D. (2009) *Effectuation: Elements of Entrepreneurial Expertise*. Cheltenham: Edward Elgar.

Sarasvathy, S.D. and Dew, N. (2005) 'New market creation through transformation', *Journal of Evolutionary Economics*, 15(5), pp. 533–565.

Sarasvathy, S.D., Dew, N., Velamuri, S.R. and Venkataraman, S. (2005) 'Three views of entrepreneurial opportunity'. In Acs, Z. and Audretsch, D. (eds) *Handbook of Entrepreneurship Research*. New York: Springer, pp. 141–160.

Savoia, A. (2011) *Prototype it: Make sure you are building the right it, before you build it right*. Available at: www.pretotyping.org/uploads/1/4/0/9/14099067/pretotype_it_2nd_pretotype_edition-2.pdf (Accessed: 31 May 2014).

Shane, S. and Venkataraman, S. (2000) 'The promise of entrepreneurship as a field of research', *Academy of Management Review*, 25(1), pp. 217–266.

Simon, H.A. (1981) *The Sciences of the Artificial*. Cambridge, MA: MIT Press.

Sorenson, O. and Stuart, T.E. (2008) 'Entrepreneurship: A field of dreams?', *Academy of Management Annals*, 2(1), pp. 517–543.

Steyaert, C. (2004) 'The prosaics of entrepreneurship'. In Hjorth, D. and Steyaert, C. (eds) *Narrative and Discursive Approaches in Entrepreneurship*. Cheltenham: Edward Elgar, pp. 8–21.

Stinchcombe, A.L. (1991) 'The conditions of fruitfulness of theorizing about mechanisms in social science', *Philosophy of the Social Sciences*, 21(3), pp. 367–388.

Van de Ven, A.H. (2007) *Engaged Scholarship: A Guide for Organizational and Social Research*. Oxford: Oxford University Press.

Van de Ven, A.H. and Engleman, R.M. (2004) 'Event- and outcome-driven explanations of entrepreneurship', *Journal of Business Venturing*, 19(3), pp. 343–358.

Venkataraman, S., Van de Ven, A., Buckeye, J. and Hudson, R. (1990) 'Starting up in a turbulent environment: A process model of failure among firms with high customer dependence', *Journal of Business Venturing*, 5, pp. 277–295.

Weick, K.E. (1979) *The Social Psychology of Organizing*. Reading, MA: Addison-Wesley.

Weick, K.E. (1990) *The Social Psychology of Organizing*. New York: McGraw-Hill.

Wilhite, A. (2006) 'Economic activity on fixed networks'. In Tesfatsion, L. and Judd, K.L. (eds) *Handbook of Computational Economics*, Volume 2. Cambridge, MA: Elsevier, pp. 1013–1045.

Wright, M., Pruthi, S. and Lockett, A. (2005) 'International venture capital research: From cross-country comparisons to crossing borders', *International Journal of Management Reviews*, 7(3), pp. 135–165.

Yang, T. and Aldrich, H.E. (2014) 'Who's the boss? Explaining gender inequality in entrepreneurial teams', *American Sociological Review*.

Zahra, S.A. and Wright, M. (2011) 'Entrepreneurship's next act', *Academy of Management Perspectives*, 25(4), pp. 67–83.

4 Grappling with the Kirznerian heritage in a time of economic and environmental crisis

Steffen Korsgaard

4.1 Introduction

The Austrian economic tradition is the closest thing to a Kuhnian 'normal science' as can be found in entrepreneurship research. In particular the work of Israel Kirzner has set the tone for theoretical and empirical advances in our understanding of entrepreneurship over the last two decades (Douhan, Eliasson and Henrekson 2007; Klein and Bylund 2014, Korsgaard, Berglund, Thrane and Blenker forthcoming b). Kirzner's theories suggest that entrepreneurs play a vital function in the development of markets and economies. They discover opportunities to allocate resources in better ways and in doing so make a profit. This depiction of the entrepreneurial function as one of discovery of opportunities has helped researchers cast light on important issues related to entrepreneurship, such as why some people and not others engage in entrepreneurial activity and how entrepreneurs organize their entrepreneurial ventures, as well as connect these findings to a macro-level understanding of market processes and economic development.

Kirzner's work thus constitutes a heritage that most if not all entrepreneurship researchers and educators must somehow relate to, by either working within the boundaries defined by the 'normal science' of entrepreneurship or positioning oneself in marginalized oppositional groupings challenging the mainstream (cf. e.g. Hjorth, Jones and Gartner 2008). In this chapter I will therefore argue that the Kirznerian heritage, on the one hand, represents a challenge and potentially a stumbling block for entrepreneurship research. It holds a number of anomalies, which are impossible to ignore in a time of economic and environmental crisis where policy makers and others look to entrepreneurship, to help solve our vital economic and environmental challenges (Korsgaard, Anderson and Gaddefors forthcoming a; Rae 2010). A continued rooting in the Kirznerian tradition without critically challenging its basic assumptions and interpretation of key concepts, may prevent us from conceptualizing entrepreneurship in ways that are inherently socialized, contextualized, localized, and environmentally and culturally sensitive. On the other hand, I will argue that simply abandoning the Kirznerian heritage will entail the risk of furthering the gap between mainstream entrepreneurship research and oppositional groups, as well as ignoring the concepts and ideas that, if re-interpreted, can help move entrepreneurship research forward in new directions that incorporate a broader range of entrepreneurial actions than opportunity discovery.

If we consider Kirznerian ideas as the mainstream 'normal science' for entrepreneurship research, it is expected that, over time, anomalies will appear; observations, results and problems that cannot adequately be explained within the frame of the dominant paradigm (Kuhn 1996). Such anomalies are inherent in all 'normal sciences' and will accumulate over time until such a point where they can no longer be ignored, and new streams of research will emerge that question the basic assumptions of the dominant paradigm. Such new streams of entrepreneurship research have been emerging at least since the turn of the century, primarily in Europe. Yet, these alternatives have made limited impact in the mainstream research for various reasons that lie beyond the scope of this chapter. With the onslaught of the financial crisis of 2008 and onwards this intra-field discussion has taken a new dimension. The financial crisis highlighted the economic, social and environmental consequences of the opportunistic exploitation mindset incorporated in the Kirznerian heritage (Munir 2011; Rae 2010), and provided a moral obligation for entrepreneurship researchers to critically examine the assumptions and values incorporated in how we have conceptualized entrepreneurship – although there is no moral obligation to arrive at similar conclusions as is done in this chapter (see Agarwal *et al.* 2009 for an example of a reflection on the crisis and entrepreneurship and strategic management theory that arrives at very different conclusions).

Following this line of thought, the chapter will argue that Kirznerian ideas as mainstream 'normal science' hold several anomalies, and that the current economic and environmental crises highlight these in ways that are impossible to ignore. In particular, it will be argued that anomalies exist in relation to 1) the socialized nature of entrepreneurship, 2) the role of context in entrepreneurial processes, and 3) the relation between entrepreneurship and the environment.

From these anomalies it is clear that the rooting of entrepreneurship in the Kirznerian heritage has drawbacks as well as advantages. Within an Austrian paradigm, entrepreneurial activities not undertaken for economic reasons and seeking to create non-economic (e.g. environmental, cultural and social) impacts are necessarily marginalized, and privilege is given to certain types of entrepreneurs (e.g. growth-oriented high tech success stories) (Steyaert and Katz 2004). Also, it offers a monochord response to social and environmental challenges; namely entrepreneurial discovery of market failures predicated on deregulation of markets.

On the basis of the identification of the key anomalies of the Kirznerian paradigm, the chapter focuses on key concepts in Kirzner's work in an attempt to develop new conceptualizations or readings of these, which address the anomalies. In particular the focus is on the idea of entrepreneurship as a function of value creation, uncertainty and resources. Firstly, a functional definition of entrepreneurship remains useful as it allows us to capture entrepreneurial phenomena regardless of the organizational form they take (Klein 2008b) and whichever motives drive the entrepreneurial activities. Yet it may be conducive to re-interpret how this function works and the outcomes it produces. In continuation of this, the function of entrepreneurship should be considered value creation more broadly than economic value. Entrepreneurs create multiple forms of value – deliberately or accidentally (Korsgaard and Anderson 2011). Thirdly, the concept of uncertainty becomes central when the image of opportunity discovery is challenged, and must therefore take a more central role in the conceptualization of the entrepreneurial function. Finally, the issue of resources needs to be addressed differently, and in ways that acknowledge how some resources are materially grounded and how their use has environmental, social and cultural implications (Hudson 2005, 2010).

For these concepts the chapter thus offers a re-interpretation that extends traditional Kirznerian thinking and aligns it with a vision for entrepreneurship that is more comprehensive y*et also* more modest. Comprehensive in the sense that entrepreneurship is considered a function for value creation through re-interpretation of resources across economic, social, cultural, environmental spheres, yet modest in the sense that entrepreneurship cannot be considered the one and only mechanism through which unfortunate allocation of resources can be addressed, as is often suggested in the Kirznerian tradition.

4.2 The Austrian heritage in entrepreneurship research

4.2.1 Austrian economics and the contribution of Israel Kirzner

Austrian economics has become increasingly influential in entrepreneurship research over the past decades, in particular the work of Kirzner, which for many entrepreneurship scholars is the primary reference point (Klein and Bylund 2014). Indeed, the conceptual inventory of Kirzner's discovery perspective of entrepreneurship, as developed in the 1973 book 'Competition and Entrepreneurship', has largely been copied into much of the mainstream empirical research in the field; and no less so since the introduction of Shane and Venkataraman's (Shane 2003, 2012; Shane and Venkataraman 2000) influential nexus perspective. Understanding the Kirznerian heritage and its role in entrepreneurship research is thus mainly about understanding how Kirzner's ideas of the alert entrepreneur, entrepreneurial discovery and the market as a process have been integrated and operationalised in mainstream entrepreneurship research and theory building (Douhan *et al.* 2007; Klein and Bylund 2014; Klein 2008b; Korsgaard *et al.* forthcoming b).

As is the case with most economic literature dealing with entrepreneurship, Kirzner is first and foremost concerned with the function of the entrepreneur in the economic system (Hebert and Link 1988), and hence deals with entrepreneurship as a distinct function in the market process. The cornerstone work of Kirzner's (1973) 'Competition and Entrepreneurship' offers an attempt to create a place for the entrepreneur in neo-classical equilibrium theory. In order to create this place, Kirzner questions some of the basic assumptions of neo-classical economic theory. According to Kirzner neo-classical economics assumes that individual actors make rational decisions, and that markets are in a state of equilibrium. The rational actor maximizes utility relative to a given set of ends. With this knowledge she allocates scarce resources to optimize her utility given the tastes and preferences she may have. Similarly, the market is in a state of equilibrium where resources are allocated optimally. Any divergence from the equilibrium state will immediately be remedied as information about prices and qualities are assumed to be openly available and accessible to all actors in the market.

By (wrongly) assuming this state of equilibrium, the neo-classical view renders invisible a number of key elements, including the competitive nature of the market process and the role of the entrepreneur (Kirzner 1973). It is therefore necessary to shift focus from equilibrium states to the market forces that compel changes in prices, outputs, methods of production, and the allocation of resources (Kirzner 1973). Contrary to the assumptions of neo-classical economics, the Kirznerian view assumes that actors have imperfect knowledge, and therefore constantly make errors in their assessment of prices and qualities. In equilibrium theory, where actors make 'perfect' decisions, there is no room for the role of the entrepreneur. But when actors make erroneous decisions, the entrepreneur is of vital importance.

The ignorance of other market actors and their plans leads individuals and organizations to overestimate or underestimate the real value of resources so that some will be willing to pay 'too much' for products and resources, while others will be willing to pay 'too little'. This in turn leads to a suboptimal coordination of resources in the market. An opportunity is the result of inefficient exploitation of resources caused by an absence of coordination (Kirzner 1973). This lack of coordination is expressed in price differences. A given resource may be sold at different prices in different markets. It is basically this difference that the entrepreneur discovers. An opportunity in the Kirznerian view is thus an arbitrage opportunity (Kirzner 1973). A prototypical example of an arbitrage opportunity is an entrepreneur buying a piece of land and subsequently making a profit by selling out smaller parcels of the land at a profit (Alvarez, Barney and Anderson 2013).

Unlike the neo-classical framework, Kirzner does not assume that all market actors are, in principle, equally likely to discover a given opportunity. Some actors are simply more alert than others. Kirzner contrasts the notion of alertness from search and knowledge. Alertness is not the possession of knowledge, but a 'knowing where to look for knowledge' (Kirzner 1973, p. 68). Therefore, alertness cannot be seen as a production factor that can be acquired. Similarly, alertness is different from search. The discovery of an opportunity, argues Kirzner, always involves an element of surprise (Kirzner 1997), which stems from the fact that for it to be a discovery, the actors cannot by definition have known what was to be discovered. It is therefore impossible to search for opportunities, as searching involves some knowledge of what you are searching for.

Kirzner's contribution to the entrepreneurship field can thus be argued to consist of two elements. Firstly, Kirzner's disequilibrium model demonstrates the importance of an entrepreneurial function in continually developing the market. Kirzner thus embodies what Klein (2008b) refers to as the functional definition of entrepreneurship. The functional definition of Kirzner places the entrepreneurial function at the heart of all change and development, and thus makes entrepreneurship an inevitable element in all theorizing and policy-making that seeks to create development at all levels from the global to the very local (see e.g. OECD 2006). Secondly, the conceptual inventory of Kirzner's view of entrepreneurship has been integrated into some of the most central debates and streams in the field: opportunities, discovery and alertness have thus all been subjected to theoretical development and empirical research by centrally placed and influential entrepreneurship researchers. An early example is the inquiry into whether entrepreneurs search actively for opportunities or discover them accidentally by being alert, as was suggested by Kirzner (see e.g. Busenitz 1996; Gaglio and Katz 2001; Kaish and Gilad 1991). These studies generally found limited support for the existence of entrepreneurial alertness. Also Shane and Venkataraman's (2000) influential nexus perspective draws heavily on Kirzner's work. In this perspective, as in Kirzner's view, opportunities are considered objective and independent from the entrepreneur; the entrepreneurial process is initiated by an entrepreneurial discovery; and some characteristics, although not necessarily alertness, make certain individuals more likely to discover opportunities than others (cf. Eckhardt and Shane 2003; Shane 2000, 2003; Shane and Venkataraman 2000).

Recent developments in the field relating to discovery and opportunities are thus very much related to the Kirznerian view of entrepreneurship. The psychology-informed research on how entrepreneurs discover opportunities, and how the discovery processes might be influenced by contextual and emotional factors, is a case of this (Baron 2004, 2006, 2008; Foo 2011). A fine example of this is Foo's (2011) finding that positive emotional affect has a positive effect on opportunity evaluation. Also in the discussion on whether opportunities are discovered or created, the former standpoint is clearly Kirznerian, and draws some of its legitimacy from being aligned with Austrian economic thinking (Alvarez and Barney 2007, 2010).

There has been some reservation about the interpretation of Kirzner's ideas in the entrepreneurship field. Kirzner (2009, 1999) himself has stated that the adoption of the central ideas from his 1973 book has been different from what was intended. Specifically, Kirzner suggests that the model presented in the 1973 book was a deliberately simplified one, intended to address neo-classical economists, but not intended to stipulate how actual entrepreneurial processes play out (Korsgaard *et al.* forthcoming b). As a consequence the passage of time was not taken into account, meaning that key concepts of real-life entrepreneurial processes such as uncertainty were ignored (Kirzner 1982, 1985; Korsgaard *et al.* forthcoming b). In similar fashion some have argued that entrepreneurship scholars have been reading the wrong Austrian economists, suggesting that Lachmann or Knight present better options than Kirzner, because of their emphasis on creativity and judgement as opposed to opportunity discovery

(Chiles, Bluedorn and Gupta 2007; Chiles *et al.* 2010a, 2010b, 2013; Foss and Klein 2012; Klein 2008b). It has also been suggested that Kirzner has been read in a limited or overly simplified way (Barreto 2012; Klein 2008b; Korsgaard *et al.* forthcoming b, McCaffrey forthcoming). As examples Klein (2008b) emphasizes how entrepreneurship scholars have ignored the metaphorical nature of key concepts such as alertness and opportunities, and Korsgaard *et al.* (forthcoming b) have shown that entrepreneurship scholars have embraced only a part of Kirzner's work, and arguably the parts least suited to provide a basis for exploring real-life entrepreneurial processes. These critiques are relevant and to some extent probably correct. They suggest that it is likely fruitful to revisit the conceptual inventory adopted from Kirzner into the entrepreneurship field; in particular the central ideas of opportunity, discovery and alertness that have been drawing the contours of the field for the past three decades. The critique does not, however, warrant a complete abandonment of Kirznerian ideas. It would be premature to suggest that Kirzner's work does not hold elements that would be useful in further developing entrepreneurship research and help bridge the current tradition and paradigm with new conceptualizations.

4.2.2 The heritage in a time of crisis

In times of economic growth and environmental optimism, the image of entrepreneurship inherited by the entrepreneurship field from its economics roots in general (Hebert and Link 1988; Landström 1999) and the Kirznerian heritage in particular may seem relevant and appropriate. Primarily, because it incorporates faith in the ability of economic opportunism to create social welfare and hopefulness with regards to the ability of profit driven entrepreneurship to solve environmental problems (see e.g. Cohen and Winn 2007; Dean and McMullen 2007; Pacheco, Dean and Payne 2010). Consequently, entrepreneurship research has had much to say about how to create economic growth on global, national and regional levels. The recent economic crisis and the increasingly imposing environmental problems facing our current society, has cracked the image, and poses questions (long overdue perhaps) about the relevance and appropriateness of the Kirznerian heritage. The crises make thoroughly visible the downsides of opportunism and pure profit motives.

The exact causes of the economic and environmental crises are debatable and to some extent probably dependent on the theoretical and political standpoint from which the analysis of the causes is conducted (Hudson and Maioli 2010). From the perspective of an entrepreneurship researcher it is, however, difficult to ignore the possibility that risky and opportunistic short-term entrepreneurial actions are significant contributors to the crises. The crash of the financial market in the US which triggered the international economic crisis was caused partially by risk-taking opportunism, with both house owners and loan brokers making overly risky decisions based on over-optimistic assessments of the housing market (Harvey 2011; Hudson and Maioli 2010). This type of risky opportunism helped create a short-term profit, but longer-term value destruction due to the bubble effect created by the short-termism. Similarly, profit seeking opportunism creates short-term profits at the expense of environmental externalities. The costs of these externalities are borne by others than the entrepreneurs, at least in the shorter run. As such both the economic and environmental crises may share a root cause in opportunistic entrepreneurship, of the kind promoted in the Kirznerian heritage, and that has been passed on enthusiastically in business school and public discourse on entrepreneurship (cf. Rae 2010).

As such it is not surprising that the entrepreneurship research community has had little to communicate and contribute in relation to the economic and environmental crises that we are currently facing. They have joined organization scholars at large in adopting a silent stance (Munir 2011). According to Munir (2011) business scholars have generally come too close to their subjects, becoming cheerleaders for big business, continually seeking out new ways for firms to make profits. This is certainly the case in entrepreneurship research (Rae 2010). With the exception of emerging oppositional forces (see e.g. Hjorth 2005; Steyaert and Katz 2004) it is a generally accepted credo that the role of entrepreneurship research is to facilitate entrepreneurship and growth, and to persuade entrepreneurs to grow their business as fast and big as possible. In other words exercise the kind of opportunistic behaviour that is embodied in the Kirznerian heritage.

Rae (2010) refers to this approach as 'old entrepreneurship' and suggests that while economies are growing and employment rising, the negative consequences of this form of entrepreneurship are overlooked. But not so in a financial crisis. In particular Rae emphasizes how the focus on opportunities without regards to the resources, quoting Stevenson and Jarillo (1990), leads to a focus on short-term economic profit and less concern for the responsible stewardship of finite resources. The economic and environmental crises highlight a paradox that is difficult to ignore. On the one hand it is likely that 'opportunistic' (Kirznerian) entrepreneurship is at the core of the capitalist system producing the crises. Yet, on the other hand at the same time entrepreneurship is aggressively promoted at the research and policy level as *the* way to (re)create economic growth (see e.g. OECD 2006, 2010). A resolution of this paradox, inevitably must involve some re-examination of the image of entrepreneurship, towards what Rae (2010) refers to as 'new entrepreneurship'.

4.3 The Kirznerian heritage as normal science and its anomalies

The extensive application of the Kirzner-based discovery view of entrepreneurship has constituted a period of Kuhnian 'normal science', with most empirical research taking place under a broadly shared understanding of what the key theoretical concepts are and the nature of the phenomenon (Shane

2012). This has allowed the field to progress rapidly and increase the output of research in both entrepreneurship and broader management journals.

As would be expected in a Kuhnian perspective, anomalies accumulate during a period of normal science, with a rising number of empirical observations that cannot be explained properly by the dominant paradigm. While these anomalies have always been there, they have become even more prevalent and visible during the financial crisis; to a point where they can and must not be ignored. The anomalies are numerous and presenting a complete list is beyond the scope of this chapter (for examples of critical examinations of Kirzner and entrepreneurship with a focus on other anomalies see e.g. Foss and Klein 2012; Klein 2008a, 2008b; Klein and Bylund 2014; Korsgaard *et al.* forthcoming b; McCaffrey forthcoming). The focus will therefore be on anomalies that are both highly relevant in a time of economic and environmental crises, as well as relevant to some of the theoretically most interesting discussions emerging in the field. Three anomalies will be discussed further in the following sections: the social dimension of entrepreneurship, the context of entrepreneurial processes, and the connection between entrepreneurship and the environment.

4.3.1 *The socialized nature of entrepreneurship*

The first anomaly relates to the socialized nature of entrepreneurship. One indication of the presence of this anomaly is the emergence of social entrepreneurship as a distinct phenomenon and research field. This suggests that existing theorizing on entrepreneurship has problems accounting for entrepreneurial phenomena associated with social motives and outcomes (Dey and Steyaert 2010) and that dominant entrepreneurship theories cannot readily be applied to social entrepreneurship (Korsgaard 2011). Indeed, the social plays a diminutive role in the Kirznerian heritage, which is largely individualistic. While Kirzner does not necessarily explicitly state that the entrepreneur is an individual, this is certainly the case in the subsequent empirical research on (Kirznerian) opportunity discovery and evaluation (Dimov 2007a). The discovery function of entrepreneurship is conceptualized as cognitive and moderated by factors that affect the individual such as education, prior experience, emotions etc. (Baron 2008; Foo 2011; Shane 2000; Shaver and Scott 1991; Welpe, Spörrle, Grichnik, Michl and Audretsch 2012). This stance has been subjected to severe criticism, suggesting that the discovery view blatantly overlooks social elements of the entrepreneurial process (cf. Korsgaard 2013).

Also, the Kirznerian heritage defines entrepreneurship as an economic activity undertaken for economic reasons only. A profit motive sparks the entrepreneurial process (Kirzner 1973). Consequently, the success of an entrepreneurial venture is measured by its economic outcomes. The emergence of socially, environmentally and culturally motivated forms of entrepreneurship question this assumption. Empirical research shows that many entrepreneurs pursue entrepreneurial ventures for many different reasons (Austin, Stevenson and Wei-Skillern 2006). It is also evident that entrepreneurial ventures create multiple types of outcomes, not just economic, and that treating these as externalities of secondary importance does not capture the full complexity of entrepreneurial phenomena (Anderson, Dodd and Jack 2012; Korsgaard and Anderson 2011).

In the Kirznerian view entrepreneurship is the fundamental mechanism through which the economy develops and growth is realised in society. Stifle entrepreneurship and suffer the consequences of a declining economic growth (Kirzner 1973). Following this line of thinking, Venkataraman (1997, p. 133), in a precursor to the seminal 2000 article with Shane, states that the connection between the individual entrepreneur's profit-seeking behaviour and the creation of social wealth is 'the very raison d'être of the field'. It is because entrepreneurs create growth in the economy as a whole that they become a worthy object of study. Indeed, in many cases, growth is seen as the only satisfactory outcome of entrepreneurial activity. So entrepreneurship and growth has at least two dimensions: Entrepreneurship as a driver of economic growth generally, and firm growth as an entrepreneurial pursuit and outcome. As a consequence economic performance of some variety is oftentimes used as the dependent variable in entrepreneurship studies (Leitch, Hill and Neergaard 2010).

The unidimensional connection between entrepreneurship and economic motives and growth is an anomaly. It does not fit with what is observed empirically. Achtenhagen, Naldi and Melin (2010) observe that researchers and practitioners have different conceptions of what growth is, and what it means to grow a business. Furthermore, considering economic growth, not all entrepreneurs want to grow their businesses (Cliff 1998; Davidsson 1989; Leitch *et al.* 2010; Lewis 2008; Morris, Miyasaki, Watters and Coombes 2006). Many entrepreneurs balance different considerations when making strategic choices, of which the ambition to grow the venture is one of many (Müller 2013; Wiklund, Davidsson and Delmar 2003).

The underlying problem is the overly narrow conception of value in the Kirznerian view. Value for Kirzner, as well as the research following the Kirznerian tradition considers value to be only economic value, and, therefore, cannot adequately describe entrepreneurial ventures that create non-economic forms of value (e.g. social entrepreneurship), and where entrepreneurs are driven by the motives related to non-economic value creation and appropriation. Consequently, there have been several calls for research that seeks to create conceptualisations and theories that embody multidimensional views of value in relation to entrepreneurship (Korsgaard and Anderson 2011; Leitch *et al.* 2010). The current financial and environmental crises make this need abundantly clear. Entrepreneurial activities, in order to contribute to recovery from the current crises and long-term economic and ecological resilience, need to balance multiple values, and incorporate a balanced view of the complex trade-offs between economic, social, cultural, environmental value (cf. Korsgaard and Anderson 2011). It is simply not enough to just create economic value and profit for the entrepreneur. The entrepreneurial activities must be sensitive to the social and spatial contexts in which they are embedded, and the long-term effects of the entrepreneurial activities on these contexts (cf. Hudson 2010; Korsgaard *et al.* forthcoming a; Rae 2010). This ambition, however, is not easily realised within or aligned with the Kirznerian heritage.

4.3.2 Entrepreneurship and context

The second anomaly relates to the issues of context in entrepreneurial processes. Several scholars have pointed to the need for a better understanding of context in entrepreneurial processes (Hindle 2010; Welter 2011; Zahra 2007). And certainly, the Kirznerian economic perspective offers outstanding possibilities for conceptualizing and researching the economic context (cf. Hindle 2010). It is less clear to what extent a discovery-based model is able to explore the temporal, spatial and institutional context. That is, how do the time/timing, location and institutional setting influence the entrepreneurial processes? Research focusing on the two latter issues indicates that entrepreneurial activity occurs in complex dynamic interrelations with the spatial and institutional environment, where a model built only on a discovery mechanism at best captures only parts of this interrelation (Buenstorf 2007; Luksha 2008).

According to several scholars the Kirznerian discovery view fails to make explicit the spatial, institutional and temporal context of entrepreneurial processes (Andersson 2005; Dimov 2007a, 2007b; McMullen and Dimov 2013; Stam and Lambooy 2012; Zahra 2007). Firstly, according to Zahra (2007), researchers must be careful not to generalize theories too far. As an example institutional settings impact severely on entrepreneurial processes (Mair and Marti 2009), and the distinction between opportunity and necessity entrepreneurship suggests that entrepreneurial discovery of an objectively existing opportunity by an alert entrepreneur is not a universally applicable model (Hechavarria and Reynolds 2009). Secondly, the arbitrage opportunity of Kirzner's 1973 book, which served as the model for the discovery and nexus perspectives (Shane and Venkataraman 2000), is devoid of a temporal dimension (McMullen and Dimov 2013). As Kirzner himself pointed out, the basic arbitrage model of entrepreneurship deliberately ignored the passage of time, and how the passage of time influenced the presence of, for example, uncertainty in the entrepreneurial process (Kirzner 1982, 1999, 2009; Korsgaard *et al.* forthcoming b). Consequently, the discovery model adopted from Kirzner, really only works when nothing of consequence happens between the initial idea or discovery and the subsequent exploitation of the opportunity. Thirdly, the Kirznerian view does not make explicit the spatial dimension of entrepreneurship (Andersson 2005; Stam and Lambooy 2012). According to Andersson (2005, p. 21) 'Kirzner's theory is non-spatial'. Consequently, it does not incorporate questions that relate to the uneven spatial distribution of opportunities, and how entrepreneurial processes have spatial consequences such as increased urbanization. This has lead entrepreneurship scholars to largely overlook the socio-spatial embeddedness of entrepreneurial opportunities (Anderson 2000; Hindle 2010). And even when the spatial dimension has been integrated, the aim has been to explore how spatial barriers can be circumvented. The entrepreneur depicted by Kirzner and subsequent entrepreneurship research is thus overly detached from the context in which the entrepreneurial processes occur, and this constitutes an important anomaly. The presence of this anomaly becomes all the more obtrusive as the financial and environmental crises have increased the gap between lagging and challenged regions both internationally and regionally. In such a situation entrepreneurship theorizing that is sensitive not only to which resources entrepreneurs can extract from the context, but most importantly to the particular needs and circumstances of the communities becomes all the more important (Hudson 2010; Korsgaard *et al.* forthcoming a; Rae 2010).

4.3.3 Entrepreneurship and the environment

The third anomaly relates to entrepreneurship and the environment. Kirzner's work builds on Hayek's idea of the market as a learning process. Here the market is seen as a dynamic process, where entrepreneurial actions continually improve the overall allocation of resources through the discovery of better ways of using resources – again with value measured solely in economic terms. The optimized allocation of resources is understood to lead to improved overall societal and environmental outcomes. Following this rationale, environmental problems of pollution and degradation of natural resources are considered to be essentially market failures caused by skewed incentive structures related to, for example, inappropriate government regulation. Examples of this line of thought include Cohen and Winn (2007) and Dean and McMullen (2007) suggesting that market failures such as flawed pricing mechanisms, inappropriate government interventions, monopoly power and information asymmetries, are the root of environmental problems. While it is perfectly possible that some environmental, economic and socio-spatial challenges are in fact market failures, this view re-produces, at a system level, the narrow view of the entrepreneurial function and entrepreneurial outcomes by providing explanations that one-dimensionally focus on economics and the market. In other words, it assumes that the invisible hand and learning process of the market will not only lead to economically better outcomes, but also improve socio-spatial and environmental conditions.

Paraphrasing Stevenson and Jarillo's (1990) definition of entrepreneurship, Kirznerian entrepreneurship pursues opportunities without regard to the resources involved (Rae 2010; Stevenson and Jarillo 1990). The existence of profit opportunities calls forth entrepreneurship, and leads to an economically optimized allocation of resources, in the Kirznerian view. But whether the allocation is environmentally optimal is another question. The presence of environmentally motivated entrepreneurs that compromise economic concerns for environmental ones, suggests that sometimes the two might conflict (Anderson 1998; Harbi, Anderson and Ammar 2010; Schaper 2002). It has recently been argued that Kirznerian entrepreneurship does not take into account how production and consumption are grounded in material nature, and therefore cannot adequately provide an explanation of why entrepreneurs do (and should) care for the environment as they engage in entrepreneurial activities (cf. Hudson 2005; Hudson 2010; Korsgaard *et al.* forthcoming a). What may be economically optimal in the short term may, from a multifaceted and balanced perspective, be sub-optimal, because the focus on short-term opportunistic behaviour obscures longer-terms environmental concerns. Consequently, it would be naïve to adopt the Kirznerian and Hayekian assumption that the presence of economic profit in itself assures that the entrepreneurial process reflects some learning about a better allocation of resources. The presence of economic profit is positive, but needs to be balanced by considerations of the possible destruction of other forms of value (environmental as well as social and cultural).

4.4 Discussion

In the above sections three anomalies of the Kirznerian heritage were identified and discussed. The Kirznerian view of entrepreneurship was criticized for underestimating the socialized nature of entrepreneurship, depicting entrepreneurial processes as overly detached from their institutional, temporal and spatial contexts, and wanting in its ability to capture the environmental aspects and consequences of opportunistic entrepreneurship. These anomalies, it was argued, are impossible to overlook in a time of economic and environmental crisis.

A logical consequence of these anomalies would be to suggest a complete abandonment of the Kirznerian heritage in favour of other theoretical foundations. Yet, in the remainder of the chapter, I will attempt to develop three concepts which are explicitly or implicitly present in the Kirznerian heritage, and which I believe are well worth exploring further in an attempt to create new ways of understanding entrepreneurship; new ways that connect to and engage in dialogue with the mainstream Kirznerian heritage. Connecting to the Kirznerian heritage is important for several reasons. Firstly, it discourages the creation of more fragmented and partly isolated groupings within the entrepreneurship field. Secondly, it allows for a better use of valuable empirical and theoretical development over the last twenty years. Needless to say, despite the anomalies of the Kirznerian heritage, research building on this heritage has led to many insightful and useful findings that the field would sorely miss if the Kirznerian heritage was abandoned.

Addressing the three anomalies will require developing the Kirznerian heritage in ways that take into account the socialized nature of entrepreneurship, a more contextualized understanding of entrepreneurial processes, and an increased sensitivity to the environmental consequences of entrepreneurial actions. This is no easy fix, but focusing on a functional definition of entrepreneurship as value creation, along with the concepts of uncertainty and resources can help extend the Kirznerian heritage into a new understanding that addresses the anomalies.

In particular the extended conceptualization of entrepreneurship as a value-creating function which includes the creation of economic as well as social, environmental, cultural etc. values addresses the need for a more socialized and contextualized understanding of entrepreneurship. Similarly, the emphasis on uncertainty and resources, seeks to underline the importance of integrating environmental concerns in entrepreneurship.

4.4.1 A functional definition of entrepreneurship

In the original Kirznerian view entrepreneurship is the function through which the market develops (Kirzner 1973). The function of the entrepreneur is not necessarily connected to particular individuals or firms, but is seen as a mundane activity in which all market actors can engage (Foss and Klein 2012). Drawing on this tradition, entrepreneurship can be understood as the recombination of resources to create value. To what extent this activity is manifested in the creation of a new firm, or whether it's an individual that performs the function or a collective of actors, becomes an empirical question rather than one of definition.

This definition is a key contribution of the (Austrian and) Kirznerian perspective. Klein (2008b) distinguishes between structural, occupational and functional definitions of entrepreneurship. Structural definitions emphasize the firm as the unit of analysis, and suggest that entrepreneurial firms are small and/or new firms. The focus in research embracing a structural definition will often be on industry dynamics at the macro-level. Occupational definitions position the individual as the unit of analysis and will focus either on the (e.g. psychological) characteristics of the entrepreneur or explore the reasons for self-employment. According to Klein (2008b) both these definitions are overly restrictive by focusing on the firm or individual.

Maintaining a functional definition is important for several reasons. Firstly, even with an expanded conceptualization of value (see below), the creation of a new firm is in and of itself neither a sufficient nor a necessary condition for the recombination of resources to create value. Nor can we assume that entrepreneurship involving the creation of new firms by definition is more valuable or more likely to succeed than entrepreneurial activities through other organizational forms. Consequently, the adoption of a non-functional definition might support unfortunate monochord policies focusing on the creation of new firms, for the sake of creating new firms. Secondly, new organizational forms are constantly emerging where the formal setup of a company is not present or an undistinctive feature of the organization, for example, in different forms of community entrepreneurship (Borch *et al.* 2008; Imas, Wilson and Weston 2012; Johannisson and Nilsson 1989; Johannisson and Olaison 2007; Peredo and Chrisman 2006). Also, occasionally the government or public authorities may need to act as entrepreneur (Link and Scott 2010).

Ideally, a definition of entrepreneurship would thus be able to encompass that entrepreneurship can happen in all sorts of organizations and not just new/ small firms. It will also be able to conceptualize those aspects of the process that are not individual, and reside with an individual entrepreneur. A functional definition manages both these aspects. By considering entrepreneurship to be a function, a process, it becomes possible to explore entrepreneurship in a broad range of settings, and without restricting analysis to the individual entrepreneur (see also Shane and Venkataraman 2000).

The financial crisis has shown that not all forms of entrepreneurship are equally valuable to society in general. Short-term opportunistic entrepreneurship on the part of, for example, financial institutions managing housing loans, real estate speculators and similar market actors have by most accounts contributed significantly to the destabilization of economies (Harvey 2011). What is central is not the presence of profit, firms or enterprising individuals but the function of value creation. Focusing on occupational or structural definitions of entrepreneurship might obscure the functional nature of entrepreneurship regardless of its organizational manifestations. The key is exploring how the function is enacted and the consequences of the function in relation to the creation and destruction of value.

A functional definition of entrepreneurship does not invalidate the study of the many different organizational forms in which it occurs, and the relative (contextually moderated) efficacy of these forms. Indeed, it actually requires such studies. It is therefore imperative, under a functional definition, for entrepreneurship scholars to continuously explore new organizational forms, contexts and manifestations of entrepreneurial value creation (Sarasvathy and Venkataraman 2011).

Where the Kirznerian functional definition needs to be extended, is in its one-dimensional focus on economic value creation. Entrepreneurs create many different forms of value, and place a different relative emphasis on these different forms (Leitch *et al.* 2010). A new conceptualization of entrepreneurship needs to take a step further in the exploration of value creation in several ways. It is absolutely imperative to develop multidimensional conceptions of value and growth. To be able to conceptually manage the fact that entrepreneurs deliberately and inadvertently create many different forms of value, and that these are intertwined (Korsgaard and Anderson 2011). It is also important to understand how the different forms of value creation may be destructive of other forms of value (see e.g. Tonts and Greive 2002). As evidenced by the financial crisis, the creation of economic value is all too often accompanied by the destruction of other forms of value. In a way this is part and parcel of the entrepreneurial process of creative destruction (cf. Schumpeter 1950). A singular focus on economic value, however, invites researchers to obscure the complex interrelations between different forms of value creation and destruction in research, teaching and general societal debate. Thereby, we run the risk of inhibiting a critical reflection on which forms of value creation to prioritize and which forms of value destruction to accept in policy-making, teaching and actual entrepreneurial practice (Steyaert 2007; Steyaert and Katz 2004).

The further exploration of different forms of value creation (and destruction) is an important avenue for future research in the entrepreneurship field. Such research will likely benefit from a firm grounding in a functional definition of entrepreneurship, as this will combine the greatest definitional precision with the greatest flexibility in where we search for new emerging forms of entrepreneurial value creation. It will be a search, that most importantly, identifies enactments of the entrepreneurial function which help communities and regions to recover from the crises and create long-term resilience.

4.4.2 Uncertainty

As pointed out by the several critics of the discovery view, the issue of uncertainty has been unduly downplayed in much of the recent entrepreneurship research (Chiles *et al.* 2007; Foss and Klein 2012; Klein 2008b). Indeed, uncertainty is typically not considered a central theme in the Kirznerian heritage. The discovery view, as rooted in Kirzner's work, operates within the confines of risk, with risk as the conceptual opposition to uncertainty (cf. Alvarez and Barney 2005, 2007). In the discovery view the information held in the opportunity as such incorporates enough knowledge to assess possible future outcomes and probabilities (cf. Shane 2003). Therefore, discovery-based research naturally emphasizes business planning and market analysis (cf. Delmar and Shane 2004). The abandonment of discovery as the key operation shifts the emphasis to uncertainty. The classic Knightian distinction between risk and uncertainty posits uncertainty as a decision-making context in which the information needed to assess possible outcomes and probabilities is not available (Knight 1921). In the Austrian economic tradition the passage of time and uncertainty are linked, so that whenever an entrepreneurial process unfolds over time it is uncertain. The fundamental action of the entrepreneur is thus not risk taking, but decision-making under uncertainty (Foss and Klein 2012; Knight 1921).

An entrepreneur obviously takes a kind of risk, in the sense that she is not certain to succeed, but it is in the common sense usage of the word, and not the theoretical sense invoked by, for example, Alvarez and Barney (2007, 2010), where risk refers to the possibility of calculating risk based on available information about the relevant outcomes and their probabilities. Therefore, as soon as we have the passage of time in an entrepreneurial process, the distinction between risky and uncertain decision-making contexts is unwarranted. Accordingly, the application of two types of opportunities in empirical research (see e.g. Hmieleski and Baron 2008; Mitchell, Mitchell and Smith 2008; Zahra 2008), often based on Alvarez and Barney's (2007, 2010) work, appears pre-mature in so far as it assumes that entrepreneurial processes exist, where the passage of time is either absent (pure arbitrage) or has no consequence (nothing of importance changes in the decision-making context). Some cases may well be imagined, but they would constitute a small minority.

In times of economic growth it is all too easy to forget the fundamental volatility of all markets. Entrepreneurial action based on opportunity discovery in risky contexts, may tend to ignore the fundamental volatility, as it dives into and analyses recent market trends (most pointing steeply upwards until the crash of the US financial markets) (Wiltbank *et al.* 2006). When economic indicators and markets develop positively it is difficult to feel uncertainty and take action to mitigate the passage of time in entrepreneurial processes, because the assumptions (e.g. continued growth in housing prices and markets for new products) are not necessarily challenged, at least at the industry level. The financial crisis, however, was an unpleasant reminder of the need to organize in ways that are more resilient to external shocks (cf. Hudson 2010; Simmie and Martin 2010; Zolli and Healy 2012).

Notably, the emergence of some of the recent popular normative models for entrepreneurship, lean start up and customer development, were developed in response to the dot com bubble of the early 00s. Following the sobering experience of the limits to growth in the emerging dot com markets, entrepreneurs such as Steve Blank came to realize that entrepreneurs need to organize in ways that take into account the fundamental uncertainty involved in all entrepreneurial processes (cf. Blank 2005, 2013).

Within the entrepreneurship research field, similar theoretical development is present, with effectuation, bricolage, exaptation etc. describing modes of entre-preneurship that are more resilient to uncertainty than traditional opportunity discovery (Baker and Nelson 2005; Dew, Sarasvathy and Venkataraman 2004; Sarasvathy 2001, 2008). The Kirznerian heritage, however, being associated with risk-based theorizing, may potentially hinder the further conceptual and empirical development of our understanding of uncertainty.

4.4.3 Resources

While opportunities and resources are inexorably intertwined, there has been a strong tendency to focus on opportunities rather than resources in entrepre-neurship research (cf. Short *et al.* 2010). This is a consequence of the somewhat limited or trending reading of the Austrians that the entrepreneurship research community has done. Kirzner as well as other Austrians have written at length about the heterogeneity of capital/resources (Foss and Ishikawa 2007; Foss and Klein 2012; Foss *et al.* 2007). Nonetheless, the historical legacy, perhaps passed on from seminal studies of entrepreneurial versus managerial opportunity dis-covery (Busenitz and Barney 1997; Kaish and Gilad 1991) have dictated a focus on opportunities rather than resources. Consequently, much effort has gone into studying the nature of opportunities (Ardichvili, Cardozo and Ray 2003; Buenstorf 2007; Chiasson and Saunders 2005; Companys and McMullen 2007; Dimov 2007a, 2007b) and how entrepreneurs discover opportunities (Baron 2004, 2006; Gaglio and Katz 2001), and much less effort has gone into dis-cussing the nature of resources in entrepreneurial processes, and how entre-preneurs creatively engage with resources to create new products and services.

It may well be argued that even within a Kirznerian view, resources are ontologically and temporally prior to opportunities. Opportunities arise from how individuals and markets assess the value of resources. From this, it is in fact a small step to acknowledging that opportunities are created from resources (Sarasvathy 2001). Indeed, Kirzner himself suggested that entrepreneurs may actually through their actions create the future reality they envisage: 'The futurity that entrepreneurship must confront introduces the possibility that the entrepreneur may, by his own creative actions, in fact construct the future as he wishes it to be' (Kirzner 1985, p. 155). Shifting the focus from opportunities to resources or resourcefulness does therefore not entail a break with Kirznerian ideas. While it would certainly need to downplay the role of opportunity discovery, much would be gained from taking into account Kirzner's ideas on capital heterogeneity (cf. Foss *et al.* 2007), as well as the idea of the market as a dynamic learning process.

The Kirznerian concept of entrepreneurship as discovery is linked to a notion of the market as a learning process (Hayek 1945; Kirzner 1997). Through entrepreneurial discovery, learning about the true value of resources and hence improved allocation of these resources is achieved. The learning, however, engages only with the exchange value of resources, that is to say the market price, as opposed to, for example, the use value. Considering the proposed extension of value to incorporate multiple forms of value, we might consider all entrepreneurial activity as an experimental learning process, which, with each little or big success and failure, increases society's knowledge of how resources can be combined to create (and destroy) different types of values. Indeed, the central (Austrian and) Kirznerian ideas on resource/capital heterogeneity and the learning process function of entrepreneurship could provide a useful platform from which the study of entrepreneurial processes can be extended.

An environmentally sensitive re-interpretation of Kirzner's heritage, would emphasize that the current environmental crisis is not simply a pollution crisis, but also a crisis of resource scarcity. The priority given to resources over opportunities must thus assume that resources are limited and that the entrepreneurial function needs to make the most of the resources already available at appropriate levels of analysis (venture, community, regional, etc.). This frugal attitude to resources focuses attention not just to creating more value, but to creating more value with less; with lessened overall resource consumption (Hudson 2005; Korsgaard *et al.* forthcoming a). As suggested by Rae (2010), such an environmental sensitivity needs to be ingrained in all entrepreneurial activities, and promoted in all institutions seeking to facilitate future entrepreneurial activity.

4.5 Implications and conclusion

In the sections above I have tried to grapple with the Kirznerian heritage in light of the recent financial crisis. This was done through the identification and discussion of three anomalies in the Kirznerian heritage as 'normal science'. On the basis of this, three themes were further developed to explore how we might develop entrepreneurship conceptualization and research further to address the anomalies while still retaining useful aspects of the Kirznerian heritage. In particular the emphasis was placed on retaining a functional definition of entrepreneurship with an extended conception of value to include non-economic forms of value; a continued exploration of uncertainty, despite this being a somewhat marginalized theme in the Kirznerian heritage; and a shift in focus from opportunities to resources.

These developments have implications for the kinds of research we may want to conduct as a field, what we would wish to pass on to our students, and what we might wish to advise to policy-makers. Some brief comments on these implications conclude the chapter.

For research the ideas presented in this paper in some way merely reiterate existing calls for a continued and relentless exploration of entrepreneurial practices, both existing and new forms (Sarasvathy and Venkataraman 2011; Steyaert 2007; Steyaert and Katz 2004). As stated above, a functional definition of entrepreneurship, combined with an extended conception of value to include non-economic value, provides a good reference point for such explorations. A certain focus, however, seems particularly important; namely the interrelations between multiple forms of value creation and destruction. This would enable a more complex and sensitive understanding of the positive and negative outcomes of entrepreneurial processes; be they economic (cf. our current financial crisis), environmental or social.

For teaching purposes, the attempt to grapple with the Kirznerian heritage, brings attention to the theories, images, role models and tools we present to our students. Too many textbooks convey the traditional model of profit-driven opportunity discovery inspired by the Kirznerian heritage (cf. Edelman, Manolova and Brush 2008), without sight for the value destructive potentials of short-sighted opportunistic entrepreneurship. The anomalies identified above, would suggest a critical reflection, which I suspect is already happening in very many entrepreneurship courses and programs, about the forms of entrepreneurship we introduce. Also the increasing use of lean start-up methods and similar tools will better equip the students to build and manage entrepreneurial ventures in ways that are more resilient to the fundamental uncertainty under which entrepreneurship occurs.

Finally, in terms of policy advice, the reconceptualization of entrepreneurship that follows from a critical engagement with the Kirznerian heritage on the one hand involves a more comprehensive understanding of entrepreneurship, where entrepreneurship as a function could/should be part of policy-making across a broad spectrum including culture, welfare, regional development, environmental issues, etc., which is already happening across the globe. Entrepreneurial value creation can potentially help to create all forms of value across sectors and domains, and independently of organizational forms. On the other hand, the complex relations between value creation and destruction suggest a more modest view of entrepreneurship. From a policy perspective it cannot be simply a monochord 'the more entrepreneurship the better'. Some forms of entrepreneurship, despite being fully legal, may not be forms of entrepreneurship that the society would benefit from promoting. One example of this is discussed on several occasions by resilience scholars, emphasizing that regional policies seeking to support entrepreneurial activities, which are strongly embedded in global input and output flows (e.g. the kind of entrepreneurial activities that can be incited with lowered company taxes), might create short-term economic development in a region, but do also leave these regions exposed and vulnerable to external shocks, such as the recent financial crisis (Bristow 2010; Hudson 2010; Simmie and Martin 2010; Zolli and Healy 2012). Increasing global integration of production may also have negative environmental consequences. Accordingly, not all entrepreneurship is created equal and of equal value from a societal perspective. The support of entrepreneurship and certain types is a political choice, which must be discussed as such. And perhaps entrepreneurship is not always the best response; let us not overestimate the ability of profit-driven entrepreneurs to solve all the problems of the world.

References

Achtenhagen, L., Naldi, L. and Melin, L. (2010) 'Business growth – do practitioners and scholars really talk about the same thing?', *Entrepreneurship Theory and Practice*, 34(2), pp. 289–316.

Agarwal, R., Barney, J.B., Foss, N.J. and Klein, P.G. (2009) 'Heterogeneous resources and the financial crisis: Implications of strategic management theory', *Strategic Organization*, 7(4), pp. 467–484.

Alvarez, S.A. and Barney, J.B. (2005) 'How do entrepreneurs organize firms under conditions of uncertainty?', *Journal of Management*, 31(5), pp. 776–793.

Alvarez, S.A. and Barney, J.B. (2007) 'Discovery and creation: Alternative theories of entrepreneurial action', *Strategic Entrepreneurship Journal*, 1(1–2), pp. 11–26.

Alvarez, S.A. and Barney, J.B. (2010) 'Entrepreneurship and epistemology: The philosophical underpinnings of the study of entrepreneurial opportunities', *Academy of Management Annals*, 4(1), pp. 557–583.

Alvarez, S.A., Barney, J.B. and Anderson, P. (2013) 'Forming and exploiting opportunities: The implications of discovery and creation processes for entrepreneurial and organizational research', *Organization Science*, 24(1), pp. 301–317.

Anderson, A. (1998) 'Cultivating the Garden of Eden: Environmental entrepreneuring', *Journal of Organizational Change Management*, 11(2), pp. 135–144.

Anderson, A. (2000) 'Paradox in the periphery: An entrepreneurial reconstruction?', *Entrepreneurship and Regional Development*, 12(2), pp. 91–109.

Anderson, A.R., Dodd, S.D. and Jack, S.L. (2012) 'Entrepreneurship as connecting: Some implications for theorising and practice', *Management Decision*, 50(5), pp. 958–971.

Andersson, D.E. (2005) 'The spatial nature of entrepreneurship', *Quarterly Journal of Austrian Economics*, 8(2), pp. 21–34.

Ardichvili, A., Cardozo, R. and Ray, S. (2003) 'A theory of entrepreneurial opportunity identification and development', *Journal of Business Venturing*, 18(1), pp. 105–123.

Austin, J., Stevenson, H. and Wei-Skillern, J. (2006) 'Social and commercial entrepreneurship: Same, different, or both?', *Entrepreneurship Theory and Practice*, 30(1), pp. 1–22.

Baker, T. and Nelson, R.E. (2005) 'Creating something from nothing: Resource construction through entrepreneurial bricolage', *Administrative Science Quarterly*, 50(3), pp. 329–366.

Baron, R.A. (2004) 'The cognitive perspective: A valuable tool for answering entrepreneurship's basic "why" questions', *Journal of Business Venturing*, 19, pp. 221–239.

Baron, R.A. (2006) 'Opportunity recognition as pattern recognition: How entrepreneurs connect the dots to identify new business opportunities', *Academy of Management Perspectives*, 20(1), pp. 104–120.

Baron, R.A. (2008) 'The role of affect in the entrepreneurial process', *Academy of Management Review*, 33(2), pp. 328–340.

Barreto, I. (2012) 'Solving the entrepreneurial puzzle: The role of entrepreneurial interpretation in opportunity formation and related processes', *Journal of Management Studies*, 49(2), pp. 356–380.

Blank, S. (2005) *The Four Steps to the Epiphany*. Stanford, CA: Cafe Press.

Blank, S. (2013) 'Why the lean start-up changes everything', *Harvard Business Review*, 91(5), pp. 63–72.

Borch, O.J., Førde, A., Rønning, L., Vestrum, I.K. and Alsos, G.A. (2008) 'Resource configuration and creative practices of community entrepreneurs', *Journal of Enterprising Communities: People and Places in the Global Economy*, 2(2), pp. 100–123.

Bristow, G. (2010) 'Resilient regions: Re-"place"ing regional competitiveness', *Cambridge Journal of Regions, Economy and Society*, 3(1), pp. 153–167.

Buenstorf, G. (2007) 'Creation and pursuit of entrepreneurial opportunities: An evolutionary economics perspective', *Small Business Economics*, 28(4), pp. 323–323.

Busenitz, L.W. (1996) 'Research on entrepreneurial alertness', *Journal of Small Business Management*, 34(4), pp. 35–44.

Busenitz, L.W. and Barney, J.B. (1997) 'Differences between entrepreneurs and managers in large organizations: Biases and heuristics in strategic decision-making', *Journal of Business Venturing*, 12(1), pp. 9–30.

Chiasson, M. and Saunders, C. (2005) 'Reconciling diverse approaches to opportunity research using the structuration theory', *Journal of Business Venturing*, 20(6), pp. 747–767.

Chiles, T.H., Bluedorn, A.C. and Gupta, V.K. (2007) 'Beyond creative destruction and entrepreneurial discovery: A radical Austrian approach to entrepreneurship', *Organization Studies*, 28(4), pp. 467–493.

Chiles, T.H., Elias, S.R.S.T.A., Zarankin, T.G. and Vultee, D.M. (2013) 'The kaleidic world of entrepreneurs: Developing and grounding a metaphor for creative imagination', *Qualitative Research in Organizations and Management: An International Journal*, 8(3), pp. 276–307.

Chiles, T.H., Tuggle, C.S., McMullen, J.S., Bierman, L. and Greening, D.W. (2010a) 'Dynamic creation: Extending the radical Austrian approach to entrepreneurship', *Organization Studies*, 31(1), pp. 7–46.

Chiles, T.H., Vultee, D.M., Gupta, V.K., Greening, D.W. and Tuggle, C.S. (2010b) 'The philosophical foundations of a radical Austrian approach to entrepreneurship', *Journal of Management Inquiry*, 19(2), pp. 138–164.

Cliff, J.E. (1998) 'Does one size fit all? Exploring the relationship between attitudes towards growth, gender', *Journal of Business Venturing*, 13(6), pp. 523–543.

Cohen, B. and Winn, M.I. (2007) 'Market imperfections, opportunity and sustainable entrepreneurship', *Journal of Business Venturing*, 22(1), pp. 29–49.

Companys, Y.E. and McMullen, J.S. (2007) 'Strategic entrepreneurs at work: The nature, discovery, and exploitation of entrepreneurial opportunities', *Small Business Economics*, 28(4), pp. 301–322.

Davidsson, P. (1989) 'Entrepreneurship – and after? A study of growth willingness in small firms', *Journal of Business Venturing*, 4(3), pp. 211–226.

Dean, T.J. and McMullen, J.S. (2007) 'Toward a theory of sustainable entrepreneurship: Reducing environmental degradation through entrepreneurial action', *Journal of Business Venturing*, 22(1), pp. 50–76.

Delmar, F. and Shane, S. (2004) 'Legitimating first: Organizing activities and the survival of new ventures', *Journal of Business Venturing*, 19(3), pp. 385–410.

Dew, N., Sarasvathy, S.D. and Venkataraman, S. (2004) 'The economic implications of exaptation', *Journal of Evolutionary Economics*, 14(1), pp. 69–84.

Dey, P. and Steyaert, C. (2010) 'The politics of narrating social entrepreneurship', *Journal of Enterprising Communities: People and Places in the Global Economy*, 4(1), pp. 85–108.

Dimov, D. (2007a) 'Beyond the single-person, single-insight attribution in understanding entrepreneurial opportunities', *Entrepreneurship Theory and Practice*, 31(5), pp. 713–731.

Dimov, D. (2007b) 'From opportunity insight to opportunity intention: The importance of person-situation learning match', *Entrepreneurship Theory and Practice*, 31(4), pp. 561–583.

Douhan, R., Eliasson, G. and Henrekson, M. (2007) 'Israel M. Kirzner: An outstanding Austrian contributor to the economics of entrepreneurship', *Small Business Economics*, 29(1), pp. 213–223.

Eckhardt, J.T. and Shane, S.A. (2003) 'Opportunities and entrepreneurship', *Journal of Management*, 29(3), pp. 333–349.

Edelman, L.F., Manolova, T.S. and Brush, C.G. (2008) 'Entrepreneurship education: Correspondence between practices of nascent entrepreneurs and textbook prescriptions for success', *Academy of Management Learning and Education*, 7(1), pp. 56–70.

Foo, M.-D. (2011) 'Emotions and entrepreneurial opportunity evaluation', *Entrepreneurship Theory and Practice*, 35(2), pp. 375–393.

Foss, K., Foss, N.J., Klein, P.G. and Klein, S.K. (2007) 'The entrepreneurial organization of heterogeneous capital', *Journal of Management Studies*, 44(7), pp. 1165–1186.

Foss, N.J. and Ishikawa, I. (2007) 'Towards a dynamic resource-based view: Insights from Austrian capital and entrepreneurship theory', *Organization Studies*, 28(5), pp. 749–772.

Foss, N.J. and Klein, P. (2012) *Organizing Entrepreneurial Judgment: A New Approach to the Firm*. Cambridge: Cambridge University Press.

Gaglio, C.M. and Katz, J.A. (2001) 'The psychological basis of opportunity identification: Entrepreneurial alertness', *Small Business Economics*, 16(2), pp. 95–111.

Harbi, S.E., Anderson, A.R. and Ammar, S.H. (2010) 'Entrepreneurs and the environment: Towards a typology of Tunisian ecopreneurs', *International Journal of Entrepreneurship and Small Business*, 10(2), pp. 181–204.

Harvey, D. (2011) *The Enigma of Capital and the Crisis of Capitalism*. London: Profile Books.

Hayek, F.A. (1945) 'The use of knowledge in society', *American Economic Review*, 35(4), pp. 519–530.

Hebert, R.F. and Link, A.N. (1988) *The Entrepreneur: Mainstream Views and Radical Critiques*. New York: Praeger.

Hechavarria, D.M. and Reynolds, P.D. (2009) 'Cultural norms and business start-ups: The impact of national values on opportunity and necessity entrepreneurs', *International Entrepreneurship and Management Journal*, 5(4), pp. 417–437.

Hindle, K. (2010) 'How community context affects entrepreneurial process: A diagnostic framework', *Entrepreneurship and Regional Development*, 22(7–8), pp. 599–647.

Hjorth, D. (2005) 'Organizational entrepreneurship: With de Certeau on creating heterotopias (or spaces for play)', *Journal of Management Inquiry*, 14(4), pp. 386–398.

Hjorth, D., Jones, C. and Gartner, W.B. (2008) 'Introduction for recreating/recontextualising entrepreneurship', *Scandinavian Journal of Management*, 24(2), pp. 81–84.

Hmieleski, K.M. and Baron, R.A. (2008) 'Regulatory focus and new venture performance: A study of entrepreneurial opportunity exploitation under conditions of risk versus uncertainty', *Strategic Entrepreneurship Journal*, 2(4), pp. 285–299.

Hudson, R. (2005) 'Towards sustainable economic practices, flows and spaces: Or is the necessary impossible and the impossible necessary?', *Sustainable Development*, 13(4), pp. 239–252.

Hudson, R. (2010) 'Resilient regions in an uncertain world: Wishful thinking or a practical reality?', *Cambridge Journal of Regions, Economy and Society*, 3(1), pp. 11–25.

Hudson, R. and Maioli, S. (2010) 'A response to reflections on a global financial crisis', *Critical Perspectives on International Business*, 6(1), pp. 53–71.

Imas, J.M., Wilson, N. and Weston, A. (2012) 'Barefoot entrepreneurs', *Organization*, 19(5), pp. 563–585.

Johannisson, B. and Nilsson, A. (1989) 'Community entrepreneurs: Networking for local development', *Entrepreneurship and Regional Development*, 1(1), pp. 3–19.

Johannisson, B. and Olaison, L. (2007) 'The moment of truth – reconstructing entrepreneurship and social capital in the eye of the storm', *Review of Social Economy*, 65(1), pp. 55–78.

Kaish, S. and Gilad, B. (1991) 'Characteristics of opportunities search of entrepreneurs vs. executives: Sources, interests, general alertness', *Journal of Business Venturing*, 6(1), pp. 45–62.

Kirzner, I. (2009) 'The alert and creative entrepreneur: A clarification', *Small Business Economics*, 32(2), pp. 145–152.

Kirzner, I.M. (1973) *Competition and Entrepreneurship*. Chicago, IL: University of Chicago Press.

Kirzner, I.M. (1982) 'Uncertainty, discovery, and human action: A study of the entrepreneurial profile in the Misesian system'. In Kirzner, I.M. (ed.) *Method, Process, and Austrian Economics*. Lexington, MA: Lexington Books, pp. 139–159.

Kirzner, I.M. (1985) 'Uncertainty, discovery, and human action'. In Kirzner, I. (ed.) *Discovery and the Capitalist Process*. Chicago, IL: Chicago University Press, pp. 40–67.

Kirzner, I.M. (1997) 'Entrepreneurial discovery and the competitive market process: An Austrian approach', *Journal of Economic Literature*, 35(1), pp. 60–85.

Kirzner, I.M. (1999) 'Creativity and/or alertness: A reconsideration of the Schumpeterian entrepreneur', *Review of Austrian Economics*, 11(1–2), pp. 5–17.

Klein, P. (2008a) 'The mundane economics of the Austrian School', *Quarterly Journal of Austrian Economics*, 11(3), pp. 165–187.

Klein, P. and Bylund, P. (2014) 'The place of Austrian economics in contemporary entrepreneurship research', *Review of Austrian Economics*, 27(3), pp. 1–21.

Klein, P.G. (2008b) 'Opportunity discovery, entrepreneurial action, and economic organization', *Strategic Entrepreneurship Journal*, 2(3), pp. 175–190.

Knight, F.H. (1921) *Risk, Uncertainty, and Profit*. New York: Houghton Mifflin.

Korsgaard, S. (2011) 'Opportunity formation in social entrepreneurship', *Journal of Enterprising Communities: People and Places in the Global Economy*, 5(4), pp. 265–285.

Korsgaard, S. (2013) 'It's really out there: A review of the critique of the discovery view of opportunities', *International Journal of Entrepreneurial Behaviour and Research*, 19(2), pp. 130–148.

Korsgaard, S. and Anderson, A.R. (2011) 'Enacting entrepreneurship as social value creation', *International Small Business Journal*, 29(2), pp. 135–151.

Korsgaard, S., Anderson, A.R. and Gaddefors, J. (forthcoming a) 'Entrepreneurship as re-sourcing: Towards a new image of entrepreneurship in a time of financial, economic and socio-spatial crisis', *Journal of Enterprising Communities*.

Korsgaard, S., Berglund, H., Thrane, C. and Blenker, P. (forthcoming b) 'A tale of two Kirzners: Time, uncertainty and the nature of opportunities', *Entrepreneurship Theory and Practice*.

Kuhn, T.S. (1996) *The Structure of Scientific Revolutions*. Chicago, IL: University of Chicago Press.

Landström, H. (1999) 'The roots of entrepreneurship research', *New England Journal of Entrepreneurship*, 2(2), pp. 9–20.

Leitch, C., Hill, F. and Neergaard, H. (2010) 'Entrepreneurial and business growth and the quest for a "comprehensive theory": Tilting at windmills?', *Entrepreneurship Theory and Practice*, 34(2), pp. 249–260.

Lewis, K. (2008) 'Small firm owners in New Zealand: In it for the good life or growth?', *Small Enterprise Research*, 16(1), pp. 61–69.

Link, A.N. and Scott, J.T. (2010) 'Government as entrepreneur: Evaluating the commercialization success of SBIR projects', *Research Policy*, 39(5), pp. 589–601.

Luksha, P. (2008) 'Niche construction: The process of opportunity creation in the environment', *Strategic Entrepreneurship Journal*, 2(4), pp. 269–283.

Mair, J. and Marti, I. (2009) 'Entrepreneurship in and around institutional voids: A case study from Bangladesh', *Journal of Business Venturing*, 24(5), pp. 419–435.

McCaffrey, M. (forthcoming) 'On the theory of entrepreneurial incentives and alertness', *Entrepreneurship Theory and Practice*.

McMullen, J.S. and Dimov, D. (2013) 'Time and the entrepreneurial journey: The problems and promise of studying entrepreneurship as a process', *Journal of Management Studies*, 50(8), pp. 1481–1512.

Mitchell, R.K., Mitchell, J.R. and Smith, J.B. (2008) 'Inside opportunity formation: Enterprise failure, cognition, and the creation of opportunities', *Strategic Entrepreneurship Journal*, 2(3), pp. 225–242.

Morris, M.H., Miyasaki, N.N., Watters, C.E. and Coombes, S.M. (2006) 'The dilemma of growth: Understanding venture size choices of women entrepreneurs', *Journal of Small Business Management*, 44(2), pp. 221–244.

Munir, K.A. (2011) 'Financial crisis 2008–2009: What does the silence of institutional theorists tell us?', *Journal of Management Inquiry*, 20(2), pp. 114–117.

Müller, S. (2013) *Entrepreneurship and Regional Development: On the Interplay between Agency and Context*. Aarhus: Aarhus University.

OECD (2006) *The New Rural Paradigm: Policies and Governance*. Paris: OECD.

OECD (2010) *SME's, Entrepreneurship and Innovation*. Paris: OECD.

Pacheco, D.F., Dean, T.J. and Payne, D.S. (2010) 'Escaping the green prison: Entrepreneurship and the creation of opportunities for sustainable development', *Journal of Business Venturing*, 25(5), pp. 464–480.

Peredo, A.M. and Chrisman, J.J. (2006) 'Toward a theory of community-based enterprise', *Academy of Management Review*, 31(2), pp. 309–328.

Rae, D. (2010) 'Universities and enterprise education: Responding to the challenges of the new era', *Journal of Small Business and Enterprise Development*, 17(4), pp. 591–606.

Sarasvathy, S.D. (2001) 'Causation and effectuation: Toward a theoretical shift from economic inevitability to entrepreneurial contingency', *Academy of Management Review*, 26(2), pp. 243–264.

Sarasvathy, S.D. (2008) *Effectuation: Elements of Entrepreneurial Expertise*. Cheltenham: Edward Elgar.

Sarasvathy, S.D. and Venkataraman, S. (2011) 'Entrepreneurship as method: Open questions for an entrepreneurial future', *Entrepreneurship Theory and Practice*, 35(1), pp. 113–135.

Schaper, M. (2002) 'The essence of ecopreneurship', *Greener Management International*, 38, pp. 26–30.

Schumpeter, J.A. (1950) *Capitalism, Socialism, and Democracy*. New York: Harper and Row.

Shane, S. (2000) 'Prior knowledge and the discovery of entrepreneurial opportunities', *Organization Science*, 11(4), pp. 448–469.

Shane, S. (2003) *A General Theory of Entrepreneurship: The Individual-Opportunity Nexus*. Cheltenham: Edward Elgar.

Shane, S. (2012) 'Reflections on the 2010 AMR Decade Award: Delivering on the promise of entrepreneurship as a field of research', *Academy of Management Review*, 37(1), pp. 10–20.

Shane, S. and Delmar, F. (2004) 'Planning for the market: Business planning before marketing and the continuation of organizing efforts', *Journal of Business Venturing*, 19(6), pp. 767–785.

Shane, S. and Venkataraman, S. (2000) 'The promise of entrepreneurship as a field of research', *Academy of Management Review*, 25(1), pp. 217–226.

Shaver, K.G. and Scott, L.R. (1991) 'Person, process, choice: The psychology of new venture creation', *Entrepreneurship Theory and Practice*, 16(2), pp. 23–46.

Short, J.C., Ketchen, D.J.J., Shook, C.L. and Ireland, R.D. (2010) 'The concept of opportunity in entrepreneurship research: Past accomplishments and future challenges', *Journal of Management*, 36(1), pp. 40–65.

Simmie, J. and Martin, R. (2010) 'The economic resilience of regions: Towards an evolutionary approach', *Cambridge Journal of Regions, Economy and Society*, 3(1), pp. 27–43.

Stam, E. and Lambooy, J. (2012) 'Entrepreneurship, knowledge, space, and place: Evolutionary economic geography meets Austrian economics', *Advances in Austrian Economics*, 16, pp. 81–103.

Stevenson, H.H. and Jarillo, J.C. (1990) 'A paradigm of entrepreneurship – entrepreneurial management', *Strategic Management Journal*, 11, pp. 17–27.

Steyaert, C. (2007) 'Entrepreneuring as a conceptual attractor? A review of process theories in 20 years of entrepreneurship studies', *Entrepreneurship and Regional Development*, 19(6), pp. 453–477.

Steyaert, C. and Katz, J. (2004) 'Reclaiming the space of entrepreneurship in society: Geographical, discursive and social dimensions', *Entrepreneurship and Regional Development*, 16(3), pp. 179–196.

Tonts, M. and Greive, S. (2002) 'Commodification and creative destruction in the Australian rural landscape: The case of Bridgetown, Western Australia', *Australian Geographical Studies*, 40(1), pp. 58–70.

Venkataraman, S. (1997) 'The distinctive domain of entrepreneurship research: An editor's perspective'. In Katz, J. and Brockhaus, R. (eds) *Advances in Entrepreneurship.* Greenwich: JAI Press, pp. 119–138.

Welpe, I.M., Spörrle, M., Grichnik, D., Michl, T. and Audretsch, D.B. (2012) 'Emotions and opportunities: The interplay of opportunity evaluation, fear, joy, and anger as antecedent of entrepreneurial exploitation', *Entrepreneurship Theory and Practice*, 36(1), pp. 69–96.

Welter, F. (2011) 'Contextualizing entrepreneurship – conceptual challenges and ways forward', *Entrepreneurship Theory and Practice*, 35(1), pp. 165–184.

Wiklund, J., Davidsson, P. and Delmar, F. (2003) 'What do they think and feel about growth? An expectancy-value approach to small business managers' attitudes toward growth', *Entrepreneurship Theory and Practice*, 27(3), pp. 247–271.

Wiltbank, R., Dew, N., Read, S. and Sarasvathy, S.D. (2006) 'What to do next? The case for non-predictive strategy', *Strategic Management Journal*, 27(10), pp. 981–998.

Zahra, S.A. (2007) 'Contextualizing theory building in entrepreneurship research', *Journal of Business Venturing*, 22(3), pp. 443–452.

Zahra, S.A. (2008) 'The virtuous cycle of discovery and creation of entrepreneurial opportunities', *Strategic Entrepreneurship Journal*, 2(3), pp. 243–257.

Zolli, A. and Healy, A.M. (2012) *Resilience: Why Things Bounce Back.* New York: Free Press.

5 Portfolio entrepreneurial households

Extending the individual and single opportunity focus

Gry Agnete Alsos

5.1 Introduction

Studies of entrepreneurship traditionally focus on the individual or the firm, which are often seen as a duality and referred to as the individual-opportunity nexus (Eckhardt and Shane 2003; Shane 2003; Venkataraman 1997). The opportunity-based view of entrepreneurship (Shane and Venkataraman 2000) was introduced as a perspective that focuses less on the characteristics of the individual entrepreneur and instead on entrepreneurship as involving the combination of individuals and opportunities. Furthermore, by differentiating between the opportunity and its mode of exploitation, this perspective allowed for seeing entrepreneurial processes as taking place not only through new organizations but also within existing firms and other organizations. Although this perspective has been beneficial by helping more clearly define the scope of entrepreneurship as a field of research and by introducing new research questions, it still hinges on the focus of the individual entrepreneur and his/her endeavours. In this chapter, I will argue that the individual-opportunity nexus has a focus on the individual entrepreneur and the single opportunity, which conceals important insights to be made about entrepreneurial processes.

First, the focus on the single individual as the entrepreneur in this nexus disregards the fact that very many firms are started by teams (Schjoedt *et al.* 2013). Moreover, the increased appreciation of the need to understand the context in which a start-up is embedded, particularly the role of the family and the household of the entrepreneur, implies that not even non-team start-ups involve a single individual alone (Alsos, Carter and Ljunggren 2014; Jennings and Brush 2013). The importance of interaction between individuals in entrepreneurial processes is well accepted, and it is studied, for instance, in the literature on entrepreneurial networks and social capital, entrepreneurial teams, and in the so-far scarce literature on the embeddedness of entrepreneurship. However, the mainstream literature continues to discuss entrepreneurship in terms of the individual (key) entrepreneur.

Second, the focus on the single opportunity also has limitations: it hides the potential connection between different opportunities. Implicitly or (more seldom) explicitly, the opportunity-based view considers opportunities to be random and discrete entities (Felin *et al.* 2014). However, several insights from the entrepreneurship literature suggest otherwise. Studies of habitual entrepreneurs indicate that they develop cognitive frames through which they selectively access and use information, which facilitates opportunity identification within their area of expertise but also hampers the identification of more distant opportunities (Sarasvathy, Menon and Kuechle 2013; Ucbasaran *et al.* 2008). In relation to entrepreneurship within existing firms, the relatedness or similarity of a new opportunity to the current activities or knowledge base of the firm has been put forward as important for the decision of exploitation (Davidsson and Tonelli 2013; Gregoire and Shepherd 2011). Furthermore, on a more general level, the literature on technological change shows how major technologies create a set of interconnected opportunities that can be exploited by economic agents (Castellacci 2008). These literature streams suggest that instead of being discrete entities, the opportunities identified can be strongly related to other opportunities previously invested in and pursued.

In this chapter, I argue that entrepreneurship should be seen neither as basically a single individual activity nor as the result of an opportunity disconnected from other opportunities. Using an illustrative example of a portfolio entrepreneurial household, I first discuss the weaknesses related to a single individual-single opportunity perspective, showing how it may hide important connections in empirical cases. Furthermore, building on the integration of the household perspective to entrepreneurship with insights from the portfolio entrepreneurship literature, I discuss one example of a perspective that can help us understand the interconnectedness of individuals and opportunities in entrepreneurship. This perspective illuminates the role of several individuals in the processes of opportunity identification and exploitation and increases awareness of the relationship between the opportunities identified and developed by the household. This perspective is not universal but limited to entrepreneurial activities where the household is involved; nonetheless, it gives important insights that can be developed further in other contexts. To illustrate this potential, I also seek to relate these insights to the context of opportunity identification within existing firms where this is relevant.

5.2 The individual-opportunity nexus

In their influential article, Shane and Venkataraman (2000) defined entrepreneurship as the discovery, evaluation and exploitation of opportunities to create future goods and services. Their focus was that entrepreneurship could not be defined by focusing on the characteristics and behaviour of the entrepreneur because entrepreneurship involves (at least) two phenomena to be present: an opportunity and a person acting upon it, described as the individual-opportunity nexus (see also Eckhardt and Shane 2003). This reorientation of entrepreneurship research extended the focus from firm creation, which previously had been defined as a scholarly field (Low and MacMillan 1988). Instead, putting opportunity at the core shifted the emphasis from the new firm to the individuals' discovery and exploitation of opportunities. Consequently, entrepreneurship can take place through the start-up of new firms, through opportunity exploitation in existing firms, communities, or social enterprises or through other 'modes of exploitation' (Shane 2012). Moreover, they argued that the individual was not in focus as a type of person but instead as an actor in the entrepreneurial process (Shane 2012). Hence, they seem to view entrepreneurship as individual behaviour (Gartner 2001). Nevertheless, and importantly, they asserted that the individual alone does not constitute entrepreneurship: 'To have entrepreneurship you must first have entrepreneurial opportunities' (Shane and Venkataraman 2000, p. 220).

This 'new'[1] definition of the field generated debate, as should be expected, because it could not be ascribed 'to the majority of the research currently undertaken by scholars in the entrepreneurship field' (Gartner 2001, p. 31). However, it was generally well received and was soon picked up on by other scholars (see Busenitz *et al.* 2003; Short *et al.* 2010), who both critically discussed and built upon it. It has since laid an important foundation of scholarly development within entrepreneurship, and Shane and Venkataraman (2000) was recently reported to be the most impactful publication within the field of entrepreneurship since 1985 (Busenitz *et al.* 2014). Although still debated and critically addressed, it has been acknowledged that the nexus perspective has important benefits; i.e., it puts the focus on the early stages of new economic activity, extends the person-focused explanations of entrepreneurship (Davidsson and Tonelli 2013) and allows for an understanding of entrepreneurial activity in forms other than the creation of a new firm (Shane 2012). For instance, in my previous studies of portfolio entrepreneurs, the opportunity-based perspective lets me analyse the creation of new economic activity without paying too much attention to whether new legal firms were formed (e.g. Alsos 2007; Alsos and Carter 2006; Alsos, Ljunggren and Pettersen 2003; Alsos *et al.* 2014). I could then compare the entrepreneurial processes of current business owners when seeking to create new economic activity and treat the formation of a legal entity as a strategic choice rather than the definition of entrepreneurship *per se*. In this chapter, I utilize insights from these studies to discuss some weaknesses with the individual-opportunity nexus approach, such as its over-emphasis on the single individual and its tendency to treat opportunities as discrete, unconnected entities.

Shane and Venkataraman (2000) defined entrepreneurial opportunities as 'those situations in which new goods, services, raw materials, and organizing methods can be introduced and sold at a greater price than their cost of production' and as 'new means–ends relationships' (p. 220). They further assert that the existence of opportunities demands asymmetry of information and beliefs.[2] Because the price and cost comparison cannot be known *ex ante*, individuals develop conjectures about the existence of an opportunity and act based on these conjectures (Eckhardt and Ciuchta 2008). Shane and Venkataraman (2000) responded to the question of why some people and not others discover and make conjectures about particular opportunities with two broad categories: prior information and the cognitive properties of individuals. In line with the shift in focus from the firm to the individual, they discussed these categories in terms of individuals' information corridors and individuals' cognitive properties, and framed the decision to exploit as an individual (cognitive) decision that depends on personal willingness and the perceived expected value of the opportunity in question. Eckhardt and Shane (2003) explicitly state the individual focus. They describe the process of discovery as follows: 'individuals acting alone, or within firms, perceive of a previously unseen or unknown way to create a new means-ends framework' (p. 339). They further explain, 'Because the discovery of an opportunity is a cognitive act, it is also an individual act' (p. 347). In this chapter, I argue that this extensive focus on individual cognition conceals situations in which several individuals are involved. These include situations where prior information on several people is needed (or used) for the opportunity to be discovered or where the decision to exploit is not an individual one, such as within a firm, within a team or within a family.[3]

Moreover, Shane and Venkataraman (2000) claimed that opportunities are objective phenomena that exist independently of their discovery by entrepreneurs. However, the recognition or discovery of opportunities is seen as a subjective process and involves some creation by the entrepreneurs as new means-ends relationships are constructed. This often implies that the entrepreneur constructs the means, the ends, or both (Eckhardt and Shane 2003). This perspective is further elaborated by Eckhardt and Ciuchta (2008), who argue that opportunities are independent of human cognition and consist of characteristics that are unchangeable but that the exploitation of opportunities requires human creativity. Hence, they see opportunity as an objective phenomenon. This perspective has since been the subject of significant debate. Others have argued that the imperfection in the market that constitutes an opportunity may be created by the actions of the entrepreneur (Alvarez and Barney 2007). Against the view that opportunities are objective phenomena, arguments have been made that entrepreneurial opportunities encompass a social learning process (Dimov 2007), that subjective enactment is an important part of the process of opportunity emergence (Alvarez and Barney 2007), and that opportunities do not at all pre-exist but are created as result of a process that involves dynamic interaction and negotiation between stakeholders (Sarasvathy *et al.* 2011). Although acknowledging the important insights resulting from the debate on the objectivity or subjectivity of opportunities, I will not address these issues further in this chapter. Instead, I will discuss the problem that decoupling opportunity from the individual(s) discovering it leads to an understanding of an opportunity as an isolated entity that is not connected to other opportunities. Because the identification of opportunities relies on the prior knowledge (or other resources) of the individuals involved (Shane 2000), the prior entrepreneurial actions taken by the individuals involved (Alvarez and Barney 2007), and/or the interaction between the individuals involved (Sarasvathy *et al.* 2011) or individuals in the environment (Dimov 2007), they are not isolated from other opportunities previously identified by the individuals involved or others.

5.3 Empirical examples of interconnected individuals and opportunities

Before I continue by discussing these issues, I present an empirical example of entrepreneurship, which I will use as an illustrative element in the discussion. The case 'Entrepreneurial activities at the family farm' comes out of a study of rural entrepreneurship in which we focused on farmers establishing new business activities in addition to their farm business, thereby becoming farm-based portfolio entrepreneurs. The data were gathered through interviews with the husband and wife, who were both involved in a variety of business activities taking place on the farm premises, some of which have been organized as separate legal entities and others of which have been organized within the family farm business. I will use this case as an illustrative element in the discussion and in the development of the perspective on portfolio entrepreneurial households at the end of this chapter. Later, I additionally present three shorter examples of opportunity development within existing firms (Box 5.1), to illustrate that the points made are also transferable to other contexts.

5.3.1 Entrepreneurial activities on the family farm

George and Anne, a couple in their late 30s, own a farm in a rural community in the western part of Norway. George is the sixth generation on the family farm, which he took over as the eldest son. His parents, now retired, still live on the farm. George has been involved in all activities on the farm since he was a boy, and he always knew he would take over the farm. He was not very interested in schoolwork when he grew up, but he enjoyed practical work and taking part in all of the activities on the farm. He did not continue school, and before he and his wife took over the farm, he took on various practical jobs, particularly within carpentry, including owning his own business. Anne grew up on a neighbouring farm. She is an educated pre-school teacher and works half time at the local school. The rest of her work capacity is spent on the various ventures on the farm. The couple have three children, aged four to nine years.

The farm estate is relatively large and includes a forest estate. In addition to forestry, milk production was the main farming activity for the previous generations. When George and Anne took over the farm ten years ago, the dairy activity had been closed down, and the milk quota had been sold a few years prior. They continued with grain and grass production as the main farming activities. Forestry had been an important activity for generations and a great interest of both George and his father's. Because of the topography, the forest estate is not very suitable for modern machinery, and the importance of forestry for farm incomes gradually reduced. Nonetheless, forestry and wood production remained an interest for them both.

However, as George stated, 'It is the tradition here that conventional farming has been a side activity.' Other business activities have been operated from the farm for generations. A salmon river runs across the estate and has been the main resource for tourism business for generations, along with many and large traditional buildings suitable for weddings and similar events. For George's grandparents, the tourism business was a very important income source. British and German nobility were among their visitors, some coming back year after year. The tourism activity was closed down by George's parents, who did not want to raise their children in a tourism business. They instead worked with racing horses as an activity in addition to farming and had a regionally famous stable for breeding and training horses for harness racing. However, a few of the regular visitors and their families have been visiting the farm since, and the stabbur (a traditional storehouse on pillars) is still used as accommodation for visitors. George and Anne have recently started planning to re-establish the tourism activity in a somewhat different manner. They plan to build a new guesthouse for accommodation close to the riverside instead of having visitors in the farm buildings. Moreover, they rent out hunting rights at their large forest and mountain estate during the hunting season.

A sawmill is currently the main business activity on the farm. It was established by George and his father as co-entrepreneurs a few years before George and Anne took over the farm. At the time, George owned a carpentry business with a companion; they specialized in lafting, a traditional technique for cog joint production. George explains the origin of the sawmill as follows:

> Maybe it was me who saw the opportunity ... or maybe we saw it together, my father and I ... my father and I have always been interested in sawing. We had a lot of knowledge of it. So we started with carpentry from our own forest, and then, we also bought from the neighbouring estates. I used to have a carpentry firm with a friend ... My father and I sawed the material we needed, particularly for lafting [cog joint construction]. There are many lafting firms around here ... We stopped lafting ourselves and did more and more sawing. As a result, my carpentry colleague and I split up, and my father and I established the sawmill. It has grown extensively since then.

The initial customer basis for the sawmill was local lafting firms, including a large producer of traditional cottages, creating a demand for specially sawed wood planks. The family's strong local embeddedness, their long-time involvement in forestry, and George and his father's expertise related to wood and carpentry were all important inputs to the start-up of the sawmill that gave them access to networks, information and knowledge. The local firms are still important customers, but the sawmill has grown and now delivers special sawed planks to a wider geographical area. The sawmill currently constitutes 80 per cent of the income from the portfolio of business activities on the farm, with a turnover of more than 10 million NOK and six employed person-years. George's father has now retired, and Anne has replaced him as a part-owner. She is currently also working part-time at the sawmill office.

Additionally, George and Anne are engaged in horse breeding. Anne offers riding therapy for children with special needs as a side activity, thereby combining the tradition of horses at the farm with her own education and special interests. The stables at the farm and George's parents' expertise from racing horses are also important resources. The family wants to develop this activity further, and although it builds on Anne's competence and interests, George is actively included in developing the business idea further; he has ideas for expansions and new markets. In general, George and Anne often discuss their current businesses and new business opportunities 'around the kitchen table' and in the wider family. Indeed, the distinction between family matters and business matters seems unclear.

5.3.2 Learnings from the case 'Entrepreneurial activities at the family farm'

Taking the individual-opportunity nexus as a starting point, we may ask, where is the nexus in this story? One way to analyse it would be to take the viewpoint of one of the individuals and one of the opportunities. In many senses, George appears to be a 'typical' entrepreneur, eager about starting new projects and more interested in action than in theoretical knowledge. He first started a firm with a friend. He thereafter closed it down and started a sawmill with his father. It was successful and grew fairly large, with several employees. The opportunity behind the sawmill can be identified. The local lafting firms, particularly a large producer of traditional cottages that would benefit from specially sawed wood planks, represent the end. George's own forest and neighbouring estates, with forests, premises and other resources on the farm, and George's and his father's competence in sawing and wood represent the means to create a new means-end relationship. However, limiting the analysis of this case to these elements conceals important knowledge that can be learned from it.

First, George did not act alone entrepreneurially. He started the sawmill with his father, and he cannot tell who came up with the idea, who saw the opportunity and developed it. Instead, the opportunity discovery and development appears to have happened in the interaction between George and his father. Furthermore, business ideas were discussed around the kitchen table and within the family. George and Anne were in the business activities together, although they divided the tasks and responsibilities between them. This blurred line is illustrated by the joint discussion and development of the salmon fishing tourism, where it was not clear who was the main entrepreneur. The horse riding therapy business was also a joint effort. Although it was Anne's area of competence and her main responsibility, the husband and the farm context, including the traditions of horse breeding on the farm, were important for identifying and exploiting the opportunity.

Second, Anne and George clearly developed several opportunities. The sawmill was organized as a separate company in addition to the farm business, which also included the horse riding, the salmon tourism business under development and several other smaller business activities. However, these opportunities did not represent separate, unconnected means-end relationships. They were clearly linked together in several ways. They were all related to the traditions and resources of the farm. Without the farm, the means side of the opportunity would not have been in place for the sawmill, the horse riding or the salmon tourism opportunities. Furthermore, their identification and development were related to other opportunities, such as the sawmill, which was partly spun out from the carpentry business and the forestry, the riding therapy business, which was partly related to the tradition of having racing horses on the farm, and the new tourism business opportunity, which was clearly identified in relation to the previous tourism business of George's grandparents. Hence, this case clearly illustrates that opportunity identification may be dependent on the prior knowledge and experiences of the entrepreneurs (Shane 2000) and their family members and on previous activities and resource endowments in a current business transferred into new business activities (Alsos and Carter 2006). Hence, opportunities are not only random imperfections in the market but also path-dependent and inter-connected.

A single individual-single opportunity approach hides the important connections between individuals involved and between opportunities, as illustrated by the case of Anne and George. In the following, I challenge this focus and suggest a perspective that can better embrace the connectedness of individuals and opportunities.

5.4 Challenging the single-individual focus

The question of where business opportunities come from has generated significant debate (Alvarez and Barney 2007; Sarasvathy *et al.* 2011). Opportunities are seen as 'recognized' through deductive processes of information search and analysis (Caplan 1999), as 'discovered' by particularly alert individuals (Kirzner 1997), or as 'created' by the entrepreneur through an abductive process (Sarasvathy *et al.* 2011). Although these perspectives are grounded in different ontological and epistemological standpoints (Alvarez and Barney 2007) and may be seen as related to different situations (Sarasvathy *et al.* 2011), they all have one common feature: they view the individual entrepreneur at the centre of the way opportunities emerge. The individual entrepreneur searches for and recognizes opportunities; is alert and discovers opportunities; or is creative and creates opportunities. None of these perspectives takes into account that opportunity emergence may be a process that involves several individuals in teams or families (Alsos *et al.* 2014) or teams. Hence, this is not a problem related to the Shane and Venkataraman (2000) perspective alone.

Nevertheless, the individual entrepreneur is not always the most suitable unit of analysis when examining how opportunities are identified and pursued; many such processes involve teams of entrepreneurs (Lim, Busenitz and Chidambaram 2013; Schjoedt *et al.* 2013). When opportunities are identified and exploited within existing firms, it may not always be possible to identify a single individual who identified the opportunity. Although the opportunity-based view in principle allows for studying the discovery and exploitation of opportunities within existing firms, we still have limited conceptual frameworks to capture how firms address opportunities (Short *et al.* 2010).

Box 5.1 illustrates examples of opportunity development in existing firms. First, the opportunity identification processes are described as joint processes among several individuals involved in the firm. The senior executives of the ship's furniture manufacturing firm deliberately sat down to identify new opportunities and discuss how existing offerings in the market could be improved. In the experience hotel firm, opportunity identification is generally described as the interaction between several individuals with different capabilities. Second, it is clear that new opportunities are developed in relation to the firms' current competencies and activities. The founders of the ship's furniture firm looked for opportunities within the ship's furniture because that was where their competencies and experience lay. The software firm described its identification of the opportunity for a new IT management system for schools as originating from its previous activities of selling IT systems to school authorities. Furthermore, the experience hotel was developed 'opportunity by opportunity' from a traditional hotel to an experience provider, taking advantage of a stream of opportunities, where the exploitation of one opportunity led to another.

Box 5.1 Examples of opportunity development in existing firms[4]

New firm in furniture manufacturing for ships

This firm was established when a group of employees chose, after a disagreement over strategic choices, to leave an existing firm that manufactured furniture for ships. They decided to use their extensive experience in the industry to establish a new firm. This is how they describe their opportunity development process:

> We sat down together and asked ourselves the question: 'What can be done better?' This resulted in reflection on possible new designs that can reduce production costs. In addition, we put focus on how the logistics chain can be more cost efficient. This process resulted in an idea for a design that will reduce the use of materials by 15 per cent, reduce the number of operations needed in the manufacturing from approximately 300 to 120, and that will make installation easy enough for the furniture to be transported flat packed and assembled aboard the ship.

Established firm in software development

A software firm that produces IT management systems sought to exploit the opportunity of a new IT management system for schools that was better adapted to the particular needs in this sector. They describe the identification of this opportunity as follows:

The background was the experience we had acquired during 2012, when we worked together with Intel to promote our [previous IT management system for schools] to school authorities and distributors. We soon discovered that our system (like no one else's) did not fully meet the schools' needs. In addition, there is a paradigm shift in the school market as more solutions are cloud-based, which creates heavy demands on broadband capacity and as tablets are replacing PCs at full speed. Through our research in the market as well as feedback from the school authorities, we found that we should develop a completely new system that addressed the needs and challenges of schools.

The small hotel and experience firm

The small, independent hotel has in the last 20 years transformed from a traditional hotel business into a firm that delivers a range of services related to the experience industry:

We turned our approach from being a supplier of accommodation and catering services into being an experience and activity provider with the hotel as a base.

In addition to accommodation and conferences in the original hotel, the business activities include the organizing of large-scale events with food service with various locations and concepts and several experience products, such as whiskey tasting, a sea eagle safari, a team-building trail (inspired from Amazing Race), fishing trips and deep sea rafting. An important success factor has been its ability to continuously identify or create and exploit new opportunities and thereby develop the business activities of the firm. The development is explained as 'creating development by virtue of several managing to build something together'. The opportunity development builds on the integration of the varied competencies and networks of the people involved: the chef, with a long and varied experience accrued from hotels, restaurants and event organizing; the experienced property developer; and the creative idea spinner. The transformation from a hotel to an activity and experience provider has been taken step by step – or opportunity by opportunity. One idea leads to another. The experiences from the first large-scale event stunts are developed further into more regular activities and utilized in the development of new opportunities.

In the case of George and Anne, it was also evident that opportunity identification and exploitation were often driven by individuals in interaction. George and his father jointly developed the sawmill. They built on each other's competence, interests, networks and information and 'saw' an opportunity to produce specialty wood planks for the cottage producers and the lafting industry. George and Anne jointly discussed the opportunity to provide riding therapy lessons for special needs children, based on her interest in riding therapy, his interest in creating business activities and George's parents' interests in horse breeding. The idea to resume the salmon tourism activity was discussed over the kitchen table and developed further between Anne and George, with input from George's parents. Hence, the interactions nurturing entrepreneurship are not necessarily formalized through teams or work groups but in this case happened naturally between individuals who, for other reasons, met and talked to each other on a regular basis. None of the opportunities in question were identified or exploited by a single person.

The single-person, single-insight understanding of entrepreneurial opportunities has also previously been criticized. Dimov (2007) argued that instead of viewing opportunities as single insights, they should be seen as emerging through continuous shaping and development from an initial insight to an idea acted upon through a social learning process. In this process, the opportunity is shaped from contextual and social influences, where entrepreneurs interact with others. Hence, Dimov sees opportunity development as a socially embedded process, where potential entrepreneurs are actively engaged in information and value creation with a surrounding community. Consequently, whether a person acts upon an opportunity is based not only on individual skills and characteristics but also on the situations and information to which he/she is exposed and, not least of all, the people with whom he/she interacts and discusses ideas. This argument is consistent with Sarasvathy's (2008) focus on opportunity creation and the role of pre-commitments from stakeholders in this process, although Dimov puts more focus on the enactment process, where ideas are developed into opportunities through interaction with others, including people who are not necessarily stakeholders or in any way committed to the venture.

Although the focus on the social embeddedness of opportunity development takes steps to show how entrepreneurs are influenced by the context during the entrepreneurial process, it still emphasizes the individual entrepreneur as driving this process through interactions with the environment. Hence, it does not account for situations in which several individuals take part in the same process of opportunity development and later exploitation, as in the example with Anne and George. This is a problem because it is an established fact that a substantial share of new ventures are established by teams of entrepreneurs (Lim *et al.* 2013; Schjoedt *et al.* 2013). Although teams *can* be put together by a single entrepreneur who first identifies an opportunity and then establishes a team to help exploit it, it is not likely that this is the situation in all (or even most) of the team start-ups. Instead, it is probable that several team starts are initiated by a joint opportunity identification and development that involves several team members, as in the case with the ship furniture firm from Box 5.1. Opportunity exploration and exploitation within existing firms is even more likely to be initiated by teams as more or less organized development activities within the firms. In the case of the software firm, the opportunity was identified among the group of employees working with the implementation of one of the firm's previous products, and the development was organized as a project that involved several individuals internal and external to the firm. In the experience hotel, the team of owners and executives acted as a 'creative hub' where new opportunities were developed as a continuous stream. So far, scholarly research has failed to acknowledge the involvement of several individuals in discovery or creation processes, and theorizing on opportunity identification and development still hinges on the single individual perspective.

Research on the drivers of opportunities has primarily discussed the individuals identifying opportunities (Short *et al.* 2010) and has paid little attention to opportunities that emerge as a result of interactions between individuals. Although the entrepreneur's prior knowledge is seen as crucial to recognizing, discovering and creating opportunities (Shane 2000; Sarasvathy *et al.* 2011; Shepherd and DeTienne 2005), it is normally assumed that if the prior knowledge of several individuals is needed for opportunity identification, this knowledge should first be transferred to one individual who can then recognize or create the opportunity. However, because the relevant prior knowledge for opportunity identification may be tacit, it cannot always easily be transferred or told to another individual so that a 'cognitive act' of opportunity recognition can take place. More subtle communication may be needed, which may take place only through the joint development of an opportunity.

5.4.1 Extending the single individual perspective: entrepreneurial households

The example of George and Anne shows that more than one individual may be involved in the same entrepreneurial activity beyond what is normally treated as an entrepreneurial team. In entrepreneurial households, new opportunities and their development may be part of the daily conversations and activities within the household (Alsos, Carter and Ljunggren 2015). A household is defined as the smallest social unit where human and economic resources are administered (Wheelock and Ougthon 1996) and is a setting where the normative systems of the family (affect, altruism, tradition) and the utilitarian system (economic rationality) are combined (Brannon, Wiklund and Haynie 2013). The concept of 'household' partly overlaps with but is also distinct from the concept of 'family'. The household typically includes the nuclear or the extended family (Brush and Manolova 2004) but may also include individuals in the larger family or persons who are not family members (Wheelock and Ougthon 1996). More importantly, the household concept emphasizes economic activities, work and residence, whereas the family concept considers the kinship and marriage relationships that tie people together (Gullestad 1984). Within the sociological literature, the household perspective emphasizes the tight connection between the business and the household in enterprising families (Wheelock and Mariussen 1997; Wheelock and Ougthon 1996), recognizing the blurred boundaries between the business and the private spheres for small-firm owners. Household decisions and business decisions are both made within the household, and business strategies are interwoven with household strategies (Alsos *et al.* 2014). Consequently, opportunity identification and exploitation is a household matter and a matter for the business.

Looking at entrepreneurial households, such as in the example of Anne and George, it becomes clear that opportunities may emerge from the joint efforts of several connected individuals. On the one hand, entrepreneurial teams may consist of several household or family members (Brannon *et al.* 2013; Kaikkonen 2005), something that brings family relations into the entrepreneurial venture. Trust and shared knowledge between family members may create an open space for the discussion of entrepreneurial opportunities (Alsos *et al.* 2015), allowing for exchanges of the information and knowledge needed for the identification or creation of new opportunities. Supporting this view, Discua Cruz, Howorth and Hamilton (2013) found that in enterprising families, the search for new entrepreneurial opportunities was a collective effort in which both the senior and the junior generation participated and that certain opportunities resulted only from the joint effort where the knowledge of both generations was involved.

On the other hand, as emphasized in the sociological literature, business decisions, such as the development and exploitation of new opportunities, are often embedded in the household even when only one or a few household members are formally working in the business (Baines, Wheelock and Oughton 2002). Consequently, household strategies and business strategies are interlinked because strategic decisions are made within entrepreneurial households, and household members may be involved in business strategy decisions regardless of whether they are formally part of the business. In entrepreneurial households, business decisions are also household decisions; the household provisions itself for one or more businesses (Baines *et al.* 2002). Consequently, business decisions may be discussed 'around the kitchen table', and the daily talk within the household may involve identification of opportunities and the considerations related to the choice to exploit them. In a study of enterprising households in rural areas, Alsos *et al.* (2014) found that several household members were involved in opportunity identification and development. Individual household members took different roles in the process, some as initiators and others as developing the opportunity further, but opportunities were also discussed within the households through informal conversations.

Hence, a household perspective offers a way to examine the embeddedness of economic activities, such as entrepreneurship, in households and families, thereby acknowledging the embeddedness of entrepreneurship within the family (Aldrich and Cliff 2003) and challenging the individualism permeating entrepreneurship research (Jennings and Brush 2013). In the context of small entrepreneurial firms or family firms, the borders of the firm may be blurry because several household members may be involved in business decisions and activities without having formal roles in the firm. A household perspective allows for analysing the influence of several individuals in the process of opportunity identification and exploitation, acknowledging that these processes can take place within or outside the firm or in the interphase between the firm and the household. Amongst other things, this perspective makes it possible to examine the extent to which opportunity decisions are made in consultation with family members, which has been previously called for (Jennings and Brush 2013). As an extra benefit, this perspective also lets us see how different businesses and opportunities may be connected; enterprising households may be involved in more than one venture at a time. Through the household, different ventures may be connected even though the ownership or individuals formally involved may not show this connection. This point will be discussed further in the following.

5.5 Challenging the single-opportunity focus

Entrepreneurship is not necessarily a once-in-a-lifetime experience. Research has documented that portfolio entrepreneurs, individuals who found, own, manage and control more than one business at the same time, constitute a substantial proportion of entrepreneurs (Alsos and Kolvereid 1998; Carter and Ram 2003; Rosa and Scott 1999; Westhead and Wright 1998). The reported incidence of portfolio entrepreneurship has varied between 12 per cent and 34 per cent, with variations between industry, geography and gender (Alsos 2007). Consequently, calls have been made to take the entrepreneur rather than the firm as the unit of analysis in entrepreneurship research (Scott and Rosa 1996; Sarasvathy *et al.* 2013). Hence, it is widely acknowledged that one person may identify more than one opportunity and exploit new opportunities by establishing new firms or within their existing firms (Alsos 2007; Wiklund and Shepherd 2008), thereby demonstrating that entrepreneurship should not be understood as a phenomenon where a single event defines the entrepreneur. However, a question that has received limited scholarly attention so far is whether or how the different opportunities an individual is involved in are inter-connected. As argued above, the literature generally treats opportunities as discrete, unconnected entities.

The case of Anne and George's business activities, however, showed that opportunities do not emerge from 'nothing'. Instead, their identification or creation was connected to other opportunities that were currently or previously exploited at the farm. This connection was in some cases related to knowledge developed from previous experiences, as in the example of the sawmill, where the experience from forestry and from the carpenter business in combination represented important input to the identification of the opportunity. The connection could also be related to the resources available from current business activities, such as the farm's forest estate for the sawmill, the farm's buildings for the salmon tourism idea, and the stables and horse equipment for the horse therapy activity. Furthermore, the connection could be on the market side, as was the case in the tourism activity, where relatives of visitors from George's grandparents' tourism business were still in contact with the family, demonstrating a potential market for a new tourism venture.

The interconnectedness of opportunities was also apparent in the short cases of opportunity identification within firms, where the firms clearly built on the existing competencies and activities of the firm when identifying new, and related, opportunities. Opportunity relatedness was a liberating strategy, such as in the case of the ship furniture manufacturer, or a result of new opportunities that emerged from current activities, such as in the case of the software firm. For the experience hotel, it was both – their strategy was to let new opportunities emerge from existing activities and to organize their firm so that they were able to take advantage of the opportunities that emerged.

Shane (2000) discussed the role of prior knowledge for opportunity discovery. He examined eight entrepreneurial opportunities that stemmed from one single invention from MIT, demonstrating that the opportunities discovered were clearly different based on the prior knowledge of the different entrepreneurs/ entrepreneurial teams. This means, he argued, that an invention does not represent an opportunity in itself but that the combination with (new or old) prior knowledge of the entrepreneurs is needed to identify the means-end framework that constitutes an opportunity. Although Shane does not explicitly make that point, his study demonstrates that different opportunities may be interconnected. First and most obvious, the eight opportunities examined are connected through the one invention on which they all build, which constitute joint means in the means-ends relationship. Second, the role of prior knowledge indicates that entrepreneurs may utilize knowledge gained from previous opportunity development and exploitation in the process of identifying new opportunities and hence create the connection between prior and new opportunities. Without the first, the next would not exist.

That one opportunity may lead to another has previously been noted from analyses of serial and portfolio entrepreneurs. Ronstadt (1988) found that most entrepreneurs continued their entrepreneurial careers by exploiting new opportunities and starting new ventures after establishing their first one. He introduced the 'corridor principle'; i.e., "the act of starting a new venture moves an entrepreneur down a venture corridor that allows him or her to see intersecting corridors leading to new venture opportunities that they could not see before getting into business" (Ronstadt 1988, p. 34). The corridor principle relates to the understanding that entrepreneurs identify opportunities because prior knowledge triggers the recognition of the value of information (Shane 2000). Often, the opportunity identification process starts in the base of the experience and knowledge of the entrepreneurs involved (Hills, Shrader and Lumpkin 1999). Experiences from current entrepreneurial activities may be particularly relevant information sources for new opportunity identification because they may, for instance, give access to information about customer needs or a particular aspect of production. Entrepreneurial opportunities identified this way are likely to be related to the current activity because they build on information developed from them. Moreover, the opportunity corridor principle indicates that in business, exploiting a previously identified opportunity is important for gaining access to this information. Hence, the current involvement in opportunity exploitation may be a source of information not available to others, which may be one reason why some people and not others identify the opportunity, as noted by Shane and Venkataraman (2000). However, it also makes one opportunity identification dependent on a previous opportunity identification. Analysing how opportunities are 'nested' and come in 'bundles' may reveal new knowledge of the characteristics of opportunities and identification processes that cannot be seen if opportunities are treated as independent of each other. Acknowledging that opportunities may be interlinked allows for considering that future opportunities may spin out of the ones currently exploited. An entrepreneur who acts on one opportunity may see this not necessarily as the end goal but as a learning experience or a temporal project, an investment that at a later point can lead to something else (Sarasvathy *et al.* 2013).

This insight is important for several reasons. It has relevance for understanding the evaluation of opportunities. Although it is impossible *ex ante* to assess the value of a new opportunity, the entrepreneur makes some sort of judgement on whether the opportunity is worth pursuing. The potential of an opportunity exploitation to lead to new opportunities could be a part of this evaluation. Similarly, it has relevance for understanding entrepreneurial careers and entrepreneurs' motivations. Ronstadt (1988) suggested that entrepreneurs should select earlier ventures based on their potential to reveal follow-up opportunities to increase the likelihood of succeeding in building a career as an entrepreneur. Furthermore, it supports the argument that the identification of new opportunities is path dependent (Alvarez and Busenitz 2001). Early decisions to exploit opportunities may create paths for the future development of the venture, including the new opportunities emerging, which can be exploited later on. In the case of Anne and George, the path-dependent nature of the opportunities exploited is evident, as explained above.

5.5.1 Extending the single-opportunity perspective: portfolio entrepreneurial households

To further discuss the interconnectedness of opportunities, I now return to the household perspective, this time focusing on portfolio entrepreneurial households. Also portfolio entrepreneurship hinges on the household-business nexus, for which the key may be both the family circumstances that influence business decisions and the economic conditions facing the business (Carter and Ram 2003; Welter 2011). It has been argued that moving the unit of analysis from the firm to the individual is needed to understand entrepreneurial activity (Scott and Rosa 1996, 1997) and is particularly relevant to examine how entrepreneurs are involved in the exploitation of several opportunities and hence how different opportunities are interconnected. Adopting a household perspective in portfolio entrepreneurship extends this argument further. Although the groups of businesses created by portfolio entrepreneurs can be complex in the sense that they involve partnerships between different owners (Iacobucci and Rosa 2005; Rosa 1998), portfolio entrepreneurship processes may also be seen as embedded within the household and involve several household members or family entrepreneurial teams (Discua Cruz *et al.* 2013). Hence, the arguments made above regarding how several individuals may be involved in opportunity identification and exploitation certainly also hold for portfolio entrepreneurship.

In the example of Anne and George, we saw that the opportunities identified by the household were interconnected not only through the experience gained from one single individual's entrepreneurial career but also through the experiences, resources and activities taking place in connection to the family farm, which involved various individuals. This dynamic was apparent in how the different business activities on the farm were connected but even more visible in the way newly identified opportunities were dependent upon previous opportunities exploited, including by earlier generations of farm owners. Thus, the interconnectedness of opportunities goes beyond a single individual and the current team. Furthermore, the example shows that current businesses, such as a farm, act as a seed-bed for new opportunities to be developed (Carter 1996) and that (sparse) resources of the current business may be input to new opportunity identification (Alsos and Carter 2006).

The focus on portfolio entrepreneurial households also extends the household perspective on entrepreneurship and small business. As argued by Discua Cruz *et al.* (2013), moving the focus of research from family enterprises to enterprising families gives the potential to encompass the full range of opportunities identified, developed and exploited, in which the household is involved. Embracing this complexity allows for the study of how different entrepreneurial opportunities are interconnected and hence facilitates a deeper understanding of core questions within entrepreneurship. Where do opportunities come from? Why are steps taken to exploit them?

Basically, I have argued that examining portfolio entrepreneurial households is one way of learning more about the interconnectedness of opportunities and individuals in entrepreneurship and hence an area in which to study entrepreneurship while avoiding an overly single-individual, single-opportunity focus. In this setting, studies of how several individuals may be, more or less, equally involved in opportunity identification and simultaneously how different opportunities are interlinked can be conducted to develop theoretical knowledge of the nature of opportunities and how they are identified and exploited. In portfolio entrepreneurial households, one can also see that connections between opportunities and business activities are created not only through formal owner positions in firms but also through more informal connections, such as within the household or the wider family.

5.6 Conclusions

The aim of this chapter has been to put a focus on the limitations inhabited in the single individual-opportunity focus and raise concerns related to the way the identification and exploitation of opportunities are discussed in the literature. The main argument is that the complexity of entrepreneurial processes remains hidden through the simplification of focusing on the single entrepreneur and the single opportunity in the individual-opportunity nexus. Instead of treating opportunities as discrete entities identified and developed by single entrepreneurs, we should acknowledge that opportunity identification, development and exploitation is a social process (Dimov 2007) that involves several inter-connected individuals and that opportunities are path dependent (Alvarez and Busenitz 2001) and may emerge based on previous efforts made by the individuals involved or their connections. This acknowledgement embraces the complexity of entrepreneurial processes and raises many new questions, such as, what are the roles of different individuals in opportunity identification and exploita-tion? What role does the interaction between individuals play in these processes? What is the path-dependent nature of opportunities? What is path depen-dent, and what is created in the process? How does the interaction between individuals and opportunities shape the process? To be able to examine such questions, multiple levels of analysis need to be included.

These questions are of a general nature and refer to entrepreneurship as such. Currently, theoretical and conceptual frameworks to capture the complex and multi-level nature of these issues are not well developed. In this chapter, I have discussed one setting where the interconnections between individuals and opportunities in entrepreneurship come to the surface and therefore can be studied: the context of portfolio entrepreneurial households. I have shown that a household perspective can give insights in this area, which complements research with an individual focus. The household perspective emphasizes the embeddedness of business decisions within the household, where several indi-viduals and their relationships constitute an entity for economic decisions. I suggest using this perspective to study the involvement of several individuals and their interactions in opportunity identification, development and exploita-tion processes because it helps us understand the social aspects of opportunity processes that also involve individuals without formal roles in the business(es). Furthermore, it helps us understand the path-dependent nature of opportunities and their interconnectedness, not only within the formal unit of one single firm but also related to the portfolio of opportunities where the household members are involved.

Although the perspective presented here addresses portfolio entrepreneurial households, similar processes may take place in other entrepreneurial teams. Entrepreneurial process often involves teams of entrepreneurs working together. Team members' interactions and the connectedness to their previous endea-vours are also likely to influence opportunity identification, development and exploitation, also outside the household context. These arguments may therefore be extended beyond the context of enterprising households. Although it has not been within the scope of this chapter to make this extension, where applicable, I have also brought in the firm context. I have provided examples of joint opportunity identification in the firm context, and these examples show how new opportunities identified and developed within a firm can be strongly related to the opportunities the same firm currently exploits. These arguments relate to issues within corporate entrepreneurship, innovation teams and other subjects discussed within strategic management and innovation research, where an entrepreneurship perspective can provide a different angle. It has been argued that we lack the conceptual frameworks to capture how firms address opportunities (Short *et al.* 2010). In firms, where team processes are usual, the single individual-single opportunity nexus may be even more problematic. An extension of the framework to examine the interconnectedness between opportunities and the involvement of several actors may therefore be useful to understand opportunity identification, development and exploitation within existing firms.

My starting point was the individual-opportunity nexus, and my main argument has been that we should talk about individuals, opportunities and nexuses as interconnected. This is challenging but important to better understand the entrepreneurial processes taking place in practice. Hence, instead of avoiding these issues to simplify the discussion of the individual-opportunity nexus, scholars should embrace the complexity that results from the interconnectedness of several opportunities and several individuals in the nexus.

Acknowledgements

I would like to thank Mariell Opdal Jørstad for conducting the interview on the experience hotel, and Karin Andrea Wigger for assisting with the identification of the cases on the software firm and the ship furniture producer. I would also like to thank Hans Landström and two anonymous reviewers for constructive and very helpful comments on previous versions of this chapter. Parts of this research are funded by the Norwegian Research Council.

Notes

1 Although this definition is ascribed to Shane and Venkataraman (2000), it is a result of a discussion within the field where several authors had asserted similar opinions, including the focus on the process rather than the entrepreneur as type of person (e.g. Gartner 1988; Low and MacMillan 1988), opportunity (e.g. Krueger 2000), and on entrepreneurship taking place in existing firms (e.g. Sharma and Chrisman 1999). It is also based on previous arguments by Venkataraman (1997).
2 This argument is in some sense contradictory to the argument that opportunities are objective phenomena that exist independently of the recognizing individual because asymmetry cannot exist independently of the individuals who have (or do not have) certain information or beliefs. However, their argument is that if the opportunity is known to all, it will already be exploited, and no entrepreneurial rent can be created. Hence, for it to be an opportunity that involves something that can be introduced and sold with profit, it cannot be known to all at a given time.
3 Caution should be stated: although I criticize Shane and Venkataraman (2000) and related research for an overemphasis on the single individual in entrepreneurship, I do not assert they necessarily disagree that such a focus is a simplification. On the contrary, Shane (2012), in his retrospective on the 2000 article, weakly modifies this focus by including in parentheses in his explanation of what entrepreneurship is: 'entrepreneurship focuses on an individual's (or set of individuals') choices relative to his or her (their) other alternatives'. Even more clearly, Venkataraman *et al.* (2012), in their parallel retrospective, state that 'much entrepreneurship is a team and/or community endeavour, rather than an individual one … highlighting the role of collective

interaction, negotiation, and shared experience in shaping and reshaping opportunities' (p. 22). My argument has rather been that the inter-individual nature of entrepreneurship needs to be further developed and explored to better understand the entrepreneurial processes taking place in practice.

4 These illustrative cases are taken from two different research projects in which I am currently involved. The data for the hotel case were gathered through an interview with the daily manager, informal talks with the marketing director and internet sources. The data for the two other cases is based on written sources, where the firms describe an opportunity they seek to develop through R&D activity as a means to secure tax credit for the R&D costs. The tax credit application includes questions on the nature of the opportunity, the opportunity identification, plans for further development and extensive information on other aspects.

References

Aldrich, H.E. and Cliff, J.E. (2003) 'The pervasive effects of family on entrepreneurship: toward a family embeddedness perspective', *Journal of Business Venturing*, 18, pp. 573–596.

Alsos, G.A. (2007) *Portfolio entrepreneurship: General and farm contexts.* PhD thesis. Bodø, Norway: Bodø Graduate School of Business.

Alsos, G.A. and Carter, S. (2006) 'Multiple business ownership in the Norwegian farm sector: Resource transfer and performance consequences', *Journal of Rural Studies*, 22, pp. 313–322.

Alsos, G.A., Carter, S. and Ljunggren, E. (2014) 'Kinship and business: How entrepreneurial households facilitate business growth', *Entrepreneurship and Regional Development*, 26, pp. 97–122.

Alsos, G.A., Carter, S. and Ljunggren, E. (2015) 'Entrepreneurial families and households'. In Baker, T. and Welter, F. (eds) *The Routledge Companion to Entrepreneurship.* Abingdon: Routledge, pp. 165–178.

Alsos, G.A. and Kolvereid, L. (1998) 'The business gestation process of novice, serial and parallel business founders', *Entrepreneurship Theory and Practice*, 22, pp. 101–114.

Alsos, G.A., Ljunggren, E. and Pettersen, L.T. (2003) 'Farm-based entrepreneurs: What triggers the start-up of new business activities?', *Journal of Small Business and Enterprise Development*, 10, pp. 435–443.

Alvarez, S.A. and Barney, J.B. (2007) 'Discovery and creation: Alternative theories of entrepreneurial action', *Strategic Entrepreneurship Journal*, 1, pp. 11–26.

Alvarez, S.A. and Busenitz, L.W. (2001) 'The entrepreneurship of resource-based theory', *Journal of Management*, 27, pp. 755–775.

Baines, S., Wheelock, J. and Oughton, E. (2002) 'A household-based approach to the small business family'. In Fletcher, D.E. (ed.) *Understanding the Small Family Business.* London and New York: Routledge, pp. 168–179.

Brannon, D.L., Wiklund, J. and Haynie, J.M. (2013) 'The varying effects of family relationships in entrepreneurial teams', *Entrepreneurship Theory and Practice*, 37(1), pp. 107–132.

Brush, C.G. and Manolova, T.S. (2004) 'The household structure variables in the PSED Questionnaire'. In Gartner, W.B., Shaver, K.G., Carter, N.M. and Reynolds, P.D. (eds) *Handbook of Entrepreneurial Dynamics: The Process of Business Creation.* Thousand Oaks, CA: Sage, pp. 39–48.

Busenitz, L.W., Plummer, L.A., Klotz, A.C. and Rhoads, K. (2014) 'Entrepreneurship research (1985–2009) and the emergence of opportunities', *Entrepreneurship, Theory and Practice*, 38(5), pp. 981–1000.

Busenitz, L.W., West III, G.P., Shepherd, D., Nelson, T., Chandler, G.N. and Zacharackis, A. (2003) 'Entrepreneurship research in emergence: Past trends and future directions', *Journal of Management*, 29(3), pp. 285–308.

Caplan, B. (1999) 'The Austrian search for realistic foundation', *Southern Economic Journal*, 65, pp. 823–838.

Carter, S. (1996) 'The indigenous rural enterprise: Characteristics and change in the British farm sector', *Entrepreneurship and Regional Development*, 8, pp. 345–358.

Carter, S. and Ram, M. (2003) 'Reassessing portfolio entrepreneurship: Towards a multidisciplinary approach', *Small Business Economics*, 21, pp. 371–380.

Castellacci, F. (2008) 'Technological paradigms, regimes and trajectories: Manufacturing and service industries in a new taxonomy of sectoral patterns of innovation', *Research Policy*, 37, pp. 978–994.

Davidsson, P. and Tonelli, M. (2013) 'Killing our darling: Why we need to let go of the entrepreneurial opportunity construct'. In Davidsson, P. (ed.) *Australia Centre for Entrepreneurship (ACE) Research Exchange Conference*. Brisbane: Australia Centre for Entrepreneurship, Queensland University of Technology.

Dimov, D. (2007) 'Beyond the single-person, single-insight attribution in understanding entrepreneurial opportunities', *Entrepreneurship Theory and Practice*, 31, pp. 713–731.

Discua Cruz, A., Howorth, C. and Hamilton, E. (2013) 'Intrafamily entrepreneurship: The formation and membership of family entrepreneurial teams', *Entrepreneurship Theory and Practice*, 37, pp. 17–46.

Eckhardt, J.T. and Ciuchta, M.P. (2008) 'Selected variation: The population-level implications of multistage selection in entrepreneurship', *Strategic Entrepreneurship Journal*, 2, pp. 209–224.

Eckhardt, J.T. and Shane, S. (2003) 'Opportunities and entrepreneurship', *Journal of Management*, 29, pp. 333–349.

Felin, T., Kauffman, S., Koppl, R. and Longo, G. (2014) 'Economic opportunity and evolution: Beyond bounded rationality and phase space', *Strategic Entrepreneurship Journal*, 8(4), pp. 269–282.

Gartner, W.B. (1988) 'Who is an entrepreneur? Is the wrong question', *American Journal of Small Business*, 12(1), pp. 11–31.

Gartner, W.B. (2001) 'Is there an elephant in entrepreneurship? Blind assumptions in theory development', *Entrepreneurship Theory and Practice*, 25(4), pp. 27–39.

Gregoire, D. and Shepherd, D. (2011) 'Technology-market combinations and the identification of entrepreneurial opportunities: An investigation of the opportunity-individual nexus', *Academy of Management Journal*, 55(4), pp. 753–785.

Gullestad, M. (1984) 'Sosialantropologiske perspektiver på familie og hushold [Social anthropological perspectives on family and household]'. In Rudie, I. (ed.) *Myk start – hard landing*. Oslo: Universitetsforlaget, pp. 37–58.

Hills, G.E., Shrader, R.C. and Lumpkin, G.T. (1999) 'Opportunity recognition as a creative process'. In *Frontiers of Entrepreneurship Research*. Wellesley, MA: Babson College, pp. 216–227.

Iacobucci, D. and Rosa, P. (2005) 'Growth, diversification, and business group formation in entrepreneurial firms', *Small Business Economics*, 25, pp. 65–82.

Jennings, J.E. and Brush, C.G. (2013) 'Research on women entrepreneurs: Challenges to (and from) the broader entrepreneurship literature?', *Academy of Management Annals*, 7, pp. 663–715.

Kaikkonen, V.A. (2005) *Essays on the Entrepreneurial Process in Rural Micro Firms*. Department of Business and Management, Kuopio: University of Kuopio.

Kirzner, I.M. (1997) 'Entrepreneurial discovery and the competitive market process: An Austrian approach', *Journal of Economic Literature*, XXXV, pp. 60–85.

Krueger, N.F. (2000) 'The cognitive infrastructure of opportunity emergence', *Entrepreneurship Theory and Practice*, 24(3), pp. 5–23.

Lim, J.Y.-K., Busenitz, L.W. and Chidambaram, L. (2013) 'New venture teams and the quality of business opportunities identified: Faultlines between subgroups of founders and investors', *Entrepreneurship Theory and Practice*, 37(1), pp. 47–67.

Low, M.B. and MacMillan, I.C. (1988) 'Entrepreneurship: Past research and future challenges', *Journal of Management*, 25, pp. 17–25.

Ronstadt, R. (1988) 'The corridor principle', *Journal of Business Venturing*, 3, pp. 31–40.

Rosa, P. (1998) 'Entrepreneurial processes of business cluster formation and growth by habitual entrepreneurs', *Entrepreneurship Theory and Practice*, 22, pp. 43–61.

Rosa, P. and Scott, M. (1999) 'The prevalence of multiple owners and directors in the SME sector: Implications for our understanding of start-up and growth', *Entrepreneurship and Regional Development*, 11, pp. 21–37.

Sarasvathy, S.D. (2008) *Effectuation: Elements of Entrepreneurial Expertise*. Cheltenham: Edward Elgar.

Sarasvathy, S.D., Dew, N., Velamuri, S.R. and Venkataraman, S. (2011) 'Three views of entrepreneurial opportunity'. In Acs, Z.J. and Audretsch, D.B. (eds) *Handbook of Entrepreneurship Research: An Interdisciplinary Survey and Introduction*. New York: Springer, pp. 77–96.

Sarasvathy, S.D., Menon, A.R. and Kuechle, G. (2013) 'Failing firms and successful entrepreneurs: Serial entrepreneurship as a temporal portfolio', *Small Business Economics*, 40, pp. 417–434.

Schjoedt, L., Monsen, E., Pearson, A., Barnett, T. and Chrisman, J.J. (2013) 'New venture and family business teams: Understanding team formation, composition, behaviors, and performance', *Entrepreneurship, Theory and Practice*, 37(1), pp. 1–15.

Scott, M. and Rosa, P. (1996) 'Opinion: Has firm level analysis reached its limits? Time for a rethink', *International Small Business Journal*, 14, pp. 81–89.

Scott, M. and Rosa, P. (1997) 'New business from old: The role of portfolio entrepreneurs in the start-up and growth of small businesses'. In Ram, M., Deakins, D. and Smallbone, D. (eds) *Small Firms: Enterprising Futures*. London: Paul Chapman Publishing, pp. 33–46.

Shane, S. (2000) 'Prior knowledge and the discovery of entrepreneurial opportunities', *Organization Science*, 11, pp. 448–469.

Shane, S. (2003) *A General Theory of Entrepreneurship: The Individual-Opportunity Nexus*. Cheltenham: Edward Elgar.

Shane, S. (2012) 'Reflections on the 2010 AMR Decade Award: Delivering on the promise of entrepreneurship as a field of research', *Academy of Management Review*, 37, pp. 10–20.

Shane, S. and Venkataraman, S. (2000) 'The promise of entrepreneurship as a field of research', *Academy of Management Review*, 25, pp. 217–226.

Sharma, P. and Chrisman, J.J. (1999) 'Towards a reconciliation of the definitional issues in the field of corporate entrepreneurship', *Entrepreneurship Theory and Practice*, 11–27.

Shepherd, D.A. and DeTienne, D.R. (2005) 'Prior knowledge, potential financial reward, and opportunity identification', *Entrepreneurship Theory and Practice*, 29, pp. 91–112.

Short, J.C., Ketchen, D.J., Shook, C.L. and Ireland, R.D. (2010) 'The concept of "opportunity" in entrepreneurship research: Past accomplishments and future challenges', *Journal of Management*, published online: October 19, 2009, doi: 10.1177/0149206309342746.

Ucbasaran, D., Alsos, G.A., Westhead, P. and Wright, M. (2008) 'Habitual entrepreneurs', *Foundations and Trends in Entrepreneurship*, 4, pp. 309–450.

Venkataraman, S. (1997) 'The distinctive domain of entrepreneurship research'. In Katz, J.A. (ed.) *Advances in Entrepreneurship Research: Firm Emergence and Growth*. Greenwich, CT: JAI Press, pp. 119–138.

Venkataraman, S., Sarasvathy, S.D., Dew, N. and Forster, W.R. (2012) 'Reflections on the 2010 AMR Decade Award: Whither the promise? Moving forward with entrepreneurship as a science of the artificial', *Academy of Management Review*, 37(1), pp. 21–33.

Welter, F. (2011) 'Contextualizing entrepreneurship – conceptual challenges and ways forward', *Entrepreneurship Theory and Practice*, 35, pp. 165–184.

Westhead, P. and Wright, M. (1998) 'Novice, portfolio, and serial founders: Are they different?', *Journal of Business Venturing*, 13, pp. 173–204.

Wheelock, J. and Mariussen, Å. (1997) *Household, Work and Economic Change: A Comparative Perspective*. Boston, MA, Dordrecht and London: Kluwer Academic Publishers.

Wheelock, J. and Ougthon, E. (1996) 'The household as a focus for research', *Journal of Economic Issues*, XXX, pp. 143–159.

Wiklund, J. and Shepherd, D.A. (2008) 'Portfolio entrepreneurship: Habitual and novice founders, new entry, and mode of organizing', *Entrepreneurship Theory and Practice*, 32, pp. 701–725.

6 Challenging assumptions and bias in entrepreneurship research

Paul Nightingale and Alex Coad

6.1 Introduction

Outside academia it is almost universally accepted in both popular and political culture (European Commission 2008; USA 2010) that entrepreneurship has a positive impact on the economy. It seems strange to many people that this view is not universally shared by economists. This positive view was captured nicely by President Bush II when he highlighted:

> We often think of pioneers as those hardy settlers who tamed the American frontier. ... However, small business people also stand among our Nation's greatest pioneers. They, too, are men and women of vision. They, too, have the courage to take risks and the willingness to make their ideas work. Industrious and self-reliant, small business men and women continually lead the way in the development of new technology and products and in the creation of economic opportunity for all Americans. Indeed, small business is the lifeblood of America's free enterprise system. It is within this vital sector of our economy that most workers find their first jobs and training. Small businesses account for two out of every three new jobs created in the United States.[1]

Presidents Clinton and Obama have made similar points, and the EU is equally smitten (European Commission 2008; Obama 2009).[2] So much so, that when Bradley and Roberts (2004, p. 38) suggested that "the contemporary period is the 'era of the entrepreneur', in which the entrepreneur is viewed increasingly as a folk hero" it was mirrored across the Atlantic by Blanchflower and Oswald (1998, p. 28) who similarly suggested we live in "the era of the entrepreneur. After years of neglect, those who start and manage their own businesses are viewed as popular heroes."[3]

Economists find the evidence for this heroic view rather inconclusive, as research suggests entrepreneurial activity has a rather marginal impact on the economy (Davidsson 2007; Nightingale and Coad 2014). In previous work (Nightingale and Coad 2014) we highlighted this mismatch and some of the reasons for its existence, surveying the literature and re-evaluating the evidence on the economic contribution of entrepreneurial firms to job creation, productivity, innovation, and well-being. In this chapter, we extend this previous work to explore in more detail how ideological and methodological biases can combine to support a Kuhnian paradigm with a strong positive bias. Our motivation is the possibility that some of the emerging policy recommendations influenced by this paradigm may be similarly biased and hence potentially damaging for the economy.

As the chapter will argue, this paradigm is stabilized by both external-demand and internal-supply side factors. Ideological biases, path-dependent framing effects and the existence of politically powerful small-firm lobbies (who are eager to exploit plentiful rent-seeking opportunities) contribute towards a powerful demand for positive interpretations of entrepreneurship that constrains the diffusion of more realistic research-backed interpretations. The supply of more realistic evaluations has been further constrained by publication (and funding) biases and methodological problems related to: poor quality data, survivor bias, skewed statistics, unrepresentative samples, flexible definitions, regression to the mean, conceptual slides, lack of attention to randomness, and endogeneity problems. These methodological problems mean that the evidence on the impact of entrepreneurship is typically ambiguous, allowing the selection of positive interpretations and the dismissal of negative findings as anomalies.

However, over time, as methods and data have improved, anomalies have accumulated, and more sober evaluations have emerged that are often at odds with the received paradigm (Hall and Woodward 2010; Hamilton 2000; Moskowitz and Vissing-Jorgensen 2002; Nightingale and Coad 2014; Santarelli and Vivarelli 2007; Shane 2009). As we highlighted in our previous work, it seems entrepreneurial firms are less innovative, less productive, and do not seem to be associated with GDP growth (Nightingale and Coad 2014). They do seem to contribute to job creation *in their first year,* but this is positive by construction (firms can't lose jobs that didn't exist) and does not imply that more market entry would generate more new jobs. The jobs that are created, like typical small firm jobs, tend to be lower quality, more volatile, less productive, and hence employees are typically paid less and have fewer benefits, while being subject to more work-related accidents.

On the positive front, a small subpopulation of new firms help open up new industries and self-employed individuals are happier. Entrepreneurial start-ups may also play important roles in providing marginal, less skilled individuals with human capital, and providing jobs to individuals who might otherwise be unemployed. Overall, however, the relatively poor performance of entrepreneurial start-ups means that it is difficult to justify the substantial subsidies already in place for entrepreneurs (see Storey 2006). Given the 'deadweight' problems associated with these subsidies, they could be distorting the market in a socially suboptimal way. Indeed, the low survival rates, profitability and productivity of new firms is consistent with *excessive* low quality entrepreneurship (Santarelli and Vivarelli 2002, 2007).

In the rest of this chapter we aim to generate a better understanding of the mismatch between recent research and the widely held view that entrepreneurial activity is always 'a good thing'. We extend Nightingale and Coad's (2014) emphasis on demand side changes in models of political economy, that are linked to biases on the supply side, to explore the emergence, consolidation and then weakening of a Kuhnian scientific paradigm that mediates the supply of, and demand for, research.

In Section 6.2 we explore how the paradigm emerged as a receptive environment was created by a change in the underlying model of political economy that linked to flexible conceptual frameworks and paradigmatic empirical studies. Together these influenced the design of policy, creating rent-seeking opportunities and funding streams that helped consolidate the paradigm. In Section 6.3 we move from the macro to micro-level and explore how the supply of research within the paradigm is influenced by biases. Section 6.4 illustrates the dynamics of the resulting paradigm, as better methods to address biases and higher quality data-sets, have changed understanding of entrepreneurship and its links to employment. Section 6.5 discusses the implications and draws conclusions.

6.2 Establishing a paradigm

While Kuhn's ideas have been subject to considerable criticism by historians and sociologists of science, his notion of a paradigm is a useful heuristic for understanding the dynamics of entrepreneurship research. For Kuhn, paradigms are widely recognized scientific achievements that provide guidance to a community of researchers on how to define and solve research problems. They consist of 'a constellation of beliefs, values, techniques and methods' that provide a 'mind set', in the form of an intuitive *a priori* backdrop of expectations for executing normal science by defining legitimate problems and methods (Turro 1986, p. 886). As paradigms get established they help co-ordinate activity and resources, as new sources of funding, PhD programmes, and journals and other outlets for research, are established.

The establishment of the current paradigm in entrepreneurship research was partly driven by a shift in the ideological context of research that created new public policy questions for researchers to address, and new sources of funding. The paradigm was established when these questions were linked to shared models and theoretical frameworks, and paradigmatic empirical studies (of which David Birch's work was key) with their associated standard methods and data. These all combined to generate a widely shared view of how the world is, how it should be researched and what kinds of findings are, and are not, legitimate and should be published and taught.

What was, and is, interesting about the standard heroic paradigm in entrepreneurship research is how, firstly, powerful social actors have political and financial interests in maintaining the paradigm against competing views. Secondly, how it is supported by a set of methodological biases that tend to support misleadingly positive research outcomes. These two features interact to support each other and help strengthen the paradigm in a self-perpetuating way.

6.2.1 New context

The heroic paradigm is surprisingly new. For most of the 20th century interest in small firms and entrepreneurs was limited (Landström, Harirchi and Åström 2012). Instead, attention focused on large firms, given their higher levels of productivity, innovation and employment (Chandler 1990; Henrekson 2005; Schumpeter 1942). This shift in paradigm was explained in Nightingale and Coad (2014) in relation to the emergence of a receptive political and ideological context. This emerged because of a shift away from the post-war consensus around Keynesian demand management (Briggs 1968; Hogan 1989; Ruggie 1982). This had involved governments, industrialists and unions co-operating to maintain demand and support large national-champion firms to exploit economies of scale in (protected) national markets (Dannreuther 2009). While this generated three decades of growth, high employment, rising equality and low inflation (Goldin and Margo 1992), after the oil shocks of the 1970s this success abruptly ended: inflation and unemployment soared, economies deindustrialized, and protected nationalized industries performed poorly (Goldthorpe 1984). The share of employment in small firms, which had been declining since the 1920s started to reverse in 1971 (Storey 1994, p. 26). Ironically, in the UK this reversal in employment trends coincided with was establishment of the Bolton Committee to examine, what was assumed to be, the terminal decline of small firms.

The alternative model, pushed by the Reagan and Thatcher governments, was based on the idea that the economy could be improved by entrepreneurial small firms (not large firms), co-ordinated by markets (not governments), achieving scale by competing in free international markets (not protected national markets) (Dannreuther 2009). This new model involved a counter-factual assertion, common in Cold War debates at the time, that outcomes would 'always' be better off with 'more' markets' co-ordination, undertaken by entrepreneurs, and 'less' state intervention. These ideas had been propagated in networks of think-tanks, rather than universities, often supported by small firm lobbies who had been partially excluded from post-war 'consensus' decision-making (Dannreuther 2009).[4] While these ideas were developed outside the academic mainstream, they were informed by academic theories and empirical research. The studies that arguably defined the paradigm were undertaken by David Birch. His groundbreaking research on small (new) firms and job creation was extremely influential inside and outside academia at a time of high and rising unemployment, and played an important role in discrediting the older large-firm based model of political economy (Birch 1979, 1987; see also Birch *et al.* 1993; Kassicieh *et al.* 2002; Kirchhoff 1994; Kirchhoff and Phillips 1988).

6.2.2 Theoretical underpinnings

Birch's empirical research was linked to the new model of political economy by three theoretical frameworks that helped underpin the new paradigm by providing a way of interpreting empirical evidence. The first was provided by

Mansfield's (1962) standard textbook theoretical framework for understanding entrepreneurship. This barriers-to-entry model suggested that an unexploited pool of potential entrepreneurs can be triggered into entrepreneurship when expected profit-levels make it a rational way to allocate time and resources. The model provides a simple, but very powerful, framework for generating public policy. Because market failures reduce profits, they create barriers to entry, which policy should remove to incentivize a stream of entrepreneurs to enter the market. An additional assumption, not necessarily part of the model, but normally implicitly accepted, is that this will generate economic growth.

This assumption is often drawn from the Austrian tradition which provides the second theoretical framework. It suggests that entrepreneurship provides the process that co-ordinates prices in the economy. As Shane (2000) notes: "By buying or selling goods and services in response to the discovery of price misalignments, an individual can earn entrepreneurial profits or incur entrepreneurial losses. Collectively, this process of decision making about prices moves an economy from disequilibrium to equilibrium." Hence entrepreneurship "is a mechanism through which temporal and spatial inefficiencies in an economy are discovered and mitigated" (Shane and Venkataraman 2000, p. 219) which is why there is so much theoretical emphasis in the Austrian's tradition on opportunity recognition and discovery (Kirzner 1997, p. 72).

The third theoretical framework was provided by Schumpeter (1942) who added a more dynamic, innovation-based emphasis that complements the previous focus on static co-ordination. Schumpeter saw economic development as an evolutionary process driven by charismatic entrepreneurs who 'creatively destroy' existing industrial structures through revolutionary innovations and their associated changes in production and markets. He argued that entrepreneurs' charismatic power eventually dissipates and reduces as they increasingly manage using organizational routines. This eventually generates a new status quo of routine production which provides opportunities for another generation of entrepreneurs to begin a new cycle of innovation.

6.2.2.1 Theoretical weaknesses

All three of these frameworks have major weaknesses. Mansfield's model adopts many of the simplifying assumptions of traditional economic thinking. It frames the economy in terms of static allocation, assumes entrepreneurs have perfect knowledge of the future profits they will inevitably make (and assumes they are highly capable). In reality, however, entrepreneurs are typically misinformed and over-optimistic: most entrepreneurial entry decisions are mistaken, and are rapidly followed by an early exit, often with significant personal and financial costs. Even successful entrepreneurs, on average, receive remuneration below the levels they would receive working in an established firm, except perhaps for a small number at the very top of the distribution (Frankish *et al.* 2014; Hamilton 2000; Moskowitz and Vissing-Jorgensen 2002; Mwaura and Carter 2015; see also Levine and Rubinstein 2013).

The problems with the Austrian school are more significant as they misleadingly frame entrepreneurs as the people who generate economic success, which is true 'in the model' only if one assumes privileged knowledge. Hayek's (1944, 1945, 1960) idea (developed in the context of Cold War debates contrasting the market-based economies of the West with the centrally planned USSR) was that entrepreneurs have better access to distributed (partially tacit) knowledge than governments. This is true, but irrelevant to current concerns as new firms compete with established firms not North Korean central planners. By defining entrepreneurship as the process which coordinates prices, the Austrian approach conflates two distinct activities: founding firms and co-ordinating the economy. Whether entrepreneurs (as people who found firms) help co-ordinate the economy is an entirely separate 'empirical' question. Because economic co-ordination is not just market co-ordination, the Austrians largely miss the role played by managers of established firms and the technological infrastructure underpinning market co-ordination (e.g. in global financial markets). By reading history backwards from atypical success stories, the Austrians over-emphasize the benefits of entrepreneurship and conflate opportunity entrepreneurship (a minority of cases of new firm starts) with necessity and life-style entrepreneurship (see Box 6.1). Most entrepreneurs act upon incorrectly perceived opportunities, and perform poorly. As a result, entrepreneurship may well multiply rather than mitigate inefficiencies in the economy, moving it further into disequilibrium. Low quality entrepreneurial start-ups can free-ride on the credentials of less risky entrants, bringing down average investor returns, increasing factor prices, and disrupting financial markets (de Meza 2002).

Box 6.1 Opportunity, necessity, and lifestyle entrepreneurship

The founding of new firms may have little to do with opportunity entrepreneurship and the unexpected surprise at cleverly spotting a new market opportunity. Necessity entrepreneurship, for example, arises when an individual starts a firm to escape unemployment. In addition, 'lifestyle' entrepreneurship occurs when new businesses are started by individuals with lifestyle preferences or psychological issues that prevent them from working for others. This is often seen in terms of positive features, but could reflect psychological problems. Handler and Kram (1988, p. 363) for example write that "since the entrepreneur can have unresolved conflicts with his father, he starts the business to escape the authority of a powerful figure ... In other words, the entrepreneur aspires to run his own empire as a result of his ongoing 'need for control' ... a need evidenced by the serious difficulty that he has addressing issues of dominance, submission, and suspicion about 'authority' ... the business can represent an extension of himself, and therefore succession issues get mixed up with the founder's 'desire for applause'."

In recent work (Nightingale 2015), we have suggested Schumpeter's ideas were heavily influenced by the German theologian Adolf Harnack. Harnack had a theory of the evolution of religions driven by a series of entrepreneurial, charismatic leaders (Moses, Jesus, Martin Luther) who creatively destroy established religions. Leaders are touched by God and receive special insight that allows them to start new religions through charismatic force of personality. However, over time as the cults they form grow into new religions they become increasingly routinized, creating the conditions for a new cycle of innovation.[5] Applying a theological theory where prophets have God-given insight, to entrepreneurs introduces a number of serious shortcomings: innovation is misunderstood as an inventive 'event', driven by unique (almost magical) insight, which generates innovations in a fully developed state, rather than an experimental *process* that develops inventions from their initial primitive state, into commercially viable innovations. In reality, this process typically takes a long time, is expensive, requires considerable capability and does not end when the product is launched (Rosenberg 1976). Schumpeter's theory of innovation, is in effect, a theory of invention with the innovation left out. By mistakenly assuming new innovations are fully formed, the Schumpeterian framework over-emphasises new radical innovations, misses the economic importance of incremental changes and diffusion, falsely assumes capturing value from innovations is unproblematic, and is unrealistic about how new firms can outcompete incumbents and disrupt existing industries.

As a result, the Schumpeterian model mistakenly implies new firms will have an absolute advantage over existing firms, and hence are likely to be the best places to commercialize new technology. But innovation isn't invention and most start-ups typically lack the capital and resources needed to develop technology, compared with large, established firms. They cannot diversify the risks of research and innovation as well as large firms and hence find it harder to access external funding. Moreover, they find it difficult to apply the outcomes and capture the benefits from investing in innovation (which has high-variance, highly skewed returns) as they lack market power and the diversified outputs of larger firms (Cohen and Klepper 1996; Ortega-Argiles, Vivarelli and Voigt 2009).

Given these problems, the Schumpeterian story of entrepreneurs creating new industries therefore needs to be carefully examined. The electronics industry in Silicon Valley, is typically taken as a poster boy for entrepreneurship, but was initially formed by the fragmentation of William Shockley's lab in Beckman Instruments, a large firm, with the backing of Fairchild, another large firm. The founder of Intel, Gordon Moore, who was one of the scientists who left the lab, observed that "successful start-ups almost always begin with an idea that has ripened in the research organization of a large company (or university). Regions without larger companies at the technology frontier or research organizations of large companies will probably have fewer companies starting or spinning off" (quoted in Auerswald and Branscomb 2003, p. 236; see also Hvide (2009) on the higher quality of entrepreneurs leaving large firms).

6.2.3 Consolidating the paradigm

Taken together the model of political economy, Birch's studies on employment, and these three frameworks provided policy-makers and politicians with a flexible way to understand entrepreneurs. The weaknesses of the frameworks strengthen the paradigm as they give it a self-reinforcing character, as the connections between theoretical models and definitions immunizes the paradigm from falsification through a network of mutually supporting assumptions. For example, the view that entrepreneurs 'do' generate growth, is not falsified by empirical evidence that they 'do not' because that anomaly can be explained away by suggesting the existence of major barriers to entry that constrain entrepreneurship. These can be addressed by policy (e.g. by removing financial constraints, creating a more entrepreneurial culture, or reducing 'red tape' (see e.g. EVCA 2010, p. 6)). If evaluations suggest these policies don't work, then the paradigm can be used to imply that 'more' policy is needed, as not enough was done.

Hence, the new way of understanding the role of entrepreneurship in the economy, generated its own new policies which helped consolidate it further. The American government introduced the Small Business Policy Act (1980), and the Small Business Innovation Development Act in 1982, amongst a range of other interventions.[6] Across the Atlantic, the supposedly free-market British Conservative government introduced 103 new policies to support small firms between 1979 and 1983 (Mason and Harrison 1986). Over time this support has become substantial. Storey (2006, p. 248) estimates that its costs have now expanded to approximately £7.9 billion for the UK, which is more than the UK spends on the police force or universities. Similarly, in Sweden the total SME support costs were recently estimated to be SEK 46.5 billion (Lundström *et al.* 2014).

This level of spending has created a substantial industry of rent-seeking lobbyists and a strong and politically powerful political constituency benefiting from, and hence supportive of, the policies and subsidies. Hence from the 1980s there has been growing political and policy 'demand' for research on the value of entrepreneurs to the economy. New academic positions were funded, journals were set up and funding streams created, to formalize the paradigm. To the credit of many of the people involved, this did not excessively constrain the generation of counter-paradigmatic evidence, but arguably did lead to problems with publication bias as 'the entrepreneurial virtues of new businesses are often assumed rather than examined' (Holtz-Eakin 2000, p. 284). Given the importance of publications, this in turn led to biases in appointments to tenured positions in universities. It would be an interesting empirical exercise to compare research from economics departments with research from business schools, and to contrast focal findings on topics with published results for control variables to assess this potential bias.

As the next section will show, these external features that reinforce the paradigm are complemented by major methodological difficulties in researching new firms that often bias research towards positive interpretations.

6.3 Methodological biases supporting the paradigm

One of the lessons of recent research in the history of science is that the outputs of research (how supply and demand are mediated) are heavily influenced by local research practices. Studying entrepreneurial firms is no different, and is subject to numerous methodological and statistical challenges and biases at the micro-level that are rarely properly addressed (Macpherson and Holt 2007, p. 177). We define biases, following Ioannidis (2005, p. 124) as:

> … the combination of various design, data, analysis, and presentation factors that tend to produce research findings [any relationship reaching formal statistical significance] when they should not have been produced. … Bias should not be confused with chance variability that causes some findings to be false by chance even though the study design, data, analysis and presentation are perfect. Bias can entail manipulation in the analysis or reporting of findings. Selective or distorted reporting is a typical form of such bias.

The biases and methodological problems in entrepreneurship research are significant. They were covered in Nightingale and Coad (2014) and are extended here to include:

Data quality and size

Small firms typically have less rigorous reporting requirements, to reduce their administrative burdens. As a result, coverage of small and young firms in administrative datasets is less comprehensive and less detailed. Data often do not exist, and where they do exist, they are often poor quality. They typically receive less scrutiny despite the potential for deliberate misreporting (for tax evasion), which creates measurement error problems. Datasets are often small which reduces the power of studies and the likelihood that findings are true (Ioannidis 2005, p. 124). Finally, a lack of representative data on new ventures means that researchers are often required to collect the data themselves. This leads to datasets with low response rates that are vulnerable to selection bias, that are cross-sectional (hence, dynamic effects cannot be investigated), and typically involve self-reported data (which may be a further source of bias; see Bertrand and Mullainathan 2001).[7]

Survivor bias

Entrants typically experience very high exit rates, with some 20–40 per cent of entrepreneurial firms exiting within two years (Audretsch 1995; Bartelsman, Scarpetta and Schivardi 2005), and about 50 per cent of entering UK businesses exiting in their first three years (Anyadike-Danes and Hart 2014; Frankish *et al.* 2013). These exit events are predominantly failures, although a minority might correspond to so-called 'successful death' events such as voluntary closure (Coad 2014). Note that mergers, acquisitions, trade sales and Initial Public Offerings are very rare for new small firms, and also are not true cases of business exit, because the business continues to operate. Firms that die shortly after entry are less likely to provide information on their activities than firms that succeed and grow. This creates survivor bias as it under-represents unsuccessful small firms, leading to a misleadingly positive picture. These problems with data quality and survivor bias combine to create an 'uncertainty principle' that trades off quality against coverage. This bias is increased because most statistical data-analysis programs react to missing observations for individual variables by automatically removing the entire firm, creating more positive bias by further under-sampling poor performance firms.

Extremely skewed statistics

The uncertainty-principle problem is made worse by the extremely skewed nature of most statistics on entrepreneurial firms (such as start-up size, longevity, innovation, financial and other performance; see e.g. Crawford *et al.* 2015). Most entrepreneurial firms perform poorly while a tiny minority drive the average performance of a cohort of firms (Storey 1989). Shane (2008, p. 168) notes that since 1970 about 820 of the two million start-ups in the USA each year are VC-backed but:

> In 2000, the 2,180 publicly traded companies that had received VC backing between 1972 and 2000 comprised 20 per cent of all public companies, 11 per cent of sales, 13 per cent of profits, 6 per cent of employees, and one third of total market value, a figure in excess of $2.7 trillion dollars.

If so much impact comes from such a small atypical subsample, it is clear that results are likely to be highly sensitive to sampling. At the extreme, the inclusion or exclusion of a single observation, Google, can change the results (Hall and Woodward 2010). Given this problem, it is not clear how useful it is to talk about the average firm, or use categories such as SMEs or entrepreneurship, or use conventional regression strategies (such as OLS) that focus on 'the average effect for the average firm', as this misleadingly links the properties of atypical subsamples to a larger population of very different firms.

Un-representative samples

The combination of poor data and skewed statistics means sampling is extremely difficult. Unfortunately, this has been not been well addressed by the research community who often use or extrapolate from very un-representative samples. For example, Eesley and Roberts (2010) investigate entrepreneurial learning using MIT alumni, 44 per cent of whom had postgraduate degrees, and Shane's (2000) seminal study on entrepreneurial opportunities focused on entrepreneurs able to take advantage of MIT patented technology. These subsamples are a tiny, atypical, highly visible minority, that give a misleadingly positive picture of entrepreneurship in general. More recent research by Denrell and Liu (2012) suggests that the focus on these kinds of high performing firms may generate misleading results, as their high performance often indicates luck rather than ability (a point we return to later).

Definitional flexibility

These problems highlight that SMEs and entrepreneurial firms are not natural kinds, and there is considerable ambiguity about how they should be defined (Baumol 2010). Definitions are rarely consistent which increases 'researcher degrees of freedom' and hence the likelihood that findings are false (Simmons, Nelson and Simonsohn 2011). We define entrepreneurs as people who start firms (so as to avoid biases about them necessarily being successful or good for the economy), and define entrepreneurial firms as firms under 7 years old (which is approximately the time their exit rates level off). Van Praag and Versloot's (2007) influential survey defines entrepreneurial firms as "firms that satisfy *one* of the following conditions: (i) They employ fewer than 100 employees; (ii) They are younger than 7 years old; (iii) They are new entrants into the market." Entrepreneurs have also been defined in relation to competition (Dennis 2011, p. 98), being innovative (Dennis 2011, p. 99), subjective growth ambitions (Henrekson 2005, p. 439; Reynolds *et al.* 2005, p. 223), future opportunities (to create goods and services) (Shane and Venkataraman 2000, p. 218), ingenious and creative personality traits and future success in adding to their own wealth, power and prestige (Baumol 1996 [1990], p. 6). Any practical definition of entrepreneurship becomes problematic if 'entrepreneurship can also occur within an existing organization' (Shane and Venkataraman 2000, p. 219), as this implies any success, in any firm, can be credited to entrepreneurship.

These definitions may be entirely appropriate for specific studies, but the lack of common definitions complicates the comparison of research findings and makes the cumulative development of robust knowledge more difficult. It is common in the literature to use metrics that cover intentions to start firms, starting firms and the performance of new firms interchangeably. However, Parker and Belghitar (2006) use Panel Study of Entrepreneurial Dynamics data to show that only 33 per cent of nascents actually 'convert' into real entrepreneurs and this sub-set of nascents is an atypical, rather than random sample, of all nascents.

Given these difficulties it is not surprising that policy-makers suffer from a 'raging confusion ... between new, small, and entrepreneurial firms' (Dennis 2011, p. 92) that are often seen as synonymous. It is important to be clear that while most new firms are small, many small firms are old, and most new firms quickly fail (for data, see Coad and Tamvada 2012). The definition of small is equally unclear and inconsistent: in the USA they have under 500 employees, but in Europe they have less than 250, and sometimes only 20 employees.[8]

There is also often confusion between start-ups, and new plants established by older firms. While new plants can sometimes be removed from the data, it is more difficult to capture the re-incorporation of existing firms. Haltiwanger, Jarmin and Miranda's (2010) data, for example, show new firms with over 10,000 employees. A particular problem exists with firms created as 'off-balance sheet' special purpose tax-reduction vehicles for transferring Intellectual Property payments across multiple tax jurisdictions. Treating new plants or re-incorporations as new firms creates an obvious upward bias.

Defining when firms are born is also problematic. The Panel Study of Entrepreneurial Dynamics, defines firm births as the time firms become profitable. Reynolds and Curtin (2008, p. 70) define birth as the time 'monthly cash flow covering all expenses and owner's salaries had occurred in 6 or more of the past 12 months'. This creates a positive bias as it misses unprofitable firms. The GEM global report (2009, p. 13) defines birth as the point when the firm has paid wages for more than 3 months. Storey (1994, Chapter 2), defines firm births by registration, and then registration for Value Added Tax (i.e., when sales exceed £68,000). This flexibility in the definitions of dependent and independent variables makes it more likely that published research findings are false (Ioannidis 2005, p. 124).

Regression to the mean

The statistical fallacy of regression bias, associated with 'regression to the mean', is widespread in economics (Friedman 1992), and is a particular problem with studies of the job creation potential of small businesses. It arises when growing entities are sorted by their initial size. A small firm that grows large will be classified as a fast-growing small firm. If it then reverts back to its original size, it will be classified as a shrinking large firm. Growth (decline) therefore tends to be inappropriately attributed to small (large) firms. If the size of firms is measured with error, which is likely with small firms, the job creation of small firms will be further amplified (and decreased for large firms).

Conceptual slides

Other problems commonly found in the literature relate to conceptual slides, such as the slides between net and gross figures, and between levels and changes. It is common to see high growth rates (in terms of employment, productivity, etc.) in a positive light, and used to support arguments that more entrepreneurship would be good for the economy. New entrants, being smaller (level) often have higher growth rates (a change), but this is because they start from low performance levels. This becomes clearer if we use an example from Nightingale and Coad (2014): high performing athletes (a level) cannot easily improve (change) their high performance. By contrast, people who are extremely unfit (level) can and do benefit (change) from exercise. However, we rarely see it suggested that unfit people, rather than high performing athletes, should make up the Olympic team.

Projecting onto random outcomes

It has been known since Bacon that there is an inherent tendency for researchers to project causality onto situations governed by randomness. In a series of important papers Denrell and colleagues (e.g. Denrell, Fang and Liu 2015) have highlighted the dangers of overlooking the role of randomness in driving outcomes. They conclude that when outcomes are partly random and subject to amplification effects, high performance and ability are unlikely to coincide. Moreover, since high performance is subject to large variance in outcomes, in both positive and negative directions, it may well be that 'on average' copying the behaviour of the most successful firms would generate negative returns.

Only recently have researchers started to control for randomness. In our work on firm growth, we have found that entrepreneurial skill and learning largely disappear when we take into account the distributions of growth that one would expect if it were random (Coad *et al.* 2013, 2014b). Indeed, we have argued that entrepreneurial learning is largely a myth (Frankish *et al.* 2013 and references therein). When challenged to explain why subsequent entrepreneurial start-ups improve in performance compared with the first, we have shown that subsequent start-ups are larger, and the performance effect disappears once you control for the larger size of subsequent firms – a result entirely consistent with the random-luck 'gamblers' ruin' model in which gamblers with more chips play longer (Coad *et al.* 2013, 2014b; Storey 2011). It seems prior ownership experience has either no effect on subsequent business performance or a negative effect if the exit is the result of bankruptcy and debt (Gottschalk *et al.* 2014; Metzger 2006). These findings are important because it is common in Europe to assert that the US economy performs better because the USA is culturally more accepting of failure. However, any link seems questionable, and failing entrepreneurs' worse subsequent performance may instead be due to lack of quality, or more likely, because they have a reduced asset base, which makes early period survival less likely.

While it is tempting to assume that entrepreneurial performance will automatically improve with time because of assumed experience, this is an empirical question that has, so far, been put into doubt. The 'parental learning' analogy in Frankish *et al.* (2013, p. 78) suggests that, theoretically, we may expect that the lifetime achievement outcomes of children should be worse for firstborn children than for later-born children (because the latter will benefit from higher parenting experience on the part of the parents), but instead the evidence suggests that first-born children have superior lifetime achievement compared with later-born siblings – which shows that performance can actually decrease with experience, despite possible learning effects.

Rather than being driven by learning or superior opportunity recognition, a range of results suggest that starting a firm is much like entering a lottery (Storey 2011; Vivarelli 2011, p. 201): it is subject to high failure/death rates; has skewed returns with a tiny number of highly visible winners and most players losing; growth is largely random; is not subject to learning ('learning to roll a dice')

(Frankish *et al.* 2013; Metzger 2006); there is limited (if any) control over outcomes, which are largely unrelated to education levels; and overconfidence among players, who are happier partly because they are more optimistic, which for entrepreneurs links to over-confidence (Camerer and Lovallo 1999; Parker 2004). For lottery players it is arguably irrational to play given the average payoff is less than the ticket price, similarly most entrepreneurs earn less than they would as waged workers.

Endogeneity

Endogeneity describes situations where there is bias in the estimated parameters of empirical work because explanatory variables are correlated with the error term in a regression model. Endogeneity related to reverse causality, selection bias, omitted variables bias, simultaneity and measurement error affects many facets of entrepreneurship research, and generates biased and inconsistent estimates in empirical research (Caliendo 2013). These biases tend to be positive, and as Caliendo (2013, p. 20) notes, as research has addressed endogeneity, it has often led 'to different conclusions compared to conventional estimators'. Instrumental Variable (IV) approaches can be applied to all types of endogeneity, while endogeneity arising from unobserved, time invariant effects can also be addressed by using fixed effects models with panel data. Similarly, selection problems can also be addressed using Heckman sample selection methods, although all methods have their problems.

Endogeneity is often a problem with research on the role of SMEs and entrepreneurship in economic growth and economic recovery (for a survey see e.g. Audretsch 2007a). Beck, Demirguc-Kunt and Levine (2005) find that the link between SMEs and economic growth disappears when instrumental variables are used to control for endogeneity. Similarly, the observed link between the rate of business start-ups and economic recovery could be endogenous (Koellinger and Thurik 2012; Moscarini and Postel-Vinay 2012). This is because recessions are periods of high unemployment, and individuals prefer to be self-employed than unemployed. This specific role for entrepreneurship in the business cycle does not mean that self-employment drives economic growth, or that 'more is always better', or that policy-makers should attempt to increase self-employment.

Endogeneity also influences other aspects of entrepreneurship, such as the relationship between an entrepreneur's performance and self-reported characteristics such as ability. For example, entrepreneurs often consider themselves to be 'skilled' if they succeeded and 'unlucky' if they failed – which might suggest that skill drives success. However, as noted earlier, entrepreneurial performance appears to be primarily a game of chance, with random factors having a predominant role (Storey 2011; Denrell *et al.* 2015). As these examples illustrate, many of these biases are inter-related. In the next section we illustrate these interdependencies by showing how they influence research on job creation.

6.4 Changing perceptions of entrepreneurs in research

In this section we explore how more sophisticated methods and better data have been used to address some of the biases highlighted in the last section, producing more nuanced interpretations of the impact of entrepreneurs (and small firms) on the economy.

6.4.1 David Birch's legacy

As noted earlier, David Birch's work is of historical importance as it provided the paradigmatic study for future entrepreneurship research. His work on the role of SMEs and entrepreneurs in job creation addressed the growing demand for studies showing the positive impact of entrepreneurial (small firm) activity. His early work found that between 1969 and 1976, 66 per cent of new jobs came from firms with 20 or under employees, and 81.5 per cent from firms with 100 and under employees. His later (1987) study showed (p. 16) small firms created roughly 88 per cent of all net jobs (1981–1985). These findings were widely publicized, because they addressed a key policy issue: job creation, and in doing so helped to validate the new paradigm.

Birch's positive results were driven, in part, by some of the biases highlighted previously. If we start with data quality, his findings had a positive bias because he could not distinguish between jobs created in new establishments, and jobs created in new plants owned by larger, established firms (Brown, Hamilton and Medoff 1990; see Disney, Haskel and Heden 2003 for the UK, and Foster, Haltiwanger and Kirzan 2006 for the USA on productivity similarly largely being driven by new entry by established firms).

There were also data problems with the jobs themselves, as Birch was not comparing like with like. Employees in SMEs generally tend to have lower human capital (i.e., experience and education) (Troske 1999; Winter-Ebmer and Zweimuller 1999), and lower capital-skill complementarity (Troske 1999). In general, they are less productive, and tend to provide lower, more volatile remuneration with fewer benefits (such as pension schemes, or training opportunities), lower returns to experience and education (Oosterbeek and Van Praag 1995) and more work-related accidents (Storey 1994). As a consequence, comparing jobs between large and small firms needs to be done with care. More jobs in small firms at the expense of large firm employment may simply be a societal wealth transfer. This is important as Baldwin (1998) found that "while small producers have increased their employment share dramatically, they have barely changed their output share" (p. 349). When he controlled for job quality (proxied by remuneration) he found that the employment creation advantage of small producers vanishes as increases in small firm jobs are offset by their lower productivity.

The extrapolation of the results to the general population of firms is also subject to 'survivor bias', and problems with 'skewed' distributions and 'sampling'. When Birch's (1985–1987) data were re-examined it was found that 75 per cent of the employment gains came from 0.3 per cent of the 1985 cohort that already employed more than 100 workers when they were first launched (Harrison 1994). In Birch's later work (1994) he recognized the extensive skew in the distribution of job creation and highlighted that roughly 4 per cent of firms generate approximately 70 per cent of new jobs, with most new firms having a tiny impact on long-term job creation. This created an interest in what Birch called Gazelles, or high growth firms. However, recent work (Coad *et al.* 2014) suggests that rather than there being a special subset of high growth firms, growth is non-persistent beyond what one would expect from randomness. So while a small percentage of firms generate most jobs in a given period of time (Henrekson and Johansson 2010; Stangler 2010), it is a different small percentage in each time period (Daunfeldt and Halvarsson 2015; Holzl 2014; Parker, Storey and Witteloostuijn 2010).

Davis, Haltiwanger and Schuh (1996) highlighted that Birch's paradigmatic study was distorted by 'regression to the mean' (though later Davidsson, Lindmark and Olofsson (1998) found that even though the bias was significant, when it is controlled for, small firms still make a strong contribution to job creation). Recently, Haltiwanger *et al.* (2010) used high quality data and methods that control for regression bias to find that it is young rather than small firms that create more jobs, and the very smallest don't grow at all. However, after their founding year, cohorts of firms have a negative effect on job creation because failing firms' job losses exceed survivors' job creation. They note, new firms' job creation in their first year is positive by construction, because new firms have no jobs to lose from the previous year and so have to create jobs (it is like comparing profit in the first year to profit and loss in subsequent years). Hence, one needs to be very careful about jumping from 'new firms create jobs in their first year' to the conclusion that start-ups generate more jobs.

6.4.2 Conceptual slides linking entrepreneurship to job creation

Recent research also highlights the problems created by the common conceptual slides that conflate 'net' and 'gross' job creation. Policy reports commonly suggest SMEs create jobs, which is technically true, but very misleading if one doesn't take into account job losses. In 2005 14 out of every 10 new jobs in the US economy (i.e., 3.5m of the 2.5m) consisted of entrepreneurs (Haltiwanger *et al.* 2010). This is because most jobs created by small firms quickly disappear (Brown *et al.* 1990). It sounds very positive that Storey (1994, p. 165) found that small firms with less than 20 workers were responsible for 54 per cent of gross employment gains, until he points out that they also generated 54 per cent of gross employment losses. Taking job losses into account dramatically changes how the job creation potential of small firms is understood. Shane (2009, p. 144) suggests it takes 43 new firms to generate nine jobs in a decade.

The other obvious conceptual slide is the conflation of changes and levels. So while small firms create most jobs, more people are employed in large firms (levels), which is the key issue. A quarter of the US population work in firms with over 10,000 employees, while only 16.6 per cent work in firms with less than 20 employees (Bartelsman *et al.* 2005; Haltiwanger *et al.* 2010). Moreover, it is misleading to treat SMEs and large firms in isolation in academic research, as they interact in complex ways in the economy (Harrison 1994). The last conceptual slide relates to whether higher growth rates are a sign of strength or weakness. There is now strong evidence that smaller firms grow faster (see Coad 2009, Chapter 4 for a survey), even after controlling for regression to the mean and survivor bias (see Calvo 2006; Hart and Oulton 1996; and Konings 1995 on not following Gibrat's law). However, this needs to be carefully interpreted. If the firms are initially below the minimum efficient size for their industry they may simply be dashing for growth in order to survive (Beesley and Hamilton 1984; Lotti and Santarelli 2004; Santarelli and Vivarelli 2007, p. 467). This weak starting point is why we repeatedly observe a fringe of sub-optimal 'revolving door' firms at the bottom of the performance distribution, continuously entering and exiting the market (Santarelli and Vivarelli 2007, p. 457). As Santarelli and Vivarelli note, "if entry were driven mainly by technological opportunity, growing sales and profit expectation, one should observe a negative cross sectional correlation between entry and exit rates, in particular over short time intervals. On the contrary, exit and entry rates are positively and significantly correlated and market 'churning' emerges as a common feature of industrial dynamics across different sectors and different countries" (2007, p. 457; see also Geroski 1995).

One of the reasons for this is that being small and young entrepreneurial firms lack the scale and accumulated capabilities needed to achieve the productivity levels required to compete effectively (Cowling, Nightingale and Siepel 2011). The labour and total factor productivity levels of small firms are lower than for larger firms (Brouwer, De Kok and Fris 2005; Castany, Lopez-Bazo and Moreno 2005), so when they experience faster productivity growth this is typically a 'catch-up effect', i.e., a sign of weakness not strength. In the traditional economic model it was assumed that competition would cause these lower productivity firms to leave the market and be displaced by higher productivity firms, generating a convergence in productivity levels in the economy. The evidence is clear that this does not happen. Productivity levels are strongly persistent and characterized by a long tail of poor performance firms. As Hughes (2008, p. 134) notes of the 4.7 million enterprises in the UK economy in 2007, 3.5 million employed no one, and while these sole proprietors generated 17 per cent of employment, they only produced 8 per cent of turnover.

With productivity, as with employment, the key issue is total levels not individual rates. Disney *et al.*'s (2003, p. 682) study of UK productivity growth in manufacturing (1980–1992) finds the largest contribution to labour productivity comes from learning and organizational change in established multiplant/group firms (44.6 per cent), with a smaller contribution from net entry of single-plant firms (15.89 per cent) and only a marginal contribution from productivity growth within single-plant start-ups (0.58 per cent). The second largest contribution to labour productivity growth was from established multiplant firms opening and closing plants (33.2 per cent), which was roughly double the effect of entry by start-ups (15.9 per cent). Taking an alternative indicator of productivity (i.e., total factor productivity instead of labour productivity), established group firms contribute 19 times more to total factor productivity 'within effects' than single-plant firms (4.37 per cent v 0.23 per cent), 126 times more to 'between effects' (13.9 per cent v 0.11 per cent), 53 times more to 'cross effects' (23.2 per cent v 0.43 per cent) and three times more to 'net entry' effects (41 per cent v 12.7 per cent).

Nor does it seem that innovation will always help entrepreneurial firms (Freel 2000). Van Praag and Versloot (2007, p. 377) summarize the evidence as follows: "Entrepreneurs do not spend more on R&D than their counterparts. They produce fewer patents [see Almeida and Kogut 1997; and Sorensen and Stuart 2000], new products and technologies. Moreover, the percentage of radical innovations is lower among entrepreneurial firms." Astebro (2003) found that 93 per cent of 1091 Canadian innovator-entrepreneurs failed to get to market, and most of the ones that did lost money with average financial returns of −7 per cent. Acs and Audretsch (1990) found that small firms generate more innovations per employee than large firms. However, it is important to note their definition of small (less than 500 employees) included many firms that would be judged largely by European standards; and the metric of 'innovations per employee' suffers from aggregation problems (Kleinknecht and Verspagen 1989). It does seem to be the case that a small minority of small firms can exploit their nimbleness and achieve more with less in certain sectors (Rothwell and Zegweld 1982). Large (small) firms drive R&D and innovation in (less) concentrated sectors, with (high) low entry rates, higher (lower) appropriability and fewer (more) technological opportunities (Ortega-Argiles *et al.* 2009, p. 5). Innovative new firms tend to be atypical, and often innovate in combination with large firms (i.e., in the biotech sector).

So it would seem that rather than entrepreneurs having any special insight, the industrial dynamics we see are consistent with growth having a large random element, and the economy is subject to substantial churn at the bottom end of the performance distribution. Indeed, one way of understanding self-employment is to see it as a consequence of failures in normal labour markets, rather than anything uniquely special or positive beyond 'small businesses provid[ing] a safety net against unemployment by big businesses' as 'when recessions occur and large businesses lay-off employees, a significant number of the displaced employees either start small businesses or are absorbed into employment by the small business sector' (Robbins *et al.* 2000, p. 295).

6.5 Discussion and conclusion

As this chapter has highlighted, the dominant paradigm in entrepreneurship research, and the dominant view of entrepreneurs in society, is very positive. The paradigm has been stabilized by a combination of internal and external factors. The external factors relate to changes in the model of political economy, shifting political ideologies, and the emergence of lobbying groups inside and outside academia with economic and political interests in maintaining the paradigm. The internal factors relate to questionable models and frameworks that allow researchers to disregard empirical anomalies that may emerge despite the serious methodological problems that tend to promote an unrealistically positive view. As the previous sections have shown, recent research that addresses these biases reaches much more sober views of the value of entrepreneurship.

A small number of start-ups, that start small and grow fast, clearly have a very positive economic impact in terms of new job creation, innovations and economic benefits (Birch *et al.* 1993; Henreksson and Johansson 2010; Mitchell 1980; Storey 1980). However, as we noted previously (Nightingale and Coad 2014) "most of the time, for most of the firms, and for most of the performance metrics, the economic impact of entrepreneurial firms is poor". The relative performance of entrepreneurial firms seems to be negative for: "wage levels; renumeration levels; renumeration volatility; benefits; number/frequency of patents; new products and technologies; percent of radical innovations; importance of innovations; adoption of innovation; labour productivity; and total factor productivity" (Nightingale and Coad 2014; see also van Praag and Versloot 2007). Start-ups' higher growth of value added, labour productivity and total factor productivity, may simply reflect their lower initial performance levels. However, entrepreneurs do seem to be happier and have better job satisfaction, and new firms create jobs in their first year, but this is positive by construction and needs to be carefully interpreted.

This weak, rather than strong performance for entrepreneurial firms, helps explain a number of stylised facts about their industrial dynamics (Nightingale and Coad 2014, p. 131):

> Market entry is very common (particularly for smaller firms), survival rates are low, and there is a positive correlation between entry and exit (suggesting entry drives churn rather than growth); growth is difficult and takes a long time for entrants to compete with incumbents; growth is rarely persistent (Parker *et al.* 2010; Holzl 2014) and is approximately as persistent as a random coin toss (Coad *et al.* 2013); adjustment costs are very high (and penalise large scale entry and rapid post-entry growth); and survival improves for older and larger firms (Geroski 1995; Stam 2010).

This reassessment of the evidence led us to suggest that (Nightingale and Coad 2014, p. 131):

> ... the typically entrepreneur is not someone like Bill Gates. ... The typical entrepreneur is more like someone who starts from an underprivileged position (people with good jobs are less likely to start firms), uses their savings to start a low productivity firm (e.g. a fish-and-chip shop), in an established, highly competitive market (e.g. a town with two

fish-and-chip shops, but a market that can only support one). As a result, if they are still around in two years, which is unlikely, it is only because they have displaced a similar marginal firm. Such firms create a lot of jobs, but also destroy a lot of jobs, and while their owners are happier, they have a fairly marginal impact on the economy.

Given the skewed distribution of impacts, the analytic value of a single category of 'entrepreneurial firms' is questionable. We have suggested that analytic precision would be improved by dividing the performance continuum into (at least) two sub-categories to capture atypical high impact firms at one end, and the long tail of more typical poor performing firms at the other (ibid.). The high impact firms often have atypical management structures, links to professional investors and large firms, and can have external equity funding a thousand times higher than the investment in a typical start-up (i.e., ~£40m v ~£4,000). To make the distinction clear, we refer to these poorer performing firms as muppets – 'marginal undersized poor performance enterprises' – with the intention to capture a more realistic picture of the median small business and market entrant. They are marginal because they typically don't grow or innovate, exit quickly and are often missed by statistics and research studies. They are under-sized because they are below the minimum efficient size in their sectors which causes them to have low productivity and hence poor performance.

Thinking in this way, creates a new way of understanding public policy as it suggests growth is hard (not easy), market entry is easy (not hard) and poor performance typically reflects weaknesses within firms (not external market failures). Hence, limited investment in start-ups may suggest problems with firms' internal management and the external environment that allows them to grow, rather than with banks and capital markets. Unfunded firms exiting the market is often a sign of a well-functioning capitalist economy (the entrepreneurs experimented with an idea that unfortunately did not work out), and is not, in itself, an indication of the need for huge subsidies (Coad 2010).

From a policy perspective, subsidies that encourage more market entry may be dysfunctional (Santarelli and Vivarelli 2007; Vivarelli 2004) as entry is already high and arguably excessive (Shane 2009). Indeed, more quantity may mean lower quality (Greene, Mole and Storey 2004). Deadweight and policy selection effects may mean that policy interventions simply increase the number of poor performance start-ups (Branstetter *et al.* 2014), generating more churn, and constraining the growth of other firms (Santarelli and Vivarelli 2007). Rather than increasing the number of start-ups, policy might be more effective if it focused on (a) improving the quantity and quality of the tiny minority of high potential firms, (b) on improving the long tail of existing poor productivity enterprises (which might include policies to encourage them to exit the market) (see Smallbone, Baldock and Burgess 2002; Santarelli and Vivarelli 2007), and (c) making changes to the regulatory environment to encourage innovation driven growth and industrial disruption (e.g. by improving competition law and making intellectual property regimes innovation rather than incumbent friendly).

In summary, the evidence in the current research literature seems to be a long way from the dominant paradigm that takes entrepreneurship to be a universally 'good thing'. As Blanchflower (2004, p. 30) notes, he sees "no convincing evidence of any kind in the literature that either increasing the proportion of the workforce that is self-employed, or having a high level of self-employment produces any positive macroeconomic effects." (See also Henrekson and Sanandaji 2014; Lerner 2010; Sanandaji 2010; Shane 2009.) Despite this academic reassessment, the internal and external feature of the paradigm described earlier have been enough to keep it stable and it has not been displaced. For example, despite the major reassessment and arguable reversal of Birch's work, Birch's findings are still trumpeted by the US Small Business Association (Neumark, Wall and Zhang 2011, p. 16).

We have suggested that this stability comes from the inter-connected nature of the paradigm, which suggests individual studies that address biases and come up with more realistic conclusions are unlikely on their own to have much impact. Instead, an approach is needed which is also more systemic and links evidence to categories and frameworks, and builds out from academic studies to influence journals and funders, promotion boards, public opinion and public policy. Perhaps the key issue now is the development of improved panels of data to study both the nascent process and new venture process. These panels need to be large scale, representative and comprehensive. While panels of data dealing with earliest stages will have to rely on self-reported data, which has significant problems, data on new ventures can be much more robust. Such data, when combined with robust research designs and methods that can deal with endogeneity and generate causal analysis are likely to be much more robust and hence are more likely to be able to generate findings that will be influential. The sums of money involved in public policy, and the political power of the small firm lobby, means this more robust research is unlikely to easily influence the wider world. Retooling in academia, as in industry, is expensive and time-consuming, but the need for it, we suggest, is clear.

Notes

1 George Bush Proclamation 6131, Small Business Week, 1990. Small Business Administration, http://clinton4.nara.gov/WH/Accomplishments/Small_Business.html. We are grateful for John Haltiwanger's help in providing the US quotes.
2 Remarks by the President on small business initiatives, Metropolitan Archives, Landover, Maryland, 21 October 2009. www.barackobama.com, The American Small Business League Endorses Barack Obama, 26 February 2008.
3 See also "The Entrepreneurial Society" by Gavron *et al.* (1998) and Audretsch (2007b).
4 This was only the case in the USA and UK. In Continental Europe small firm organizations had been integrated into the political system as part of a post-War denazification process, which explains 'the variety of capitalisms', why the shift towards market-based governance was so strong in the USA and UK, and why it was and is resisted more in continental Europe, where the obsession with entrepreneurs has shallower roots (Dannreuther 2009).

5 Thus Moses creatively destroyed the religion of the pagans, but Judaism became increasingly routinized and law driven, allowing the charismatic prophet Jesus to creatively destroy it and create Christianity. This, in turn, became routinized in the teachings of the Catholic Church, creating the conditions for Martin Luther to launch the Reformation.
6 Note however that the SBA (Small Business Administration) was founded in 1953, well before small firms were as politically important as they are today.
7 In the context of entrepreneurship research, Saridakis, Marlow and Storey (2014) report some interesting differences between what self-report data tell you and what statistical analysis tells you. The authors observe that self-report data point to females being less influenced by economic factors in entering self-employment than males. However, the time-series econometric data show that, in some cases, economic variables can better explain female rather than male self-employment activity.
8 The EU definition of SMEs has an upper limit of 250 employees (http://ec.europa.eu/research/sme-techweb/pdf/sme-definition_en.pdf).

References

Acs, Z.J. and Audretsch, D.B. (1990) *Innovation and Small Firms*. Cambridge, MA: MIT Press.
Almeida, P. and Kogut, B. (1997) 'The exploration of technological diversity and geographic localization in innovation: Start-up firms in the semiconductor industry', *Small Business Economics*, 9(1), pp. 21–31.
Anyadike-Danes, M. and Hart, M. (2014) *All grown up? The fate after 15 years of the quarter of a million UK firms born in 1998*. September 14th, Mimeo.
Astebro, T. (2003) 'The return to independent invention: Evidence of unrealistic optimism, risk seeking or skewness loving?', *Economic Journal*, 113(484), pp. 226–239.
Audretsch, D.B. (1995) 'Innovation growth and survival', *International Journal of Industrial Organization*, 13(4), pp. 441–457.
Audretsch, D.B. (2007a) 'Entrepreneurship capital and economic growth', *Oxford Review of Economic Policy*, 23(1), pp. 63–78.
Audretsch, D.B. (2007b) *The Entrepreneurial Society*. Oxford: Oxford University Press.
Auerswald, P.E. and Branscomb, L.M. (2003) 'Valleys of death and Darwinian seas: Financing the invention to innovation transition in the United States', *Journal of Technology Transfer*, 28, pp. 227–239.
Baldwin, J.R. (1998) 'Were small producers the engines of growth in the Canadian manufacturing sector in the 1980s?', *Small Business Economics*, 10, pp. 349–364.
Bartelsman, E., Scarpetta, S. and Schivardi, F. (2005) 'Comparative analysis of firm demographics and survival: Evidence from micro-level sources in OECD countries', *Industrial and Corporate Change*, 14(3), pp. 365–391.
Baumol, W.J. (1996) 'Entrepreneurship: productive, unproductive, and destructive', *Journal of Business Venturing*, 11, pp. 3–22.
Baumol, W. (2010) *The Microtheory of the Innovative Entrepreneur*. Princeton, NJ and Oxford: Princeton University Press.
Beck, T., Demirguc-Kunt, A. and Levine, R. (2005) 'SMEs, growth and poverty: Cross-country evidence', *Journal of Economic Growth*, 10, pp. 199–229.
Beesley, M.E. and Hamilton, R.T. (1984) 'Small firms' seedbed role and the concept of turbulence', *Journal of Industrial Economics*, 33(2), pp. 217–231.
Bertrand, M. and Mullainathan, S. (2001) 'Do people mean what they say? Implications for subjective survey data', *American Economic Review*, 91, pp. 67–72.

Birch, D.L. (1979) *The Job Generation Process*. Cambridge, MA: MIT program on neighborhood and regional change, Massachusetts Institute of Technology.

Birch, D.L. (1987) *Job Creation in America: How Our Smallest Companies Put the Most People to Work*. New York: Free Press.

Birch, D., Haggerty, A., Parsons, W. and Rossel, C. (1993) *Entrepreneurial Hot Spots*. Boston, MA: Cognetics.

Blanchflower, D.G. and Oswald, A.J. (1998) 'What makes an entrepreneur?', *Journal of Labor Economics*, 16(1), pp. 26–60.

Blanchflower, D.G. (2004) 'Self-employment: More may not be better', *Swedish Economic Policy Review*, 11, pp. 15–73.

Bradley, D.E. and Roberts, J.A. (2004) 'Self-employment and job satisfaction: Investigating the role of self-efficacy, depression and seniority', *Journal of Small Business Management*, 42(1), pp. 37–58.

Branstetter, L., Lima, F., Taylor, L.J. and Venancio, A. (2014) 'Do entry regulations deter entrepreneurship and job creation? Evidence from recent reforms in Portugal', *Economic Journal*, 124(577), pp. 805–832.

Briggs, A. (1968) 'The world economy: Interdependence and planning'. In Mowat, C.L. (ed.) *The New Cambridge Modern History*. Cambridge: Cambridge University Press.

Brouwer, P., De Kok, J. and Fris, P. (2005) *Can firm age account for productivity differences?* EIM SCALES-paper N200421, Zoetermeer, the Netherlands.

Brown, C., Hamilton, J. and Medoff, J. (1990) *Employers, Large and Small*. Cambridge, MA: Harvard University Press.

Calvo, J.L. (2006) 'Testing Gibrat's law for small, young and innovating firms', *Small Business Economics*, 26(2), pp. 117–123

Caliendo, M. (2013) *Endogeneity in Entrepreneurship Research*. Mimeo, University of Potsdam, Germany.

Camerer, C. and Lovallo, D. (1999) 'Overconfidence and excess entry: An experimental approach', *American Economic Review*, 89, pp. 306–318.

Castany, L., Lopez-Bazo, E. and Moreno, R. (2005) *Differences in total factor productivity across firm size. A distributional analysis*. Working Paper, University of Barcelona, Spain.

Chandler, A.D. (1990) *Scale and Scope: The Dynamics of Industrial Capitalism*. Cambridge, MA: Harvard University Press.

Coad, A. (2009). *The Growth of Firms. A Survey of Theories and Empirical Evidence*. Cheltenham: Edward Elgar.

Coad, A. (2010) 'Neoclassical vs evolutionary theories of financial constraints: Critique and prospectus', *Structural Change and Economic Dynamics*, 21(3), pp. 206–218.

Coad, A. (2014) 'Death is not a success: Reflections on business exit', *International Small Business Journal*, 32(7), pp. 721–732.

Coad, A., Frankish, J.S., Nightingale, P. and Roberts, R.G. (2014) 'Business experience and start-up size: Buying more lottery tickets next time around?', *Small Business Economics*, 43(3), pp. 529–547.

Coad, A., Frankish, J., Roberts, R. and Storey, D. (2013) 'Growth paths and survival chances: An application of gambler's ruin theory', *Journal of Business Venturing*, 28, pp. 615–632.

Coad, A., Cowling, M., Nightingale, P., Pellegrino, G., Savona, M. and Siepel, J. (2014) *Innovative Firms and Growth*. BIS Research Reports 14–643, Crown Copyright.

Coad, A., Daunfeldt, S., Hölzl, W., Johansson, D. and Nightingale, P. (2014) 'High-growth firms: Introduction to the special section', *Industrial and Corporate Change*, 23(1), pp. 91–112.

Coad, A. and Tamvada, J.P. (2012) 'Firm growth and barriers to growth among small firms in India', *Small Business Economics*, 39, pp. 383–400.

Cohen, W.M. and Klepper, S. (1996) 'A reprise of size and R&D', *Economic Journal*, 106, pp. 925–951.

Comanor, W.S. (1967) 'Market structure, product differentiation, and industrial research', *Quarterly Journal of Economics*, 81, pp. 639–657.

Cowling, M., Nightingale, P. and Siepel, J. (2011) *The 30 year climb: The relative dynamics of entrepreneurial inefficiency.* Unpublished Working Paper.

Crawford, G.C., Aguinis, H., Lichtenstein, B., Davidsson, P. and McKelvey, B. (2015) 'Power law distributions in entrepreneurship: Implications for theory and research', *Journal of Business Venturing*, 30(5), pp. 696–713.

Dannreuther, C. (2009) 'The political economy of entrepreneurship', *International Small Business Journal*, 27, pp. 522–524.

Daunfeldt, S.-O. and Halvarsson, D. (2015) 'Are high-growth firms one-hit wonders? Evidence from Sweden', *Small Business Economics*, 44(2), pp. 361–383.

Davidsson, P. (2007) *Strategies for dealing with heterogeneity in entrepreneurship research.* Paper presented at the Academy of Management Conference, Philadelphia, August.

Davidsson, P., Lindmark, L. and Olofsson, C. (1998) 'The extent of overestimation of small firm job creation – an empirical examination of the regression bias', *Small Business Economics*, 11, pp. 87–100.

Davis, S.J., Haltiwanger, J.C. and Schuh, S. (1996) *Job Creation and Destruction.* Cambridge, MA: MIT Press.

de Meza, D. (2002) 'Overlending', *Economic Journal*, 112, pp. F17–F31.

Dennis, W.J. (2011) 'Entrepreneurship, small business and public policy levers', *Journal of Small Business Management*, 49(1), pp. 92–106.

Denrell, J., Fang, C. and Liu, C. (2015) 'Chance explanations in the management sciences', *Organization Science*, 26(3), pp. 923–940.

Denrell, J. and Liu, C. (2012) 'Top performers are not the most impressive when extreme performance indicates unreliability', *PNAS*, 109(24), pp. 9331–9336.

Disney, R., Haskel, J. and Heden, Y. (2003) 'Restructuring and productivity growth in UK manufacturing', *Economic Journal*, 113(489), pp. 666–694.

Eesley, C.E. and Roberts, E.B. (2010) Cutting your teeth: Learning from rare experiences, unpublished working paper. MIT, Boston, MA.

Eesley, C. and Roberts, E.B. (2012) *Cutting your Teeth: Learning from Entrepreneurial Experiences.* Academy of Management Proceedings, Meeting Abstract Supplements, pp. 1–6.

European Commission (2008) *Think Small First. A Small Business Act for Europe*, Brussels, 25. 6. 2008, COM Communication from the Commission to the Council, the European Parliament, the European Economic and Social Committee and the Committee of the Regions.

EVCA (2010) *Closing Gaps and Moving Up a Gear: The Next Stage of Venture Capital's Evolution in Europe.* Brussels: EVCA.

Foster, L., Haltiwanger, J. and Kirzan, C.J. (2006) 'Market selection, reallocation, and restructuring in the U.S. retail trade sector in the 1990s', *Review of Economics and Statistics*, 88(4), pp. 748–758.

Frankish, J., Roberts, R., Coad, A., Spears, T. and Storey, D. (2013) 'Do entrepreneurs really learn? Or do they just tell us that they do?', *Industrial and Corporate Change*, 22(1), pp. 73–106.

Frankish, J.S., Roberts, R.G., Coad, A. and Storey, D.J. (2014) 'Is entrepreneurship a route out of deprivation?', *Regional Studies*, 48(6), pp. 1090–1107.

Freel, M.S. (2000) 'Do small innovating firms outperform non-innovators?', *Small Business Economics*, 14, pp. 195–210.

Friedman, M. (1992) 'Do old fallacies ever die?', *Journal of Economic Literature*, 30(4), pp. 2129–2132.

Galbraith, J.K. (1967) *The New Industrial State*. London: Hamish Hamilton.

Gavron, R., Cowling, M., Holtham, G. and Westall, A. (1998) The entrepreneurial society. Institute of Public Policy Research, London.

Geroski, P.A. (1995) 'What do we know about entry?', *International Journal of Industrial Organization*, 13, pp. 421–440.

GEM (2009) *Global Entrepreneurship Monitor 2009 Annual Report*. London and Boston, MA: GEM.

Goldin, C. and Margo, R.A. (1992) 'The great compression: The wage structure in the United States at mid-century', *Quarterly Journal of Economics*, 107(1), pp. 1–34.

Goldthorpe, J.H. (1984) *Order and Conflict*. Oxford: Oxford University Press

Gottschalk, S., Greene, F.J., Hoewer, D. and Mueller, B. (2014) *If You Don't Succeed, Should You Try Again? The Role of Entrepreneurial Experience in Venture Survival*. ZEW – Centre for European Economic Research Discussion Paper No. 14–009.

Greene, F.J., Mole, K. and Storey, D.J. (2004) 'Does more mean worse? Three decades of enterprise policy in the Tees Valley', *Urban Studies*, 41, pp. 1207–1228.

Hall, R.E. and Woodward, S.E. (2010) 'The burden of the nondiversifiable risk of entrepreneurship', *American Economic Review*, 100, pp. 1163–1194.

Haltiwanger, J.C., Jarmin, R.S. and Miranda, J. (2010) *Who creates jobs: Small vs large vs young*. NBER Working Paper 16300, Washington, DC: NBER.

Hamilton, B.H. (2000) 'Does entrepreneurship pay? An empirical analysis of the returns to self-employment', *Journal of Political Economy*, 108(3), pp. 604–631.

Handler, W.C. and Kram, K.E. (1988) 'Succession in family firms: The problem of resistance', *Family Business Review*, 1(4), pp. 361–381.

Harrison, B. (1994) 'The small firm myth', *California Management Review*, 36(3), pp. 146–158.

Hart, P.E. and Oulton, N. (1996) 'Growth and size of firms', *Economic Journal*, 106(438), pp. 1242–1252.

Hayek, F.A. (1944) *The Road to Serfdom*. In Caldwell, B. (ed.) Chicago, IL: Chicago University Press.

Hayek, F.A. (1945) 'The use of knowledge in society', *American Economic Review*, 35(4), pp. 519–530.

Hayek, F.A. (1960) *The Constitution of Liberty*. Chicago, IL: Chicago University Press.

Henrekson, M. (2005) 'Entrepreneurship: A weak link in the welfare state?', *Industrial and Corporate Change*, 14(3), pp. 437–467.

Henrekson, M. and Johansson, D. (2010) 'Gazelles as job creators: A survey and interpretation of the evidence', *Small Business Economics*, 35(2), pp. 227–244.

Henrekson, M. and Sanandaji, T. (2014) 'Small business activity does not measure entrepreneurship', *Proceedings of the National Academy of Sciences*, 111(5), pp. 1760–1765.

Hogan, M.J. (1989) *The Marshall Plan: America, Britain and the Reconstruction of Western Europe, 1947–1952*. Cambridge, MA: Cambridge University Press.

Holtz-Eakin, D. (2000) 'Public policy toward entrepreneurship', *Small Business Economics*, 15(4), pp. 283–291.

Holzl, W. (2014) 'Persistence, survival, and growth: A closer look at 20 years of fast-growing firms in Austria', *Industrial and Corporate Change*, 23(1), pp. 199–231.

Hudson, M.C. (1996) 'To play the hegemon: Fifty years of US policy toward the Middle East', *Middle East Journal*, 50(3), pp. 329–343.

Hughes, A. (2008) 'Entrepreneurship and innovation policy: Retrospect and prospect', *Political Quarterly*, 79, pp. 133–152.

Hvide, H.K. (2009) 'The quality of entrepreneurs', *Economic Journal*, 119, pp. 1010–1035.

Ioannidis, J.P.A. (2005) 'Why most published research findings are false', *PLOS Medicine*. DOI: 10.1371/journal.pmed.0020124.

Kassicieh, S.K., Kirchhoff, B.A., Walsh, S.T. and McWhorter, P.J. (2002) 'The role of small firms in the transfer of disruptive technologies', *Technovation*, 22(11), pp. 667–674.

Konings, J. (1995) 'Gross job flows and the evolution of size in U.K. establishments', *Small Business Economics*, 7(3), pp. 213–220.

Kirchhoff, B.A. (1994) *Entrepreneurship and Dynamic Capitalism: The Economics of Business Firm Formation and Growth*. Westport, CT: Praeger Publishers.

Kirchhoff, B.A. and Phillips, B.D. (1988) 'The effect of firm formation and growth on job creation in the United States', *Journal of Business Venturing*, 3(4), pp. 261–272.

Kirzner, I. (1997) 'Entrepreneurial discovery and the competitive market process: An Austrian approach', *Journal of Economic Literature*, 35, pp. 60–85.

Kleinknecht, A. and Verspagen, B. (1989) 'R&D and market structure: The impact of measurement and aggregation problems', *Small Business Economics*, 1, pp. 297–301.

Koellinger, P.D. and Thurik, R.A. (2012) 'Entrepreneurship and the business cycle', *Review of Economics and Statistics*, 94(4), pp. 1143–1156.

Landström, H., Harirchi, G. and Åström, F. (2011) 'Entrepreneurship: Exploring the knowledge base', *Research Policy*, 41(7), pp. 1154–1181.

Lerner, J. (2010) 'The future of public efforts to boost entrepreneurship and venture capital', *Small Business Economics*, 35, pp. 255–264.

Levine, R. and Rubinstein, Y. (2013) *Smart and illicit: Who becomes an entrepreneur and does it pay?* CEP Discussion Paper No 1237.

Lotti, F. and Santarelli, E. (2004) 'Industry dynamics and the distribution of firm sizes: A nonparametric approach', *Southern Economic Journal*, 70(3), pp. 443–466.

Love, J.H. and Ashcroft, B. (1999) 'Market versus corporate structure in plant-level innovation performance', *Small Business Economics*, 13(2), pp. 97–109.

Lundström, A., Vikström, P., Fink, M., Meuleman, M., Glodek, P., Storey, D.J. and Kroksgard, A. (2014) 'Measuring the costs and coverage of SME and entrepreneurship policy: A pioneering study', *Entrepreneurship Theory and Practice*, 38(4), pp. 941–957.

Macpherson, A. and Holt, R. (2007) 'Knowledge, learning and small firm growth: A systematic review of the evidence', *Research Policy*, 36, pp. 172–192.

Mansfield, E. (1962) 'Entry, Gibrat's Law, innovation and the growth of firms', *American Economic Review*, 52, pp. 1023–1051.

Mason, C. and Harrison, R. (1986) 'The regional impact of public policy towards small firms in the UK'. In Keeble, D. and Wever, E. (eds) *New Firms and Regional Development in Europe*. London: Routledge.

de Meza, D. (2002) 'Overlending?', *Economic Journal*, 112, pp. F17–F31.

Metzger, G. (2006) *Once bitten twice shy? The performance of entrepreneurial re-starts*. Discussion Paper 6–83, ZEW, Mannheim.

Mitchell, J.A. (1980) *Small Firms: A Critique*. London: Three Banks Review.

Moscarini, G. and Postel-Vinay, F. (2012) 'The contribution of large and small employers to job creation in times of high and low unemployment', *American Economic Review*, 102(6), pp. 2509–2539.

Moskowitz, T.J. and Vissing-Jorgensen, A. (2002) 'The returns to entrepreneurial investment: A private equity premium puzzle?', *American Economic Review*, 92(4), pp. 745–778.

Mwaura, S. and Carter, S. (2015) *Does entrepreneurship make you wealthy? Insights from the UK wealth and assets survey.* ERC Research Paper No. 25.

Neumark, D., Wall, B. and Zhang, J. (2011) 'Do small businesses create more jobs? New evidence for the United States from the National Establishment Time Series', *Review of Economics and Statistics*, 93(1), pp. 16–29.

Nightingale, P. (2015) 'Schumpeter's theological roots? Harnack and the origins of creative destruction', *Journal of Evolutionary Economics*, 25, pp. 69–75.

Nightingale, P. and Coad, A. (2014) 'Muppets and gazelles: Ideological and methodological biases in entrepreneurship research', *Industrial and Corporate Change*, 23(1), pp. 113–143.

Obama, B. (2009) *Remarks by the President on Small Business Initiatives.* Metropolitan Archives, Landover, MD.

Oosterbeek, H. and Van Praag, M. (1995) 'Firm-size wage differentials in the Netherlands', *Small Business Economics*, 7(3), pp. 173–182.

Ortega-Argiles, R., Vivarelli, M. and Voigt, P. (2009) 'R&D in SMEs: A paradox?', *Small Business Economics*, 33, pp. 3–11.

Parker, S.C. (2004) *The Economics of Self-employment and Entrepreneurship.* Cambridge: Cambridge University Press.

Parker, S.C., Storey, D.J. and van Witteloostuijn, A. (2010) 'What happens to gazelles? The importance of dynamic management strategy', *Small Business Economics*, 35, pp. 203–226.

Parker, S.C. and Belghitar, Y. (2006) 'What happens to nascent entrepreneurs? An econometric analysis of the PSED', *Small Business Economics*, 27(1), pp. 81–101.

Robbins, D.K., Pantuosco, L.J., Parker, D.F. and Fuller, B.K. (2000) 'An empirical assessment of the contribution of small business employment to US state economic performance', *Small Business Economics*, 15, pp. 293–302.

Rothwell, R. and Zegweld, W. (1982) *Innovation and the Small and Medium Sized Firm.* London: Pinter Publishers.

Reynolds, P., Bosma, N., Autio, E., De Bono, H., Servais, H. and Lopez-Garcia, P. (2005) 'Global entrepreneurship monitor: Data collection design and implementation 1998–2003', *Small Business Economics*, 24, pp. 205–231.

Reynolds, P.D. and Curtin, R.T. (2008) 'Business creation in the United States: Panel study of entrepreneurial dynamics II initial assessment', *Foundations and Trends in Entrepreneurship*, 4(3), pp. 155–307.

Rosenberg, N. (1976) *Perspectives on Technology.* Cambridge: Cambridge University Press.

Ruggie, J. (1982) 'International regimes, transactions, and change: Embedded liberalism in the postwar economic order', *International Organisation*, 36(2), pp. 379–415.

Sanandaji, T. (2010) *Self-employment Does Not Measure Entrepreneurship.* Chicago, IL: University of Chicago.

Santarelli, E. and Vivarelli, M. (2002) 'Is subsidizing entry an optimal policy?', *Industrial and Corporate Change*, 11(1), pp. 39–52.

Santarelli, E. and Vivarelli, M. (2007) 'Entrepreneurship and the process of firms' entry, survival and growth', *Industrial and Corporate Change*, 16(3), pp. 455–488.

Saridakis, G., Marlow, S. and Storey, D.J. (2014) 'Do different factors explain male and female self-employment rates?', *Journal of Business Venturing*, 29(3), pp. 345–362.

Schumpeter, J.A. (1942) *Capitalism, Socialism and Democracy.* New York: George Allen and Unwin.

Shane, S. (2000) 'Prior knowledge and the discovery of entrepreneurial opportunities', *Organization Science*, 11(4), pp. 448–469.

Shane, S. and Venkataraman, S. (2000) 'The promise of entrepreneurship as a field of research', *Academy of Management Review*, 25(1), pp. 217–226.

Shane, S. (2008) *The Illusions of Entrepreneurship: The Costly Myths that Entrepreneurs, Investors and Policy Makers Live By*. New Haven, CT: Yale University Press.

Shane, S. (2009) 'Why encouraging more people to become entrepreneurs is bad public policy', *Small Business Economics*, 33(2), pp. 141–149.

Simmons, J.P., Nelson, L.D. and Simonsohn, U. (2011) 'False-positive psychology: Undisclosed flexibility in data collection and analysis allows presenting anything as significant', *Psychological Science*, 22(11), pp. 1359–1366.

Smallbone, D., Baldock, R. and Burgess, S. (2002) 'Targeted support for high-growth start-ups: Some policy issues', *Environment and Planning C*, 20(2), pp. 195–220.

Sorensen, J.B. and Stuart, T.E. (2000) 'Aging, obsolescence, and organizational innovation', *Administrative Science Quarterly*, 45(1), pp. 81–112.

Stam, E. (2010) 'Growth beyond Gibrat: Firm growth processes and strategies', *Small Business Economics*, 35(2), pp. 1–7.

Stam, E., Thurik, R. and van der Zwan, P. (2010) 'Entrepreneurial exit in real and imagined markets', *Industrial and Corporate Change*, 19(4), pp. 1109–1139.

Stangler, D. (2010) *High-growth firms and the future of the American economy*. Available at SSRN 1568246.

Storey, D.J. (1980) *Job Generation and Small Firm Policy in Britain*. Centre for Environmental Studies, Policy Series 11, London.

Storey, D.J. (1989) 'Firm performance and size: Explanations from the small firm sector', *Small Business Economics*, 1(3), pp. 175–180.

Storey, D.J. (1998) *The Ten Percenters*. Fourth Report: Fast Growing SMEs in Great Britain, London: Deloitte & Touche Tohmatsu.

Storey, D.J. (1994) *Understanding the Small Business Sector*. London: Routledge.

Storey, D.J. (2006) 'Evaluating SME policies and programmes: Technical and political dimensions'. In Basu, A., Casson, M., Wadeson, N. and Yeung, B. (eds) *The Oxford Handbook of Entrepreneurship*. Oxford: Oxford University Press, pp. 248–268.

Storey, D.J. (2011) 'Optimism and chance: The elephants in the entrepreneurship room', *International Small Business Journal*, 29(4), pp. 303–321.

Troske, T.R. (1999) 'Evidence on the employer size-wage premium from worker-establishment matched data', *Review of Economics and Statistics*, 81(1), pp. 15–26.

Turro, N.J. (1986) 'Geometric and topological thinking in organic chemistry', *Angew. Chem. International*, 25(10), pp. 882–901.

USA (2010) *Presidential Proclamation–National Entrepreneurship Week*, 15th November.

Van Horn, R. and Mirowski, P. (2009) 'The rise of the Chicago School of Economics and the birth of neoliberalism'. In Mirowski, P. and Plehwe, D. (eds) *The Road from Mont Pèlerin: The Making of the Neoliberal Thought Collective*. Boston, MA: Harvard University Press, pp. 149–163.

van Praag, C.M. and Versloot, P.H. (2007) 'What is the value of entrepreneurship? A review of recent research', *Small Business Economics*, 29, pp. 351–382.

Vivarelli, M. (2004) 'Are all the potential entrepreneurs so good?', *Small Business Economics*, 23, pp. 41–49.

Vivarelli, M. (2011) 'Baumol, W.J.: The microtheory of innovative entrepreneurship', *Journal of Economics*, 103, pp. 199–202.

Winter-Ebmer, R. and Zweimuller, J. (1999) 'Firm-size wage differentials in Switzerland: Evidence from job-changers', *American Economic Review Papers and Proceedings*, 89(2), pp. 89–93.

Part II

Dissensus challenges

7 A critical review of critical perspectives in entrepreneurship research

Denise Fletcher and Paul Seldon

7.1 Introduction

Reflecting on 'what entrepreneurship is and how entrepreneurship might be studied', Gartner (2004, p. 199) used the notion of 'critical mess' to invoke an image of a 'pile of scholarship' and mass of non-scholarly material on entrepreneurship that has been generated as 'data' for developing stories, theories, concepts, policies and insights for understanding the phenomena of entrepreneurship. One of Gartner's (2004) main concerns in this essay was to use the phrase 'critical mess' to argue that academics might practise different forms of entrepreneurship scholarship by 'enlarging what we currently consider to be the relevant kinds of evidence' (p. 202) and to use these different forms of evidence as a basis for theory development.

Ten years on, the story of entrepreneurship research is one that is characterized by fast growth, expansion and diversification, as the social, economic or cultural significance of entrepreneurship has been recognized and advanced through the application of multiple disciplinary approaches, definitions, concepts, units of analysis, dynamic principles and modes of explanation. Moreover, an extensive evidence base has been created using traditional empirical data sources (surveys and large data sets), immersive methodologies (such as ethnography, participant observation), practice-oriented approaches (such as action research or enactive research) as well as heuristic (i.e., auto-ethnography; autobiography) and discourse-based methods of inquiry (i.e., narrative analysis or story-telling).

In this period, we have also seen a growing interest in broadening out the functional economic role of the entrepreneur (Schumpeter 1912/1961, etc.) to take account of entrepreneurship as a social, historical and cultural phenomenon (Cole 1959; Fletcher 2006) and a general societal force that permeates everyday life (Steyaert and Katz 2004). Furthermore, we have been made aware of how it is possible to claim a 'double sociality' for entrepreneurial endeavours, in the sense that they produce social change and transformation at the same time as having a social nature (Steyaert and Hjorth 2006, p. 1). This has the effect not only of disclosing and contextualizing entrepreneurial endeavour as a part of society, but also of emphasizing entrepreneurship as an action-centred 'shaping process' (Ardichvili, Cardozo and Ray 2003; Dimov 2007).

We can also observe a closer examination of the relation between human action (or agency) and social environment (or structure), whether in terms of the nexus of individual entrepreneur and antecedent market opportunity (i.e., the 'individual-opportunity nexus', Shane and Venkataraman 2000) or the 'action-interaction nexus' between individual and social context (Venkataraman *et al.* 2012). These analytical categories are based on a subject-object dichotomy or inner-outer distinction, which cue explanatory elements that are 'internal' to the individual (such as cognitive structures or decision-making) and 'external' to the individual (such as social interactions, firm processes and market opportunities) (Venkataraman *et al.* 2012). Structuration theory has also been used to argue that the relationship between entrepreneurial action and context is a 'reflexive' process in which the entrepreneur reflects on and responds to the consequences of their own actions (Sarason, Dean and Dillard 2006). In addition, there has been consideration of the causal significance of structural contexts, such as market systems, social networks and firm structures (Aldrich and Kenworthy 1999; Chiles *et al.* 2010; McKelvey 2004; Mole and Mole 2010), as well as material contexts, such as technologies and resources (Baker and Nelson 2005; Garud and Karnøe 2003), that have properties that are mutually constituted with action, but which endure separately and have their own dynamic with entrepreneurial action.

We can also read about entrepreneurship as a 'phenomenon' or 'process' associated with the creation of new ventures, organizations, opportunities, commodities and markets, rather than as a type of 'setting', such as small business or owner-managed business (McMullen and Dimov 2013; Shane and Venkataraman 2000; Wiklund *et al.* 2011). Seeing entrepreneurship as a phenomenon, event or process recognizes that entrepreneurship is context-specific, time-specific and multi-dimensional in time and space. This fuels even more the diversification of the field into new spaces of inquiry (Landstöm 2005) that include not only a multiplicity of contexts, from universities (Shane 2003) to urban spaces (Dobers 2003), households (Mason 2011) and rural settings Fletcher and Watson (2006), but also time-relative analyses that examine how entrepreneurial events emerge/unfold over time through interrelationships between actions, contexts and outcomes (Aldrich 2001; Dimov 2011; McMullen and Dimov 2013; Mohr 1982; Sarasvathy 2008, Shane 2003).

As even this limited overview of the shifts and developments in entrepreneurship scholarship demonstrates, the more inclusive evidence base and 'critical mass/mess' that Gartner (2004) called for, is being realized. A pertinent question for entrepreneurship scholarship ten years on, therefore, relates to the 'critical' dimension of the phrase 'critical mess'. Naturally, most, if not all, scientific research incorporates some levels of critical thinking defined as: 'the intellectually disciplined process of actively and skilfully conceptualizing, applying, analysing, synthesizing, and/or evaluating information gathered from, or generated by, observation, experience, reflection, reasoning, or communication, as a guide to belief and action'.[1] In practising critical thinking, inquirers critique extant research positions, authenticate the evidence bases used and 'strive to avoid speculative arguments and erroneous conclusions' (Alvesson and Ashcraft 2009). At the same time, however, the term 'critical' is often associated with particular intellectual traditions such as Postmodern Thinking, Critical Theory and Post-Structuralist theories, as well as streams of research such as Critical Management Studies (CMS).

In entrepreneurship scholarship, there has been widespread usage of the term 'critical' to signify a search for alternative ways of knowing and understanding what constitutes entrepreneurial activity and how these activities/practices may be studied. It is not immediately apparent, however, the extent to which this interest in criticality is symptomatic of the post-positivist expansion of entrepreneurship research and the inclusive critical thinking quest for a 'critical mess' of evidence and multiple perspectives (Gartner 2004; Jennings, Perren and Carter 2005). Or, whether, and perhaps simultaneously, this interest is indicative of 'critique inspired' analyses in the sense conceptualised by Alvesson and Deetz (2000, p. 8) where critique re-examines social institutions, ideologies, and discourses in terms of representation and domination.

In this chapter we evaluate the collection of studies using the terms 'critical' and 'entrepreneurship' in order to make transparent the kinds of questions, issues and concerns being addressed through critical inquiry. Our main interest is to offer a reflection on the process of critical inquiry in entrepreneurship research and to draw attention to how different inquirers engage with criticality in order to stimulate alternative ways of attending to entrepreneurship. In the first section of what is to follow, we outline the core assumptions, meanings, tactics and principles that are central to critical research. Next, we undertake a review of the entrepreneurship literature to identify the research problems being addressed through the use of critical research tactics and we distinguish some defining characteristics of the approaches, tactics and methods explored. In the discussion section, based on this analysis, we consider the extent to which critical work/critique is becoming more visible within entrepreneurship inquiry and gaining momentum (Hjorth and Steyaert 2010, p. 192). We conclude with some suggestions for sharpening critical engagement and reflexivity in entrepreneurship research.

7.2 What is critical research?

In the broadest sense, critical tactics are widely employed in entrepreneurship research to substantiate the systematic, disciplined and rigorous approach to scientific research efforts. Referring to Glaser (1941, p. 5), 'critical thinking calls for a persistent effort to examine any belief or supposed form of knowledge in the light of the evidence that supports it and the further conclusions to which it tends'. When undertaking scientific research, therefore, three key principles are important: (1) 'an attitude of being disposed to consider in a thoughtful way the problems and subjects that come within the range of one's experience;

(2) knowledge of the methods of logical enquiry and reasoning; and (3) [demonstrating] some skill in applying those methods' (Glaser 1941, p. 5). Practising these principles, therefore, is the starting point for engaging critically with our research material.

From this perspective, critical research tactics can be applied either to uncover the differentiating and critical factors that explain variance in entrepreneurial performances or to redirect research attention onto contexts and issues that have been under-examined. Here, traditional 'critical thinking' methods, as mentioned above, would be applied to examine taken for granted or supposed forms of knowledge to challenge, expose or illuminate 'hidden' or lesser known explanations.

Additionally, critical tactics can be used to transform arguments into ideological critiques that challenge received wisdom and knowledge about society, the economy and the various organizational, institutional and managerial practices that constitute the socio-economic world. Here, criticism and critical thinking principles are extended into 'critique inspired' analyses which go beyond rational evaluation to involve: (1) 'identifying and challenging assumptions behind ordinary ways of perceiving, conceiving and acting; (2) recognizing the influence of history, culture and social positioning on beliefs and actions; (3) imagining and exploring/ explores extraordinary alternatives, ones that may disrupt routines and established orders; (4) being appropriately skeptical about any knowledge or solution that claims to be the only truth or alternative' (Alvesson and Deetz 2000, p. 8, referring to Brookfield 1987).

With these kinds of interests in mind, inquirers draw, whether directly or indirectly, on a range of intellectual traditions. These include, but are not limited to, Critical Theory, Postmodernism and Poststructuralist Ideas – each of which contributes a set of intellectual resources with which to undertake critical research. A short summary of each of these intellectual streams is now outlined to distinguish critique from a critical thinking approach.

Critical theory (CT) is not a theory that can be easily recognized for signifying a unified position or standpoint. It is not characterized by a set of unified principles. Nor do the ideas of CT cohere into a clear blueprint for research action. Instead, as aptly asserted by Willmott (2008), CT is a 'refreshing reservoir of ideas ... drawn from sociology, philosophy, economics, psychology' (p. 66). CT – or, more accurately, the body of work associated with critical theorists – was inspired by an intellectual movement known as the Frankfurt School (involving people such as Horkheimer, Adorno, Marcuse, Fromm, Habermas and many others).[2] In so far as a definition of CT is possible, therefore, it may be defined as a self-conscious social critique directed at social change and emancipation through enlightenment and which does not cling dogmatically to its own doctrinal assumptions (Horkheimer 1972 [1937]). These theorists had in common concerns with how economic and social systems produced oppression, exploitation, repression, unfairness and asymmetrical power relations through hierarchical positions and asymmetry involving class, gender or ethnicity (Alvesson and Deetz 2000).

Another set of core interests of theorists working within a critical tradition stem from a need to differentiate from modernist ideas, assumptions and ways of thinking. By 'modernist', in a management and organisation context, Alvesson and Deetz (2000):

> ... draw attention to the instrumentalisation of people and nature through the use of scientific-technical knowledge (modelled after positivism and other rational ways of developing safe, robust knowledge) to accomplish predictable results, measured by productivity, and technical problem solving leading to the 'good' of economic and social life, primarily defined by accumulation of wealth by production investors and consumption by consumers.
>
> (p. 13)

As a reaction to the perceived limitations of modernism, with its underpinnings in a rational and reductionist logic of representation, an alternative set of reactionary 'post-modern' and post-structuralist ideas began to evolve.[3] This broad movement of critical ideas eschews research processes and theories that attempt to 'order, dissect and represent fluid living experiences in order to make them more amenable to instrumental control and manipulation' (Chia 1995, 2008, p. 162). They also reject the overconfidence in positivist science's acceptance of the robustness of empirical data and a preoccupation with confirmation of empirical regularities and data (Smircich and Calas 1987). Instead, research attention centres on 'giving voice and legitimacy to those tacit and oftentimes unpresentable forms of knowledge that modern epistemology inevitably depends upon yet, conveniently overlooks or glosses over' (Chia 2008, p. 162). This means that critical research projects often challenge 'the human subject as a coherent entity with natural rights and potential autonomy' and they are concerned with 'non-enlightened voices [and] the human possibilities that are suppressed' (Alvesson and Deetz 2000, p. 15). In addition, with the post-structuralist emphasis on deconstruction, language, discourse, meaning and symbols, epistemological matters and issues of method are brought to the centre of analysis (Alvesson and Skoldberg 2000, p. 150). Relating to Derrida, Nietzsche, Foucault, Lacan and Deleuze, for example, the poststructuralist signals new ways of looking at the language, theory and politics of our research. More specifically, poststructuralists 'demote the subject from its central position – decentre it, that is – to shift the emphasis as regards what constructs perceptions, thoughts, emotions and actions to the linguistic and discursive context, which socially creates forms and expressions of subjectivity limited in time and space' (Alvesson and Sköldberg 2000, p. 164).

It is not the intention in this chapter to give a detailed discussion of the various critical traditions. What is important is to signal that different intellectual ideas and resources are drawn upon to shape the landscape of critical inquiry. For example, in organizational research various methodological and theoretical approaches can be found such as critical ethnography (Thomas

1993), critical realism (Reed 2009), critical methodology (Alvesson and Ashcraft 2009), critical contexts of research (Buchanan and Bryman 2007), feminist analyses (Calas and Smircich 2009) and the 'doing' of critical management research (Alvesson and Deetz 2000; Alvesson and Sköldberg 2000). In addition, many critical ideas and orientations are employed in the CMS stream of research with its interests in critical questioning and denaturalisation of dominant ideologies and institutions, social reform and 'the recognition that "real" conditions constrain choice and action...' (Alvesson and Aschcraft 2009, p. 63). As a result of these multifarious interests, critical research can be found in many streams of thought such as: critical realism, pragmatism, interpretivism, phenomenology, feminism, hermeneutics, symbolic interactionism, ethnomethodology, social constructionism and post-structuralism – and each 'would likely portray key features [of critical management research] quite differently' (Alvesson and Aschraft 2009, p. 63).

7.3   First stirrings of critical research in entrepreneurship

Turning now to entrepreneurship inquiry, the first stirrings of 'the cool if not cold wind of critique' (Weiskopf and Steyaert 2009, p. 7) can be noted in the early seminal commentaries by Nodoushani and Nodoushani (1999), Ogbor (2000) and Armstrong (2005). Nodoushani and Nodoushani's (1999) work, for example, was one of the first to deconstruct the ideological roots of entrepreneurship with its purported avant-garde and 'anti-management lyricism' (p. 48). Ogbor (2000) was also concerned with 'deconstruction in order to denaturalize or call into question the knowledge claims of the entrepreneurial texts/discourses, and to reveal how they present as inherently neutral the ways things are always done' (p. 607). Adding to these, Armstrong's critique (2001) also revealed the dysfunctional and ideologically controlling effects of the concept of entrepreneurship.

In these works, for the first time in entrepreneurship research, the functionalist, essentialist, entitative and representational assumptions behind traditional ways of perceiving, conceiving and knowing entrepreneurship were challenged. In particular, entrepreneurship inquirers were invited to explore extraordinary alternatives in order to disrupt routines and established orders that eulogized the entrepreneur as a heroic figure and associated discourses. We might also say that a 'dissensus discourse' (Alvesson and Deetz 2000, pp. 23–24) began to emerge that disturbed the traditional foundations of entrepreneurship and where, instead of 'being celebrated as the epitome of the autonomous [freely acting] individual, the entrepreneur [became] a target of critique' (Weiskopf and Steyaert 2009, p. 8). By 'dissensus discourse', Alvesson and Deetz (2000) are invoking an analytic distinction upon which to contrast different research perspectives based on the extent to which certain research practices either 'work within' (consensus discourse) or 'disrupt' (dissensus discourse) 'a dominant set of structurings of knowledge, social relations, and identities' (p. 24). Although one could readily think about consensus and dissensus in terms of agreement and disagreement, it is their intention to see the two discourses as 'the presentation of unity or of difference; and the continuation or disruption of any prevailing discourse' (p. 25).

In the wake of the three generative critiques of Nodoushani and Nodoushani (1999), Ogbor (2000) and Armstrong (2005), three issues are worth addressing. First, it is not clear from the critical stream of research that has since emerged in entrepreneurship, if there are common or collective interests and preoccupations that are shaping critical entrepreneurship studies. Second, is the adoption of critical entrepreneurship research stances symptomatic of a consensus discourse and the ongoing analytical quest for multiplicity and new perspectives, concepts or contexts of entrepreneurship that affirm and mirror entrepreneurial phenomena that exist 'out there'? Or, is critical entrepreneurship research (perhaps simultaneously) indicative of a dissensus discourse and the disruption of the philosophical and ideological bases of entrepreneurship inquiry as implied in the three above-mentioned critique-inspired articles? Third, there are few studies that offer a reflection on the process of critical inquiry in entrepreneurship research.[4]

In what is to follow, therefore, we draw attention to how different inquirers in entrepreneurship research engage with criticality in order to stimulate alternative ways of attending to entrepreneurship. To do this, we draw up a list of articles that capture the different ways in which critical knowledge production is developing in entrepreneurship research. To derive this list, a general search in Google Scholar was undertaken using the terms (1) 'critical' and 'entrepreneurship/entrepreneurial'; and (2) 'critique' and 'entrepreneurship/entrepreneurial'. The rationale for using these specific search terms was not only to provide some boundaries for the search but also because it is presumed that in using the word 'critical' or 'critique' in the title, authors are denoting something distinctive about their intended approach or form of analysis. However, we are aware that many studies are critical in orientation without necessarily using the term 'critical' or 'critique'. These issues are discussed further below.

7.4 A review of critical perspectives in entrepreneurship research

The Google Scholar search identified 143 entries that use the terms critical or critique and entrepreneurship/entrepreneurial in the title of books, book chapters, journal articles and conference papers.[5] At first glance, therefore, it appears that critical tactics are fairly well employed in entrepreneurship research, but, as noted previously, this might be expected in scientific inquiry in the sense that critical thinking and the practice of systematic, disciplined and rigorous procedures are the hallmarks of scholarly/analytical work. For purposes of closer analysis and also manageability, a final list was derived from the complete list by selecting only journal articles and books published between 2000 and 2014 (and by leaving out thesis entries, book chapters and articles not related to the field of business, management and entrepreneurship). It should also be noted that, in this search, we included all journals regardless of whether or not they were SSCI-ranked. This yielded 55 articles for closer analysis and enabled us to identify a range of studies and their preoccupations regardless of the ranking of the journal.

The entries have been listed according to the range of questions, issues and concerns being addressed by the authors with a view to evaluating whether critical tactics are employed as a means of signifying something distinctive about the intended approach or form of analysis. It should be noted that the search revealed some studies that have not been included in the final table. Two studies were found that specifically addressed critical thinking in entrepreneurship education (Colakoglu and Sledge 2013; Drummond 2010). Their focus was how experiential and dialectic learning processes can enhance critical engagement and for this reason they are critical in the general sense outlined earlier. In addition, a set of eight studies were found that are critical in the sense that they identify critical success factors for developing entrepreneurial behaviours and compe-tencies (Ahsan and Cheng 2006; Hyvonen and Touminen 2006; Littunen 2003; Sebora, Lee and Sukasame 2009), entrepreneurial courage (Vozikis and Mescon 2010), networking (Hoyos-Ruperto *et al.* 2013), e-commerce (Sebora *et al.* 2009) and education or training (Glaub and Frese 2013; Matlay 2009). A further four studies were also found that emphasized the positive and enabling features of entrepreneurship activities for economic development (Archibong 2010; Baldacchino and Dana 2012; Glăvan 2008; Setiawan 2012). These studies are not included in the table, however, because their main preoccupations are to identify the key ingredients that make entrepreneurship 'successful' and to affirm/ promote some universally productive features of entrepreneurship that can be promoted and transferred into generic success factors for other contexts. Furthermore, these studies aim to prescribe 'what should be' on the basis of an assumed robustness of the nature of empirical data. For this reason, they tend to be functionalist in orientation in the sense that researchers regularize and normalize entrepreneurial experiences into a set of social (economic) order factors that can be generalized across contexts. This left 42 articles to be categorized (see Appendix to Chapter 7, Table A.1).

Publications are grouped under the following four research interests: (1) critical reviews, such as the scrutiny of particular topics, themes or policies; (2) critical standpoints that highlight practice and under-represented voices or social groups; (3) the critiquing of entrepreneurial practices and its discourses in the form of 'critical entrepreneurship'; and (4) critical research practices that question the assumptions underlying research practices (such as critical realism).

The first entries at the head of the table are critical reviews of sub-topics/themes within entrepreneurship research. Examples are: entrepreneurship education and learning (Cope 2003; Grüner and Neuberger 2006; Ibrahim and Soufani 2002; Komulainen, Korhonen and Räty 2013; McLarty 2003), firm behaviour, off the books entrepreneurship and informal entrepreneurship (Williams and Youseff 2014; Williams *et al.* 2013), international entrepreneurship (Kiss *et al.* 2012; Peiris, Akoorie and Sinha 2012; Wright, Westhead and Ucbasaran 2007), trust (Welter 2012), the network concept (O'Donnell *et al.* 2001), social entrepreneurship

(Dacin, Dacin and Tracey 2011; Dey and Steyaert 2012; Teasdale and Mason 2012), e-entrepreneurship (Lewis *et al.* 2010; Lewis, Thomas and Sanders 2013) and transnational entrepreneurship (Yeung 2009). The aim here is to critique extant positions and sub-themes within the entrepreneurship literature in order to potentiate and realize under-realized viewpoints, conceptualizations and methodologies. The critical 'drive' in this category of critical research is to expand or enrich the field of studies by exposing limitations of extant research and identifying empirical, conceptual or methodological gaps that have not been addressed. These research efforts, therefore, involve an inclusive critical thinking approach to advancing the field, concerned with keeping entrepreneurship 'fresh', although 'not dangerous', to use Day and Steyaert's (2010) terminology.

Studies in the second category of Table A.1 are concerned with generating contextualized understandings of social groups that are marginalized or under-represented in mainstream research. We refer to these studies as 'standpoint' critiques – a term from feminist analyses which means to expose the local and particularized perspectives of minority or disadvantaged groups. Examples from the table are: women entrepreneurs in developing countries (Kumbhar 2013; Lau, Haug and Wright 2012; Sarbapriya and Ray 2011; Singh 2012), issues of gender (Marlow and McAdam 2012), African entrepreneurship (Ojo 2012; Onuoha 2008) and ethnic or immigrant entrepreneurship (Basu and Werbner 2001; Rath and Kloosterman 2000). These studies take the form of 'stories from the street' (Tedmanson *et al.* 2012, p. 36, referring to Imas, Wilson and Weston 2012) and are concerned with uncovering hidden or under-examined practices such as the transitioning of transnational entrepreneurs from enclave to diaspora (Ojo 2012). These research interests have the effect of 'keeping entrepreneurship critical' (Verduijn and Dey 2014) by exposing tensions, contradictions, nuances, subtleties, pluralistic viewpoints and marginalized experiences.

The third listing of entries, 'critical research practices', identifies a range of studies that question the philosophical foundations of entrepreneurship. These studies are critical in the sense that they challenge the ontological and epistemological bases of entrepreneurship knowledge often in the form of critical realist arguments (Leca and Naccache 2006; Matthyssens, Vandenbempt and Van Bockhaven 2013; Mole 2012; Mole and Mole 2010a). For those advocating a critical realist position, the key issue is how to consider the simultaneous influence of both actors' actions and the structures in which they are embedded, without conflating them (Leca and Naccache 2006, p. 627). A debate about the nature of opportunities in relation to entrepreneurial agency led Mole and Mole (2010) to recognize opportunities as distinct ontological entities. Here, critical research efforts are concerned with promoting an epistemological reflexivity and a de-naturalizing ontology that 'seeks to show how objects of inquiry are constructed through ongoing social processes…' (Spicer 2011, p. 151).

The last category in Table A.1 captures those commentaries and studies that are explicitly 'critical of entrepreneurship' (Verduijn and Dey 2014) within the context of the Critical Theory, Postmodern or Post-structuralist tradition. For this reason, this set of entries is categorized as 'critical entrepreneurship.' Critical entrepreneurship emphasizes the need to overturn 'the taken for granted norms of entrepreneurship scholarship as a whole, including its ideologies, dominant assumptions, grand narratives, samples and methods' (Tedmanson *et al.* 2012, p. 532) – especially those that centre on neo-liberal orthodoxies. Within this category of articles is an ideologically oriented intention to challenge the universality of market-based, wealth-creating, job stimulating and emancipatory assumptions about entrepreneurship (Ogbor 2000; Tedmanson *et al.* 2012; Verduijn *et al.* 2014). For example, Ogbor (2000) discusses the dysfunctional effects of ideological control in entrepreneurial discourses and praxis. Also, Armstrong (2005) and Spicer (2011) draw attention to the hegemonic discourse of entrepreneurship and how it functions as a political ideology that serves 'conservative political or economic (capitalist) ends' (Tedmanson *et al.* 2012, p. 536). Spicer (2011) argues that critical theory 'prompts us to rethink the entrepreneur in a number of ways': (1) 'challenging pre-existing assumptions'; (2) 'revealing existing political presuppositions that lurk below the discussion of entrepreneurship'; (3) 'confronting the implicit assumptions around knowledge production that have led to a narrow account of entrepreneurship'; and (4) 'seek[ing] to intervene in the subject(s) that they study' (pp. 150–151). Finally, in Verduijn *et al.* (2014), the authors use the notion of criticality to examine the complex relationality between entrepreneurial emancipation and oppression. Ideologically oriented critiques, therefore, aim to 'bust myths' and de-normalize discourses and in so doing radicalize entrepreneurship by exposing power effects and generating controversy or doubt (Dey and Steyaert 2012). They are also politically anti-performative (i.e., un-tethering knowledge production from means-end calculation) and have at their core a concern with emancipatory interests (Spicer 2011, p. 151).

Having reviewed the results of our search, it should be noted that there is a range of studies that have also contributed to the stirrings of a critical tradition in entrepreneurship research without necessarily using the terms 'critical' or 'critique' in the title. For instance, in 2004, Steyaert and Katz encouraged us to reconsider which (economic) discourses have been privileged in the study of entrepreneurship with a view to asking what other (social) discourses could be considered to open up new perspectives and be inclusive of non-traditional contexts. At the same time, the Movements in Entrepreneurship mini-series of publications (Hjorth and Steyaert 2004, 2010; Steyaert and Hjorth 2003, 2006) sponsored and endorsed 'a critical and crucial discussion' that 'creates a chance to change our understanding of entrepreneurship itself' (Steyaert and Hjorth 2006, p. xi). Throughout this mini series, new concepts, contexts, perspectives and 2dialectical discourses, involving enactment, narration, discourse, dialogicality, poetics, aesthetics, prosaics, rhetorics, politics and ethics, contributed an alternative (critical) theoretical and methodological landscape for entrepreneurship research.

Jones and Spicer's (2005) work was also emblematic in its reflection on the continued failure within entrepreneurship research 'to find the character of the entrepreneur' and how this signals that the notion of the entrepreneur is 'an empty signifier' that exists to 'structure phantasmic attachment' to an enterprise discourse (p. 235). Such arguments seek to challenge the myths of entrepreneurship (Dodd and Anderson 2007; Rhen *et al.* 2013). They also challenge the political representation and ideological bases of entrepreneurship discussed earlier (Jones and Spicer 2005, 2009; Perren and Jennings 2005), and conceive of entrepreneurship as a political (Jones and Murtola 2012) and ethical project, concerned with the 'practice of freedom' (Weiskopf and Steyaert 2009, p. 22). Calas and Smircich (2009), for example, criticize the universality of the market-based concept of entrepreneurship and argue for the re-framing of the nexus of opportunities in terms of social change in order to eliminate barriers that disadvantage women entrepreneurs. Other studies are concerned with issues of power, as well as the emancipatory potential (Goss *et al.* 2011; Rindova 2009), suppression (Verduijn *et al.* 2014) and/or subjugation (Perren and Jennings 2005), that entrepreneurial endeavours bring about. With these interests in mind, inquirers seek to highlight standpoint critiques and expose the 'darker' sides of entrepreneurial practices (i.e., Rehn and Talas 2004) to highlight relations of power, or asymmetry, related, for instance, to gender or ethnicity (Essers and Benschop 2007, 2009; Essers, Benschop and Doorewaard 2010; Marlow and McAdam 2012; Tedmanson 2012). In so doing, they give attention to local particularities and the social production of acts of resistance or forms of consent.

Finally, other critical orientations can be noted in entrepreneurship research that is concerned with exposing and challenging the dominant epistemological/ontological assumptions of entrepreneurship knowledge. For example, Jennings *et al.* (2005) question, from a philosophical perspective, the (dominant) functionalist nature of mainstream entrepreneurship research. Likewise, Fletcher (2006) referred to social constructionist thinking to provide for an alternative and more relational view of how entrepreneurial opportunities are enacted. An additional debate has emerged concerning the different categories of realism that are distinctive for explaining the nature of discovery and creation (Alvarez *et al.* 2014; Alvarez and Barney 2010).

7.5 Discussion: a spectrum of critical studies

In the preceding section, we have identified a range of studies that have adopted critical research tactics in order to reflect upon the process of critical inquiry in entrepreneurship research and to clarify what is distinctive in the various interests and preoccupations that are shaping critical research. A spectrum of critical studies can be identified by invoking the analytic distinction introduced early on concerning the extent to which certain research practices either 'work within' (consensus discourse) or 'disrupt' (dissensus discourse) a 'dominant set of structurings of knowledge, social relations, and identities' (p. 24).

On the left side of the spectrum there are those review articles that engage in critical thinking to scrutinize a particular concept or theme of entrepreneurship. These analyses use critical evaluation and logical inquiry in thoughtful yet creative ways to identify gaps and invoke new concepts, themes and methodologies (i.e., transnational entrepreneurship; entrepreneurial learning; trust) that are important for keeping entrepreneurship current and relevant. In the main, these studies demonstrate a consensual orientation in their examination of social orders in that 'they seek order and treat order production as the dominant feature of natural and social systems' (Alvesson and Deetz 2000, p. 26). Placing critical reviews on the left hand side, however, does not preclude critical reviews that work with a dissensus discourse (i.e., Dey and Steyaert 2012).

In the middle of the spectrum, there are two categories of articles. One category is the locally contextualized 'street stories' of marginalized and underrepresented social groups, the exposure and analysis of which have the effect of keeping entrepreneurship replete with new 'standpoints' and perspectives. Shaping such 'standpoint' critiques is an ethics of equality and a quest for an inclusivity of pluralistic voices, as well as insights that reduce 'otherness' and take account of situated and grounded experiences in the context of localized socio-cultural norms. The second category includes a small number of critical-philosophical reflections that discuss the meaning and relevance of different ontologies for entrepreneurship (i.e., realism and its different expressions including critical realism, pragmatic realism and realism in the construction of social reality) (Alvarez and Barney 2010, 2014; Fletcher 2006; Mole 2012; Watson 2013). Central to these commentaries are issues about dualities and dualisms, structure and agency, entitative-ness and relationality, as well as discovery versus creation. These perspectives provide a healthy epistemological (and ontological) reflexivity that is necessary for recognizing the value and importance of 'alternative ways of attending to the world' (Deetz 2009, p. 24).

On the right-hand side of the spectrum, it is possible to observe a closer alignment with the core interests of Critical Management Studies and the use of critical-ideological arguments that seek to doubt, disrupt, disturb and de-naturalize prevailing discourses. For this reason, studies on the right of the spectrum are more closely aligned with a dissensus discourse and the disruption of a dominant way of knowing and traditional research practices. Here, as implied by the strongest sense of the word 'critical', critical tactics are used to expose 'institutions, structures and forms of organizing that are deemed dominant, [or] in some way harmful, and/or under-challenged' (Alvesson and Ashcraft 2009, p. 63). This stance promotes emancipation from, reform to, and transformation of, dominating norms and structures. We can observe this in standpoint perspectives that focus on practice and localized experiences. Furthermore, we can also discern the ways in which critical research becomes extended into 'critique' and 'the examination of social institutions, ideologies, discourses (ways of constructing and reasoning about the world through the use of a particular language) and forms of consciousness in terms of representation and domination' (Alvesson and Deetz 2000, p. 8).

7.6 Conclusion

The shift towards a critical scholarship is inevitable as the entrepreneurship area of research expands, deepens its knowledge base and becomes progressively more probing and questioning of established ways of knowing. Reflecting on these developments is important, as some (neo-positivist) scientific domains 'do not spend much time thinking about [such matters]. [As a result], they accept the world as it appears to them in their science, procedures and language, as simply real and there' (Deetz 2009, p. 23).

For this reason, we have drawn attention to the different treatments, expressions and meanings behind the usage of the terms 'critical' and 'critique' to consider the linguistic, political, ethical, moral and ideological interests and preoccupations they serve. Whilst it might be the case that, as Spicer (2011) argues, the emergence of the studies in the category of 'critical entrepreneurship' can be attributed to developments in Critical Management Studies, in our review we can also observe more nuanced treatments of criticality that are less ideologically oriented and more concerned with highlighting critical conditions for entrepreneurship. This is sometimes expressed as the difference between being critical 'for' or 'of' entrepreneurship (Dey and Verduijn 2014). Such a duality is helpful for highlighting the different purposes that criticality serves especially in terms of the range of studies that seek to keep entrepreneurship critical (i.e., working within a consensus discourse) compared to those that are critical of entrepreneurship and working within a dissensus discourse.

At the same time, this duality masks more complex and multifarious nuances about the origin of concepts and research problems, such as the extent to which such problems are either generated a priori to the research, or introduced (and transformed) via localized, situated experiences (Alvesson and Deetz 2000). An a priori position privileges the theoretical interests, language system and interpretations of the researcher/scientific community; while a situated approach emphasizes an 'ontology of otherness' and adopts research practices that privilege multi-voiced-ness and local systems of meaning (Alvesson and Deetz 2000, p. 29).

Over the fourteen years covered by this review, it can be seen that there has been a visible and steady output of critical knowledge production relating to entrepreneurship.

This demonstrates that, in the last ten years, the critical dimension of the phrase 'critical mess' (Gartner 2004) is being addressed. The largest set of outputs using the term 'critical' is the category of 'critical reviews of a sub-theme', and the identification of gaps and alternative concepts, themes and topics, which coheres, to a great extent, with the general growth and expansion of the entrepreneurship field. The category that critiques epistemological/ontological assumptions has also received steady interest. Current debates about the nature of realism (Alvarez and Barney 2010, 2014) have boosted this set of critical outputs. Standpoint critiques have been increasing in number over the last few years as have 'critical entrepreneurship' entries that, latterly, are emphasizing enactive stances for critical research. An enactive stance concerns both 'inheriting approaches' that involve contextualizing, historicizing and socializing, as well as 'intervening approaches' that encourage participation, spatializing and minorizing (Dey and Steyaert 2012). Such research practices help to advance theory development in the sense of more nuanced interpretations of critical notions, such as emancipation (Verduijn *et al.* 2014). At the same time, they keep critical research tactics anchored in localized practices and meanings systems, as just discussed.

From the listing, a wide range of journals is identified as publishing critically oriented studies. However, there are a higher number of lower-ranked journals than higher-ranked entrepreneurship journals. For example, *Entrepreneurship Theory and Practice* (ETP) appears in the publication list only once, as does the *Journal of Small Business Management,* and the *Journal of Business Venturing* appears twice. These tend to be review articles (i.e., human capital and entrepreneurship; structuration/opportunity; and trust). Management and organization journals also feature (*Organization Science* once and *Journal of Management Studies* once) and the critical journal *Organization* also appears once. Field-specific journals can also be noted (*Regional Studies* and *Progress in Human Geography*). Topic-specific journals are especially prominent for publishing standpoint critiques (i.e., *Journal of African Business; Journal of Business Diversity; Ethnic and Racial Studies,* etc.).

In spite of the steady increase in the volume of critical studies, there is (still) too much reliance on the robustness of empirical data and a tendency to privilege the confirmation of theory and empirical data. In the main, there are still many studies that privilege the freely acting autonomy of entrepreneurs and their stewardship, agency or decision-making efforts. There is a scarcity of consideration regarding the struggles, conflicts and tensions experienced in these processes (excepting work on business failure and emotions). There is also a lingering trace of 'possessive individualism' (Dachler, Hosking and Gergen 1995) and its associated assumptions that entrepreneurial behaviours and endeavours are 'possessions' that are owned by knowing and alert individuals rather than being communally or relationally constructed (Fletcher 2006). Moreover, excepting processual approaches, research phenomena are often still regarded as fixed and discoverable through the research process which leads to reification and affirmation of 'what exists'. There is too much preoccupation with norms and descriptions that are thought to mirror (entrepreneurial) entities that exist in the external world in a relatively fixed state. There is often also a privileging of the particular language system of the researcher and the expertise of the research community (Alvesson and Deetz 2000, p. 28). With the exception of a small number of studies (Weiskopf and Steyaert 2009), there is a denial of the role of moral-practical concerns in processes of social development and the presumption that the ends of human existence are self-evident (Willmott 2008, p. 67).

Whether or not critical theories, tactics and research in entrepreneurship studies can help to overcome some of these challenges depends upon whether we see a greater number of substantive empirical studies that use critically inspired enactive research strategies. At the same time, the future of critically oriented studies also depends upon how we deal with the proclivity of critical research to emphasize the need for more dialogue, understanding, exposure, insight, technology, awareness, etc. (Alvesson and Deetz

2000, p. 15). Being receptive towards more critical approaches takes us some way to keeping entrepreneurship critical and fresh (and maybe even dangerous as mentioned earlier with reference to Steyaert and Dey 2010), but it also leads us into a circular conclusion: which is that we need more critical studies.

In writing the concluding sentences of this chapter, we find ourselves caught in our own epistemological bind, therefore: how to review critical inquiry in entrepreneurship research without concluding that we need yet more critical studies. We don't claim that we can address this. Perhaps this is an issue for further research. In fact, we argue that there is still space for further critical studies especially empirical works that utilize enactive and interventionist strategies as previously discussed. In particular, critical perspectives and stances are significant for theory development. For example, much attention has been awarded to *what* aspects of a phenomenon are being represented in theoretical explanations (i.e., individual actors, networks, opportunities, decisions, events, environmental changes, actions, cognitive processes, journeys, etc.). With the influence of processual approaches, we are now seeing a shift as entrepreneurship inquirers become concerned about how, when and why the units of a theory are related (Dubin 1978; Whetten 1989). We see a lot of potential, therefore, for critically inspired or enactive research to address 'why', 'how' and 'when' particular entrepreneurial practices, contexts, actions or interactions produce relations of power, gender, relationality, asymmetry, coerciveness, autonomy, control, conflict and harmony, participation, restorative practice and so forth. Here are some further suggestions for sharpening critical engagement and reflexivity in entrepreneurship research that relate to and draw from many of the authors referred to and points previously made in this chapter. Engaging in critique-inspired research practices means:

a   Examining why entrepreneurial contexts are sites for the production of discourse, power, gender, relationality, asymmetry, coerciveness, autonomy, control, conflict *and* harmony, participation, restorative practice.
b   Emphasizing process, time and context relativity.
c   Avoiding the regularizing and normalizing entrepreneurial experiences into a set of social orders factors that can be generalized across contexts.
d   Avoiding an entitative stance (where essences, components and elements of organizational life are seen and theorized as the 'properties' of actors).
e   Evaluating issues of power/asymmetry by connecting to wider discourses, materialities and ideologies.
f   Searching for alternative (or pluralistic) ways of understanding the world.
g   Privileging multi-voicedness in research accounts (by demonstrating inter-subjective exchanges, hidden speech, sub-textual interpretations, dialogue, and conversations between organizational actors).
h   Being non-representational (avoid truth claims about how our research work captures, mirrors or represents, rather than constructs, social reality).
i   Inspiring creative forms of authorship.

j   Having an interest in contextualization processes (Buchanan and Bryman 2007).
k   Making explicit the emotions, politics and ethics of research practice.
l   Engendering reflexivity and responsiveness of researchers and engaging the participants in research processes.
m   Accommodating the complex issues drawn from everyday experience and interpretations (to expose under-represented topics (class, ethnicity) and marginal social groups).
n   Accommodating a political and ethical stance as the researcher becomes concerned with how deep social formations constrain human behaviours, affect autonomy and decision-making.

Finally, we find inspiring for future critical work Weiskopf and Steyaert's (2009, p. 15) conception of entrepreneurship as 'critical engagement in the world'. This, we think, keeps critical entrepreneurship work anchored in a social ontology, which, rather than promising what might be if only there were more critical perspectives, emphasizes issues of relatedness, reflexivity, practice, power and the social/moral accountability of this critical engagement.

Notes

1   The National Council for Excellence in Critical Thinking, www.criticalthinking. org/pages/the-national-council-for-excellence-in-critical-thinking/406 (downloaded 1 May 2015).
2   Theodor W. Adorno, *One Last Genius*, by Detlev Claussen, translated by Rodney Livingston, Cambridge, MA: Harvard University Press, 2008. Originally published as Theodor W. Adorno, *Einletztes Genie*, Frankfurt am Main: S. Fischer VerlagGmbh, 2003.
3   See Alvesson and Sköldberg 2000, pp. 149–153 for a more detailed consideration of the analytical nuances between postmodernist and poststructuralist ideas.
4   Two exceptions, however, are Steyaert and Dey (2010) and Verduijn *et al.* (2014). The former authors, offer in the context of social entrepreneurship, nine verbs for keeping that field of research 'dangerous'. In the latter study, the authors use the attribute 'critical' as a sensitizing concept to emphasize entrepreneurship's role in overcoming extant relations of exploitation, domination and oppression.
5   Between 2000 and 2015 – search in Google Scholar including book chapters, journal articles and conference papers (downloaded 19 January 2015).

References

Ahsan, K. and Cheng, P. (2006) 'Critical issues of starting entrepreneurship in Kazakhstan', *IUP Journal of Entrepreneurship Development*, 3(2), pp. 43–51.
Aldrich, H.E. and Kenworthy, A. (1999) 'The accidental entrepreneur: Campbellian antinomies and organizational foundings'. In Baum, J.A.C. and McKelvey, B. (eds) *Variations in Organization Science: In Honor of Donald T. Campbell*. Newbury Park, CA: Sage, pp. 19–33.

Aldrich, H.E. (2001) 'Who wants to be an evolutionary theorist: Remarks on the occasion of the Year 2000 OMT Distinguished Scholarly Career Award Presentation', *Journal of Management Inquiry*, 10(2), pp. 115–127.

Alvarez, S.A. and Barney, J.B. (2010) 'Entrepreneurship and epistemology: The philosophical underpinnings of the study of entrepreneurial opportunities', *Academy of Management Annals*, 4(1), pp. 557–583.

Alvarez, S.A., Barney, J.B., McBride, R. and Wuebker, R. (2014) 'Realism in the study of entrepreneurship', *Academy of Management Review*, 39(2), pp. 227–231.

Alvesson, M. and Ashcraft, K.L. (2009) 'Critical methodology in management and organization research'. In Buchanan, D. and Bryman, A. (eds) *The Sage Handbook of Organizational Research Methods*. London: Sage, pp. 61–77.

Alvesson, M. and Deetz, S. (2000) *Doing Critical Management Research*. London: Sage.

Alvesson, M. and Sköldberg, K. (2000) *Reflexive Methodology: New Vistas for Qualitative Research*. London: Sage.

Alvesson, M. and Willmott, H. (1992) *Critical Management Studies*. London: Sage.

Archibong, A. (2010) 'Entrepreneurship as a critical and missing factor in economic development of poor nations: A systematic analysis of factors of production', *IUP Journal of Business Strategy*, 7(1), pp. 7–20.

Ardichvili, A., Cardozo, R. and Ray, S. (2003) 'A theory of entrepreneurial opportunity identification and development', *Journal of Business Venturing*, 18(1), pp. 105–123.

Armstrong, P. (2005) *Critique of Entrepreneurship: People and Policy*. Basingstoke: Palgrave Macmillan.

Baker, T. and Nelson, R.E. (2005) 'Creating something from nothing: Resource construction through entrepreneurial bricolage', *Administrative Science Quarterly*, 50, pp. 329–366.

Baldacchino, G. and Dana, L.P. (2006) 'The impact of public policy on entrepreneurship: A critical investigation of the protestant ethic on a divided island jurisdiction', *Journal of Small Business and Entrepreneurship*, 19(4), pp. 419–430.

Banerjee, B. and Tedmanson, D. (2010) 'Grass burning under our feet: Indigenous enterprise development in a political economy of whiteness', *Management Learning*, 41(2), pp. 147–165.

Basu, D. and Werbner, P. (2001) 'Bootstrap capitalism and the culture industries: A critique of invidious comparisons in the study of ethnic entrepreneurship', *Ethnic and Racial Studies*, 24, pp. 236–262.

Bergmann, H., Mueller, S. and Schrettle, T. (2014) 'The use of global entrepreneurship monitor data in academic research: A critical inventory and future potentials', *International Journal of Entrepreneurial Venturing*, 6(3), pp. 242–276.

Brookfield, S.D. (1987) *Developing Critical Thinkers: Challenging Adults to Explore Alternative Ways of Thinking and Acting*. San Francisco, CA: Jossey-Bass.

Bruni, A., Gherardi, S. and Poggio, B. (2004) 'Doing gender, doing entrepreneurship: An ethnographic account of intertwined practices', *Gender, Work and Organization*, 11(4), pp. 406–429.

Buchanan, D. and Bryman, A. (2007) 'Contextualising methods choice in organizational research', *Organizational Research Methods*, 10(3), pp. 483–501.

Calas, M.B. and Smircich, L. (2009) 'Feminist perspectives on gender in organizational research: What is and is yet to be'. In Buchanan, D. and Bryman, A. (eds) *The Sage Handbook of Organizational Research Methods*. London: Sage, pp. 246–269.

Calas, M.B., Smircich, L. and Bourne, K.A. (2009) 'Extending the boundaries: Reframing "entrepreneurship as social change" through feminist perspectives', *Academy of Management Review*, 34(3), pp. 552–569.

Casson, M. (1982) *The Entrepreneur: An Economic Theory*. Totawa, NJ: Barnes and Noble.

Chia, R. (1995) 'From modern to postmodern organizational analysis', *Organization Studies*, 16(4), pp. 579–604.

Chia, R. (2008) 'Postmodernism'. In Thorpe, R. and Holt, R. (eds) *The Sage Dictionary of Qualitative Management Research*. London: Sage, pp. 162–163.

Chiles, T.H., Tuggle, C.S., McMullan, J.S., Bierman, L. and Greening, D.W. (2010) 'Dynamic creation: Extending the radical Austrian approach to entrepreneurship', *Organization Studies*, 31(7), 7–46.

Cho, A.H. (2006) 'Politics, values and social entrepreneurship: A critical appraisal'. In Mair, J., Robinson, J. and Hockerts, K. (eds) *Social Entrepreneurship*. New York: Palgrave Macmillan, pp. 34–56.

Colakoglu, S.N. and Sledge, S.A. (2013) 'The development of critical thinking skills through a service-learning oriented entrepreneurship course', *Journal of Entrepreneurship Education*, 16, pp. 115–124.

Cole, A.H. (1959) *Business Enterprise in a Social Setting*. Cambridge, MA: Harvard University Press.

Cope, J. (2003) 'Entrepreneurial learning and critical reflection: Discontinuous events as triggers for "higher-level" learning', *Management Learning*, 34, pp. 429–450.

Dachler, H.P., Hosking, D.M. and Gergen, K.J. (1995) *Relational Alternatives to Individualisation: Management and Organisation*. Aldershot: Avebury.

Dacin, M.T., Dacin, P.A. and Tracey, P. (2011) 'Social entrepreneurship: A critique and future directions', *Organization Science*, 22(5), pp. 1203–1213.

Deetz, S. (2009) 'Organizational research as alternative ways of attending to and talking about structures and activities'. In *The SAGE Handbook of Organizational Research Methods*. London: Sage, pp. 21–38.

Dey, P. and Steyaert, C. (2012) 'Social entrepreneurship: Critique and the radical enactment of the social', *Social Enterprise Journal*, 8(2), pp. 90–107.

Dimov, D. (2007) 'Beyond the single-person, single-insight attribution in understanding entrepreneurial opportunities', *Entrepreneurship Theory and Practice*, 31(5), pp. 713–731.

Dimov, D., (2011) 'Grappling with the unbearable elusiveness of entrepreneurial opportunities', *Entrepreneurship Theory and Practice*, 35(1), pp. 57–81.

Dobers, P. (2003) 'Image of Stockholm as an IT city: Emerging urban entrepreneurship'. In Steyaert, C. and Hjorth, D. (eds) *New Movements in Entrepreneurship*. Cheltenham: Edward Elgar.

Dodd, S.D. and Anderson, A.R. (2007) 'Mumpsimus and the mything of the individualistic entrepreneur', *International Small Business Journal*, 25(4), pp. 341–360.

Drummond, C.K. (2010) 'Team-based learning to enhance critical thinking skills in entrepreneurship education', *Academy of Entrepreneurship*, 16(2), p. 18.

Dubin, R. (1978) *Theory Building*. Revised Edition. New York: Free Press.

Essers, C. (2009a) *New Directions in Postheroic Entrepreneurship: Narratives of Gender and Ethnicity*. Malmö: Liber.

Essers, C. (2009b) 'Reflections on the narrative approach: Dilemmas of power, emotions and social location while constructing life-stories', *Organization*, 16(2), pp. 163–181.

Essers, C. and Benschop, Y. (2007) 'Enterprising identities: Female entrepreneurs of Moroccan and Turkish origin in the Netherlands', *Organization Studies*, 28(1), pp. 49–69.

Essers, C. and Benschop, Y. (2009) 'Muslim businesswomen doing boundary work: The negotiation of Islam, gender and ethnicity within entrepreneurial contexts', *Human Relations*, 62(3), pp. 403–424.

Essers, C., Benschop, Y. and Doorewaard, H. (2010) 'Female ethnicity: Understanding Muslim migrant businesswomen in the Netherlands', *Gender, Work and Organization*, 17(3), pp. 320–340.

Fletcher, D. (2007) '"Toy Story": The narrative world of entrepreneurship and the creation of interpretive communities', *Journal of Business Venturing*, 22(5), pp. 649–672.

Fletcher, D.E. and Watson, T.J. (2006) 'Entrepreneurship, shifting life orientations and social change in the countryside'. In Steyaert, C. and Hjorth, D. (eds) *Entrepreneurship as Social Change*, Cheltenham: Edward Elgar, pp. 145–164.

Fournier, V. and Grey, C. (2000) 'At the critical moment: Conditions and prospects for critical management studies', *Human Relations*, 53(1), pp. 7–32.

Gartner, W.B. (2004) 'Achieving "critical mess" in entrepreneurship scholarship'. In Katz, J.A. and Shepherd, D. (eds) *Advances in Entrepreneurship, Firm Emergence, and Growth*. Greenwich, CT: JAI Press, pp. 199–216.

Garud, R. and Karnøe, P. (2003) 'Bricolage versus breakthrough: Distributed and embedded agency in technology entrepreneurship', *Research Policy*, 32(2), pp. 277–300.

Glaser, B. (1941) *An Experiment in the Development of Critical Thinking*. New York: Bureau of Publications, Teachers College, Columbia University.

Glaub, M. and Frese, M. (2011) 'A critical review of the effects of entrepreneurship training in developing countries', *Enterprise Development and Microfinance*, 22(4), pp. 335–353.

Glăvan, B. (2008) 'Coordination failures, cluster theory, and entrepreneurship: A critical view', *Quarterly Journal of Austrian Economics*, 11(1), pp. 43–59.

Goss, D., Jones, R., Betta, M. and Latham, J. (2011) 'Power as practice: A micro-sociological analysis of the dynamics of emancipatory entrepreneurship', *Organization Studies*, 32(2), pp. 211–229.

Grüner, H. and Neuberger, L. (2006) 'Entrepreneurs' education: Critical areas for the pedagogic-didactic agenda and beyond', *Journal of Business Economics and Management*, 7(4), pp. 163–170.

Habermas, J. (1984) *The Theory of Communicative Action, Vol. 1: Reason and the Rationalization of Society*. Translated by T. McCarthy. Boston, MA: Beacon Press.

Hjorth, D. and Steyaert, C. (2004) *Narrative and Discursive Approaches in Entrepreneurship: A Second Movements in Entrepreneurship Book*. Cheltenham: Edward Elgar.

Hjorth, D. and Steyaert, C. (eds) (2010) *The Politics and Aesthetics of Entrepreneurship: A Fourth Movements in Entrepreneurship Book*. Cheltenham: Edward Elgar.

Hoang, H. and Antoncic, B. (2003) 'Network-based research in entrepreneurship: A critical review', *Journal of Business Venturing*, 18(2), pp. 165–187.

Horkheimer, M. (1972 [1937]) *Traditional and Critical Theory. Selected Essays*. Translated by Matthew J. O'Connell. New York: Herder and Herder.

Horkheimer, M. and Adorno, T. (1947) *The Dialectics of Enlightenment*. London: Verso.

Hoyos-Ruperto, D., Romaguera José, M., Carlsson, B. and Lyytinen, K. (2013) 'Networking: A critical success factor for entrepreneurship', *American Journal of Management*, 13(2), pp. 55–72.

Hyvonen, S. and Touminen, M. (2006) 'Entrepreneurial innovations, market-driven intangibles and learning orientation: Critical indicators for performance advantages in SMEs', *International Journal of Management and Decision Making*, 7(6), pp. 643–660.

Ibrahim, A.B. and Soufani, K. (2002) 'Entrepreneurship education and training in Canada: A critical assessment', *Education +Training*, 44(8/9), pp. 421–430.

Imas, J.M., Wilson, N. and Weston, A. (2012) 'Barefoot entrepreneurs', *Organization*, 19(5), pp. 563–585.

Jaafar, M., Abdul-Aziz, A.-R. and Ali, R. (2010) 'Entrepreneurship: A critical outlook on housing developers in Malaysia', *International Journal of Construction Management*, 10(4), pp. 75–99.

Jennings, P.L., Perren, L. and Carter, S. (2005) 'Guest editors' introduction: Alternative perspectives on entrepreneurship research', *Entrepreneurship Theory and Practice*, 29(2), pp. 145–152.

Jones, C. and Spicer, A. (2005) 'The sublime object of entrepreneurship', *Organization*, 12(2), pp. 223–246.

Jones, C. and Spicer, A. (2009) *Unmasking the Entrepreneur*. Cheltenham: Edward Elgar.

Jones, C. and Murtola, A.M. (2012) 'Entrepreneurship and expropriation', *Organization*, 19(5), pp. 635–655.

Kirzner, I. (1973) *Competition and Entrepreneurship*. Chicago, IL: University of Chicago Press.

Kiss, A.N., Wade, M.D. and Cavusgil, S.T. (2012) 'International entrepreneurship research in emerging economies: A critical review and research agenda', *Journal of Business Venturing*, 27(2), pp. 266–290.

Knight, F.H. (1921) *Risk, Uncertainty and Profit*. New York: Houghton Mifflin.

Komulainen, K.J., Korhonen, M. and Räty, H. (2013) 'On entrepreneurship, in a different voice? Finnish entrepreneurship education and pupils' critical narratives of the entrepreneur', *International Journal of Qualitative Studies in Education*, 26(8), pp. 1079–1095.

Kumbhar, V.M. (2013) 'Some critical issues of women entrepreneurship in rural India', *European Academic Research*, 1(2), pp. 192–200.

Landström, H. (2005) 'The emergence of an academic field'. In Landström, H. (ed.) *Pioneers in Entrepreneurship and Small Business Research*. New York: Springer, pp. 55–93.

Lau, L.K., Haug, J.C. and Wright, L.B. (2012) 'A critical study of the entrepreneurship development process among women', *Journal of Business Diversity*, 12(1), pp. 107–121.

Leca, B. and Naccache, P. (2006) 'A critical realist approach to institutional entrepreneurship', *Organization*, 13(5), pp. 627–651.

Lepoutre, J. and Heene, A. (2006) 'Investigating the impact of firm size on small business social responsibility: A critical review', *Journal of Business Ethics*, 67(3), pp. 257–273.

Levinsohn, D. (2013) 'Disembedded and beheaded? A critical review of the emerging field of sustainability entrepreneurship', *International Journal of Entrepreneurship and Small Business*, 19(2), pp. 190–211.

Lewis, A., Daunton, L., Thomas, B. and Sanders, G. (2010) 'A critical exploration into whether E-Recruitment is an effective E-Entrepreneurship method in attracting appropriate employees for enterprises', *International Journal of E-Entrepreneurship and Innovation*, 1(2), pp. 30–44.

Lewis, A., Thomas, B. and Sanders, G.M. (2013) 'Pushing the right buttons? A critical exploration into the effects of social media as an innovative E-Entrepreneurship method of recruitment for enterprises', *International Journal of E-Entrepreneurship and Innovation*, 4(3), pp. 16–37.

Littunen, H. (2003) 'Management capabilities and environmental characteristics in the critical operational phase of entrepreneurship: A comparison of Finnish family and nonfamily firms', *Family Business Review*, 16, pp. 183–197.

Marcuse, H. (1964) *One-dimensional Man: Studies in the Ideology of Advanced Industrial Society*. Boston, MA: Beacon Press.

Marlow, S. and McAdam, M. (2012) 'Advancing debate: An epistemological critique of the relationship between gender, entrepreneurship and firm performance', *International Journal of Entrepreneurial Behaviour and Research*, 19(1), pp. 6–26.

Mason, C. (2011) 'Up for grabs: A critical discourse analysis of social entrepreneurship discourse in the United Kingdom', *Social Enterprise Journal*, 8(2), pp. 123–140.

Matlay, H. (2009) 'Entrepreneurship education in the UK: A critical analysis of stakeholder involvement and expectations', *Journal of Small Business and Enterprise Development*, 16(2), pp. 355–368.

Matthyssens, P., Vandenbempt, K. and Van Bockhaven, W. (2013) 'Structural antecedents of institutional entrepreneurship in industrial networks: A critical realist explanation', *Industrial Marketing Management*, 42(3), pp. 405–420.

McClelland, D.C. (1961) *The Achieving Society*. Princeton, NJ: Van Nostrand.

McKelvey, B. (2004) 'Towards a complexity science of entrepreneurship', *Journal of Business Venturing*, 19, pp. 313–342.

McLarty, R. (2003) 'Graduate entrepreneurship: A critical review of problems, issues and personal competencies', *International Journal of Entrepreneurship and Innovation Management*, 3(5), pp. 621–636.

McMullen, J.S. and Dimov, D. (2013) 'Time and the entrepreneurship journey: The problems and promise of studying entrepreneurship as a process', *Journal of Management Studies*, 50(8), pp. 1481–1512.

Mohr, L. (1982) *Explaining Organizational Behaviour*. San Francisco, CA: Jossey-Bass.

Mole, K. (2012) *Critical Realism in Entrepreneurship*. Working paper. Available at: http://wrap.warwick.ac.uk.

Mole, K. (2012) 'Critical realism in entrepreneurship'. In Mole, K. and Ram, M. (eds) *Perspectives in Entrepreneurship: A Critical Approach*. Basingstoke: Palgrave Macmillan.

Mole, K.F. and Mole, M. (2010a) 'Entrepreneurship as the structuration of individual and opportunity: A response using a critical realist perspective', *Journal of Business Venturing*, 25(2), pp. 230–237.

Mole, K.F. and Mole, M. (2010b) 'Entrepreneurship as the structuration of individual and opportunity: A response using a critical realist perspective: Comment on Sarason, Dean and Dillar', *Journal of Business Venturing*, 25(2), pp. 230–237.

Mullen, M.R., Budeva, D.G. and Doney, P.M. (2009) 'Research methods in the leading small business–entrepreneurship journals: A critical review with recommendations for future research', *Journal of Small Business Management*, 47(3), pp. 287–307.

Nodoushani, O. and Nodoushani, P.A. (1999) 'A deconstructionist theory of entrepreneurship: A note', *American Business Review*, 17(1), pp. 45–49.

O'Donnell, A., Gilmore, A., Cummins, D. and Carson, D. (2001) 'The network construct in entrepreneurship research: A review and critique', *Management Decision*, 39(9), pp. 749–760.

Ogbor, J. (2000) 'Mythicizing and reification in entrepreneurial discourse: Ideology-critique of entrepreneurial studies', *Journal of Management Studies*, 37(5), pp. 605–635.

Ojo, S. (2012) 'Ethnic enclaves to diaspora entrepreneurs: A critical appraisal of black British Africans' transnational entrepreneurship in London', *Journal of African Business*, 133(2), pp. 145–156.

Onuoha, B.C. (2008) 'A critical analysis of impediment to entrepreneurship development of Nigeria', *African Journal of Entrepreneurship*, 1(1), p. 31.

Peiris, I., Akoorie, M. and Sinha, P. (2012) 'International entrepreneurship: A critical analysis of studies in the past two decades and future directions for research', *Journal of International Entrepreneurship*, 10(4), pp. 279–324.

Peredo, A.M. and McLean, M. (2006) 'Social entrepreneurship: A critical review of the concept', *Journal of World Business*, 41(1), pp. 56–65.

Perren, L. and Jennings, P.L. (2005) 'Government discourses on entrepreneurship: Issues of subjugation, legitimisation and power', *Entrepreneurship Theory and Practice*, 29(2), pp. 173–184.

Pio, E. (2005) 'Knotted strands: Working lives of Indian women migrants in New Zealand', *Human Relations*, 58(10), pp. 1277–1300.

Poon, P.S., Zhou, L. and Chan, T.S. (2009) 'Social entrepreneurship in a transitional economy: A critical assessment of rural Chinese entrepreneurial firms', *Journal of Management Development*, 28(2), pp. 94–109.

Prieto, L.C., Phipps, S.A. and Friedrich, T.L. (2012) 'Social entrepreneur development: An integration of critical pedagogy, the theory of planned behavior and the ACS model', *Academy of Entrepreneurship Journal*, 18(2), pp. 1–15.

Rath, J. and Kloosterman, R. (2000) 'Outsiders' business: A critical review of research on immigrant entrepreneurship', *International Migration Review*, 34(3), pp. 657–681.

Reed, M. (2009) 'Critical realism: Philosophy, method or philosophy in search of a method?'. In Buchanan, D. and Bryman, A. (eds) *The Sage Handbook of Organizational Research Methods*. London: Sage, pp. 430–448.

Rehn, A. and Taalas, S. (2004) 'Crime and Assumptions in Entrepreneurship'. In Hjorth, D. and Steyaert, C. (eds) *Narrative and Discursive Approaches in Entrepreneurship. A Second Movements in Entrepreneurship Book*. Cheltenham: Edward Elgar, pp. 144–159.

Rehn, A., Brännback, M., Carsrud, A. and Lindahl, M. (2013) 'Challenging the myths of entrepreneurship?', *Entrepreneurship and Regional Development*, 25(7–8), pp. 543–551.

Rideout, E.C. and Gray, D.O. (2013) 'Does entrepreneurship education really work? A review and methodological critique of the empirical literature on the effects of university-based entrepreneurship education', *Journal of Small Business Management*, 51(3), pp. 329–351.

Rindova, V., Barry, D. and Ketchen Jr., D.J. (2009) 'Entrepreneuring as emancipation', *Academy of Management Review*, 34(3), pp. 477–491.

Sarason, Y., Dean, T. and Dillard, J.F. (2006) 'Entrepreneurship as the nexus of individual and opportunity: A structuration view', *Journal of Business Venturing*, 21, pp. 286–305.

Sarasvathy, S.D. (2008) *Effectuation: Elements of Entrepreneurial Expertise*. Cheltenham: Edward Elgar.

Sarbapriya, R. and Ishita, A.R. (2011) 'Women entrepreneurship in India: Some critical issues and challenges', *Journal of Contemporary Business Studies*, 2(8), p. 6.

Sarbapriya, R. and Ray, A. (2011) 'Some aspects of women entrepreneurship in India', *Asian Journal of Management Research*, 2(1), pp. 1–13.

Schumpeter, J.A. (1961 [1912]) *The Theory of Economic Development*. New York: Oxford University Press.

Sebora, T.C., Lee, S.M. and Sukasame, N. (2009) 'Critical success factors for e-commerce entrepreneurship: An empirical study of Thailand', *Small Business Economics*, 32(3), pp. 303–316.

Setiawan, I. (2012) 'Economic development and entrepreneurship: A critical review from a socio-cultural perspective', *Asia-Pacific Management and Business Application*, 1(1), pp 9–27.

Shane, S. (2003) 'When are universities the locus of invention'. In Steyaert, C. and Hjorth, D. (eds) *New Movements in Entrepreneurship*. Cheltenham: Edward Elgar, pp. 145–159.

Shane, S. and Venkataraman, S. (2000) 'The promise of entrepreneurship as a field of research', *Academy of Management Review*, 25(1), pp. 217–226.

Singh, R. (2012) 'A critical study of the entrepreneurship development process among women', *Journal of Business Diversity*, 12(1), pp. 88–106.

Smircich, L. and Calas, M. (1987) 'Organizational culture: A critical assessment'. In Jablin, F., Putnam, L., Roberts, K. and Porter, L. (eds) *Handbook of Organizational Communication*. Newbury Park, CA: Sage, pp. 228–263.

Spedale, S. and Watson, T.J. (2014) 'The emergence of entrepreneurial action: At the crossroads between institutional logics and individual life-orientation', *International Small Business Journal*, 32(7), pp. 759–776.

Spicer, A. (2011) *Critical Theories of Entrepreneurship: Perspectives on Entrepreneurship*. London: Palgrave Macmillan.

Steyaert, C. (2007) 'Entrepreneuring as a conceptual attractor? A review of process theories in 20 years of entrepreneurship studies', *Entrepreneurship and Regional Development*, 19(6), pp. 453–477.

Steyaert, C. and Hjorth, D. (eds) (2003) *New Movements in Entrepreneurship*. Cheltenham: Edward Elgar.

Steyaert, C. and Hjorth, D. (eds) (2006) *Entrepreneurship as Social Change: A Third Movements in Entrepreneurship Book*. Cheltenham: Edward Elgar.

Steyaert, C. and Katz, J. (2004) 'Reclaiming the space of entrepreneurship in society: Geographical, discursive and social dimensions', *Entrepreneurship and Regional Development*, 16(3), pp. 179–196.

Steyaert, C. and Dey, P. (2010) 'Nine verbs to keep the social entrepreneurship research agenda "dangerous"', *Journal of Social Entrepreneurship*, 1(2), pp. 231–254.

Swami, S. and Porwal, R.K. (2005) 'Entrepreneurship, innovation and marketing: conceptualization of critical linkages', *Journal of Advances in Management Research*, 2(2), pp. 54–69.

Tedmanson, D., Verduyn, K., Essers, C. and Gartner, W.B. (2012) 'Critical perspectives in entrepreneurship research', *Organization*, 19, pp. 531–541.

Thomas, J. (1993) *Doing Critical Ethnography*. Newbury Park, CA: Sage.

Venkataraman, S., Sarasvathy, S.D., Dew, N. and Forster, W.R. (2012) 'Reflections on the 2010 AMR Decade Award: Whither the promise? Moving forward with entrepreneurship as a science of the artificial', *Academy of Management Review*, 37(1), pp. 21–33.

Verduijn, K. and Dey, P. (2014) *Critical entrepreneurship studies – taking stock and Looking ahead*. Paper presented at the Research in Entrepreneurship (RENT) Conference, University of Luxembourg, November.

Verduijn, K., Dey, P., Tedmanson, D. and Essers, C. (2014) 'Emancipation and/or oppression? Conceptualizing dimensions of criticality in entrepreneurship studies', *International Journal of Entrepreneurial Behavior and Research*, 20(2), pp. 98–107.

Vozikis, G.S. and Mescon, T.S. (2010) 'Developing international interdisciplinary programs in management and technology entrepreneurship in Eastern Europe: The critical success factors for developing entrepreneurial courage', *Journal of Small Business and Entrepreneurship*, 23(1), pp. 785–796.

Watson, T.J. (2013) 'Entrepreneurial action and the Euro-American social science tradition: Pragmatism, realism and looking beyond the entrepreneur', *Entrepreneurship and Regional Development*, 25(1–2), pp. 16–33.

Weiskopf, R. and Steyaert, C. (2009) 'Metamorphoses in entrepreneurship studies: Towards an affirmative politics of entrepreneuring'. In Hjorth, D. and Steyaert, C. (eds) *The Politics and Aesthetics of Entrepreneurship. A Fourth Movements in Entrepreneurship Book*. Cheltenham: Edward Elgar, pp. 183–201.

Welter, F. (2012) 'All you need is trust? A critical review of the trust and entrepreneurship literature', *International Small Business Journal*, 30(3), pp. 193–212.

Welter, F. and Smallbone, D. (2006) 'Exploring the role of trust in entrepreneurial activity', *Entrepreneurship Theory and Practice*, 30(4), pp. 465–475.

Whetten, D.A. (1989) 'What constitutes a theoretical contribution?', *Academy of Management Review*, 14(4), pp. 490–495.

Wiklund, J., Davidsson, P., Audretsch, D. and Karlsson, C. (2011) 'The future of entrepreneurship research', *Entrepreneurship Theory and Practice*, 35(1), pp. 1–9.

Williams, C.C., Nadin, S., Newton, S., Rogers, P. and Windebank, J. (2013) 'Explaining off-the-books entrepreneurship: A critical evaluation of competing perspectives', *International Entrepreneurship and Management Journal*, 9(3), pp. 447–463.

Williams, C.C. and Youseff, Y. (2014) 'Tackling informal entrepreneurship in Latin America: A critical evaluation of the neo-liberal policy approach', *Journal of Entrepreneurship and Organizations Management*, 3(1), pp. 1–22.

Willmott, H. (2008) 'Critical theory'. In Thorpe, R. and Holt, R. (eds) *The Sage Dictionary of Qualitative Management Research*. London: Sage, pp. 66–68.

Wood, M.S. and McKinley, W. (2010) 'The production of entrepreneurial opportunity: A constructivist perspective', *Strategic Entrepreneurship Journal*, 4, pp. 66–83.

Wright, M., Westhead, P. and Ucbasaran, D. (2007) 'Internationalization of small and medium-sized enterprises (SMEs) and international entrepreneurship: A critique and policy implications', *Regional Studies*, 41(7), pp. 1013–1030.

Yeung, H.W. (2009) 'Transnationalizing entrepreneurship: A critical agenda for economic geography', *Progress in Human Geography*, 33, pp. 210–235.

Yuehua, Z. (2005) 'Critical factors for science park development: The case of the Singapore Science Park', *International Journal of Technology Transfer and Commercialisation*, 4(2), p. 1.

8 Engaged scholarship

Taking responsibility for the politics of method mediation

Ester Barinaga

8.1 Introduction

> ... this essay is an argument for situated and embodied knowledges and an argument against various forms of unlocatable, and so irresponsible, knowledge claims. Irresponsible means unable to be called into account.
>
> (Haraway 1988, p. 583)

At the heart of this essay is the relationship between, on the one hand, the phenomenon in the world we researchers are interested in studying and, on the other hand, the descriptions we offer of that phenomenon in the world. Mediating the relationship between the world and our descriptions of it is method; mediating in the sense that methods help us select and craft such descriptions of the world, a process that is never neutral. Most often, however, we relate to methods as if these were neutral operations for accessing and describing a particular pattern in the world, thereby ignoring the mediation of method and disregarding the set of assumptions about reality (ontology) and about the nature and value of knowledge (epistemology) that guide the crafting of our descriptions.

While the relation between the world and our descriptions of it has been largely discussed as a problem of (too much or too little) interpretation, a matter of perspective (Strathern 1987), the performative turn has taught us that interpretation is not the only step that stands between the world and our descriptions of it. The categories we use to describe the world, the social and semiotic relations we build throughout our research processes, and the models we build to account for a particular phenomenon (actively) enact particular realities. In crafting our descriptions our methods contribute to create reality. This insight constitutes the essence of my argument for an engaged scholarship. Not because I want everybody to stop using methods other than those I refer to as engaged; but because we need a larger variety of methods that enable us to enact multiple realities.

Although the argument is valid across the phenomena studied by and descriptions offered by the social sciences, I believe it is particularly relevant for researchers of entrepreneurship. One, because entrepreneurship is the process through which particular actors actively and intentionally construct organizational, economic and social realities. To study such a phenomenon with methods that do not take responsibility for their own role in constructing the realities studied is a contradiction in approaches to the world. On the one hand, such studies acknowledge reality as the result of a process of socio-material (and entrepreneurial) construction; on the other, they pay no heed to their own role in constructing the realities thus described. Two, because crafting a reality implies a political and ethical responsibility for the uses and the consequences of that reality. Often inspired by mainstream entrepreneurship research, many entrepreneurship support programs are driven by an ambition to spread an entrepreneurial spirit across society, reduce unemployment and work towards social inclusion (Högberg *et al.* forthcoming). The direction to which our descriptions contribute to shape such programs and their ambitions, depends on the extent to which we take responsibility for the realities we contribute to enact.

That is, to argue for engaged scholarship in entrepreneurship research I need first to discuss the work of mediation between the world and our descriptions of it conducted through our methods, what John Law refers to as method mediation (Law 2005). This will be done in the next two sections, each of which focus, one at a time, on a specific aspect of that work of mediation. The third and final step of my argument suggests an alternative methodological approach that negotiates both the location and the limitations of method mediation. Having shown the way in which the methods we use are deeply involved in the relationship between the world and our descriptions of it, I try to elucidate the requirements for increased awareness concerning the mediating work of method.

8.2 The operation of method mediation: simplification

One of the first aspects to consider when discussing method mediation is the question of what the steps making up the process of describing a particular phenomenon in the world are. And what their sequence is. What happens when we go from a phenomenon to a description of that phenomenon? What is captured, what is transformed, what is enacted and what disappears from view? And what does our reliance on a specific set of methods have to do with it? To answer this question, let me first take a look at the operations that build up the research processes through which we craft our descriptions.

A typical method book will characteristically offer a generalized and idealized linear description of the research process (Law and Mol 2002), a linearity that is often followed in the method section of research articles on a variety of social phenomena, including that of entrepreneurship. The starting point of such linear descriptions is the research question. A good research question, we learn, is one that clearly identifies the unit of analysis to be followed throughout the research process, thus guiding our design of the set of methods to be used, directing us through the generation of empirical material as well as shaping the analysis of that material. An example: asking about the behaviour of immigrant or female entrepreneurs clearly identifies the group of immigrant or female entrepreneurs as the subjects of study. This subsequently guides the research design towards a combination of survey, interview and (for those more adventurous) ethnographic methods applied on a population of entrepreneurs whose utmost characteristic is defined by their ethnicity or gender. As empirical material is generated, the focus is kept on the immigrant-ness or female-ness of the study objects, relating the questions and tensions that may emerge in the empirical material to this, their defining trait. Analysis and the ulterior report of it are similarly organized along the ethnic or gender lines that framed the initial question and delimited the object of study. Whether it is to conclude that such traits matter or do not matter, the work of analysis focuses on eliciting clear patterns related to the ethnicity or gender of the entrepreneur. A research question, that is, clearly and neatly identifies a phenomenon in the world that is to be the object of study, consequently shaping the research process and giving structure to our descriptions of that phenomenon.

Although the above description of a typical research process may seem somewhat of a caricature, my intention is not to make ridicule of it. Rather the opposite. The clear focus set by well-delimited research questions and rigorously designed research processes is needed if we want to give accounts that are consistent throughout. Because clear, consistent and thorough descriptions make for solid bases for making decisions concerning the world thus described. The alternative, vague and contradictory descriptions, make poor bases for decision-making.

Yet, needed as clear and consistent accounts of the world may be, the process of crafting them has at least two implications that are important for our relationship to the world so described.

First, such research processes promote an identification of the object of study from the comfort of the chair in one's office, using gap-spotting in the existing literature as its main technique to formulate research questions (Alvesson and Sandberg 2013; Sandberg and Alvesson 2011). We need, beforehand, something specific to describe, a well-delimited phenomenon's description has thus far been unsatisfactory, a well-bounded unit of analysis. The 'immigrant entrepreneur' or 'immigrant entrepreneurship' to continue with the example above. Through reading extant descriptions in the literature on the particular phenomenon, we locate a hole, a gap in the collection of academic descriptions, that has yet to be accounted for. Such as the type and density of networks of entrepreneurs identified as immigrant (Light, Bhachu and Karageorgis 2004) or the relation between national background and business ownership (Evans 1989). That hole is made into the epicentre of our research practices, thus directing our observations of the complex world into a simplified reality, a reality that may stress the ethnocultural assimilation of such entrepreneurs at the expense of ignoring, for example, 'structural changes in the urban economy and the institutional framework … within which entrepreneurs operate' (Rath and Kloosterman 2000).

As a result, and this is the second implication of the way we craft our descriptions of the world, the starting point of our descriptions is an already made social reality. The identification of the object of study previous to immersion in the field assumes the existence of a singular reality to be studied – the group of 'immigrant entrepreneurs' – which exists prior to the researcher setting to studying it, and whose definite, unambiguous nature makes it possible to capture (Law 2005). The researcher may endorse philosophies of science based on social constructivism, maintain that actors construct the world around them, and that we as students of those constructed realities can merely offer partial descriptions of them. Yet, the scientific practice of observing the construction of realities as if these existed previous to our study leads us to ignore our own role in constructing the reality that one claims to merely document. We go about recording the particular social phenomena as if we found ourselves thrown into it. To continue with the example, to maintain that we study immigrant entrepreneurs neglects the fact that groups on paper are not factual groups (Bourdieu 1985), that 'immigrant entrepreneurs' is a category that does not reflect the existence of a homogeneous or organized group, and that those that are studied through those lenses may not accept the lenses through which they are being described. Studying the pre-defined reality of 'immigrant entrepreneurship' assumes that the external imposition of a category (by the researcher among others) equals either individual identification with the category or the existence of a uniform group (Jenkins 1997). The immigrant lens reduces the complexity of situations of the so identified entrepreneurs and their everyday practices into simplified and incomplete accounts of their condition, in which all that is important becomes their being or not being an immigrant, thus ignoring other facets of their quotidian realities and other contextual and institutional factors.

Simplification, the first operation of method mediation, may be best explained through the distinction between world and reality. As Luc Boltanski indicates, whereas the world is considered as being 'everything that is the case', reality is regarded as 'what appears to hang together' (Boltanski 2011, pp. 57–58). 'We can construct the project of knowing and representing reality, [yet] describing the world, in what would be its entirety, is not within anyone's grasp' (ibid.). Instead, we select and craft simplified descriptions of the world, stories (scientific or otherwise) that make reality hang together. Although using a different vocabulary, other philosophers of science had earlier made this point. From Kuhn's paradigms and blindness for anomalies that do not fit the paradigm (Kuhn 1970) to Feyerabend's conquest (reduction) of the abundance in the world around us through academic attention and research method (Feyerabend 1975, 1999). In this sense, the mediating work of method implies the construction of fictional realities, fictional in the sense that they do not cover 'everything that is the case' but instead craft 'realities that hang together' (see Figure 8.1).

Now, it is easy to denounce simplification as fictional and violent at worst, partial and lacking at best as much poststructuralist writing does (see Derrida 1976; Foucault 1979; Lyotard 1979), consequently reacting by refusing to offer linear, ordered descriptions. Yet, instead of denouncing simplification, I would prefer to plainly realize, that such is the result of method mediation, whatever

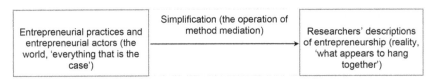

Figure 8.1 Simplification

the method. Accept it. And work with it. On this basis, I will argue for a greater variety of methods, so that we can increase the number and variety of simplified descriptions. But before I go into looking for requirements to increase the variety of our descriptions, I need to take a look into a second aspect of method mediation.

8.3 The effects of method mediation: performativity

A second aspect to consider in any discussion about the mediating work of method is performativity. Performativity, an increasingly popular notion in the social sciences today, has to do with the effects of our descriptions on the practices and the actors the sciences claim to merely observe.[1]

In the most intuitive understanding of performativity, it refers to the indirect effect of academic descriptions on the reality described through the influence these descriptions may have on the policies regulating that reality as well as through the teaching of those descriptions to future actors in that reality. That is, in this understanding, descriptions per se do not shape reality, at least not directly. The people who read our descriptions and have the power to regulate or intervene in the reality so described may however alter it through the changes they may introduce as a consequence of their reading. Figure 8.2 represents with a simple diagram the intuitive understanding of the performativity of method.

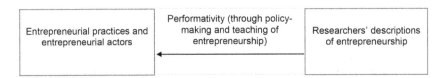

Figure 8.2 Intuitive performativity

Connecting Figure 8.2 with the one visualizing the simplifying work of method mediation we saw in the previous section (Figure 8.1), we obtain a snapshot of the most common understanding of the research process (Figure 8.3).

This linear understanding of the research process separates professional descriptions from lay readings, scientific accounts from how regulators and practitioners act on the basis of these accounts. In this view, method mediates between the world and the descriptions given by researchers, whereas lay actors

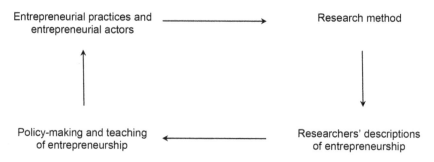

Figure 8.3 Common understanding of the research process

mediate back between academic descriptions and the world in which their actions are inserted. It is as if method itself was separate and distinct from the reality it purports to describe, as if one could stop at any single step of this circular process and thereby prevent the potential influence of our descriptions on the world. This assumes the existence of a certain, positive world on the one side – an immigrant category that distinguishes entrepreneurs – and, on the other, scientific, more or less rigorous and detailed descriptions of that world – the distinct motivations and behaviours of the pre-defined group of immigrant entrepreneurs (Basu and Altinay 2002). It implies a world that is set apart from the knower and the practices of her knowing – immigrant entrepreneurship exists independently of the methods we use to apprehend entrepreneurship and the categories we apply to describe it. It demands methods that are able to capture that separate world; and it results in descriptions that can easily be distinguished from the social world thus depicted.

8.3.1 A more sophisticated version of performativity

This however is not the whole story of how the research process works. The world, the methods for its study, and the descriptions such methods come up with, are not as separate as that linear understanding makes it seem. For one, through our research practices researchers '*participate in, reflect upon* and *enact* the social' realities studied (Law and Urry 2004, p. 392).[2] The categories we use to design our studies shape our research questions, direct our method practices and structure our descriptions, thus rendering reality visible, and actionable, to us (Asplund 1970). That is, knowledge of the social world also guides the actions of researchers and practitioners. Both types of actors, that is, contribute to produce the social world they know. This argument has been made with force for economics, Callon showing us the extent to which that form of knowledge has contributed to create that of which it speaks.[3] This is so not only for the more quantitative, harder versions of the social sciences; but also for its qualitative, softer variations, which, in turn, claims to 'make sense only if they are located in the contexts that produced them' (Law and Urry 2004, p. 392).

Developing this line of argument, a more sophisticated understanding of performativity looks at the way in which the very language[4] used in our methods and descriptions intervenes in and shapes the world we claim to merely depict. That is, what appears to be neutral descriptions of particular groups and actors implies no neutral work. First, because in the effort to identify and classify actors and entities, academic descriptions and method practices have a tendency to *prescribe* traits and behaviours to the individuals so classified. To continue with the example of the 'immigrant entrepreneur', just like other group categories, this is a prescription disguised as description (Bourdieu 1991a). The high-tech entrepreneur of foreign origin is rarely, if ever, included in that category; a silent demarcation of the group, this, that tells of traits and behaviours prescribed in the seemingly neutral 'immigrant' tag. Second, because each description encourages a way to look at and divide the world to the detriment of other, different, ways. To choose ethnicity (or gender) as a principle to group people, illustrate their behaviour and describe social dynamics is also to dismiss other ways to understand people, their behaviour and the social world they live in. Economic background, educational level, or political awareness could, just as well, have been used to understand, and act on, individual behaviours and social dynamics.

8.3.2 *Performativity highlights the political in scientific methods and descriptions*

It is here that descriptions, scientific or not, as well as methods become political. The terms we use to identify, classify and describe a particular group or specific actors do more than simply elicit that group and those actors. They put forward a principle of vision and division, a boundary that may not be explicit but that divides the social world thus described. To refer to someone as 'immigrant' forces an ethnic boundary into our organization of the social, a boundary that actively divides the social world into particular groups. Even if that group only exists on paper (Bourdieu 1985), where one's roots once were becomes the important aspect in the description, ethnicity becoming the boundary structuring scientific debate and conjuring up social reality. One may choose to accept or reject that categorical boundary, but regardless of one's position, one needs to refer to the group so created. That is, the methodological struggle to articulate descriptions is also a struggle to demarcate and organize reality.

Even if the researcher is satisfied to offer a description of 'what appears to hang together', the description changes 'that which is the case' (Bourdieu 1991b, p. 222). To put it in the terms used in this essay: Even if the researcher is satisfied to offer a simplified description of reality, the description changes the world. To continue with the example of the 'immigrant entrepreneur': Nobody can deny that there are names and surnames that do not belong to the national tradition. Uncontroversial facts such as skin colour, country of birth, or residential neighbourhood become the basis for 'natural' group categories grounded on 'natural' observations. Helped by the boundaries that organize our research descriptions – immigrant-ness – 'natural' (real) facts acquire a social meaning that is superimposed to facts related to skin, country, or neighbourhood. Facts are made 'to hang together' through the categories imposed on the people described – 'immigrant' vs. 'non-immigrant'. Yet both the dividing boundary as well as where it is drawn are arbitrary. Social groups defined along other criteria do not always coincide. The 'immigrant' group would include different sets of individuals depending on whether the criteria for the group's demarcation is an individual's country of birth, the country of birth of one's parents, length of residence in the new country, the economic situation of one's family, or educational level (Sassen 2003). A different boundary would have resulted in a different description and thereby in a different group reality.

This is what Bourdieu calls 'theory effect'; that is, the effect of forcing a principle of vision and division that occurs in attempts to describe (Bourdieu 1991a, p. 132). '[B]y expressing in a coherent and empirically valid discourse what was previously ignored, i.e., what was implicit or repressed, it transforms the representation of the social world as well as simultaneously transforming the social world itself, at least to the extent that it renders possible practices that conform to this transformed representation' (ibid., p. 133).[5] From the decision of the entrepreneur concerning who to partner with, to the practices of business support organisations concerning support to entrepreneurs (Högberg *et al.* forthcoming), or the political responses to thusly framed immigrant entrepreneurs (e.g. Collins 2003), these acts are grounded on descriptions based on the arbitrary boundary. And in what relates research practices, we may in various ways try to deem whether there exists or not an ethnic distinction among entrepreneurs; but first, one needs to look at those actors through ethnic lenses.

8.3.3 From observing to intervening

Performativity, in both its intuitive and sophisticated versions, is thus the second operation of method mediation: the idea that method, through either the relationships it makes or the categories it chooses to focus on, contributes to craft the realities it purports to merely register. It is in this sense that the insight of performativity goes beyond those of perspectivism and constructivism. While perspective is about the standpoints from which to look at the world and tell our descriptions, constructivist stories are most often about the plurality of alternatives that could have been possible some time in the past but disappeared before they ever had a chance (Mol 1999). Both perspective and construction *look at* reality from a distance, either as given or as already made. Both base the work of method on a metaphor of vision: observing the world as it is either given to us or constructed by us. Performativity, on the other hand, moves away from such vision metaphors and uses those of intervention, of performance (ibid.). The scientist is not an actor separate from the reality studied. Although through a different set of practices – scientific, methodological – the scientist is an active actor shaping the reality she describes. Returning to Boltanski's distinction between the world and reality, the insight of the performativity of method helps us add some nuance about the nature of reality: rather than simply being 'what *appears* to hang together' (a definition that builds on the metaphor of vision), reality is 'what *is made* to hang together', 'made' also by the researcher through method mediation.

The implications of this argument are radical for the practice of social research as it both liberates researchers from strict method protocols and gives them responsibility for the realities described. If, as performativity indicates, the singular, definite, prior and simplified realities arrived at through method mediation are also made, enacted – and enacted in part by us through our categories and method practices – then, we have room to arrange different realities by negotiating our methods. Rather than adopting a nihilist attitude where anything goes, the matter is one of discussing what type of realities *we wish* to enact, a discussion that, as I have been arguing, is entangled with that of method mediation. Accordingly, the relationship knower-known-knowledge becomes not only a matter of methods and epistemologies but also a question of ethics and politics (Haraway 1988). How to start tackling such ethical and political conundrums? As a first step, let me suggest moving the starting point of our descriptions.

8.4 Engaged scholarship: moving the starting point of our descriptions

By highlighting the effects of our method practices and our descriptions on the reality studied, performativity is an argument that transforms the linearity of the research process that is so often implied in method books into an iterative, everemergent process in which reality, descriptions and research practices are mutually constitutive. The known, the knowledge and the knower – in the sense of the scientific practices that define her – are inextricably woven together. Such is the work of method mediation. As a result, the research process becomes a process that both retro-actively and pro-actively enacts that of which it speaks. The reality described coalesces with the methods and the language of the knower. A reformulation of Figure 8.3 may help visualize this understanding of method mediation in the research process (Figure 8.4).

No longer is the reality to describe something prior to the researcher's entry into the field. Nor is it separate. Instead, the reality to describe is being produced as it is being described. As many Swedish citizens born from foreign parents become painfully aware of when they come out of the neighbourhood where they grew up, the dominant gaze describes them along identity lines which they did not use previous to that encounter but through which they learn to see the world and themselves after they have been so described.[6] Reality, that is, results from a practice of naming and relating, a practice that researchers conduct through method mediation. In other words, reality arises contemporaneously to the research process.

If this is the case, then, where do we start our descriptions from? If 'reality is a relational effect produced in arrangements generated in social science' (Law

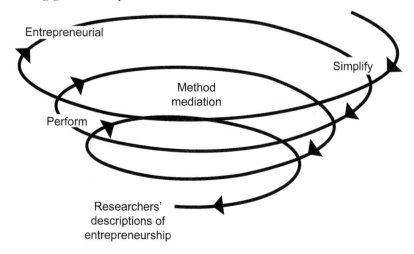

Figure 8.4 Method mediation

and Urry 2004, p. 394), then, there are several possible entry points to start our descriptions from. Not only is there space to design different arrangements for method mediation (Law 2005, see next section), there is also room for moving the place and time from which we start our mediations. From the singular, definite and prior realities implied in a separate world, to the multi-voiced, unspecified and concurrent realities of an emergent world.

This is the move taken by a 'scholarship of engagement' (Boyer 1996). With engaged scholarship I refer to a participatory approach that builds on an analysis of the broader power structures embedded both in the research relation as well as in the realities being studied.[7] Attending to issues of power in the research process, it proposes engagement in the communities studied as a way to deal with the political-theoretical twosome. Experimenting with different forms to build reciprocal, collaborative relations with those studied, engaged scholars aim at the co-production of knowledge, the articulation of research methods/ practices embedded in communities, and the remaking of reality. In such research processes there is both an awareness of the politics of method as well as a commitment to develop practices that may carve spaces for transformative politics.

Let me elaborate. The engaged scholar moves her practices and methods straight into the field, into the reality that is in the process of being constructed, or rather, co-constructed together with other actors in the field. Method mediation becomes one with the realities mediated. Engagement, that is, implies a situated and active, yet reflexive, involvement with the world that the scholar aims to describe (Barinaga and Parker 2013) but that she is also contributing to produce. The fly on the wall is long gone. Aware of the impossibility leading an existence that is separate and distinct to the realities studied, the engaged scholar takes responsibility for the performativity of method by consciously siding with certain realities in the field.

Put differently, the argument of simplification achieved through method mediation is also an argument that locates the starting point of our descriptions in a moment posterior to, and at a place separate from, the realities described. As if realities existed prior to and distinct from the researcher and her method practices; or there was a singular, definite reality that the researcher is able to capture with her methods after the fact. Moving the starting point of our descriptions from an already made social reality to the social world in the process of being made (Boltanski 2011, pp. 43–44), starting our descriptions from the moment the scholar makes realities together with other actors in the field studied, has the potential to offer more varied descriptions. And thereby, more varied realities. Such a change of starting point implies actively and consciously engaging with the realities described/enacted, thus changing both the realities so described and our descriptions of them. To the knower-known-knowledge triad, we are adding the knower's position in time and place. It is not only a matter of research practices; it is also a question of the location of those practices.

The argument on simplification is an argument about knowledge, about the nature of the knowledge of the world that we are able to generate with our methods. That is, simplification is, in essence, an epistemological argument. Performativity, on the other hand, is an argument about reality, about the effects of our methods on the reality that we claim to only register. That is, performativity is in character an ontological argument, an argument on the ontological politics of method (Mol 1999; Mol and Law 2002). As a corollary of this line of argument: moving the starting point of our descriptions from a prior, already made reality to an ever-emergent reality in which the researcher is engaged has implications both for the character of the knowledge generated as well as for the nature and strength of the realities enacted.

And although, as some have argued (Mol 1999, pp. 83–85), we may not have a clear choice as to which realities contribute to performance, we do have a responsibility for the politics of our method mediations. What, then, should we require of engaged method mediations?

8.5 Requirements on the engaged scholar

Just to be clear. My argument is not that our methods are wrong, our practices unmoral, and our knowledge delusional. No matter what methods we put to work or what practices we live with, our mediations are bound to simplify, singularize and enact the realities we toil with. Because the world is emergent, and complex, and messy, while our method practices are limited by the place and time from which we start (research budgets, project deadlines, university sympathies), as well as by language mechanics, we cannot but adopt a pragmatic attitude: Accept the simplification of reality performed through our mediations.

Accepting simplification however does not mean that all method mediations are to work along the same simplifying boundaries. If method entails the performance of a certain reality, then we could increase the number and variety of realities by expanding the forms and modalities of our methods. My argument is then an appeal to increase the variety of method mediations. It is a plea to experiment with a heterogeneity of method assemblages (Law 2004), with manifold engagements with the realities studied, with multiple relationships to the world.

Beware, and at risk of being repetitive: Choosing a method means choosing what reality to perform. 'Choice incorporated' as Mol refers to it (Mol 1999, p. 86). With the choice of method comes the answer to political and ontological questions such as 'what realities should we bring into being?' (Law and Urry 2004, p. 396) or 'what are the *effects* that we should be seeking?' (Mol 1999, p. 86).[8] For method and reality are tightly entangled. For not only the form of our descriptions, but also what we describe is implicit in the methods we put to work for crafting our descriptions. What reality we end up affecting is incorporated in the techniques, procedures, practices and language of our mediations.

8.5.1 *Situated*

Being responsive to ontological politics is then about taking responsibility for the politics of our methods. A first step in this direction was indicated in the previous section: Move the starting point of our descriptions into the process of scholarly enacting the realities described. This relocates research practices into the very heart of reality performance and results in what, after Haraway's 1988's influential piece, is referred to as 'situated knowledges'. This is the first requirement on a scholarship of engagement: 'Situated'. Not because traditional accounts of knowledge are not told from particular locations. As we saw, these are often told from a place posterior to the reality so known. They are indeed located, though not explicitly localized. 'Knowledge*s*', in the plural, not because traditional accounts of knowledge are not varied, but because they are told from a position of totalizing vision.

This first requirement necessarily forces the researcher to acknowledge her body. Localized knowledge practices are positioned in a specific place, within a stream of actions, and in a particular body. In traditional accounts of knowledge, as we have seen, vision was 'used to signify a leap out of the marked body and into a conquering gaze from nowhere' (Haraway 1988, p. 581), or rather, a gaze from an un-acknowledged posterior reality. And yet, as I have argued, vision is always from somewhere. A somewhere that is both a place and a body. As many an ethnographer is mindful of, respondents and observed react to the social categories that mark the body of the researcher (Coffey 1999), the researcher's body thus shaping the accounts elicited from the field. Received by those studied as a female or male body, a white or coloured body, a young or aged body – some of the explicit categories framing the body – the scholar is awarded various degrees of recognition and thus given more or less space to intervene in the field. A coloured young female body has better prospects of being embraced by poor female subordinated micro-entrepreneurs than the white mature male body of her research colleague. That is, engaged scholarship is necessarily embodied, shaped by the relationships between the embodied researcher and the bodies of those researched.

8.5.2 *Reflexive*

Because of the nature and depth of access granted to particular researcher bodies, situated knowledge practices require the engaged scholar to side with particular realities. The immigrant woman will easily be able to participate in the realities of female immigrant micro-entrepreneurs. She probably won't have as easy an access to the entrepreneurial realities of elder white risk capitalists. Choice incorporated, once more. And once more, the argument is *not* not to take knowledge and facts seriously. For indeed they are serious. Knowledge and facts are enacting the realities many of us inhabit. The argument is instead to take seriously the doing, ours too, of that knowledge and those facts; to reflect on how our located and embodied knowledge practices result in a partial knowledge and a determinate reality; to be cognisant of and responsible for the politics of our method mediations. Reflexivity, that is, is the second requirement on the engaged scholar. Differently, a scholarship of engagement needs to be reflective on the scholar's own role in enacting that which she describes. Reflexive on the categories she prefers to use. Also reflexive on the concrete socio-material relations that she contributes to enact in the local realities she is immersed in.

8.5.3 *Intentionally political*

As a consequence of reflexivity, and this is the third requirement to increase the variety of method practices, engaged scholarship is intentionally political. Not because research practices located posterior to a single and determine reality are not political. Political, they always were, as vision is never passive, specific ways of seeing implying specific positions and specific ways of life. Intentionally political, however, they seldom are. By this I mean actively and consciously engaging in shaping reality, interfering to delimit actors and possibilities, getting involved in the 'making of what hangs together'. Not only aware of the ontological (and epistemological) politics involved in method mediations. But also deliberately implicated in the making of that reality. In this way, the engaged scholar stresses the importance of combining theoretical concerns and methodological pre-occupations with a serious commitment to producing socially and politically rele-vant scholarship that contributes to making different (hopefully more just) realities.

Situated and embodied, reflexive and purposely performative (Barinaga and Parker 2013), all requirements push scholarship away from the metaphor of vision and into a metaphor of intervention. Engaged scholarship is a scholarship that starts from an awareness of the ontological politics implied in our metho-dological practices; a scholarship that is responsive to the politics of domination implied in our scientific engagement; a scholarship that is not only judged by its truth value but also by criteria that has to do with the justice of the realities it contributes to enact; a scholarship that is deeply involved in the here and now, and that takes the body and its involvement in the world as the tool and strategy for research.

8.6 Open questions for researchers of entrepreneurship

How do we translate the political insight gained through an awareness of method mediations into the field of entrepreneurship studies? Through examples, this essay has focused on what simplification and performativity mean within that field. It then highlighted general requirements to demand from a scholarship that takes responsibility for the effects of its simplifications. The essay has yet to elaborate on what taking responsibility for such effects means for entrepreneurship scholars. Apart from ethnographically inspired methods that move the starting point of the research process to the midst of reality making, apart from mediations that are reflexive of their location and performativity, what do researchers of entrepreneurship need to consider if they are committed to responsible and more heterogeneous accounts of entrepreneurial practices?

I am not sure I can fully answer that question. I can however start sketching a few questions that need to be addressed in a way to develop more varied accounts (Alvesson and Sandberg 2013) and more heterogeneous realities. These questions, it is my belief, may be able to help us formulate novel research questions that challenge existing theories and produce more imaginative empirical studies.

The questions entrepreneurship scholars should ask as they craft their descriptions have to do with the position from which these descriptions are built as well as with the type of practices they engage in:

- Where to craft our accounts of entrepreneurial practices from? From after the fact? From the midst of someone else's entrepreneurial process? Why not from the embodiment of my own entrepreneurial practice?
- What are the limits of our crafting? Body included. That is, how is our position in the here and now delineating the stories we craft?
- Who do we craft our descriptions with? Or, how participatory should our methods be? To what extent and in what form are we inviting others, included those being studied, in the co-production of knowledge?
- Who is empowered by our descriptions and who is made to disappear? In the terms used throughout this essay, what, or who, are we simplifying away?
- What other practices, besides methodological, do we wish to pursue? For instance, what implications does a commitment to crafting more just realities have on the collaborations we build, on the type of funding we seek, and on the type and form of the texts we publish?
- What do we craft our descriptions for? Formulated in more general terms, what criteria do we use to assess our (and others') research?
- What happens if we do not ask these questions?

These questions relate to the form, depth and intensity of our engagement. They stem not from a metaphor of vision that puts the correspondence theory of truth at the heart of research efforts, but from a metaphor of intervention that recognizes the mutual responsiveness implicating researcher and reality into one another. Entrepreneurship scholars are responding to these questions in multiple ways. From Bengt Johanisson's experiments with the auto-ethnography of the entrepreneurial process instigated by the researcher himself (Johanisson 2005, 2011; Steyaert 2011; see also my own efforts in this direction in Barinaga 2014), or Daniel Hjorth's involvement in shaping the philosophy and program of The Creative Plot, an incubator for the cultural and creative industries (Hjorth 2013), to those that suggest novel entrepreneurial practices in blogs and practitioner-oriented journals (see for instance Soule 2013), promote novel forms of entrepreneurship through the foundation of university-business centres (e.g. Gregory Dees' Center for the Advancement of Social Entrepreneurship – CASE – at Duke University) or my own efforts to train community activists and develop manuals for community-based social entrepreneurship (Barinaga 2015).

Becoming entrepreneurs, counsellors, bloggers, and activists, these entrepreneurship scholars are exploring new ways to engage with the realities they are researching in the hope of remaking them hopefully in a better way. This brings us to the thorny issue of the criteria to use when assessing research and the realities it contributes to make. Whatever the character of the scholar's engagement, what criteria should we use to evaluate entrepreneurship research? Other values may be just as appropriate: justice, equality and personal commitment.

I am not sure about what kind of realities and what type of descriptions the many possible answers to the above questions are going to result in. Yet, because they open up the possibility for different and more responsible method mediations, such questions lead to an increased variety of descriptions; and thereby to a multiplication of realities. Varied method arrangements hold the promise of 'not always reinforc[ing] the same simplicities or impos[ing] the same silences' (Mol and Law 2002, p. 7).

The argument presented in this essay does not call for the choice between simplifying or not. Methods simplify. Full stop. The essay calls instead for a discussion of what simplification/s do we wish to perform. It is an argument for an increase in the number and variety of simplified descriptions. And to do that, we need methods that allow us to do the work of crafting differently.

Notes

1 Whereas this has been acknowledged in the social sciences for a long time – thus the exhortations to ethnographers to reduce their influence by trying to 'be the fly-on-the-wall' – Science and Technology Studies (STS) have extended this claim into the, if you want, harder natural sciences. Things of nature as well as things of technology have become socio-material networks affected by the scientific practices in place for their study. For some examples, see Latour and Woolgar 1979; Law and Callon 1988; Mol 2001.

2 Emphasis in the original.
3 For some examples, see Callon 1998; MacKenzie 2011 as well as chapters in the volume *Do Economists Make Markets? On the Performativity of Economics*, edited by MacKenzie, Muniesa and Siu 2007.
4 A swift note on what performativity scholars refer to when they talk about scientific language may be due here. They refer to (1) the *concepts* used in research accounts; and (2) the theories that identify *relations* among such concepts.
5 Both Pierre Bourdieu and Johan Asplund mention Karl Marx and his theory of class conflict as the ultimate example of theory effect since it is only after him that it is possible to describe social dynamics with the help of class and class conflict, as well as organize political parties and other social actors along class boundaries (Asplund 1970; Bourdieu 1991a).
6 A quote from my previous research illustrates the constitutive effect of descriptions: '*Cajsa*. I grew up in Bredäng, an immigrant area, you know. Much more so now than when we lived there. It's called "the Orient Express" – the underground's red line to the south because there are so many immigrants there. I went to school and hanged out with both Swedes and immigrants. They were as I was. Maybe someone had one parent coming from Sweden and the other parent from another country. I always felt Swedish. I was a Swede! If someone asked me, I always presented myself as a Swede. Grew up here, speak Swedish and have always lived here. I thought Sweden was that way. Until I started to study at KTH. My first week there was a shock. There were only Swedes, whole Swedes. They saw something in me, it must have been my behaviour or my appearance, I don't know. But they asked, "Where do you come from, actually?" Since then, I don't see myself as a Swede. I thought, "I don't think like them, I don't have the same life as them." *EB* What do you mean? *Cajsa*. They had a family and celebrated Mid-Summer with their family. I've never celebrated Mid-Summer, I've never needed to celebrate it. My friends came from other countries as well and didn't celebrate Mid-Summer either. It was that way with many things, it's many small things … You get used after a while. And now, whenever I go to the suburbs, it's just the opposite – "Wow! How many immigrants!" I get surprised that there are so many immigrants' (Barinaga 2010, pp. 155–156).
7 Note that this definition of engaged scholarship goes beyond the one popularized by Andrew H. Van de Ven (2007). Focusing on the gap between theory and practice and aiming at increasing the relevance of research, Van de Ven ignores the power dynamics involved in the research process, those discussed in this essay as simplification and performativity. A discussion on the political (and ideological) dimension of research co-constructed with those being studied is completely absent in Van de Ven's approach. He bases his discussion as a purely epistemological problem – the theory-practice gap – without reference to the subversive potential of engaged scholarship – the ontological politics that the next section of this essay elaborates more on.
8 Emphasis in the original.

References

Alvesson, M. and Sandberg, J. (2013) *Constructing Research Questions: Doing Interesting Research*. Thousand Oaks, CA: Sage.
Asplund, J. (1970) *Om undran inför samhället*. Lund: Argos.
Barinaga, E. (2010) *Powerful Dichotomies: Inclusion and Exclusion in the Information Society*. Stockholm: EFI.
Barinaga, E. (2014) *Social Entrepreneurship: Cases and Concepts*. Lund: Studentlitteratur.
Barinaga, E. (2015) *Betongen berättar: Handbok för muralaktivister (Handbook for Community Activists)*. Stockholm: ETC.

Barinaga, E. and Parker, P. (2013) 'Community-engaged scholarship: Creating participative spaces for transformative politics', *Tamara: Journal for Critical Organization Inquiry*, 11(4), pp. 5–11.

Basu, A. and Altinay, E. (2002) 'The interaction between culture and entrepreneurship in London's immigrant businesses', *International Small Business Journal*, 20(4), pp. 371–393.

Boltanski, L. (2011) *On Critique: A Sociology of Emancipation*. Cambridge: Polity Press.

Bourdieu, P. (1985) 'The social space and the genesis of groups', *Theory and Methods*, 24(2), pp. 195–220.

Bourdieu, P. (1991a) 'Description and prescription: The conditions of possibility and the limits of political effectiveness'. In *Language & Symbolic Power*. Cambridge: Polity Press.

Bourdieu, P. (1991b) 'Identity and representation: Elements for a critical reflection on the idea of region'. In *Language & Symbolic Power*. Cambridge: Polity Press.

Boyer, E.L. (1996) 'The scholarship of engagement', *Journal of Public Service and Outreach*, 1(1), pp. 11–20.

Callon, M. (1998) *The Laws of the Markets*. Oxford: Blackwell and the *Sociological Review*.

Coffey, A. (1999) 'The embodiment of fieldwork'. In *The Ethnographic Self: Fieldwork and the Representation of Identity*. Thousand Oaks, CA: Sage, Chapter 4.

Collins, J. (2003) 'Cultural diversity and entrepreneurship: Policy responses to immigrant entrepreneurs in Australia', *Entrepreneurship and Regional Development*, 15(2), pp. 137–149.

Derrida, J. (1976) *Speech and Phenomenon*. Evanston, IL: Northwestern University Press.

Evans, M.D.R. (1989) 'Immigrant entrepreneurship: Effects of ethnic market size and isolated labor pool', *American Journal of Sociology*, 54(6), pp. 950–962.

Feyerabend, P. (1975) *Against Method*. London: New Left Books.

Feyerabend, P. (1999) *Conquest of Abundance: A Tale of Abstraction Versus the Richness of Being*. Edited by Bert Terpstra. Chicago, IL: University of Chicago Press.

Foucault, M. (1979) *The Archeology of Knowledge*. New York: Harper and Row.

Haraway, D. (1988) 'Situated knowledges: The science question in feminism and the privilege of partial perspective', *Feminist Studies*, 14(3), pp. 575–599.

Hjorth, D. (2013) *Don't Sit on It! A Study of What No Longer Can Be Called Incubation*. Lund: Ideon Innovation.

Högberg, L., Schölin, T., Ram, M. and Jones, T. (forthcoming) 'Categorising and labelling entrepreneurs: Business support organisations constructing the other through prefixes of ethnicity and immigrantship', *International Small Business Journal*.

Jenkins, R. (1997) *Rethinking Ethnicity: Arguments and Explorations*. London: Sage.

Johannisson, B. (2005) *Entreprenörskapets väsen*. Lund: Studentlitteratur.

Johannisson, B. (2011) 'Towards a practice theory of entrepreneuring', *Small Business Economics*, 36(2), pp. 135–150.

Kuhn, T.S. (1970) *The Structure of Scientific Revolutions*. Chicago, IL: University of Chicago Press.

Latour, B. and Woolgar, S. (1979) *Laboratory Life: The Social Construction of Scientific Facts*. Beverly Hills, CA and London: Sage.

Law, J. (2005) *After Method: Mess in Social Science Research*. London and New York: Routledge.

Law, J. and Callon, M. (1988) 'Engineering and sociology in a military aircraft project: A network analysis of technical change', *Social Problems*, 35, pp. 284–297.

Law, J. and Mol, A. (2002) *Complexities: Social Studies of Knowledge Practices*. Durham, NC and London: Duke University Press.

Law, J. and Urry, J. (2004) 'Enacting the social', *Economy and Society*, 33(3), pp. 390–410.

Light, I., Bhachu, P. and Karageorgis, S. (2004) 'Migration networks and immigrant entrepreneurship'. In Light, I. and Bhachu, P. (eds) *Immigration and Entrepreneurship: Culture, Capital, and Ethnic Networks*. New York: Transaction Publishers.

Lyotard, J.F. (1979) *The Postmodern Condition: A Report on Knowledge*. Trans. Geoff Bennington and Brian Massumi. Manchester: Manchester University Press.

MacKenzie, D. (2011) 'The big bad wolf and the rational market: Portfolio insurance, the 1987 crash and the performativity of economics', *Economy and Society*, 33(3), pp. 303–334.

MacKenzie, D., Muniesa, F. and Siu, L. (2007) *Do Economists Make Markets? On the Performativity of Economics*. Princeton, NJ: Princeton University Press.

Mol, A. (1999) 'Ontological politics: A word and some questions'. In Law, J. and Hassard, J. (eds) *Actor Network and After*. Oxford and Keele: Blackwell and the *Sociological Review*, pp. 74–89.

Mol, A. (2001) *The Body Multiple: Artherosclerosis in Practice*. Durham, NC and London: Duke University Press.

Mol, A. and Law, J. (2002) 'Complexities: An introduction'. In Law, J. and Mol, A. (eds) *Complexities: Social Studies of Knowledge Practices*. Durham, NC and London: Duke University Press, pp. 1–22.

Rath, J. and Kloosterman, R. (2000) 'Outsiders' business: A critical review of research on immigrant entrepreneurship', *International Migration Review*, 34(3), pp. 657–681.

Sandberg, J. and Alvesson, M. (2011) 'Ways of constructing research questions: Gap-spotting or problematization?', *Organization Studies*, 18(1), pp. 23–44.

Sassen, S. (2003) 'Citizenship destabilized', *Liberal Education*, Spring, pp. 14–21.

Soule, S. (2013) 'Why design thinking is an effective tool for social entrepreneurs', *Stanford Center for Social Innovation's blog*.

Steyaert, C. (2011) 'Entrepreneurship as in(ter)vention: Reconsidering the conceptual politics of method in entrepreneurship studies', *Entrepreneurship and Regional Development*, 23(1–2), pp. 77–88.

Strathern, M. (1987) 'Out of context: The persuasive fictions of anthropology', *Current Anthropology*, 28(3), pp. 251–281.

Van de Ven, A.H. (2007) *Engaged Scholarship: A Guide for Organizational and Social Research*. Oxford: Oxford University Press.

9 Is there still a Heffalump in the room?

Examining paradigms in historical entrepreneurship research

Luke Pittaway and Richard Tunstall

9.1 Introduction

In this chapter we seek to explore the underlying assumptions of historic entrepreneurship thinking to consider its consequences for contemporary thought. Kilby (1971) is widely quoted as criticising the search for a definition of entrepreneurship through this analogy with A.A. Milne's 'Winnie-the-Pooh' where attempts are made to describe and trap a mythical Heffalump. Kilby argued that the entrepreneur as a focus of research had escaped explanation because each researcher had applied an approach that described specific aspects yet did not capture the whole. In A.A. Milne's (1926) story, the uncritical application of definitions leads to the development of traps which serve only to ensnare the hunters themselves. In this chapter, therefore, we seek to build from this idea by illustrating how common underlying meta-theories have caused a degree of myopia in entrepreneurship theory and we argue for the use of meta-theoretical diversity in entrepreneurship thought as a means to consider a wider range of approaches. We categorize this willingness to consider a diverse set of underlying philosophies as an 'interpretive' perspective to the construction of theory (Grant and Perren 2002).

Many years have passed since Kilby (1971) made this point. Thinking in entrepreneurship research has advanced and yet there is a nagging suspicion amongst many, as articulated in this book, that while research studies have become more nuanced, certain 'traps' have once again grown to dominate research (Grant and Perren 2002; Pittaway 2005). Indeed, it can be argued that other philosophies have been neglected or fragmented, obscuring our understanding of the range of phenomena associated with entrepreneurship (Davidsson, Low and Wright 2001; Jennings, Perren and Carter 2005; Sarasvathy 2004). This chapter aims to ask whether in the pursuit of common definition and measurement, entrepreneurship researchers have become too focused on constructing more intricate traps while failing to appreciate the underlying assumptions that guide them to different, and yet, not completely incompatible views of entrepreneurship. As we present them later, the common traps appear to include: an overriding desire on the part of some researchers to create a scientific rather than a social scientific discipline; a common under-estimation of social and institutional factors; and, an assumption that entrepreneurs are 'special' individuals.

This chapter builds on the work of Pittaway (2005) by considering historical research in entrepreneurship. It will explore the underlying meta-theories used with the aim of illustrating the dangers of applying assumptions without fully considering their implications. The chapter will then progress to consider how appreciation of such 'taken-for-granted' assumptions can inform the development of contemporary theory and research. The contribution of this work is to lay out the foundation philosophies of prior entrepreneurship theory, so that they can be appreciated and understood. By laying out these foundations we contend that researchers can more carefully consider the philosophical assumptions that guide their own research and be more aware of the implications such assumptions may have.

9.2 Meta-theory and its implications

Meta-theory is the deeper assumptions that researchers apply when they construct theories and conduct empirical research (Burrell and Morgan 1979). Researchers in many fields of study actively debate and consider these prior assumptions, yet in entrepreneurship research, these assumptions are rarely discussed (Ogbor 2000).

9.2.1 Basic philosophies

Meta-theories are basic philosophies that apply one stance on a subject and in doing so inherently exclude alternatives. They come in several forms:

- Ontological assumptions focus on the 'nature of being' and thus focus on questions about the nature of reality. The concreteness of nature beyond human consciousness and reality's interpretation by humans is a central consideration. Within entrepreneurship such assumptions may, for example, guide how researchers view 'opportunity' (Alvarez *et al.* 2014; Fischer *et al.* 1997). Is it constructed in the mind of the entrepreneur and created by independent human action or is it 'out-there' waiting to be discovered by entrepreneurs who have a special ability to sense it (Learned 1992)?
- Epistemological assumptions are focused on the 'nature of knowledge' and consider how knowledge is constructed. Debates focus on how people conceptualize and understand the world and ask questions about what constitutes knowledge. In entrepreneurship, questions about knowledge construction often revolve around issues of 'definition' and 'measurement' (Gartner 2001; Shane and Venkataraman 2000). What is the best way to capture and understand knowledge about entrepreneurship, what traps are valid and how should we use them? How should entrepreneurship be defined? And, should it be considered and researched in a 'normative scientific' manner rather than with a focus on the practical experiences of individuals?
- Axiological assumptions come in two forms: 'ethics' and 'aesthetics', and are focused on the 'nature of value'. Assumptions about 'ethics' are most

relevant and generate questions about underlying, often implicit values, that govern what is considered 'good' or 'correct' for individual and social conduct. In entrepreneurship, common axioms that exist include, for example, a focus on 'individualism', a taken-for-granted view that entrepreneurship is 'good' and an over-emphasis on the positive outcomes of entrepreneurial effort (Ogbor 2000).

- Assumptions about human nature concentrate on prior beliefs about humankind and the underlying factors that guide human behaviour. Common debates include 'nature' versus 'nurture' and 'free will' versus 'determinism' (Carland, Hoy and Carland 1988; Gartner 1989). In entrepreneurship these assumptions can influence the extent to which entrepreneurial action is considered to be learnt or naturally acquired and the extent to which entrepreneurs are influenced by their environment.

- Assumptions about the nature of society overlap both with axiology and human nature and questions are asked about the relationship between human beings and the societies they construct. A common theme focuses on 'order and stability' versus 'conflict and change' and the extent to which society can be viewed as stable or undergoing constant contradictions, stress and turbulent change. Assumptions in entrepreneurship hinge on whether the entrepreneur is considered to be a part of such change, which is best articulated through Schumpeter's concept of creative destruction (Pittaway 2005).

Within each of these areas there are many arguments and differences of position that guide debate and underpin theory. Occasionally empirical observations can undermine such taken-for-granted tenets and be the cause of 'paradigm shifts' (Kuhn 1962). Such shifts can be viewed to have occurred in the field of entrepreneurship, for example, in the early 1980s entrepreneurship researchers moved away from a focus on the 'entrepreneurial personality' to consider what entrepreneurs 'do', taking on a different set of underlying meta-theoretical assumptions (Bygrave 1989). Another shift can be observed to have occurred in the late 1990s and early 2000s when researchers began to move away from 'new venture creation' perspectives of 'doing' entrepreneurship to a focus more on the 'opportunity recognition' part of the process (Alvarez *et al.* 2014).

9.2.2 *Research paradigms*

Such shifts were observed in the field of organizational studies by Burrell and Morgan (1979), who then led debates about the nature of these meta-theories, and their impact on the construction of theory. The paradigms presented by Burrell and Morgan positioned different philosophical assumptions into dichotomous relationships (e.g. relativity versus realism and interpretive knowledge construction versus positivism) and positioned these along two dimensions, the 'objective versus subjective' dimension and the 'sociology of radical change versus the sociology of regulation' dimension. Using these dimensions four paradigms of social science were constructed (Burrell and Morgan 1979; Pittaway 2005) and these are presented in Figure 9.1.

The concept of paradigms of social science received much attention in organizational studies in the 1980s and 1990s. Within entrepreneurship Burrell and Morgan's (1979) paradigms were considered to be useful tools to review, and then reflect on, the underlying assumptions guiding prior studies (Grant and Perren 2002; Pittaway 2005). The view that they could be a useful 'tool' for unpicking implicit assumptions within subjects was supported by other fields where the paradigms were also used to make explicit taken-for-granted assumptions (Nightingale and Cromby 1999; Parker 1998; Willmott 1993).

Grant and Perren's (2002) work, for example, reviewed developments in research in entrepreneurship in the late 1990s using the paradigms to assess the

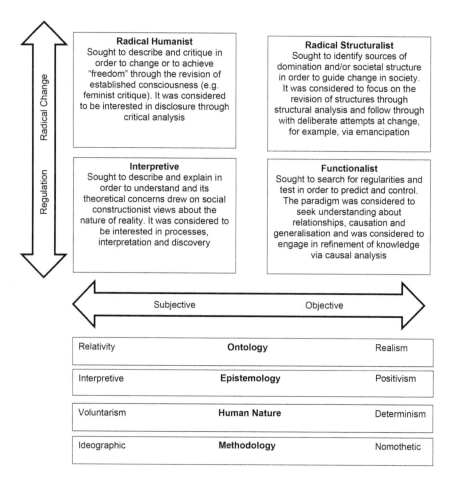

Figure 9.1 BM's sociological paradigms

underlying meta-theoretical assumptions applied and concluded that entrepreneurship research was dominated by functionalist assumptions. The study observed that entrepreneurship research had broadly applied realist, positivist, determinist meta-theoretical assumptions and nomothetic methodological assumptions (Grant and Perren 2002). Importantly for this book, it critiqued entrepreneurship research for excluding interpretive research from mainstream journals and considered that entrepreneurship research had further largely ignored 'critical studies' that were derived from assumptions applied in the radical humanist and radical structuralist paradigms (Grant and Perren 2002).

The second study in entrepreneurship that used Burrell and Morgan's (BM) paradigms (Pittaway 2005) provides the basis for the work reported here. Pittaway (2005) used the paradigms to unravel the underlying assumptions applied in historical studies of entrepreneurship in economics. The study aimed to understand the meta-theoretical assumptions applied in economic theories associated with entrepreneurship, sought to categorize these according to the BM paradigms and tried to explain the 'decline' of the entrepreneur in economic inquiry (Barreto 1989). The research found three principle sets of meta-theoretical assumptions. Like Grant and Perren (2002) the study found much of the prior work on entrepreneurship in economics to be dominated by functionalist assumptions (Pittaway 2005). It also noted the gradual removal of the entrepreneur from mainstream economic theory and concluded that extreme functionalist assumptions (in particular realism; positivism and determinism) posed problems for understanding entrepreneurship in economics because they had eliminated important alternative philosophies from inquiry, such as human action and philosophies of social and economic change (Pittaway 2005).

Taking these studies forward the work reported here uses the BM paradigms to explore further the historical studies in entrepreneurship. We focus principally on studies that take a psychological or social psychological approach in researching the entrepreneur, beginning with studies conducted in the 1960s and concluding with studies from the 1990s. Within this chapter we focus principally on this historical review of the subject for a number of reasons. First, we believe it is important to reflect on older work and its contribution to the underlying assumptions that might exist in common thought today. Research in entrepreneurship often has an 'immediacy' bias, an axiom that encourages researchers to concentrate only on what is currently fashionable within the domain, rather than looking back in a thorough manner at what has gone before. We believe there is much merit in returning occasionally to historical studies in the field to 'take stock' of the foundations of the subject to ensure that promising lines of enquiry have not been lost in time. Secondly, attempts to understand meta-theories within research require a very detailed, 'deep-dive' approach to reviewing literature, which aims to carefully unpick assumptions in a way that is consistent with the work conducted. Doing this form of review takes some considerable time and effort on behalf of the researcher and so it is important to frame the focus carefully.

In this chapter, therefore, we have thus chosen to draw the boundaries of the study around the early research in entrepreneurship that derives from psychology and social psychology and not expand our review to more contemporary work. Our rationale for drawing the boundaries around these dates is driven by the dominance of the psychological approaches to entrepreneurship during this period and we seek to fully understand the philosophies that guided this particular 'paradigm'. While there remains much merit in expanding the use of BM paradigms, as a tool, to consider other contemporary theories we contend that fully understanding the philosophical assumptions of this period of research will have merit as it is often considered to be a 'dead-end' by some commentators (Gartner 1989). Why was it a dead-end? Were there underlying philosophical assumptions, like those in the theory of the firm, that somehow led to it being a dead-end in the view of many entrepreneurship researchers? These are questions this work seeks to explore and they have merit for contemporary theory if today's researchers want to understand and perhaps avoid the 'traps' of prior research periods. Before undertaking this review, however, we explain how the BM paradigms were applied during the review process.

9.3 Methodological notes

Using BM's paradigms to review a field of literature is not without its limitations and problems despite its prior use as a tool for these purposes (Grant and Perren 2002; Nightingale and Cromby 1999; Parker 1998; Pittaway 2005; Willmott 1993). The paradigms have been widely criticized and a number of issues arise. The paradigms align forms of philosophy alongside one another (e.g. ontology and epistemology), along a subjective-objective dimension where the different forms of philosophical assumption may not be aligned. For example, making a realist ontological assumption does not inherently mean a researcher will take a positivist epistemological assumption; these are in fact independent of each other (Willmott 1993). Secondly, the paradigms present assumptions as dichotomous of each other (e.g. voluntarism versus determinism); while there are some dichotomous aspects, in most cases philosophical assumptions are significant debates with multiple alternatives (Parker 1998). Consequently, presenting them as two alternatives along a continuum rather simplifies the nature of the debates (Nightingale and Cromby 1999). Finally, the BM paradigms assume a degree of incommensurability, the paradigms are 'contiguous but separate' (Burrell and Morgan 1979, p. 22) and this aspect caused considerable debate about the nature of communication across paradigms, particularly near paradigm boundaries where assumptions are less extreme (Jackson and Carter 1991, 1993).

   To operationalize the BM paradigms as tools to consider implicit philosophical assumptions the study had to develop several techniques. It allowed for the dichotomous nature of the paradigms to continue to be represented but considered variation of approach to exist within a paradigm (e.g. assumptions about positivism in knowledge construction can be more or less extreme). The study allowed for variation between different types of assumption by developing review criteria for each type of philosophical assumption separate from each other within the objective-subjective dimension (Morgan and Smircich 1980, see Table 9.1). For the regulation-radical change dimension, where criteria had not previously been developed, the study reviewed the sociology literature and developed criteria for this dimension (Table 9.2). The review selected literature using a narrative review method and used the criteria presented to consider and report the underlying philosophical assumptions that were observed in the literature as presented in the following section.

The approach applied a narrative review method (Pittaway, Holt and Broad 2014). The narrative review method is the common form in academic research and it is iterative in nature. Narrative reviews are used extensively in management research and require the researcher to follow 'lines of inquiry'; reading literature as it is found and following selected relevant citations (Tranfield, Denyer and Smart 2003). It does have a number of weaknesses and in recent years there has been growth in the Systematic Literature Review (SLR) method, which has been designed to address some of these weaknesses (Pittaway *et al.* 2014). For example, narrative reviews can suffer from researcher bias in the selection and inclusion of studies (Hart 1998) and cannot easily be used to generalize or enable knowledge accumulation in the way that SLRs can (Greenhalgh 1997).

In this study the researchers began by sampling the conference proceedings of *Frontiers of Entrepreneurship* from 1980 through to 1990. The initial sample,

Table 9.1 A summary of the criteria used to analyse BM's subjective–objective dichotomy

	Subjectivism				Objectivism	
Ontological assumptions	Reality as a projection of human imagination	Reality as a social construction	Reality as the realm of symbolic discourse	Reality as contextual fields of information	Reality as a concrete process	Reality as a concrete structure
Epistemological assumptions	To obtain phenomenological insight, revelation	To understand how social reality is constructed	To understand patterns of symbolic discourse	To map contexts	To study systems, processes and change	To construct a positivist science
Assumptions about human nature	Man as pure spirit, consciousness, being	Man as the social constructor; the symbol creator	Man as an actor; the symbol user	Man as an information processor	Man as an adapter	Man as a responder
Favoured metaphors	Transcendental	Language game	Theatre, culture	Cybernetic	Organism	Machine
Examples	Exploration of pure subjectivity	Hermeneutics	Symbolic analysis	Contextual analysis	Historical analysis	Surveys

Source: Adapted from Morgan and Smircich (1980).

Table 9.2 A summary of the criteria used to analyse BM's radical change – regulation dichotomy

	Radical change			Regulation		
Assumptions about change to society	Every society is at every point subject to forces of radical change	Every society experiences periods of revolution and periods of stability	Every element in society is subject to incremental but continuous change	Every element in society has facilitated change to the existing social order	Every element in society responds to change imposed upon it	Every element in society is relatively stable and change occurs infrequently
Assumptions about the structure of society	Every element in society renders a contribution to internal disintegration	Every element in society displays contradiction and paradox	Every element in society is in a constant state of structural flux	Every element in society displays surface flux which obscures general structural principles	Every element in society is part of an organic system	Every society is a well integrated structure of elements and each element has a function
Assumptions about the degree of conflict in society	Every society at every point displays dissensus and conflict	Every society is based on the coercion of some of its members by others	Every group in society protects its own interests and is in open conflict with other groups	Every element of society is determined by power relationships between individuals and groups	Every functioning social structure is based on negotiation between the demands of its stake-holders	Every functioning social structure is based on a consensus of values among its members
Favoured metaphors	Anarchy and chaos	Transformation revolution	Tribal factions	Morphogenic	Organic	Mechanistic
Examples	Analysis of anarchy and chaos including action	Critical analysis of the *status quo* including action to transform	Critical analysis of the *status quo*	Analysis of functional autonomy	Analysis of the latent functions of society	Analysis of laws governing society

therefore, is likely to be somewhat biased toward US authors and a different outcome may have occurred had the researchers started with papers published at the European RENT conference; although it must also be noted that RENT conferences started somewhat later (1987) within the sample frame. The conference proceedings served as a citation bank for this study. Papers within the proceedings that focused on psychological aspects of entrepreneurship were identified and their bibliographies were comprehensively studied for highly cited papers in the field. In this stage there were around 120 relevant conference papers that included from five to 30 citations per paper.

From this review process seminal work that was highly cited was identified and consequently sourced through the narrative review method. The method used did not, therefore, favour publication outlet (i.e., book chapter versus journal paper) and did not seek judgments of quality (i.e., by using journal rankings) beyond the fact that the work was widely cited and considered seminal within the reviewed literature. The review conducted included many papers not listed in the following discussion. As is common with the narrative method of literature reviews the researchers made judgments about the critical papers to report in this review. These judgements were guided by the desire to seek out diversity in the meta-theoretical assumptions made and by an effort to include seminal studies during the review period and as such are designed to encourage creative lines of inquiry (Alvesson and Sandberg 2011, 2013).

Once papers were selected each was reviewed in detail applying the criteria developed and presented in Tables 9.1 and 9.2. Here the researcher was required to read sources multiple times to consider deeply the underlying assumptions used by theorists when considering the possible forms available (as summarized in Tables 9.1 and 9.2). The review criteria were used as guides to remind the researcher of the various forms and options during the review process. Undoubtedly, while the work was carried out in a relatively thorough manner, this process includes a degree of interpretation and judgement, and this must be considered a limitation of the work carried out.

The review focused on psychological and social psychological approaches to entrepreneurship research conducted from the 1960s to the 1990s. During this period personality trait studies dominated research in entrepreneurship and studies generally were criticized for lacking consistency in definition (Bull and Willard 1993; Gartner 1985) and it was argued that studies were largely atheoretical (Smith, Gannon and Sapienza 1989). Although studies draw on different schools of thought within these disciplines it was evident from the review that they have a common focus on the entrepreneurial 'person', as they hold in common an interest in trying to explain why some individuals act or behave in one way while others behave differently. Typically researchers in these areas are interested in explaining what makes an entrepreneur do what they do. In this sense these studies focus on the individual, their traits, motivations and behaviours.

Previous reviews of the literature on the psychology of the entrepreneur do exist (Brockhaus 1982; Brockhaus and Horwitz 1986; Chell 1985; Chell,

Haworth and Brearley 1991). These reviews provide critiques of the common approaches and categorize theories into forms but they do not consider the underlying meta-theories guiding theory. The common approaches explored during this review were categorized as: single trait; multi-trait; displacement; social development; psychodynamic; interactionism; and social constructionism. This categorization was based on both underlying meta-theoretical assumptions made and prior reviews of this literature (Chell 1997, 2000; Chell *et al.* 1991). Each of these is now explored with explicit attention paid to the meta-theories underpinning these approaches. A historic timeline of these approaches is also presented (see Figure 9.2).

9.4 A focus on single traits 1960s-1970s

There are two major types of trait theory in entrepreneurship research. In the 1960s work began by trying to seek 'single-trait' explanations that focused on seeking out one particular aspect of personality that could determine behaviour (Chell and Burrows 1991). From these grew more comprehensive multi-trait theories that attempted to identify a pattern of traits that could be used to construct personality (Hampson 1982). The most significant single trait theories in entrepreneurship were 'need for achievement', 'locus of control' and 'risk-taking propensity' and these continue to guide researchers in contemporary research, particularly when they discuss entrepreneurial competencies. The development of the achievement construct started with the work of Murray (1938) and was formalized and applied to entrepreneurship by McClelland (1955). McClelland's (1971) concept of the achievement motive and its role in

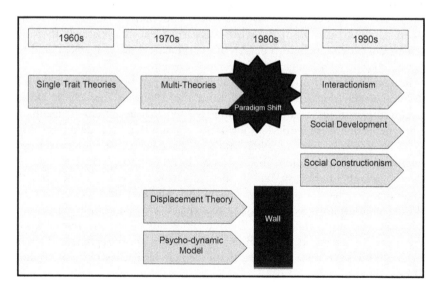

Figure 9.2 Timeline of psychological approaches to entrepreneurship (1960s to 1990s)

economic development and entrepreneurship was conceptualized as the 'desire to do well', not for social recognition or prestige, but for a sense of inner personal accomplishment.

McClelland considered motivation to be 'internal' and 'unconscious' and tested the motive through the analysis of fantasy via the Thematic Appreciation Test (TAT). After a number of studies McClelland concluded that people with a high need for achievement would exhibit certain behaviours that could predict 'entrepreneurial success'. Despite many criticisms (Frey 1984; Klinger 1966; Miner 1980; Schatz 1971) McClelland's concept was widely adopted and used in entrepreneurship research until the late 1980s (Johnson 1990). Johnson (1990), for example, compared the results of twenty-three studies using the construct in entrepreneurship research and reviewed eight different measurement techniques (see e.g. Table 9.3).

Table 9.3 Achievement measures used in entrepreneurship research

Measure	Type	Design
1. TAT (McClelland 1955)	Projective: imaginative stories	4 pictures: work situation, study situation, father-son situation, young boy
2. MSCS-Form T (Miner 1982, 1986)	Projective: sentence completion	40 sentence stems: 8 for each of five subscales: 1) self-achievement, 2) avoiding risks, 3) feedback of results, 4) personal innovation, 5) planning for the future.
3. EPPS (Edwards 1959)	Comprehensive personality scale	225-item inventory: achievement one of 15 needs measured.
4. PRF-E (Jackson 1974)	Comprehensive personality scale	352-item inventory: achievement one of 20 personality traits measured.
5. LAMQ (Lynn 1969)	Achievement questionnaire	8 yes-no questions, e.g. Do you find it easy to relax on holiday? Have you always worked hard in order to be among the best in your own line?
6. MAS (Mehrabian 1968, 1969)	Achievement questionnaire	26-item scale measuring extent of agreement or disagreement on such items as: 'I worry more about getting a bad grade than I think about getting a good grade.'
7. SCT (Mukjerhee 1968)	Achievement questionnaire	50 forced-choice triads measuring achievement values, e.g. I like • to be faithful to my friends and colleagues • to be very systematic in my work • to do my best in whatever work I undertake.
8. WOFO (Spence and Helmreich 1978)	Achievement questionnaire	3 achievement scales: 1) mastery needs, 2) work orientation, 3) inter-personal competitiveness.

Source: Johnson 1990, p. 42.

Johnson (1990) concluded that in 20 of 23 studies there was a relationship between 'entrepreneurship', however defined, and the 'need for achievement', however measured, even when there was no consistency between studies (Shaver and Scott 1991). Many commentators though have pointed to the contradictions between studies, particularly with regard to lack of definitional clarity as a major weakness of the approach (Gartner 1989).

A second key single-trait theory in entrepreneurship was 'locus of control', which began with the work of Rotter (1966); Table 9.4 summarises the research on locus of control during the review period.

Table 9.4 Research on locus of control beliefs

Authors	Research results
Ahmed 1985	Examined locus of control beliefs of Bangladesh immigrants living in the UK and concluded that the locus of control scale was positively related to entrepreneurship.
Anderson 1976	Used a longitudinal study of 90 'entrepreneurs' and discovered that those with high internal locus of control beliefs suffered less stress and employed more task-centred coping behaviours than those with external beliefs.
Begley and Boyd 1986	Found no evidence to suggest that locus of control beliefs differed between business founders and business managers.
Borland, 1974 (cited in Brockhaus 1982)	Suggested that a belief in internal locus of control was a better predictor of entrepreneurial intentions than need for achievement.
Brockhaus and Nord 1979	Found that internal locus of control scores failed to help distinguish between entrepreneurs and managers.
Brockhaus 1980	Used a criterion for success, which was that the business still existed after three years. Found that successful business founders had a higher internal locus of control than founders of those businesses that ceased to exist.
Cromie and Johns 1983	Established 'entrepreneurs' scored significantly higher than senior managers did on internal locus of control beliefs.
Durand and Shea 1974	Investigated the entrepreneurial activity of black adults engaged in operating small businesses (USA). 'Entrepreneurs' with high nArch and internal locus of control were found to be significantly more 'active'.
Hull, Bosley and Udell 1980	Failed to find any relationship between locus of control and entrepreneurial activity but did think the need for achievement motive was the more important variable.
Pandey and Tewary 1979	Provided 'empirical' evidence to suggest that people with high internal locus of control are more likely to become successful entrepreneurs.
Venkatapathy 1984	'Entrepreneurs' differed significantly from non-entrepreneurs on all the scales of the I-E inventory.

Source: Venkatapathy 1984, pp. 97–100; Chell *et al.* 1991, pp. 39–41; Shaver and Scott 1991, p. 30.

Rotter hypothesized that there were two extremes of control beliefs: internal and external. Internal control beliefs were the degree to which a person would expect outcomes to be contingent on their own behaviour while in external control beliefs they considered outcomes to be contingent on factors beyond their control, such as chance, luck or fate (Rotter 1990). Overall, this theory proposed that at the individual level people take on personal beliefs that may (or may not) guide their personal actions and their willingness to take such actions. Intuitively, it made sense to researchers to consider that entrepreneurs might have high internal locus of control beliefs (Chell *et al.* 1991) and so research focused on the entrepreneur's perception of a specific situation and how this would influence their intention to act (Liles 1974). Most research that followed in entrepreneurship tried to link locus of control beliefs to need for achievement and risk-taking propensity (McGhee and Crandall 1968) and a series of studies followed (Venkatapathy 1984; Shaver and Scott 1991). Once again results were contradictory (Chell *et al.* 1991) and the construct was criticized for being one-dimensional, in that it did not allow for varying contexts to alter locus-of-control beliefs and saw these beliefs as a fixed personality construct (Furnham 1986).

The third single trait theory that was introduced in entrepreneurship during this period was 'risk-taking propensity'. In personality theory risk-taking is not just something that the entrepreneur 'does', it is something an entrepreneur 'is', in that they have a personality which inclines them to take more risks (Brockhaus 1982). The majority of research that followed used the Choice Dilemmas Questionnaire (CDQ) (Brockhaus 1982; Brockhaus and Horwitz 1985) and sought to assess risk-taking propensity amongst respondents. The CDQ as an instrument has been criticized (Shaver and Scott 1991) and the idea that 'risk-taking propensity' could be considered a personality trait has been disputed (Timmons, Smollen and Dingee 1985). Researchers have pointed out that taking risks is often 'calculated' and that entrepreneurs can be observed to remove or reduce risk in situations (Chell *et al.* 1991; Sarasvathy 2004).

9.5 Personality and psychological approaches 1970s–1980s

9.5.1 Multi-trait theory

Dissatisfaction with the inability of single trait theories to 'predict' entrepreneurial behaviour in the late 1970s and early 1980s led to significant growth in multi-trait approaches to entrepreneurship research. Table 9.5, for example, illustrates a sample of multi-trait approaches to entrepreneurship during the review period.

Here researchers sought to assess the constellation of traits that could help predict entrepreneurial behaviour. Many different instruments were used, for example, the Behavioural Event Questionnaire (Flanagan 1954), the Edwards Personal Preference Schedule (Edwards 1959) and the Personality Research Form – E (Jackson 1974) to support the many studies taking this approach

Table 9.5 A sample of research using multi–trait perspectives

Author(s)	Sample	Characteristics
DeCarlo and Lyons 1979	Random selection of 122 individuals from a pooled listing of female entrepreneurs drawn from the business and manufacturing directories of several Mid Atlantic (USA) states, from directories of women business owners, and from directories of minority owned firms.	Age, marriage rate, education, previous entrepreneurial effort, regimentation, means of starting, achievement autonomy, aggression, independence, leadership, support conformity.
Hisrich and O'Brien 1981	21 female entrepreneurs in greater Boston area in service and construction businesses.	Self-discipline and perseverance, desire to succeed, action orientation, energy level.
Hornaday and Aboud 1971	60 entrepreneurs from East Coast (USA) in manufacturing, sales, and services businesses. No industry specified.	Need for achievement, autonomy, aggression, recognition, independence, leadership.
Hull, Bosley, and Udell 1980	57 owners or partial owners of business. 31 of the 57 had helped create the business or had been involved with the creation of a business in the past.	Interest in 'money or fame', social desirability, task preferences, locus of control, risk-taking propensity, creativity, achievement.
Litzinger 1965	15 owner-operators of motels in Northern Arizona.	Risk preference, independence, leadership, recognition, support, conformity, benevolence, structure, consideration.
McClelland 1961	Middle–level managers from Harvard and MIT executive programs, General Electric unit managers, managers from Turkey, Italy, Poland and Indian mechanics.	Achievement, optimism, affiliation, power, conscientiousness, asceticism, belief in achieved status, market morality.
Meredith, Nelson and Neck 1982	Descriptive account discussing how to be an entrepreneur.	Self-confidence, risk-taking, flexibility, need for achievement, independence.
Mescon and Mon-tanari 1981	31 real estate brokers who owned and operated their own firms in north central region of the United States.	Achievement, autonomy, dominance, endurance, order, locus of control.
Schrage 1965	22 R&D companies, less than 10 years old, in service, consulting and manufacturing.	Veridical perception, achievement motivation, power motivation, awareness of impaired performance under tension.
Wainer and Rubin 1969	51 technically based service and manufacturing companies that were spin-offs from MIT, 4–10 years old.	Achievement, power, affiliation.
Welsch and Young 1982	53 owners of small businesses. Average size of 10 full-time employees and four part-time employees. All types of industries and businesses.	Locus of control, Machiavellianism, self-esteem, risk-taking, openness to innovation, rigidity, government regulation, economic optimism.

Source: Gartner 1989, pp. 49–56.

(Gartner 1989). Like single-trait theories, multi-trait studies once again struggled to define the entrepreneur in a common way and very few studies employed the same definition and as a result the samples employed were extremely diverse (Gartner 1989). So many traits became associated with the 'entrepreneurial psychological profile' that Gartner argued that they depicted an individual who would be:

> ... larger than life, full of contradictions, and, conversely, someone so full of traits that (s)he would have to be a sort of generic everyman.
>
> (Gartner 1989, p. 57)

This crisis for personality theory in entrepreneurship in the 1980s led to a 'paradigm shift' that introduced behavioural and subsequently cognitive theories of entrepreneurship. The wider criticisms of personality theory included the inadequacies of measuring instruments, the poor definition of the population to which the traits were being applied and the inadequacy of attempts to describe and manage population samples. When applying BM's paradigms to the underlying assumptions of personality theory another picture emerges: there are clear meta-theoretical assumptions used in these studies that ultimately undermined the paradigm.

The first core assumptions of personality theory are 'stability' and 'consistency', or the axioms that personality is relatively stable and consistently influences behaviour in particular ways (Hampson 1982). Although the concept of stability does allow for some long-term development in an individual's personality over time and allows for some day-to-day variation, the axiom assumes that personality is stable, creating a second axiom that personality leads to continuity of behaviour over time and across contexts. As such, these assumptions apply the view that personality 'determines' behaviour, assuming that other factors have limited effect (e.g. personal choice or social context).

While it clearly excludes the 'nurture' aspect of behaviour it also largely excludes the 'free-will or voluntarism' view of human behaviour and as such could be described as 'extreme psychological determinism'. Individuals are effectively born with, or acquire early on in life, their personality traits and these principally guide their future behaviour. In terms of the BM paradigms this assumption in personality theory also disregards factors external to the individual (such as the social context or culture), ignoring the role of society in human behaviour. A further major assumption in personality theory is 'internality' or the idea that personality resides within an individual, is unique and that behaviour is the outward expression of individual personality (Hampson 1982).

In terms of the BM paradigms one can see the use of both relativist and realist ontologies. On the one hand, internality implies 'a unique reality' for each individual in terms of their personality. On the other hand, capturing personality via observation of common behaviours and beliefs implies realist ontology, that these 'exist' as concrete things to be observed. In reviewing personality theory we thus observe a paradox between the initial assumptions which were relativist and later implementation, which was realist. Researchers sought to 'capture' observable behaviours as if these somehow 'existed' as representations of social reality and ultimately as descriptions of an individual's personality.

Approaches to capture 'personality' via systematic quantitative instruments that test behaviours and beliefs in scientifically rigorous ways in order to predict behaviour are also positivist in terms of knowledge construction and nomothetic in terms of methodology. From the review conducted it is reasonable to consider that researchers' use of these meta-theories may also have contributed to the decline of personality theory in entrepreneurship.

9.5.2 Displacement theory

During the dominance of personality theory in entrepreneurship research there were a number of theories about entrepreneurial behaviour that were not widely adopted in mainstream studies of the subject. One such theory was displacement (Shapero 1975) and in a very similar vein Scase and Goffee's (1980) social marginality theory. The basic premise of these theories was that entrepreneurs are 'displaced' people who have been supplanted from their familiar way of life. They are unemployed, have been made redundant, or have simply become tired of their current way of life and seek more autonomy. Displacement occurs within two forms, as a consequence of either negative or positive forces. Positive forces, for example, included a close friend's suggestion, chance encounters and opportunities that unexpectedly emerge (e.g. a management buy-out). Negative forces in contrast included unemployment, divorce or economic stress.

In Shapero's (1975) work, while displacement can be led by psychological factors (e.g. internal beliefs and personality) most entrepreneurship occurs because of external drivers that are either 'push' or 'pull' in form. Push factors are mostly negative, that displace an individual from a known situation into an unknown one (e.g. redundancy). Pull factors, in contrast, may include attractive unexpected opportunities, personal tendencies (including traits) and role models. Displacement theory thus draws on wider sociological factors when considering human behaviour and suggests that significant contextual factors play a role in encouraging (or not) a tendency towards entrepreneurship. The concept of displacement was embedded in many subsequent contextual studies, such as those focused on immigrant entrepreneurship, female entrepreneurship and necessity-based entrepreneurship (Folger, Timmerman and Wooten 1992; Price and Monroe 1992; see e.g. Table 9.6).

The theory applies several meta-theoretical assumptions relevant to the BM paradigms. Displacement, for example, does allow for some 'personal choice' or free will in decisions to become an entrepreneur but predominately presents these choices as forced by circumstances. In this sense it tends to ignore prior intentions or propensity to become entrepreneurs before circumstances arose and ignores deliberate efforts. Displacement can, therefore, be considered a form of 'sociological determinism'. While social context plays a much more important role than in personality theory behaviour is still largely 'determined',

Table 9.6 A sample of research using the displacement assumption

Authors	Research
Ahmed 1985	Examined risk-taking and locus of control among the Bangladeshi immigrant community in the UK.
Folger, Timmerman and Wooten 1992	Examined the personality traits of business managers who had been laid off as a result of companies downsizing. Data were collected before an explicit decision to start a business and later contrasted with the managers' subsequent decision. Found that personality traits could help predict which managers would start a business as a result of their displacement.
Ohe, Honjo, Okada, and Miura 1992	Conducted a psychological study that compared male and female entrepreneurs in Japan and the USA. Concluded that female entrepreneurs in both countries had a higher degree of 'entrepreneurial spirit' than their male counterparts.
Price and Monroe 1992	Claimed that women and minorities were launching new enterprises six times faster than any other group in the USA. Suggested that this occurred because of the displacement caused by downsizing and because of inflexible working conditions. Researched the effectiveness of entrepreneurial training schemes for women and minorities in Colorado.
Sexton and Bowman 1986	Examined the psychological characteristics of female business students majoring in entrepreneurship, female business students majoring in functional areas of business, female entrepreneurs and female managers. Concluded that personality traits were significantly different between entrepreneurship students and business students and between female managers and entrepreneurs.
Watkins and Watkins 1986	Examined the influences leading women to adopt an entrepreneurial career in the United Kingdom. The research used in-depth interviews with 58 male and 58 female business owners. Concluded that the background and experience of women entrepreneurs differed substantially from their male counterparts. Discovered that the male control group fitted the displacement model of entrepreneurship while the female group did not. The female group was motivated more by internal push factors such as the desire for autonomy and need for achievement (not as a psychometric measure).
Moriya, Judd and File 1988	Discovered that women entrepreneurs were more values orientated than male entrepreneurs who were more profit orientated. Identified significant differences between women entrepreneurs in different segments of the same industry.

this time by exogenous factors beyond the individual's control. Even where 'choice' is applied the displacement model used personality traits as the means to assess who will choose what courses of action.

9.5.3 Psycho-dynamic model

A third approach that sat alongside personality theory but that did not enter into mainstream entrepreneurship research during the 1970s was Kets de Vries's (1977) study, which we have described as a 'psycho-dynamic model'. Kets de Vries (1977) appears to build on the displacement concept of Shapero (1975) but places more focus on the person and applies ideas based on Freudian psychology. The psychological assumptions applied lead Kets de Vries to view displacement in two ways, 'actual' displacement that occurs because of exogenous factors and 'perceived' displacement that occurs because of psycho-dynamic forces. In the second stance displacement is considered to be a psychological state. From this concept Kets de Vries (1977) portrays the 'entrepreneur' as a person who is yearning to control the environment around them and who may use innovation to rebel against the current norms and structures that are perceived to exist. He thinks these tendencies may occur because of '… reactive ways of dealing with feelings of anger, fear and anxiety' (Kets de Vries 1977, p. 35) that lead to the possession of different value systems that lead entrepreneurs to 'unconventional' behaviour.

In Kets de Vries's view a number of reasons can cause this: displacement by force; denigration of valued symbols; inconsistency between status symbols or changes in the distribution of economic power; and, non-acceptance of immigrant groups. Such feelings of displacement, he contends, will lead to a greater disposition towards 'entrepreneurial behaviour'. He also argues that prior family dynamics can lead to a sense of perceived displacement; delving deeply into these issues he considers a child's relationship with their father, their mother and inter-sibling rivalry, as well as, the role of family events like the early death of parent. Within the context of BM's paradigms it is an interesting model. On the BM continuum associated with the sociology of regulation versus radical change it makes much more pronounced assumptions about the role of societal change in encouraging entrepreneurial acts. For example, it highlights the role of displacement by force and considers how revolutionary change might encourage immigration and subsequent immigrant entrepreneurship.

While accepting significant societal change much of Kets de Vries's work concentrates on 'psychological displacement' and so focuses on internal family dynamics and personal psychology. When considering human nature, the theory appears to consider humans as adaptive within a social structure: applying a strong Freudian perspective to the construction of future behaviour. Humans are either displaced by changes to social structures or are caught within social structures against which they rebel. Entrepreneurial action within this theory is tied to a desire to change existing social structures because of beliefs that have arisen out of displacement or dissatisfaction with what exists. Kets de Vries's (1977) theory is also notable because it presents a 'darker-side' to entrepreneurial efforts and does not apply the commonly held axiom that entrepreneurship is a positive force in society (Ogbor 2000).

9.6 Importance of social psychology 1980s–1990s

9.6.1 Social development model

Another approach that did not receive much mainstream attention during the 1980s was Gibb and Ritchie's (1981) social development model. This work can perhaps be considered the forerunner of a much later study of 'entrepreneurial learning' and for this reason is considered an important focus for the study carried out (Pittaway and Thorpe 2012). The authors explicitly rejected personality theory and argued that it assumed entrepreneurs were 'born' when in fact they were 'made'. Here they suggested that '…entrepreneurship can be better understood in terms of the types of situation encountered and the social groups to which the individuals relate' (Gibb and Ritchie 1981, p. 27). In other words, individual behaviour grows, adapts and improves as individuals engage in social groups/networks, or in other words they learn through social engagement.

Gibb and Ritchie's model was one of the first to articulate the view that entrepreneurs change throughout the course of their life and that the individual's relationship with previous social contexts will mould and influence their engagement with future contexts. The model they presented, was designed to explain how different stages in the 'life course' might influence how they choose to engage in entrepreneurial effort; how it impacts on their motivations for entrepreneurship. They presented four different forms: improvisers, revisionists, superseders and reverters. Chell (1985) offered a number of criticisms of this particular model including that it was 'situational', describing behaviour as a function of social influences; was 'stereotypical' presenting a typology based on abstractions; and was somewhat limited methodologically. Despite the weaknesses, the model is interesting in the context of the BM paradigms. It considers social and individual factors, it allows for greater 'voluntarism' and choice in decisions, it places the entrepreneur within the context of social change and ultimately it allows for 'development', or learning, so that entrepreneurs can improve as they become more familiar with the contexts experienced. Evidently, it may also provide the initial foundation on which significant subsequent work has been built within theories of 'entrepreneurial learning'.

9.6.2 Interactionism

As outlined previously, a number of researchers became increasingly dissatisfied with the dominance of personality theory during the 1980s and began to provide extensive critiques undermining its use in entrepreneurship (Chell *et al.* 1991; Gartner 1989). The immediate response was a blossoming towards the late 1980s and early 1990s of what can be described as 'social psychological' theories of entrepreneurship. This equated to a paradigm shift as some researchers focused more on what entrepreneurs 'do', initially focusing on venture creation, than on what they 'are' (Gartner 1989) and theories from social psychology were used to address these new research questions. The first of these approaches was interactionism. Interactionism in social psychology describes the interaction between the individual and their environment. Within entrepreneurship a number of theories were introduced that described the interaction of a range of factors, for example, personality, self-perception, intentionality, propensity to act and situational variables (Greenberger and Sexton 1988).

These interactionist models aimed to bring together three broad concepts; 'intentionality', 'self-efficacy' and 'situational' aspects (Bird 1988; Naffziger, Hornsby and Kuratko 1994). Intentionality was viewed as the individual's desire to achieve a specific objective (goal) or a path of objectives (Bird 1988). Self-efficacy was the person's belief in their ability to achieve an objective based on mastery experiences, observational learning, social persuasion and judgements of their own psychological and physiological states (Boyd and Vozikis 1994). Situational components included aspects of the external context that had a bearing on the entrepreneur's decision or impacted on their ability to implement the chosen course of action. Models vary somewhat in terms of their concepts of 'intentionality' and 'self-efficacy' and on what situational factors they think important. All models hold in common a narrowing of the definition of entrepreneurship to 'venture creation'.

Models in the early 1990s could, however, be separated into 'cognitive interactionism' and 'processional interactionism'. The former, which is best represented by the work of Bird (1988), Boyd and Vozikis (1994) and Shaver and Scott (1991), tends towards considering how an intention to act towards venture creation becomes formed in the minds of entrepreneurs and as such tends to focus on cognitive processes (e.g. rationality and intuition). It also considers the role of temporal tension, between the individual's imagined future state, and the actions that are required in the present to bring about the outcomes desired; including the impact that self-confidence may have on implementation (Boyd and Vozikis 1994). The emphasis in 'processional interactionism' differs because the focus is more on the decision-making process during venture creation than on the individual's cognitive skills and perceptions (Greenberger and Sexton 1988; Learned 1992; Naffziger *et al.* 1994). Models tend towards focusing on the factors that go into the process of making a decision to start a venture. The meta-theoretical assumptions of these models, as defined by the BM paradigms, are interesting as they seem to continue to guide the significant contemporary study in entrepreneurship focused on 'cognition'.

There is also some diversity between approaches. Cognitive approaches tend to apply a slightly more relativist position as they see reality residing outside the individual but recognize that it is mediated by cognitive skills and interpretation. Process interactionist models in contrast are more interested in objective factors and how they impact on entrepreneurial decision-making to start a venture. The temporal nature of the models is also interesting (Bird 1988). Theorists consider that entrepreneurs can only understand the context that is presented before them at a given time and must cope with significant uncertainty about future conditions (Kirzner 1973, 1980). The view is both more relativist and more accepting of societal change than personality theory. Studies in the 'cognitive' genre do appear to see human behaviour in 'information processing' terms. Entrepreneurs collect information about their environment, use certain cognitive skills to make sense of it in a way that is different to others and consequently 'see' new opportunities, which they can then act on. In this view the opportunities were largely considered to 'exist' and were waiting to be 'discovered'. In contrast, studies in the 'process' genre tend to see human nature as an adaptive process. Inputs and outputs within the models tend to be seen as generalizable to entrepreneurial activity more broadly and entrepreneurial activity is viewed in rather homogenous terms, with little role for variation in entrepreneurial activity across different social contexts.

9.6.3 Social constructionism

Interactionist theories, it may be argued, could be developed out of dissatisfaction amongst 'normative science' researchers to achieve a reasonable level of reliability from traditional trait theories. Researchers sought to use more behaviour-oriented approaches but these approaches largely maintained a relatively realist, normative set of meta-theoretical assumptions. This dissatisfaction also led to a reconsideration of personality based on different meta-theoretical assumptions (Hampson 1982). Social constructionist approaches to researching the entrepreneur, were led and developed by Chell *et al.* (1991). Social constructionism begins from the premise that a person's perception of reality is constructed from experience and accumulated 'knowledge' about their general environment and their specific social context (Cunliffe 2008).

Underlying social constructionism is a view that individuals 'construct' knowledge about themselves and other people by labelling and categorizing their thoughts, feelings and experiences (Chell 1997). The act of labelling is perceived to be the way in which individuals externalize their thought processes and make sense of the world. In this view reality is 'relativist', unique to individual interpretation, while labels can be common; shared between people as a means to describe and explain observations and experiences (Chell 1997). The social construction of personality as applied in entrepreneurship, therefore, had a number of key features. 'Traits' were considered to be categorizing concepts that are inferred from actual behaviour, personality metaphorically 'existed' between people. The relationship between 'personality' and 'behaviour' can be viewed differently by different people. 'Traits' were considered to be prototypical categories and were thus imprecise descriptors of behaviour mediated by language and interpreted by people in varying ways (Chell *et al.* 1991).

Research using social constructionism in entrepreneurship during this period applied the critical incident interview technique and unstructured interviews to explore the behaviours that were prototypical of particular forms of entrepreneurship (Chell and Haworth 1988; Chell, Hedberg-Jalonen and Miettinen 1997). The categorization process explored behaviour and the features of behaviour that were prototypical of a particular 'trait' and categorized a set of traits that were prototypical of a category of business owner. From the research a number of prototypical categories or types of business owner were identified, 'entrepreneur', 'quasi-entrepreneur', 'administrator' and 'caretaker' (Chell *et al.* 1991) and four prototypical categories related to business growth including: 'growth', 'declining', 'rejuvenating' and 'plateauing'. The social constructionist approach to entrepreneurial personality, therefore, was keenly aware of the heterogeneity of the business owner population and demonstrated the complex relationship between growth, business context and the business owner's behavioural type. In this sense, unlike cognitive and processional interactionist approaches, the social constructionist approach accepted that not all individuals involved in venture creation behaved entrepreneurially, while also precluding the notion that entrepreneurial behaviour is internal to a 'special' person, and instead connecting entrepreneurship to behaviour exhibited in the context of venture development.

The types presented are also dynamic, allowing for social development and changes of motivation by individual business owners. From the review it was evident that the meta-theories used to underpin the social constructionist approach to entrepreneurship were derived from BM's interpretive paradigm. Ontological assumptions apply ideas from the social construction of reality, which are along the subjective part of the subjective-objective continuum and knowledge is also perceived to be fairly subjective because individual's experience and knowledge are unique, guided by prior contexts, experiences and interpretations of the world mediated by labels embedded in discourse.

9.7 Discussion and implications for contemporary study in entrepreneurship

The meta-theories underlying the different psychological and social psychological theories in entrepreneurship from the 1960s to the 1990s are summarized in Table 9.7. A number of implications for contemporary study can be drawn from this review along with its counterpart that focused on economic theories (Pittaway 2005). These implications highlight why it is important to take stock of historical approaches to entrepreneurship and in particular for contemporary researchers to consider why certain lines of inquiry did not develop further. Initially, it is clear that there are different meta-theoretical assumptions underpinning theory in entrepreneurship research and these do guide researchers to different and often contradictory views of the nature of the entrepreneur and the entrepreneurial process (Pittaway 2005). Clearly, this study supports those

Table 9.7 A summary of the meta-theories observed in the review

Theory	Ontology	Epistemology	Human behaviour	Nature of society
Trait theory	A combination of both realist and nominalist assumptions	Positivist	Psychological determinism. Personality determines behaviour	Behaviour is 'real' and represents personality but context does not play much role in explaining an individual's behaviour
Displacement theory	Reality as a concrete process	Systems building	'Man' as an adaptor	Society under-goes surface flux which hides actual structural relationships
Social development theory	Reality is a concrete process	Systems building	'Man' as a responder	Society is relatively ordered
Psycho-dynamic theory	Reality is a contextual field of information: people can be displaced and they can feel displaced	Systems building	'Man' as an adapter	Society goes through periods of radical change that can displace people but existing social order is the focus of entrepreneurial efforts for the psychologically displaced
Cognitive interactionism	Symbolic interactionism	Information exchange	'Man' as an information processor	Society is organic
Processional interactionism	Contextualism	Systems building	'Man' as an adapter	Society is organic
Social con-structionism	Social construction of reality	Symbolic discourse	'Man' as the social constructor; the symbol creator	Society has structural flux

of Grant and Perren (2002) and Pittaway (2005) and can conclude that the psychological theories of the period were dominated by functionalist assumptions.

Within psychology and social psychology, underlying disciplinary 'paradigms' have influenced the development of common approaches in entrepreneurship, for example, the social development model appears to guide initial thinking in entrepreneurial learning and interactionism seems to play a role in contemporary theories on opportunity recognition. These different approaches often apply contrasting implicit views on key meta-theories and, therefore, lead to significant differences in theoretical constructs and thus influence the research conducted. Such assumptions are nearly always applied implicitly and so it can be difficult for researchers to appreciate the implications that these have on the development of their work. Consequently, it is clear that studies need to aim to be more explicit about these guiding assumptions when developing and applying theories. 'Axioms' do exist in entrepreneurship research, for example most of the studies in this review, possibly by definition, applied an 'individualistic' axiom (Ogbor 2000) and, thus tended to obscure or minimize the role of societal factors. Research was also predominately functionalist in terms of BM's paradigms (Grant and Perren 2002; Pittaway 2005). None of the studies can be described as taking a 'radical structuralist' or 'radical humanist' approach and only a few took an 'interpretive' one.

From this review we can also conclude that extreme functionalist assumptions, which often dominate entrepreneurship research, need to be carefully applied. At least in two instances, the theory of the firm (Pittaway 2005) and traditional trait theory, their use can be considered as problematic when seeking to understand entrepreneurial activity. In the former, extreme efforts to 'objectify' and 'measure' economic activity removed purposeful behaviour and entrepreneurship from theorising (Pittaway 2005). In the latter, efforts to 'measure' and 'predict' the entrepreneurial personality led to a mass of traits that did not achieve meaningful advances in the subject (Gartner 1989). The review has found a number of interrelated philosophical assumptions from the use of BM's paradigms that may have caused these issues and that need to be more widely considered. These have also been discovered previously in reviews of economic thinking (Pittaway 2005) and within reviews of contemporary study during the 1990s (Grant and Perren 2002).

- Strong realist ontological assumptions tend to view the social world as an external structure and objectify social behaviour and yet entrepreneurship emphasizes agency and deliberate human action. Change, both incremental and discontinuous, seems to be important in entrepreneurship and entrepreneurs are thought to play a role in encouraging the occurrence of change, either through exploiting opportunities or through purposively creating them. By over-emphasizing 'externality' and 'order' realist assumptions may impinge a researcher's ability to consider how individuals and groups engage and lead reconfigurations which impact on industries and markets, and the social world more generally. Ultimately our review would suggest that concepts of 'human action' are inherently interwoven with entrepreneurship and assumptions that move towards removing a degree of relativity in human systems essentially remove the entrepreneurial function (as occurred in the theory of the firm, Barreto 1989).
- Positivism, in an extreme form, can also present challenges. Greater precision in measurement, via the use of mathematics, requires clarity of definition.

Yet, 'entrepreneurship' has been notoriously difficult to define narrowly (e.g. to define it as venture creation was one attempt) and attempts to narrow the subject so that normative science methods can be applied often lead to the exclusion of complexity, uncertainty, messiness and variety. Order and measurement, as implied by extreme positivism and certain applications of positivism (e.g. probability theory), seem to sit poorly in entrepreneurship which requires understanding of complex, chaotic systems and an appreciation of the 'unknown'.

- Determinism also presents challenges. Theories that seem to imply that behaviour is determined by something (e.g. personality, displacement, situational factor, etc.) tend towards ignoring the role of human action, choice and learning in the process of entrepreneurship. Yet, conceptions of human action, entrepreneurial learning and perseverance when acting seem to be essential (Knight 1921). If researchers erode the role of human action, in the pursuit of a 'normative science' approach, they are in fact, we would contend, removing something essential to understanding entrepreneurship as it occurs in practice (i.e., action focused on the creation of change).

- Axioms in the historic subject are also evident. The most obvious axiom is 'individualism', where the focus of research tends towards individuals rather than groups, social processes and institutional contexts. Another widespread axiom that was evident in the studies reviewed was 'success bias', where researchers tend to focus on and one could say celebrate, the successes of entrepreneurs.

These implications have resonance for contemporary study in entrepreneurship. They show the value of understanding the influence of meta-theories in the historical development of the field and lead us to look at the conceptual 'traps' that have arisen and that are being used once again by contemporary scholars to 'capture' the essence of entrepreneurship. Theories of entrepreneurship have been particularly influenced by attention to the individual and economic opportunity, largely through the enduring influence of early economic theorists and their conceptualisations (Pittaway 2005). Many early eco2nomic studies emphasized uncertainty and the nature of opportunity but applied diverse definitions about the 'individual' entrepreneur. Each theory felt that the individual entrepreneur must be important but could never quite explain how the individual contributed (Pittaway 2005).

This chapter has illustrated that the early psychological theories tried to fill this void by explaining the individual, but that in doing so they tended to understate the role of external structures and context while remaining fixated on deterministic approaches to human behaviour. Shane and Venkataraman (2000), amongst others, have provided a more recent impetus in the field by trying to explain the links between the individual, the context and interrelated processes associated with entrepreneurship (Shane and Venkataraman 2013). Such efforts, while seemingly advancing the field apply prior assumptions (in their case disequilibrium theory, Kirzner 1980) without considering the underpinning meta-theoretical assumptions inherent in such an approach.

While we may stand on the shoulders of giants, we may also unthinkingly build on their assumptions. For this reason it is important that as a field we occasionally reflect, including reflecting on underlying taken-for-granted assumptions that underpin our theory (Gartner 2001; Pittaway *et al.* 2014). Yet despite this, major theorists who have a leading impact on our field, rarely discuss the meta-theories guiding their approach nor often carefully consider alternatives. Meta-theories are choices for researchers, often they are applied implicitly without thought but it would be far better if these discussions were carried out and assumptions made in an explicit way; just as we are required to do with our methodological decisions.

This study and its counterpart show that meta-theoretical decisions made by researchers do have consequences for the ways in which entrepreneurship is conceived, conceptualized and studied. An approach which made these assumptions explicit therefore, would add value within entrepreneurship research by helping to critically engage the subject, allowing us to unpick, deconstruct and question some of our underlying assumptions. By undertaking one such critically reflective review we can present some common traps that historic researchers have occasionally fallen into and that might be avoided in future.

9.7.1 *Heffalump Trap 1: aiming to be a scientific (rather than a social scientific) discipline*

This study also outlines that there has been a tension between mainstream attempts to build theories about entrepreneurship based on 'normative science' approaches, which tend to look for causality, and the need to allow for entrepreneurs to engage in 'human action'. The reviews conducted display some tension when applying scientific philosophies of knowledge construction to a field where the focal actors, by definition, engage in action that can lead to economic and social change (Sarasvathy and Venkataraman 2011; Watson 2013a, 2013b). Causality implies prediction, either deterministically or probabilistically, and does not easily cope with randomness, luck, chaos and underdetermined multiple but unrealised futures, nor do such approaches cope well with the desire by individuals to create such futures that they imagine or appreciate their efforts to build them.

From this review philosophies applied to entrepreneurship need to be able to fully embrace both human action and relativity in future reality and common scientific methods do not inherently do this well. For example, the individual-opportunity nexus has become a key theory in entrepreneurship whereby opportunities are conceived as 'out there' to be 'discovered' (Alvarez and Barney 2013; Shane and Venkataraman 2000, 2013), yet it is evident that the construction of opportunity, imagination to visualize what is possible and human action to pursue and create opportunity are all essential components of high-impact entrepreneurial efforts (Alvarez and Barney 2007, 2010; Fischer *et al.* 1997). Current theoretical disagreements about whether opportunities are 'discovered' or 'created' reflect the tension between causality and human action, yet such arguments continue to coalesce around realist ontology (Alvarez and Barney 2013). By considering alternative paradigms, it is possible to see new avenues for opportunity creation, as a theory of entrepreneurship. These new lines of enquiry lie in both separating opportunity creation from opportunity recognition (Alvarez and Barney 2007, 2010) and considering studies which move away from realist ontology. In so doing, researchers can add value by exploring opportunity creation through employing different subjectivist, social constructionist and interpretive ontologies (Chell *et al.* 1997; Fletcher 2006; Korsgaard and Neergaard 2010).

9.7.2 Heffalump Trap 2: ignoring the role of social context, structures and institutions

Through the analysis outlined in this chapter it is possible to identify that the theory which most closely fits the stance on human beings and reality adopted by critical realists is cognitive interactionism and this stance appears to have become popular in recent research. Such a critical realist perspective has the opportunity to build ontologically appropriate theories of entrepreneurship drawn from the radical structuralist paradigm of BM's framework. Approaches of this nature can more appropriately consider the contextual, sociological and institutional factors that might guide theory and the importance of these factors has been highlighted by a growing trend in the field (Aldrich 2010; Mole and Mole 2010).

These developments show an acknowledgement of the need to expand the 'sociological' aspects of entrepreneurship research to include social structures, social context and social change and that some focus on radical structuralism (i.e., radical change to social and economic structures) might be an intriguing area for future research in this paradigm (Sarason, Dean and Dillard 2006, 2010; Zahra 2007). Our historical analysis would appear to concur with the view that such a shift could be beneficial for the field and that we should continue to expand such 'institutional' and 'critical realist' approaches. At the same time, our analysis provides a cautionary tale for these approaches. Critical realist and institutional theories continue to have fairly strong determinist overtones. Institutional frameworks and sociological structures are given more weight in guiding behaviour and human action. In contrast relativity and volition take somewhat of a back seat and yet, as with functionalist perspectives, there is a danger that the 'future yet to come' and the entrepreneur's ability to envision and enact that future remains under-appreciated. Here studies which apply alternative sociological approaches to understanding entrepreneurship, organising and social systems may prove insightful (e.g. Kostera 2013; Sarason *et al.* 2006).

9.7.3 Heffalump Trap 3: assuming entrepreneurship is about 'special' individuals

The review also outlined a key axiom that the 'individual entrepreneur' was focused on and was considered to be a 'special individual' without much reference to social aspects (e.g. teams; families; social context, etc.). Despite a growth in research concerned with the social factors of entrepreneurship the dominance of study on the individual-opportunity nexus has taken forward this axiom and reinforced a view of the entrepreneur as a 'special' individual who discovers opportunities through their unique cognitive powers. Likewise these theories rarely include a focus on the actions entrepreneurs take in pursuit of these opportunities (Venkataraman *et al.* 2012). While Alvarez and Barney (2010) provide an alternative explanation of entrepreneurs creating opportunities through interpretation, the focus remains on the individual. Even in institutional entrepreneurship where creative destruction of institutions occurs, the entrepreneur is again considered a 'special' individual, who acts relatively autonomously (Aldrich 2012). Some contemporary theory, therefore, seems to uncritically perpetuate the individualistic axiom previously identified (Ogbor 2000) without carefully considering alternatives (Dimov 2011; Johannisson 2011; Welter 2011; Zahra and Wright 2011).

From this review, and the traps presented, we can make some conclusions about the role of understanding meta-theories for future studies and the value of diversity in the research domain. We will explore these conclusions next.

9.8 Conclusions

This chapter used BM's paradigms to review and consider the meta-theoretical assumptions in the historic (1960s–1990s) psychological and social psychological approaches to entrepreneurship. The study was a companion of a similar review that explored economic theories (Pittaway 2005) and its purpose was to explore and understand the common meta-theories that have been used to guide prior theories. From this review we have been able to present some concerns about the use of extreme functionalist assumptions within the subject (e.g. realist; positivist; and deterministic assumptions) and have presented some common traps previous researchers have fallen into. The chapter, therefore, makes a number of contributions. First and foremost, prior reviews of meta-theories in entrepreneurship research show some diversity in the meta-theories used within the functionalist paradigm but a lack of diversity across paradigms. Yet most researchers rarely consider these assumptions when developing theory. While we do not wish to encourage excessive 'self-reflection', as sometimes occurs in other disciplines, we do suggest that entrepreneurship researchers need to be more reflective about these underlying assumptions and that as a field we need to engage in 'critical studies' that allow us to step back and consider our philosophies and axioms more diligently. Secondly, the review identified a number of prior traps from historic research including: a desire to create a scientific discipline;

ignoring sociological and institutional factors; and a focus on 'special' individuals. These traps suggest that there is much merit in applying BM's framework to consider new approaches and their philosophical assumptions and it might assist researchers when they seek to bring new theories into the domain (Aldrich 2012; Alvarez and Barney 2013; Sarasvathy 2001; Venkatamaran *et al.* 2012).

Our review of historic approaches also demonstrates that the functionalist paradigm in BM's framework has consistently been employed in mainstream entrepreneurship theory. While there have been some encouraging developments in recent years, and this book is an example, we still consider much contemporary research to be dominated by many of the same assumptions. As illustrated by our analysis and its counterpart (Pittaway 2005), this dominance is caused partly by the history of previous work which was functionalist in nature and by an effort to mimic scientific research via a normative science approach to the subject (Aldrich 2012). For us two issues arise. Firstly, philosophies in the more subjective domain of the BM paradigms seem to be important but somewhat overlooked. In particular human action (or volition) as a guiding philosophy behind theory seems important as does relativity when applied to unknown futures. These meta-theories seem neglected as guiding philosophies for theory in entrepreneurship and yet to us they seem essential when seeking to explain the entrepreneurial role in society. Secondly, there is merit in continuing to expand and accept research that has diverse meta-theoretical backgrounds, so long as underpinning assumptions are clear and we argue that diversity across the BM's paradigms is healthy for the subject in exploring new avenues.

In particular following the 1990s there has been growth in 'interpretive' approaches to entrepreneurship studies (Anderson and Starnawska 2008; Cope 2005; Watkins-Mathys and Lowe 2005) which seek to explore entrepreneurial experience and meaning in social contexts through approaches drawn from social constructionism, interactionism and symbolic discourse analysis (Chell 2008; Downing 2005; Lindgren and Packendorff 2009; Perren and Jennings 2012), yet these remain relatively marginal in mainstream debates which often seek to avoid competing theories (Aldrich 2012; Dimov 2011). We consider such diversity in explanations as valuable for understanding alternative explanations of various socially situated entrepreneurial phenomena.

Despite the growth of interpretive studies, there has only relatively recently been a development of approaches to entrepreneurship studies in the radical structuralist and radical humanist paradigms, as defined by BM. Early dominance of functionalist approaches, it can be argued, has limited the acceptance and legitimacy of these alternative more critical perspectives to the subject, yet some research has, however, begun to develop.

Within BMs' 'radical structuralist' paradigm, scholars adopting an approach known as 'critical entrepreneurship studies' have begun to outline the 'dark side' of entrepreneurship as a political discourse in society and markets and have argued that it reinforces the ideals of capitalism and individualism (Tedmanson *et al.* 2012). Approaches in this form outline how dominant social structures limit the extent to which an individual can act entrepreneurially and have highlighted the social mechanisms which reinforce this (Du Gay 1996; Jones and Spicer 2009). The radical structural perspective is interested in identifying sources of domination in order to identify change which will support a wider variety of entrepreneurial activity and some studies have begun to focus on this, although they remain at the periphery of the contemporary subject.

Similarly, developments have occurred in radical humanist approaches to entrepreneurship. Here, rather than being the preserve of 'special' individuals entrepreneurship is outlined as an aspect of everyday life (Spinosa, Flores and Dreyfus 1997) which is relatively 'mundane' in that it may be enacted by anyone in order to engender social change (Hjorth 2013; Johannisson 2011; Stayaert 2007), or 'disclosing new [social] worlds' (Spinosa *et al.* 1997). These approaches provide opportunities to see how entrepreneurship is part of a wider desire for change and development in society, linked to changes in personal aspiration at the level of the individual-in-the-world.

These developing approaches to entrepreneurship research illustrate the insights and opportunities to advance understanding that might be possible if we are open to diversity and encourage the development of new approaches by applying other BM paradigms in entrepreneurship studies. By closely considering meta-theoretical assumptions we may also remain aware of the limits of adopting any approach, by critically engaging our studies to better support the maturing of our field.

References

Ahmed, S.U. (1985) 'nAch, risk-taking propensity, locus of control, and entrepreneurship', *Personality and Individual Differences*, 6, pp. 781–782.

Aldrich, H.E. (2010) 'Beam me up, Scott(ie)! Institutional theorists' struggles with the emergent nature of entrepreneurship', *Research in the Sociology of Work*, 21, pp. 329–364.

Aldrich, H.E. (2012) 'The emergence of entrepreneurship as an academic field: A personal essay on institutional entrepreneurship', *Research Policy*, 41(7), pp. 1240–1248.

Alvarez, S.A. and Barney, J.B. (2007) 'Discovery and creation: Alternative theories of entrepreneurial action', *Strategic Entrepreneurship Journal*, 1(1–2), pp. 11–26.

Alvarez, S.A. and Barney, J.B. (2010) 'Entrepreneurship and epistemology: The philosophical underpinnings of the study of entrepreneurial opportunities', *Academy of Management Annals*, 4, pp. 557–583.

Alvarez, S.A. and Barney, J.B. (2013) 'Epistemology, opportunities, and entrepreneurship: Comments on Venkataraman *et al.* (2012) and Shane (2012)', *Academy of Management Review*, 38(1), pp. 154–158.

Alvarez, S., Barney, J., McBride, R. and Wuebker, R. (2014) 'Realism in the study of entrepreneurship', *Academy of Management Review*, 39(2), pp. 201–208.

Alvesson, M. and Sandberg, J. (2011) 'Generating research questions through problematization', *Academy of Management Review*, 36(2), pp. 247–271.

Alvesson, M. and Sandberg, J. (2013) 'Has management studies lost its way? Ideas for more imaginative and innovative research', *Management Studies*, 50(1), pp. 128–152.

Anderson, C.R. (1976) 'The relationship between locus of control, decision behaviours and performance in a stress setting: A longitudinal study'. In *Academy of Management Proceedings*, 1976(1), pp. 65–69, Academy of Management. Available at: http://proceedings.aom.org/content/1976/1/65 doi: 10.5465/AMBPP.1976.4975566.

Anderson, A.R. and Starnawska, M. (2008) 'Research practices in entrepreneurship; problems of definition, description and meaning', *International Journal of Entrepreneurship and Innovation*, 9(4), pp. 221–230.

Barreto, H. (1989) *The Entrepreneur in Micro-Economic Theory: Disappearance and Explanation.* New York: Routledge.

Begley, T.M. and Boyd, D.P. (1986) 'Psychological characteristics associated with entrepreneurial performance'. In *Frontiers of Entrepreneurship Research.* 6th Annual Entrepreneurship Research Conference, Babson College, Wellesley, MA, pp. 146–165.

Bird, B.J. (1988) 'Implementing entrepreneurial ideas: The case of intention', *Academy of Management Review*, 13(3), pp. 442–453.

Borland, C. (1974) *Locus of control, need for achievement and entrepreneurship.* Doctoral Dissertation, Austin, TX: University of Texas.

Boyd, N.G. and Vozikis, G.S. (1994) 'The influence of self-efficacy on the development of entrepreneurial intentions and actions', *Entrepreneurship Theory and Practice*, 18(4), pp. 63–77.

Brockhaus, R.H. (1980) 'Risk-taking propensity of entrepreneurs', *Academy of Management Journal*, 23(3), pp. 509–520.

Brockhaus, R.H. (1982) 'Psychology of the entrepreneur'. In Kent, C.A., Sexton, D.L. and Vesper, K.H (eds) *Encyclopedia of Entrepreneurship.* Englewood Cliffs, NJ: Prentice Hall, pp. 38–71.

Brockhaus, R.H. and Horwitz, P.S. (1985) 'The psychology of the entrepreneur'. In Sexton, D. and Smilor, R. (eds) *The Art and Science of Entrepreneurship.* Cambridge, MA: Ballinger, pp. 25–48.

Brockhaus, R.H. and Horwitz, P.S. (1986) 'The psychology of the entrepreneur'. In Sexton, D. and Smilor, R. (eds) *The Art and Science of Entrepreneurship.* Cambridge, MA: Ballinger, pp. 25–48.

Brockhaus, R.H. and Nord, W.R. (1979) 'An exploration of factors affecting the entrepreneurial decision: Personal characteristics vs environmental conditions'. In *Academy of Management Proceedings*, 1979(1), pp. 364–368, Academy of Management. Available at: http://proceedings.aom.org/content/1979/1/364; doi: 10.5465/AMBPP. 1979.4977621.

Bull, I. and Willard, G.E. (1993) 'Towards a theory of entrepreneurship', *Journal of Business Venturing*, 8(3), pp. 181–182.

Burrell, G. and Morgan, G. (1979) *Sociological Paradigms and Organizational Analysis.* London: Heinemann.

Bygrave, W.D. (1989) 'The entrepreneurship paradigm (I): A philosophical look at its research methodologies', *Entrepreneurship Theory and Practice*, 14(1), pp. 7–26.

Carland, J.W., Hoy, F. and Carland, J.A. (1988) 'Who is an entrepreneur? Is a question worth asking', *American Journal of Small Business*, 13, Spring, pp. 33–39.

Chell, E. (1985) 'The entrepreneurial personality: A few ghosts laid to rest?', *International Small Business Journal*, 3(3), pp. 43–54.

Chell, E. (1997) *The social construction of the entrepreneurial personality.* Paper presented at the British Academy of Management Conference, September. London: British Academy of Management.

Chell, E. (2000) 'Towards researching the "opportunistic entrepreneur": A social constructionist approach and research agenda', *European Journal of Work and Organizational Psychology*, 9(1), pp. 63–80.

Chell, E. (2008) *The Entrepreneurial Personality: A Social Construction.* London: Routledge.

Chell, E. and Burrows, R. (1991) 'The small business owner-manager'. In Stanworth, J. and Gray, C. (eds) *Bolton 20 Years On*. London: Paul Chapman, pp. 151–177.

Chell, E. and Haworth, J. (1988) 'Entrepreneurship and entrepreneurial management: The need for a paradigm', *Graduate Management Research*, 4(1), pp. 16–33.

Chell, E., Haworth, J. and Brearley, S. (1991) *The Entrepreneurial Personality: Concepts, Cases and Categories*. London: Routledge.

Chell, E., Hedberg-Jalonen, N. and Miettinen, A. (1997) 'Are types of business owner-manager universal? A cross-country study of the U.K., New Zealand and Finland'. In Donckels, R. and Miettinen, A. (eds) *Entrepreneurship and SME Research: On its Way to the Next Millennium*. Aldershot: Ashgate, pp. 3–18.

Cope, J. (2005) 'Toward a dynamic learning perspective of entrepreneurship', *Entrepreneurship Theory and Practice*, 29(4), pp. 373–397.

Cromie, S. and Johns, S. (1983) 'Irish entrepreneurs: Some personal characteristics', *Journal of Occupational Behaviour*, 4, pp. 317–324.

Cunliffe, A.L. (2008) 'Orientations to social constructionism: Relationally responsive social constructionism and its implications for knowledge and learning', *Management Learning*, 39(2), pp. 123–139.

Davidsson, P., Low, M.B. and Wright, M. (2001) 'Editor's introduction: Low and MacMillan ten years on: Achievements and future directions for entrepreneurship research', *Entrepreneurship Theory and Practice*, 25(4), pp. 5–15.

DeCarlo, J.F. and Lyons, P.R. (1979) 'A comparison of selected personal characteristics of minority and non-minority female entrepreneurs', *Journal of Small Business Management*, 17, pp. 22–29.

Dimov, D. (2011) 'Grappling with the unbearable elusiveness of entrepreneurial opportunities', *Entrepreneurship Theory and Practice*, 35(1), pp. 57–81.

Downing, S. (2005) 'The social construction of entrepreneurship: Narrative and dramatic processes in the coproduction of organizations and identities', *Entrepreneurship Theory and Practice*, 29, pp. 185–204.

Du Gay, P. (1996) *Consumption and Identity at Work*. London: Sage.

Durand, D. and Shea, D. (1974) 'Entrepreneurial activity as a function of achievement motive and reinforcement control', *Journal of Psychology*, 88, pp. 57–63.

Edwards, A.L. (1959) *Manual for the Edwards Personal Preference Schedule*. New York: Psychological Corporation.

Fischer, E., Reuber, A., Hababou, M., Johnson, W. and Lee, S. (1997) 'The role of socially constructed temporal perspectives in the emergence of rapid-growth firms', *Entrepreneurship, Theory and Practice*, 22(2), pp. 13–30.

Flanagan, J.C. (1954) 'The critical incident technique', *Psychological Bulletin*, 15, pp. 327–358.

Furnham, A. (1986) 'Economic locus of control', *Human Relations*, 39(1), pp. 29–43.

Folger, R., Timmerman, T. and Wooten, K. (1992) 'Personality predictors of entrepreneurship by outplaced managers'. In *Frontiers of Entrepreneurship Research*. 12th Annual Babson College Research Conference, Fontainebleau, France, pp. 63–74.

Frey, R.S. (1984) 'Need for achievement, entrepreneurship, and economic growth: A critique of the McClelland thesis', *Social Science Journal*, 21(2), pp. 125–135.

Fletcher, D.E. (2006) 'Entrepreneurial processes and the social construction of opportunity', *Entrepreneurship and Regional Development*, 18(5), pp. 421–440.

Gartner, W. (1985) 'A framework for describing and classifying the phenomenon of new venture creation', *Academy of Management Review*, 10(4), pp. 696–706.

Gartner, W.B. (1989) 'Who is an entrepreneur? Is the wrong question', *Entrepreneurship Theory and Practice*, 13(4), pp. 47–68.

Gartner, W. (2001) 'Is there an elephant in entrepreneurship? Blind assumptions in theory development', *Entrepreneurship Theory and Practice*, 25(4), pp. 27–39.

Gibb, A. and Ritchie, J. (1981) *Influences on entrepreneurship: A study over time*. Paper presented to the 1981 Small Business Policy and Research Conference, 20–21 November, Polytechnic of Central London.

Grant, P. and Perren, L. (2002) 'Small business and entrepreneurial research: Meta-theories, paradigms and prejudices', *International Small Business Journal*, 20(2), pp. 185–211.

Greenberger, D.B. and Sexton, D.L. (1988) 'An interactive model of new venture initiation', *Journal of Small Business Management*, 26(3), pp. 107–113.

Greenhalgh, T. (1997) 'Papers that summarise other papers (systematic reviews and meta-analyses)', *British Medical Journal*, 315(7109), pp. 672–675.

Hampson, S.E. (1982) *The Construction of Personality*. London: Routledge/Keegan Paul.

Hart, C. (1998) *Doing a Literature Review: Releasing the Social Science Research Imagination*. London: Sage.

Hisrich, R.D. and O'Brien, M. (1981) 'The woman entrepreneur from a business and sociological perspective'. In *Frontiers of Entrepreneurship Research*. Wellesley, MA: Babson College, pp. 21–39.

Hjorth, D. (2013) 'Public entrepreneurship: Desiring social change, creating sociality', *Entrepreneurship and Regional Development*, 25(1–2), pp. 34–51.

Hornaday, J.A. and Aboud, J. (1971) 'Characteristics of successful entrepreneurs', *Personnel Psychology*, 24(2), pp. 141–153.

Hull, D.L., Bosley, J.J. and Udell, G.G. (1980) 'Renewing the hunt for Heffalump: Identifying potential entrepreneurs by personality characteristics', *Journal of Small Business Management*, 18(1), pp. 11–18.

Jackson, D.D. (1974) *Personality Research Form Manual*. New York: Research Psychologists Press.

Jackson, N. and Carter, P. (1991) 'In defence of paradigm incommensurability', *Organization Studies*, 12(1), pp. 109–127.

Jackson, N. and Carter, P. (1993) 'Paradigm wars: A response to Hugh Willmott', *Organization Studies*, 14(5), pp. 721–725.

Jennings, P.L., Perren, L. and Carter, S. (2005) 'Alternative perspectives of entrepreneurship', *Entrepreneurship Theory and Practice*, 29(2), pp. 145–152.

Johannisson, B. (2011) 'Towards a practice theory of entrepreneuring', *Small Business Economics*, 36(2), pp. 135–150.

Johnson, B.R. (1990) 'Toward a multidimensional model of entrepreneurship: The case of achievement motivation and the entrepreneur', *Entrepreneurship Theory and Practice*, 14(3), pp. 39–54.

Jones, C. and Spicer, A. (2009) *Unmasking the Entrepreneur*. Cheltenham: Edward Elgar.

Kets de Vries, M.F.R. (1977) 'The entrepreneurial personality: A person at the crossroads', *Journal of Management Studies*, 14, pp. 34–57.

Korsgaard, S. and Neergaard, H. (2010) 'Sites and enactments: A nominalist approach to opportunities'. In Gartner, W.B. (ed.) *ENTER: Entrepreneurial Narrative Theory Ethnomethodology and Reflexivity*. Volume 1, Clemson, SC: Clemson University Digital Press, pp. 137–152.

Kilby, P. (1971) *Entrepreneurship and Economic Development*. New York: Free Press.

Kirzner, I.M. (1973) *Competition and Entrepreneurship*. Chicago, IL: University of Chicago Press.

Kirzner, I.M. (1980) 'The primacy of entrepreneurial discovery'. In Seldon, A. (ed.) *Prime Mover of Progress: The Entrepreneur in Capitalism and Socialism*. London: Institute of Economic Affairs, pp. 5–29.

Klinger, E. (1966) 'Fantasy need achievement as a motivational construct', *Psychological Bulletin*, 66, pp. 291–308.

Knight, F.H. (1921) *Risk, Uncertainty and Profit*. New York: Houghton Mifflin.

Kostera, M. (2013) *Organizations and Archetypes*. Cheltenham: Edward Elgar.

Kuhn, T.S. (1962) *The Structure of Scientific Revolutions*. Chicago, IL: University of Chicago Press.

Learned, K.E. (1992) 'What happened before the organization? A model of organization formation', *Entrepreneurship Theory and Practice*, 17(1), pp. 39–48.

Liles, P.R. (1974) *New Business Ventures and the Entrepreneur*. Homewood, IL: Richard Irwin.

Lindgren, M. and Packendorff, J. (2009) 'Project leadership revisited: Towards distributed leadership perspectives in project research', *International Journal of Project Organisation and Management*, 1(3), pp. 285–308.

Litzinger, W.D. (1965) 'The motel entrepreneur and the motel manager', *Academy of Management Journal*, 8, pp. 268–281.

Lynn, R. (1969) 'An achievement motivation questionnaire', *British Journal of Psychology*, 60(4), pp. 529–534.

McClelland, D.C. (1955) 'Measuring motivation in phantasy: The achievement motive'. In McClelland, D.C. (ed.) *Studies in Motivation*. New York: Appleton-Century-Crofts, pp. 401–413.

McClelland, D.C. (1961) *The Achieving Society*. Princeton, NJ: Van Nostrand.

McClelland, D.C. (1971) 'The achievement motive in economic growth'. In Kilby, P. (ed.) *Entrepreneurship and Economic Development*. New York: Free Press, pp. 108–122.

McGee, P.E. and Crandall, V.C. (1968) 'Beliefs in internal-external control of reinforcement and academic performance', *Child Development*, 39, pp. 91–102.

Mehrabian, A. (1968) 'Male and female scales of the tendency to achieve', *Educational and Psychological Measurement*, 28, pp. 493–502.

Mehrabian, A. (1969) 'Measures of achieving tendency', *Educational and Psychological Measurement*, 29, pp. 445–451.

Meredith, G.G., Nelson, R.E. and Neck, P.A. (1982) *The Practice of Entrepreneurship*. Geneva: International Labour Office.

Mescon, T. and Montanari, J. (1981) 'The personalities of independent and franchise entrepreneurs: An empirical analysis of concepts', *Journal of Enterprise Management*, 3(2), pp. 149–159.

Milne, A.A. (2010 [1926]) *Winnie-the-Pooh*. London: Egmont.

Miner, J.B. (1980) *Theories of Organizational Behavior*. Hinsdale, IL: Dryden Press.

Miner, J.B. (1982) 'The uncertain future of the leadership concept: Revisions and clarifications', *Journal of Applied Behavioural Science*, 18(3), pp. 293–307.

Miner, J.B. (1986) *Scoring Guide for the Miner Sentence Completion Scale Form T*. Atlanta, GA: Organizational Measurement Systems Press.

Mole, K.F. and Mole, M.M. (2010) 'Entrepreneurship as the structuration of individual and opportunity: A response using a critical realist perspective. Comment on Sarason, Dean and Dillard', *Journal of Business Venturing*, 25(2), pp. 230–237.

Morgan, G. and Smircich, L. (1980) 'The case for qualitative research', *Academy of Management Science*, 5(4), pp. 491–500.

Moriya, F.E., Judd, B.B. and File, K.M. (1988) 'Are women business owners the new breed of entrepreneur?'. In Lasher, H.J., Maliche, R.G. and Scherer, R. (eds) *Entrepreneurship: Bridging the Gaps Between Research and Practice.* Monteray, CA: USASBE, pp. 84–87.

Mukjerhee, B.N. (1968) 'Achievement values and scientific productivity', *Journal of Applied Psychology*, 52(2), pp. 145–147.

Murray, H.A. (1938) *Explorations in Personality.* New York: Oxford University Press.

Naffziger, D.W., Hornsby, J.S. and Kuratko, D.F. (1994) 'A proposed research model of entrepreneurial motivation', *Entrepreneurship Theory and Practice*, 19(2), pp. 29–42.

Nightingale, D.J. and Cromby, J. (1999) *Social Constructionist Psychology: A Critical Analysis of Theory and Practice.* Milton Keynes: Open University Press.

Ohe, T., Honjo, S., Okada, Y. and Miura, K. (1992) 'Female entrepreneurs in the United States and Japan: A study of perceived differences'. In *Frontiers of Entrepreneurship Research.* 12th Annual Babson College Research Conference, Fontainebleau, France, pp. 463–464.

Ogbor, J.O. (2000) 'Mythicizing and reification in entrepreneurial discourse: Ideology-critique of entrepreneurial studies', *Journal of Management Studies*, 35(5), pp. 605–635.

Pandey, J. and Tewary, N.B. (1979) 'Locus of control and achievement values of entrepreneurs', *Journal of Occupational Psychology*, 52, pp. 107–111.

Parker, I. (1998) *Social Constructionism, Discourse and Realism.* London: Sage.

Perren, L. and Jennings, P.L. (2012) 'Discursive and narrative perspectives of entrepreneurship and small firms: A systematic literature review', *International Small Business Journal*, (Virtual special issue), pp. 1–22. ISSN 0266-2426.

Pittaway, L. (2005) 'Philosophies in entrepreneurship: A focus on economic theories', *International Journal of Entrepreneurial Behaviour and Research*, 11(3), pp. 201–221.

Pittaway, L., Holt, R. and Broad, J. (2014) 'Synthesising knowledge in entrepreneurship research: The role of systematic literature reviews'. In Chell, E. and Karatas-Ozkan, M. (eds) *Handbook of Research on Small Business and Entrepreneurship.* London: FT Prentice-Hall, pp. 83–105.

Pittaway, L. and Thorpe, R. (2012) 'A framework for entrepreneurial learning: A tribute to Jason Cope', *Entrepreneurship and Regional Development*, 24(9–10), pp. 837–859.

Price, C. and Monroe, S. (1992) 'Educational training for women and minority entrepreneurs positively impacts venture growth and development'. In *Frontiers of Entrepreneurship Research.* 12th Annual Babson College Research Conference, Fontainebleau, France, 216–230.

Rotter, J.B. (1966) 'Generalised expectancies for internal versus external control of reinforcement', *Psychological Monographs*, 80(1), pp. 1–28.

Rotter, J.B. (1990) 'Internal versus external control of reinforcement', *American Psychologist*, 45(4), pp. 489–493.

Sarason, Y., Dean, T.D. and Dillard, J.F. (2006) 'Entrepreneurship as the nexus of individual and opportunity: A structuration view', *Journal of Business Venturing*, 21, pp. 286–305.

Sarason, Y., Dean, T.D. and Dillard, J.F. (2010) 'How can we know the dancer from the dance? Reply to Entrepreneurship as the structuration of individual and opportunity: A response using a critical realist perspective', *Journal of Business Venturing*, 25(1), pp. 238–243.

Sarasvathy, S.D. (2001) 'Causation and effectuation: Toward a theoretical shift from economic inevitability to entrepreneurial contingency', *Academy of Management Review*, 26, pp. 243–263.

Sarasvathy, S.D. (2004) 'The questions we ask and the questions we care about: Reformulating some problems in entrepreneurship research', *Journal of Business Venturing*, 19(5), pp. 707–717.

Sarasvathy, S.D. and Venkataraman, S. (2011) 'Entrepreneurship as method: Open questions for an entrepreneurial future', *Entrepreneurship Theory and Practice*, 35(1), pp. 113–135.

Scase, R. and Goffee, R. (1985) *Entrepreneurship in Europe: The Social Processes.* London: Groom Helm.

Schrage, H. (1965) 'The R&D entrepreneur: Profile of success', *Harvard Business Review*, 43(5), pp. 56–69.

Schatz, S.P. (1971) 'Achievement and economic growth: A critical appraisal'. In Kilby, P. (ed.) *Entrepreneurship and Economic Development.* New York: Free Press, pp. 183–190.

Sexton, D.L. and Bowman, N.B. (1986) 'Validation of a personality index: Comparative psychological characteristics analysis of female entrepreneurs, managers, entrepreneurship students and business students'. In *Frontiers of Entrepreneurship Research.* Wellesley, MA: Babson College, pp. 40–51.

Shapero, A. (1975) 'The displaced, uncomfortable entrepreneur', *Psychology Today*, November, pp. 83–88.

Shane, S. and Venkataraman, S. (2000) 'The promise of entrepreneurship as a field of research', *Academy of Management Review*, 25(1), pp. 217–226.

Shane, S. and Venkataraman, S. (2013) 'Note: The promise of entrepreneurship as a field of research', *Academy of Management Review*, 25(1), pp. 217–226.

Shaver, K.G. and Scott, L.R. (1991) 'Person, process, choice: The psychology of new venture creation', *Entrepreneurship Theory and Practice*, 16(2), pp. 23–45.

Smith, K.G., Gannon, M. and Sapienza, H. (1989) 'Selecting strategy measures for entrepreneurial research: Trade-offs and guidelines', *Entrepreneurship Theory and Practice*, 14(1), pp. 39–49.

Spence, J.T. and Helmreich, R.L. (1978) *Masculinity and Femininity: Their Psychological Dimensions Correlates and Antecendents.* Austin, TX: University of Texas.

Spinosa, C., Flores, F. and Dreyfus, H.L. (1997) *Disclosing New Worlds: Entrepreneurship, Democratic Action and the Cultivation of Solidarity.* Cambridge, MA: MIT Press.

Steyaert, C. (2007) 'Entrepreneuring as a conceptual attractor? A review of process theories in 20 years of entrepreneurship studies', *Entrepreneurship and Regional Development*, 19(6), pp. 453–477.

Tedmanson, D., Verduyn, K., Essers, C. and Gartner, W.B. (2012) 'Critical perspectives in entrepreneurship research', *Organization*, 19(5), pp. 531–541.

Timmons, J.A., Smollen, L.E. and Dingee, A.L. (1985) *New Venture Creation.* Homewood, IL: Irwin.

Tranfield, D.R., Denyer, D. and Smart, P. (2003) 'Towards a methodology for developing evidence-informed management knowledge by means of systematic review', *British Journal of Management*, 14, pp. 207–222.

Venkatapathy, R. (1984) 'Locus of control among entrepreneurs: A review', *Psychological Studies*, 29(1), pp. 97–100.

Venkataraman, S., Sarasvathy, S.D., Dew, N. and Forster, W.R. (2012) 'Reflections on the 2010 AMR Decade Award: Whither the promise? Moving forward with entrepreneurship as a science of the artificial', *Academy of Management Review*, 37(1), pp. 21–33.

Wainer, H.A. and Rubin, I.M. (1969) 'Motivation of R&D entrepreneurs: Determinants of company success', *Journal of Applied Psychology*, 53(3), pp. 178–184.

Watkins-Mathys, L. and Lowe, S. (2005) 'Small business and entrepreneurship research: The way through the paradigm incommensurability', *International Small Business Journal*, 23(6), pp. 657–677.

Watkins, J.M. and Watkins, D.S. (1986) 'The female entrepreneur: Her background and determinants of business choice – some British data'. In Curran, J., Stanworth, J. and Watkins, D. (eds) *Survival of the Small Firm*. Aldershot: Gower, pp. 220–232.

Watson, T.J. (2013a) 'Entrepreneurial action and the Euro-American social science tradition: Pragmatism, realism and looking beyond the entrepreneur', *Entrepreneurship and Regional Development*, 25(1–2), pp. 16–33.

Watson, T.J. (2013b) 'Entrepreneurship in action: Bringing together the individual, organizational and institutional dimensions of entrepreneurial action', *Entrepreneurship and Regional Development*, 25(5–6), pp. 404–422.

Welsch, H.P. and Young, E.C. (1982) 'The information source selection decision: The role of entrepreneurial personality characteristics', *Journal of Small Business Management*, 20, pp. 49–57.

Welter, F. (2011) 'Contextualizing entrepreneurship-conceptual challenges and ways forward', *Entrepreneurship Theory and Practice*, 35(1), pp. 165–184.

Willmott, H. (1993) 'Breaking the paradigm mentality', *Organization Studies*, 14(5), pp. 682–719.

Zahra, S.A. (2007) 'Contextualizing theory building in entrepreneurship research', *Journal of Business Venturing*, 22(3), pp. 443–452.

Zahra, S.A. and Wright, M. (2011) 'Entrepreneurship's next act', *Academy of Management Perspectives*, 25(4), pp. 67–83.

10 Challenging constructions of entrepreneurial identities

Deirdre Tedmanson and Caroline Essers

10.1 Introduction

Much entrepreneurship literature in the 60s, 70s and 80s tended to emphasize particular psychological traits as key to 'the' entrepreneurial identity. Notions about autonomous, innovative, creative and achievement oriented personality types are often emphasized in such discussions of people's predilection for entrepreneurialism (Ketz de Vries 1977; McClelland 1987; Thomas and Mueller 2000). Risk-taking and individualistic behaviour are also commonly eulogized in this literature as desirable features of 'the' entrepreneurial identity. More contemporary literature however has tended to move away from a focus on behavioural or personality characteristics and towards analyses which look more closely at social context (Donnellan, Ollila and Middleton 2014; Douglas and Grant 2014; Rigg and O'Dwyer 2012; Sheth 2010) and self-narration (Boje and Smith 2010; Down and Warren 2008; Harmeling 2011; Johansson 2004; Steyaert 2007) for example. This trend has enabled the development of more nuanced understandings of entrepreneurial characteristics.

However, dominant entrepreneurial archetypes often continue to portray what we argue to be a specifically male type of rationality that is purposeful, ego-driven and oriented to conquest, domination and control albeit within a more diverse range of social contexts. Such an overtly gendered identity discourse about entrepreneurship serves to both re-inscribe hegemonic patriarchy while simultaneously suggesting a concomitant female identity stereotype which is by contrast subordinate, supportive and most often also dependent (Bruni, Gherardi and Poggio 2004; Tedmanson and Essers 2015). Critical analyses of such gendered discourse by Ahl (2002, 2004) and Bruni *et al.* (2004) for example, argue that female entrepreneurs are most usually constructed as the 'other' when compared with male counterparts whose identities are assumed to be the 'norm'.

Research on ethnic minority entrepreneurs similarly asserts that non-European or non-Anglo entrepreneurs are motivated by labour market discrimination or cultural factors rather than identity issues or personality traits (Bonacich 1993; Dana 2007; Kloosterman and Rath 2003; Portes 1995; Ram and Carter 2003). Thomas and Mueller (2000) similarly show that entrepreneurs from diverse cultural backgrounds may exhibit quite different entrepreneurial traits from those conventionally accepted as the 'norm'. Amongst others, authors such as Ogbor (2000) and Essers and Benschop (2007) in particular suggest that the mainstream construction of entrepreneurial identity is both ethnocentric and patriarchal. This means that there is a strong gender and ethnocentric sub-text in the description of entrepreneurial identities. Ogbor (2000, p. 608) argues that the discourse of entrepreneurship has been particularly pernicious:

> The discourse on entrepreneurship ... has been used to further enhance the divisions among humans, race, ethnicity and gender, through processes of classification, codification, categorization and taxonomies. In other words, the discourse has delineated a certain space that privileges the dominance of the Western male mentality in Western discourse.

Discourse is of interest here as a means for understanding the way some aspects of entrepreneurial identity gain attribution and emphasis, while others do not. Particular aspects of human nature, such as risk-taking behaviour and assertiveness for example, are constantly promoted as if essential and natural attributes for an entrepreneurial identity. These attributes are privileged and assumed to have a greater hierarchical importance than others, such as a predisposition to be sociable and reflexive for example. As Ogbor explains (2000, p. 607):

> Discourse is seen as a structuring principle of society, and thus through detailed deconstruction, we can examine the working of power on behalf of specific interests and analyse the opportunities for resistance to it.

Much mainstream entrepreneurship literature presumes a particular kind of heroic masculinity as key to 'the' entrepreneurial identity and connects this also with a Eurocentric cultural bias in a binary which reproduces existing relations of power (Halford and Leonard 2006; Lutz 1991; Tedmanson *et al.* 2012). Other research (see e.g. Bruni *et al.* 2005; Alvesson, Lee Ashcraft and Thomas 2008; Alvesson 2010; Powell and Greenhaus 2010) points however to the diversity and complexity of women's lived experience. As Chasserio, Pailot and Poroli (2014, p. 129) explain, women are:

> ... socially constructed through social interactions, and ... throughout their lives they acquire diverse and multiple social identities and linked roles.

In this chapter we challenge the mainstream totalizing image of a masculine and totalizing entrepreneurial identity. Eschewing this gendered and 'white' Western construction we strive instead for more reflexive and nuanced considerations of entrepreneurship (Ahl and Marlow 2012; Jones and Spicer 2009; Tedmanson *et al.* 2012). By focusing on the rich, diverse and at times contradictory identity narratives of a group of Muslim businesswomen of Turkish descent in the Netherlands we explore the hybridity, mimicry, fluidity, resistance and resilience of women's lived experiences, their agency and identities.

We highlight particular excerpts taken from the identity narratives of Muslim businesswomen of Turkish descent living in the Netherlands to show how these stories describe quite different ways of experiencing, interpreting and responding to their marginalization. These narrative excerpts shed light on some of the underlying relations of power that, we argue, shape the entrepreneurial identities of these women. We take issue with the often taken-for-granted universal subjectivity of 'the entrepreneur' by including the identity categories of ethnicity, gender and religion (Essers and Benschop 2007, 2009). One of the more powerful insights coming from these narratives is the way in which the women create new hybrid identities which fuse their lives as Muslim women in the Netherlands with their sense of themselves as entrepreneurs. We take this concept further in this chapter by exploring the tensions inherent in the hybridity of entrepreneurial identities. An analysis of the women's own stories is used to illustrate the competing tensions in the fashioning of hybrid identities, both for and against assimilation and acceptance in the Dutch socio-political context.

In this chapter we ask: what are the identity constructions female Muslim entrepreneurs of Turkish descent fashion for themselves within the Dutch context and how does this context mediate their multiple social and work-life identities?

10.2 Socio-political context

As in many parts of the western world in contemporary times, migrants with a Muslim background are currently being targeted in what is a highly politicized discourse against 'multiculturalism' in the Netherlands. Since the 1990s, this 'Islamaphobia' has been promoted by right-wing politicians who argue vehemently that the Muslim population in the Netherlands, should 'assimilate' to Dutch culture. Such prejudiced sentiments focus on negative stereotypes of Turkish and other immigrants – especially those who happen to follow Islam (Gijsberts and Dagevos 2004). The repeated demonization of a particular group in the Dutch population creates an environment of fear and anxiety in which hatred and a popularly entrenched anti-Muslim bias takes root. The marginalization of the Muslim population accelerates in such an atmosphere of moral panic.

Moral panic (Cohen 1999) generates fear and hostility in the popular press and campaigns about the 'undesirability' of the head-scarf, opposition to the building of new mosques in the Netherlands and reunification through marriage from countries such as Turkey. There has been an escalation of racist tensions in the Netherlands as elsewhere in Europe (and globally) which is built around the construction of Muslims as a people who are different, and even dangerous, due solely to their cultural and religious heritage (Ghorashi 2003, 2006).

Turkey, which is a secular nation, has never been formally tied to the Netherlands. However, Dutch companies supported by government policies aiming to expand the pool of labour available to accelerate economic expansion in the 1960s and 70s, recruited Turkish men to work in heavy industry (see Frenkel and Shenhav 2006, p. 866). These 'guest labourers' or 'gastarbeiders' as they were termed in Dutch, held temporary work contracts which ended when the temporary work was done (Merens 2000). Once family reunification was established in international treaties however, many guest workers chose to remain in the Netherlands. With the immigration of their families made possible through policies of family reunification, Turkish women settled in the Netherlands also. While Dutch policy favoured multiculturalism in the 1980s such pluralism was viewed in a positive light.

Migrants of Turkish origin who were Muslim (amongst other Muslim groups) quickly became the targets of the discourse against 'multiculturalism' in the Netherlands in the 1990s, with right-wing politicians arguing vehemently that migrants, especially Muslims, should be forced to 'assimilate' to Dutch culture and promulgating negative stereotypes of people from Morocco and Turkey (Gijsberts and Dagevos 2004). While earlier sought after as a source of ready labour that would be productive and useful to economic growth, Turkish and other migrants who may share the Islamic faith were now shunned. As a result, past Dutch Muslim policies which accommodated and promoted multiculturalism and encouraged 'guest workers' from Turkey and other locations has now given way to fear of 'others':

> Public discourse on Muslims in the Netherlands – and Europe more broadly – has increasingly been framed around the alleged incompatibility of Islam with some idealized notion of supposed 'more civilized' Western values.
>
> (Essers and Tedmanson 2014, p. 355)

As at the last census Turkish people (around 393,000 inhabitants) constitute the largest group of migrants in the Netherlands. The total Dutch population is approximately 16.8 million. The birth rate of people of Turkish origin is higher than that of the native Dutch (CBS 2012). Combined with continuing immigration from Turkey, the percentage of this group in the whole population will continue to increase. Given the history of Turkey as a secular nation, obviously not all Turkish migrants to the Netherlands are Muslim. However, the nature of the discursive construction of Islamophobia in the Netherlands – and Europe more broadly – has been increasingly stereotyping whole ethnicities and communities, framed around some idealized notions of a supposedly 'more civilized' Western modernity (Korteweg and Yurdakul 2009, p. 218; Ryan 2011, p. 1046), irrespective of evidence to the contrary. It is within this increasingly complex socio-political context that the women who are the focus of our chapter must shape their entrepreneurial identities.

10.3 Identity and entrepreneurship

We argue in this chapter that identities are always contextually, historically and discursively constructed at the intersection of various identity categories (Essers and Benschop 2009; Tedmanson and Essers 2015). Accordingly, female entrepreneurs and minority business women may always have multiple, inter-related and evolving selves (Sardar 2005). The female entrepreneurs we focus on in this chapter for example speak of a construction of their professional identities coming in part from the values, norms, rituals and artefacts which are familiar and recurring themes in popular entrepreneurship discourse (Bruni *et al.* 2004; Essers and Benschop 2009; Ogbor 2000).

The women interviewed in this study however, also reveal how they construct their identities 'in relation to' the socio-political context in which they live and work (Essers and Benschop 2009; Essers and Tedmanson 2014; Pio 2007). It is through the narrative accounts of their lived experience that we see how the polarized nature of Muslim/non-Muslim relations in the Netherlands impacts on these women's ethnic, religious, gender and entrepreneurial identities.

It is often stated that gender is the personal and social categorization by which sense is made of biological differences between men and women while 'ethnicity' is similarly an ideological construct (Essers and Benschop 2009). People also construct their national or ethnic identities by incorporating or perceiving certain ways of being such as language, religion or cultural mores as distinctive markers of 'self-hood' (Sardar 2005). Such cultural markers or identity signatures are recognized, embraced, disparaged or eschewed according to one's sense of identification or distance from them.

Gendering entrepreneurship develops on from these concepts to challenge assumptions and accepted practices in entrepreneurship research. Considerations about the interplay of gender and ethnicity help to reveal how historical and socio-political contexts can intersect in a multiplicity of ways to shape the way entrepreneurial identities are constructed (Calas, Smircich and Bourne 2009; Essers and Benschop 2007). As we have elsewhere stated: "women are not just 'entrepreneurs', they become identified and identifiable – as 'Turkish Muslim entrepreneurs'" (Essers and Tedmanson 2014, p. 355).

Intersectionality is a concept denoting the (in)separability of people's sense of their identities in relation to ethnicity, class, gender and sexuality, and of how such multiple and intersecting identities evolve within differing social, cultural and institutional contexts (Essers and Benschop 2009; Holvino 2010; McCall 2005). The concept of intersectionality stresses the importance of the meshing of different categories of oppression and helps us analyse how these forces come together to shape the complex identities of women (Crenshaw *et al.* 1995). In the field of entrepreneurship, several studies have already been conducted on the intersections of gender, ethnic and religious identities (Essers and Benschop 2007; Essers and Benschop 2009; Essers and Tedmanson 2014). These studies point to the importance of women performing boundary work, as active agents, when gender, ethnicity and religion intersect in entrepreneurial contexts. Hence, the intersectionality of gender, ethnicity and Islam within entrepreneurship, as told by the women in the study we focus on in this chapter, reveals that extensive identity work is undertaken to enable the women concerned to be able to cope with structural inequalities and to create room for their entrepreneurship.

As Mirchandani reminds us, women are never just women but are 'always located within a particular class and of a particular ethnicity and sexuality' (1999, p. 229). Analysing the intersectionality at play in how a particular sample of women in this study combines diverse categories of difference simultaneously in the construction of their entrepreneurial identities provides a new way for analysing the hybridity inherent in their entrepreneurial identities (Crenshaw 1997).

In this chapter we use these concepts of intersectionality, hybridity, the fluidity of women's lives and the complexity of identity construction, along with insights drawn also from critical theory and postcolonial feminism (Ghandi 1998; Mohanty 2003; Narayan 1998; Rozaldo 1980; Trinh 2001; Westwood 2006) to explore the identity construction through the self-narration of three Turkish Muslim entrepreneurs, at the intersection of gender and race/ethnicity in a socio-political context. The key issue to emerge from our analysis is the less often discussed notion of hybridity in entrepreneurial identity work.

10.4 Hybridity

Elsewhere we have theorized the self-identity work of Turkish Muslim entrepreneurs in the Netherlands from an exclusively postcolonial feminist perspective (Essers and Tedmanson 2014). In this chapter we augment this work by focusing particularly on hybridity in the context of women forging their entrepreneurial identities as resistance to a dominant cultural context which is antipathetic to their cultural histories. We consider the concept of hybridity to be an important aspect of intersectionality in the context of Muslim/non-Muslim relations.

Through a strategic response to the embedded practices of 'otherizing' experienced within dominant culture settings, individuals create hybrid identities which represent an intermingling and fusion of their intersecting selves at a cultural and even psychological level (Prasad 2003, 2006). Bhabha (1994, 1997) argues however that the postcolonial Orientalist discourse of 'otherizing' is not unilateral and that the 'boundary' separating West and non-West is not a fixed one but rather a porous domain which is 'ambivalent' and liminal. He also suggests that hybridity can also be akin to mimicry, whereby people imitate a dominant group or aspects of dominant group behaviour. Sometimes the liminal space of mimicry reflects an internalization of dominant group norms and values (Bhabha 1997). This process of internalizing the constructions of 'otherness' promulgated by the dominant group is identified by Fanon (1986) as a form of postcolonial anxiety in which a sense of dependency and inferiority is produced by the negative gaze of the dominant.

Narrating new stories of oneself – in which a new identity is repositioned as positive even within the context of the dominant gaze – is a powerful gesture of survival. Inherent in the stories of the Turkish Muslim female entrepreneurs operating in the Dutch context provided in this chapter are aspects of the reproduction, in some cases, of the judgemental attitudes of the dominant Dutch society. In others however the women reframe the context within which their identities are forged to provide a new sense of themselves as agentic and powerful, despite and perhaps because of their awareness of the gaze of others.

Mahalingam and Leu (2005, p. 841) argue that intersectionality can be thought of as the 'triangulation' of subjective positioning vis à vis one's location on the axes of social categories such as class, gender, race, sexuality and age:

> The process is dynamic, multidimensional, multi-sited and historically contingent. It mediates various psychological processes such as well-being, acculturation, moral reasoning, judgement and decision making and everyday understandings of social relations.

Bhabha (1997) proposes the concept of hybridity as a way of disrupting the essentializing discourses which seek fixed and static categorizations of difference and disadvantage. Hybridity in Bhaba's view is a critical intervention which enables the deconstruction of discourses about the 'other' which focus on the bounded edges difference rather than the fluid intersections of diversity and power. By acknowledging the criss-crossing of boundaries evolving back and forth and the overlapping of subjectivities, the messiness and hence potentialities of difference can emerge (Mahalingam and Leu 2005). Root (1999) asserts the formation and naming of hybrid identities (e.g. Asian-Australian; young-Irish-athlete; Turkish-Muslim-female-entrepreneur) which reflect the multiple nature of intersectionality and subjectivities is in itself a way of challenging dominant discourses which aim to essentialize and thus disempower.

Percoud (2002) also uses the concept of hybridity to analyse the stages of acculturation and adaptation of Turkish businesses in the German economy. Percoud suggests that early in their development such sole trader self-employed Turkish-German businesses rely on a 'protected market constituted by Turkish migrants' specific needs' (p. 497). However, Percoud argues this closed economy approach changes over time as a reliance on German suppliers and interactions leads to a greater German customer base. He argues the very hybridity of the new businesses emerging leads to a form of identity assimilation. A new phase of entrepreneurial activity develops which focuses on the broader market with often employees also not being exclusively Turkish but more often German or of other non-Turkish background. Turkish entrepreneurs in this context, he argues, have gone from 'niche to market' as truly hybrid intersectional identities. Hillmann (1999), in a study of Turkish-German female entrepreneurs, notes how they do not see themselves as part of an ethnic or Turkish economy but rather as 'normal' businesswomen. The duality of minority entrepreneurship as both a critical means of human emancipation and at the same time a form of assimilationist social entrapment is thus evident in Percoud's case study as in many other such commentaries (Chan and Ong 1995; Chasserio *et al.* 2014; Tedmanson *et al.* 2012).

Hybridity as Appadurai (2006) perceives it, however, is a way of conceptualizing a new space where cultural differences are reaffirmed while at the same time unequal power relations are disrupted – transforming the identities of both dominator and dominated. Through fusing aspects of West and non-West, a third space emerges (Bhabha 1997); a domain of negotiation, translation and liminality (Narayan and Harding 1998). It is in this fluid, localized and politicized space that 'relations of alternity and positions of self-other are performed' (Westwood 2006, p. 105).

Generally in social research hybridity has been understood to refer to the intersectional mixture of characteristics in a continuum between two binary opposite axes (Grassl 2011; Makadok and Coff 2009). Grassl (2011) amongst others has provided a schema for enterprise contexts which identifies hybridity of organizational type, product status re goods and services, profit orientation and ownership model amongst other key variables, to illustrate the types of hybrid combinations which can be produced. Social entrepreneurial effort is often promoted in this way as an exemplar of a hybrid form of entrepreneurial organisation, as the focus is both business enterprise activities as well as the production of a social good.

Hybridity is also a means not of integration and absorption into a dominant cultural space but rather a means for maintaining and asserting individual and collective agency. In 'The Location of Culture' Bhabha (1994, p. 4) argues for the space:

> In between the designations of identity … an interstitial passage between fixed identifications [which] opens up the possibility of a cultural hybridity that entertains difference without an assumed or imposed hierarchy.

It is in this third space we argue that female Turkish Muslim entrepreneurs in the Netherlands are able to craft their own identities and to also morph, change and revisit how they enact and narrate themselves in order to maintain power within what otherwise might be the terrain of vulnerability. Bhabha (1994) invokes hybridity as a means for transcendence and invites us to question how we position others and to 'inhabit an intervening space' (p. 3) and to consider instead their sense of selfhood and agency 'from the interstitial perspective' (p. 7) that an understanding of the intersectional nature of hybridity offers.

10.5 Collecting identity narratives

Narayan (1998, p. 104) suggests that developing ways of research that promote an approach committed to an 'anti-essentialism' both about women and about cultures – and we argue also about entrepreneurship – 'is an urgent and important task'. Subtle, textured, nuanced ethnographies which give voice to a plurality of experience are needed in our view, to challenge the assumptions and accepted research practices in the field of entrepreneurship research.

As feminists, we hear the words of McAdams (1997), Narayan (1998), Czarniawska (1999) and Spivak (2008) amongst many others to approach our research reflexively, sensitive to the challenges of our power and place within the contexts explored. As researchers who do not identify religiously but are secular, humanist and agnostic we acknowledge the ethical challenges of researching cross-culturally. We are scholars – from Australia (first author), a Western country but not a Dutch context and the Netherlands (second author), but not Muslim or Turkish. Our identities, like those of the women we choose to work with in feminist solidarity, are shaped and constructed within the socio-political contexts and values which form our life experiences.

We acknowledge that it is the researcher who collects and interprets the stories we discuss below. We accept responsibility for 'the power that is played out in our writing' (Rhodes and Brown 2005, p. 477), in so far as it might produce and reproduce various social orders and political inequalities, despite our efforts to remain reflective and responsive. In keeping with our sense of poststructuralist feminism, we believe that as Rhodes and Brown (2005, p. 477) state:

> Producing objective truth everyone agrees upon is impossible, nor is it desirable to search for the right reading of someone's story as this would imply a particular practice of power-claiming that researchers have the ability to represent reality.

In the empirical phase of the research, in-depth life story interviews were conducted[1] – some 15 in all, lasting over 2 hours each – with female Turkish entrepreneurs, selected through migrant businesswomen's networks through snowballing. We sought to bring forward the voice of this often neglected group of entrepreneurs to profile their agency and productive contributions against the backdrop of a hostile national socio-political context. Interviews were semi-structured to elicit life narratives which provide space for respondents to convey a broader sense of their life experiences.

This qualitative method enables the intersectionality of women's lives to be made more visible, as women narrate their own journey/s and construct their own stories of identity (Czarniawska 1999; Essers and Tedmanson 2014). McAdams defines identity here as 'the internalized and evolving story that results from a person's selective appropriation of past, present and future' (1997, p. 71). Consistent with narrative techniques for unpacking the discourse, we explored each of the life stories for recurring themes, key descriptors and patterns of language. We utilized 'an interpretative, in-depth stance to identify the three stories which most clearly reflected the explicated themes ... and which were the most distinctive' (Essers and Tedmanson 2014, p. 357).

In this instance we are most concerned to focus on the qualitative theme of hybridity which comes strongly through the narratives. While the women interviewed adapt, adopt and rework their individual stories to portray their sense of their own identities differently, each portrays aspects of a hybrid 'self' fashioned in response to circumstance – and unique to the socio-political context in which they conduct their entrepreneurial activities.

Giving voice to the plurality and fluidity of women's lives aids the pursuit of a transnational feminist literacy (Spivak 2008). Extending such new literacies serves to challenge normative and essentialist notions of what an entrepreneur is and does. Bringing to life the complex, more subtle and nuanced subjective experiences of those interviewed is in itself we argue, a form of Fine's (2006) epistemic justice, which makes hybridity in women's identity work visible, worthy of respect and recognition.

10.6 The construction of 'hybrid' identities

Excerpts from the identity narratives of three Turkish Muslim women entrepreneurs follow, each denoted by a separate pseudonym to provide anonymity. In order to particularly highlight the issues of hybridity we are seeking to explore, we selected the most relevant commentaries around this theme. Of the 15 in-depth narratives collected we selected these three for the purposes of discussion on hybridity in this chapter, but also as the women articulated a particular agility with moving between contexts and fusing often competing tensions into a sense of self which works for them. Each also engaged in a reflexive analysis of why their situation enabled or alternatively necessitated them to enact such dexterity.

Elsewhere (Essers and Tedmanson 2014) we have elaborated on this research through the lens of postcolonial feminism. The excerpts cited and discussed below were selected for analysis for the way they addressed the intersectional hybridity of the women's narratives of selfhood. Their expression of construction of the transnational and hybrid nature of their identities as female Turkish Muslim entrepreneurs is our focus. We will first briefly introduce the women (pseudonyms used throughout) as follows:

- Atalya, 29 years old, owns a beauty salon for ethnic minority women, which she operates with her sister. She was born in Turkey and came to the Netherlands when she was three. Atalya was arranged to be married to a Turkish man when she was 16. She had two sons with him before and at the age of 22 years she divorced her ex-husband. She now has a new boyfriend who is Turkish, with whom she has a daughter.
- Dürrin is a 33-year-old Turkish businesswoman who owns a clothing shop and imports fashion clothes from Turkey. She came to the Netherlands when she was three and a half and has lived in the Netherlands ever since. She is divorced, and has a 12-year-old son. Recently, she married a Dutch man.
- Leila is a 41-year-old woman of Turkish origin, who is divorced and has remarried. She and her new husband who is Turkish are raising both

her two children and his two children. Leila came to the Netherlands when she was 17 and runs her own television production company.

10.7 Experiencing discrimination

All three women experience what they perceive to be discrimination within the Dutch context in which they live. However, the experiences of discrimination and 'otherizing' each recount differs in both the degree of severity and its particular manifestation. Atalya for example initially describes how, during her training as a beautician she and her sister were singled out as appearing to be different or ethnic and then treated less favourably as a result by their Dutch teachers and fellow (female) Dutch students:

> We were the only migrants there, kind of outsiders … we almost always had to practise on each other, we never got models to practise on. We eventually told the director we felt discriminated against. And then a Turkish model showed up. We heard students whispering: 'hopefully I don't get her' …

When later seeking support from the bank to establish her own beautician's business Atalya again recounts the stereotyping she experienced of her identity as a Turkish woman being the unitary focus of discussion and an attribute which was perceived by the bank to be a barrier to her being able to negotiate a loan. However, she also recalls how when she connected with a female bank officer she felt some rapport, at least on the level of being a woman seeking to establish a business:

> We had to prove much more. … If we would have been of Dutch descent. … Yes, at the bank we got [a] woman, and that went very well, she was very enthusiastic about our plan [a beauty salon specifically for migrant women]. … 'Well, it was a good thing she was a woman'.

Dürrin, who was establishing her own fashion clothing business, also narrated instances of experiencing discrimination on the basis of her gender, her ethnicity and her religion. The real estate agent she approached to rent store space from was judgemental in Dürrin's view and openly opinionated about her being a 'Turkish Muslim woman'. Dürrin felt aware of the deadening weight of the general ignorance about her cultural history. She felt she was up against a particular form of Islamophobic racism as a woman who was viewed also as one who was not 'regular Dutch':

> When I started this company, the male estate agent said: 'Are you going to sell traditional Turkish clothes?' I said: 'Man, what are you talking about, there is no such thing as traditional Turkish clothing, we

are no Moroccans, we have plain clothes.' So I thought: 'You really don't know anything about Turkey'. ...

While Atalya and Dürrin seek different adaptive strategies and ways to resist and overcome the stereotyping and discrimination they experience in the Netherlands through how they approach their entrepreneurial activity and 'do business', Leila by contrast is more centred on Turkey as the focus of her entrepreneurial activity and indeed her identity. Leila aims to develop her business in the Netherlands but to then return home to expand and succeed in her venture, after which she will make films and promote her own sense of women's advancement:

> I would like to have a branch office ... in Istanbul, between now and 3 years. And I would like to live in Istanbul also, because that really attracts me. And that means that I would like to transfer people working here to Istanbul. And that they once in a while are positioned here ... I make documentaries on female circumcision because you want that the knowledge you have developed can be used in a certain context for other women in the World ...

Leila's media work takes her between cultures and locations and the women interviewed she spoke least of being discriminated against. Leila's focus is notably transnational and she conveys a sense of herself as someone able to move across boundaries with fluidity and agency. Each of the women interviewed sees her entrepreneurialism as only a part of her identity and is happy to discuss how her entrepreneurial activity animates or furthers other aspects of her life. They are entrepreneurial women with clear aims and goals for their business ventures; however, this is one aspect of their lives only. Each cites instances of how they are using or intend to use their business activity to enhance their agency as Turkish women.

10.8 Hybridity in entrepreneurship

Hybridity is spoken about and/or exemplified differently in the narrative journeys of Atalya, Dürrin and Leila. In each of their stories there is a fusion of identities and interplay between the hitherto fixed categories within which their lives are portrayed by others. They each observe the way the dominant Dutch culture perceives their difference and in different but also complimentary ways they each construct their own identities, resisting the Dutch categorizations with which they are faced or alternatively mixing these to advance their entrepreneurial aims and/or create new identities for themselves.

Atalya and her sister turn the negation they perceive of their Turkish-ness and the reluctance of other beautician students to work with Turkish models into a plus.

That's when we thought: this is a market [as] many migrant women do not dare to go to a real beauty salon. ... And then we had to do a whole research, a survey to find out if there would be a demand for this target group, because we were the first [Turkish women doing this].

Within the discriminatory experience a niche market was identified and a new business started. Here the hybrid identities of being a woman and an entrepreneur have come together to enable and embrace the Turkish identity not only of Atalya and her sister but also their customers. As elsewhere analysed (Essers and Tedmanson, 2014, p. 359):

This realization of discrimination through negative stereotyping as Turkish, spurs Atalya to turn her identity into a positive asset with its own unique opportunities. Atalya uses her entrepreneurship to gain self-esteem (Pio 2007; Zhou 2008), targeting a unique market. Yet, in her opinion she still has to prove much more than Dutch (male) entrepreneurs. Regarding the start-up loan centre, Atalya suggests it was 'a good thing she was a woman', conveying her awareness that if the loan officer at the bank had been a man, it may have been harder (in her view) to gain a loan. Atalya's identity is as an outsider: being a female, Turkish businesswoman in the Dutch context.

Similarly for Dürrin, there is a difficult challenge, to create her fashion business at the cross-roads between the mainstream Dutch society and the intersection with a projected construction of Turkish exotica – and also for Dürrin Muslim 'otherness' – which although imagined and not representative, is nonetheless a point of business discouragement for Dürrin:

At first, everyone thought because of my appearance [Dürrin has blue eyes and light hair] that I was Italian and hence the business went better. But I'm too honest [not] to admit the clothes come from Turkey, and then it sells much less. ... First, you were a Turk, now a Muslim, nothing more. ... Since people know I'm Muslim, they do not come anymore. ... But I am practically Dutch, as I have lived here almost my whole life ...

Dürrin's identity is a hybrid one – she 'looks' Italian, she argues, because of her hair and eye colouring. Her embodiment in this sense is European, which seems to psychologically also link her to a sense of herself as more cosmopolitan and even able to 'pass' as Dutch. Yet Dürrin sells Turkish clothes and wishes to develop her clothes business in ways to expand her Dutch as well as Turkish customer base. As earlier cited, she looks to move from niche to market. While experiencing being shunned as a Muslim, Dürrin also speaks of herself as being 'practically Dutch', having lived in the Netherlands most of her life.

10.9 Competing tensions

Hybridity of identity here brings with it both positive and negative attributes. It is nevertheless a strong example of hybridity of identity in action. In this contemporary Dutch context Dürrin's identity is not fixed but something tumbled together through her own sense of selfhood mixed with the reflections of the society around her, then tempered by her experience as an entrepreneur. As Wallace (2007, p. 7) argues in her research on entrepreneurship as embodiment:

> Identity politics, in countering claims of a universal selfhood of positivist approaches has, like poststructuralist approaches, focused upon an expression of self in difference. In fact, as Kruks (2001, p. 107) points out, identity politics is based upon, a 'double-turn toward difference' – a celebration of difference and a move towards global difference (difference within women).

Dürrin is reflexive, self-aware and articulate in her life narrative interview about the fluidity of her identity and the contradictions that are inherent in her situation. Identity politics enables previously marginalized peoples to gain voice yet it may also tend to reify groups of women or those oppressed beyond those which are supported by either empirical evidence or the self-determined wishes of those deemed oppressed (Alcoff 2006).

Dürrin's entrepreneurial self knows she could 'pass' as not Turkish and in some ways she appears to be keen to pursue this integration as this would enable her to avoid the troubles which accrue to those perceived as 'other' in the contemporary politics of the Netherlands where problematizing ethnicity is on the rise. Passing as Dutch would allow Dürrin to network more easily with other entrepreneurs also. However, Dürrin's identity is also well connected to her sense of Turkish heritage and she does not want to disavow her roots, and so she sells less. In other instances Dürrin adopts an almost superior attitude in which she 'somewhat arrogantly' (as she suggests) reveals her disdain for Turkey, sharing a negative stereotyping of her own origins as well as those of other Turkish women living in the Netherlands:

> Yes, when I was 13, my old father started to talk about Turkey all the time, but he never really brought me on a real vacation there and so I had a completely different image of Turkey, just like the Dutch would have then. I had such a bad image, that I was afraid to go to Turkey. ... Some Turkish women, they wear closed clothes. I use my Turkishness more in Turkey you could say, that's my advantage. But in relation to my clients, well, it also depends on me; if I had a certain taste just like other Turkish people. ... It would have been difficult if I wouldn't have been integrated being a migrant woman ... I know the language

well; I feel, I live here, I'm going to make it here. ... I'm very against this, if you want a neighbourhood with only Turks, then go and live in Turkey.

(Essers and Tedmanson 2014, p. 360)

Perhaps this distancing is a form of psychic protection (Fanon 1986 [1952]) to avoid internalizing the negative judgements she experiences around her and to prevent its erosion of her self-esteem. Dürrin does not wish her identity to be that of the 'Other' and reveals her self-perception of her identity as, 'practically Dutch', which resonates with both the processes of hybridity and postcolonial concepts of 'mimicry' and 'mask' in the quest to 'belong' (Fanon 1986 [1952]; Narayan 1998; Narayan and Harding 2000).

Dürrin muses that she feels there are more women 'like her' in her home-country, who gain support and respect from their grassroots. She ironically (as the longest in the Netherlands) constructs an identity closer to Turks from Turkey than Turks in the Netherlands, perceiving Turkish women as having more freedom than Turkish migrants living in the Netherlands. She considers starting a business in Istanbul at one point in her story. In a juxtaposition of the concept of 'female subaltern', Dürrin perceives that migrant men of Turkish descent have a specific image of how a woman of Turkish descent should look and behave. Although eventually positive about her identity, being a female entrepreneur is equated with being Western (Dutch). In reaction, Dürrin constructs her entrepreneurial and gender identity by identifying with business-women in Turkey. Her narrative reflects her ideas about the Turkish secular state of which she seems proud.

Dürrin's observation of the real estate agent's stereotypical image of Turkey, knowing little about its 'Westernization', upsets her greatly as this is not how she sees herself. By saying 'man, what are you talking about, there is no such thing as traditional Turkish clothing', she claims agency and challenges some of the 'taken for granted' dichotomies about her identity as a Turkish woman.

By describing her kind of (Turkish) clothes as 'plain clothes', Dürrin un-others herself and reveals her sense of being a mixture of both cultures operating in a new and unique 'third' space (Bhabha 1997). Dürrin is not free of categorizing others however, as she positions herself hierarchically, being Turkish, between Italy (at the top) and Morocco (at the bottom). By saying 'we are no Moroccans', she distances herself from people she perceives to be a lesser ethnic group, or at least one portrayed as such in the Netherlands and minimizes the distance between being Turkish and being Dutch/Western. Dürrin builds a narrative which constructs a very transnational identity while simultaneously maintaining a sense of herself as a Muslim in the West.

10.10 Like us/like them?

For Leila, who often travels to Turkey for her media production company, identity as gender features prominently. Leila feels there is a gender gap in opportunities and in how her entrepreneurial activities are perceived in relation to her role as a mother:

> Men find it easier to travel for their career if necessary, every few months or so. But I don't feel any guilt, despite that women, Dutch women mind you, try to make you feel guilty by saying: 'Shouldn't you bring your kids'.

Leila discusses how she fuses her identity as a woman, a mother and a Turkish entrepreneur and compares her situation favourably to those of men and other Dutch women. She emphasizes her sense that as a woman she is entitled to the same rights as men. However, Leila recounts that she often has to defend her independent female identity to Dutch women. Leila adds to her statement above about Dutch women trying to make her feel guilty by implying she is not a good mother, travelling alone without her children, by saying that she believes Dutch women to be less emancipated than people would like to believe and less comfortable perhaps with the intersecting roles they inhabit as women, workers, wives and mothers. By portraying Dutch women as un-emancipated and less comfortable with their roles, instead of Turkish women, Leila intentionally shifts the focus of unequal power relations.

Leila is also assertive about her Turkish identity and aims to take her business to her 'home' country:

> I would like to have a branch office of F. in Istanbul, between now and 3 years. And I would like to live in Istanbul also, because that really attracts me. And that means that I would like to transfer people working here to Istanbul. And that they once in a while are positioned here in order to achieve cross-fertilization. ... I make documentaries on female circumcision because you want that the knowledge you have developed can be used in a certain context for other women in the World. ... And that's the power of entrepreneurship I believe. Because it's about combining forces, that's how I see it in society too. If we would just join our strengths, instead of pigeon-holing each other! I don't believe that quality only exists in the Dutch, nor in the Turks, but once in a while you really make great matches with both.

Leila exhibits an enabling form of hybridity in entrepreneurship. The intersections of ethnicity, gender and entrepreneurship for Leila enable her to capitalize on options. She emphasizes her ability to move across the boundaries of her gender and ethnicity, focusing on the sharing of knowledge, 'cross-fertilization', combining forces and avoiding pigeon-holes. Her feminist and hybrid Turkish/Dutch identity contribute to her entrepreneurial identity. Leila aims for example to produce new knowledge in an area of Western fascination about Muslim female oppression and share this throughout the world. She is convinced that 'making great matches with both' is 'the power of entrepreneurship' and regrets people often think in stereotypes, restraints instead of opportunities. The process of cultural hybridity enables the emergence of something different, new and unrecognizable (Essers and Tedmanson 2014). This is the 'third space' Bhabha (1994) speaks of which yields new forms of creativity through the renegotiation of meaning.

Whether viewed as the fluid liminality offered at the intersection, the breaking of bounds afforded by 'border crossing' (Narayan and Harding 1998) or a more 'dialectic' process of negotiating identities, there is movement towards new spaces of hybridity where Leila's 'hard won' agency can be exerted, on her own terms.

10.11 Resisting assimilation

Hence, we have noticed that although in several narratives Turkish business-women are disturbed that everyone else seems to speak for them, the female 'subaltern' (Spivak 2008), some women, like Dürrin, also seem to speak for this female subaltern. They distance themselves from an internalized image of 'Turkishness', copied from the Dutch context, and exhibit pride in a more hybrid identity. Thus, in order to advance entrepreneurial possibilities, Dürrin applies aspects of mimicry: using what she perceives to be her 'Turkishness' in her home-country, but emphasizing also her ability to speak Dutch and ready integration into Dutch society; constructing an identity which is also 'Westernized'. Dürrin's reactions might be influenced by a context in which not only populist politicians and media, but also mainstream parties (such as the Christian Democratic Party) stress the importance of integration. Government initiatives construct minorities as cultural 'Others', such as the Rotterdam 'Islam debates', and the national government-sponsored debate on Dutch 'norms and values' (Siebers 2009, p. 81).

Like Dürrin, Atalya distinguishes between more emancipated Turkish people, who accept female entrepreneurship, and more 'traditional' people:

> People originating from the western part of Turkey find it very normal what we [being women] do, but people from the eastern part don't. And many come from this region. We are originally from the middle, near Ankara. ... I don't have many Dutch clients, that's too bad. This is of course because we're Turkish. I don't have a lot of contact with Dutch people. ... It is true that we don't trust those [Dutch] organizations, and they don't trust us either. You could become [a] member of the ANBOS [a branch organization], but we didn't do this either.

There are complexities and paradoxes in these women's identifications. On the one hand, Atalya creates an 'us' vs 'them' dichotomy between Turkish people based on their geographical origins and perceived level of emancipation, yet on the other hand, distinguishes herself from 'the Dutch'. Accordingly, she resists the expectation of the dominant Dutch to assimilate to the Dutch culture and prefers to maintain what she perceives to be a more liberated individual form of her Turkish identity. In line with this, Atalya constructs an in-between identity, one between the Dutch and the 'old-fashioned' Turks. Although Atalya says she would favour having more Dutch clients, she admits she does not want to become a member of official Dutch organizations as she does not trust them; hence, she appears to 'other' the Dutch too and resists adjusting to Dutch entrepreneurial practices or mores, such as becoming a member of Dutch official organizations. Her distrust might stem from discriminatory experiences described earlier, or suspicion that Dutch clients are not attracted to her salon ('this is of course because we're Turkish'). Her 'Turkish way' of approaching business feels better to her, and she does not want to become part of the 'Dutch way' of doing business. Her distinct identity as a female Turkish entrepreneur is a strong source of her sense of self; hence, her entrepreneurial identity seems to sustain her Turkish self.

There is a cultural essentialism evident in comments from the interviewees. Reactivity, a negative self-image and internalization of oppression are common responses to discrimination and dis-empowerment. The idea of two separate, irreconcilable worlds seems convincing to Atalya, which discourages her from embracing a more fluid negotiable 'third space', which might contribute to her embrace of a more hybrid entrepreneurial identity.

10.12 Conclusion

In this chapter we set out to challenge the generalized masculine and western oriented entrepreneurial identity by focusing on three nuanced and at times complex identity narratives of Muslim businesswomen of Turkish descent in the Netherlands. The excerpts highlighted from the identity narratives these women shared with us, reveal the quite different ways each perceives and responds to the social marginalization they experience in the midst of the hegemonic Islamophobia taking place currently in Dutch society, as also in many other European/Westernised countries. These rich life narrative excerpts reveal how relations of power as well as gender, ethnicity and religion come together to shape entrepreneurial identities. We explore in the chapter how the hybridity, intersectionality, mimicry, resistance and resilience of these women's lived experiences, enhances their agency and identities. Hybridity is shown here, we argue, to be a unique response to the challenging experiences of Muslim businesswomen making their way in contemporary Dutch society. The focus on hybridity in context is a particular contribution we wish to make to the research on gender and ethnic minority entrepreneurship research. We believe further studies in this area are needed to increase our understanding of the creolization aspects of entrepreneurship and the extent to which this represents empowerment, resistance and/or adaptation and even assimilation to the demands of dominant cultural mores.

Each of the women interviewed has shared different stories of how they 'see' themselves within the context of their minority entrepreneurship. For example, the narrative excerpts highlight the strategic use of 'ethnicity' to resist, evade, unsettle and rework the more commonly fixed categories of identity.

Atalya is defensive about actively seeking Dutch clients and maintains her focus on Turkish clients. She speaks of her dis/'trust' of this dominant cultural positioning and focuses her entrepreneurship on the Turkish community. Fuelled by emotions such as suspicion and fear, Atalya constructs an 'in-between' identity, while differentiating herself from both the Dutch and non-emancipated people from Turkey. This makes it difficult for her to attract both clientele groups, and she speaks of feeling 'stuck' between two worlds. Atalya's experiences reflect the 'double bind' of 'racialized sexisms' (Ho 2007, p. 296), whereby Turkish women face racism and sexism from the dominant society they live and work in, while also confronting sexism and patriarchal dominations in their own communities.

Dutch women and men alike may position Atalya, Dürrin and Leila as 'female Others', less suited to being an entrepreneur. In some cases, as their narratives reveal, other Turkish women and men perceive them also as 'non-conforming', 'deviant' women, especially so in instances where entrepreneurship is not considered gender-appropriate behaviour. While not denying her religious and cultural heritage, Dürrin identifies herself with the more Western 'emancipations' of both Turkey and the Netherlands. She recognizes that the social exclusion of Muslims limits her entrepreneurship, but at the same time proclaims that she is 'practically Dutch'. Realizing she could 'pass' for an ethnicity other than Turkish, this part of her identity nevertheless remains deeply animating for her. At times, she sets herself apart from her Turkishness and other Turkish women; reminiscent of Bhabha's (1997) mimicry, she articulates sentiments that reflect the dominant discourses and norms of her Dutch location. Besides mimicking and constructing a hybrid identity while referring to women in Turkey, her identity strategy reflects an ambivalent approach to her Turkishness. Dürrin maintains a private individualized Turkish Muslim self, while co-operating but not entirely compromising with, her perceptions of Dutch attitudes, and distancing herself from less integrated Turkish women, to protect and progress her entrepreneurial identity. Dürrin expresses her resistance through this identity approach, yet seems frustrated about always being, 'almost the same, but not quite'.

Leila on the other hand muses on the potential opportunities the 'third' or hybrid space affords. She refers explicitly to 'cross-fertilization', suggesting an awareness of the advantages her hybrid identity brings. She constructs a transnational horizon for her entrepreneurial identity. The opening of this 'third space' can break down racialized identities as well as unitary perspectives on gendered roles. Negotiating a hybrid sense of self is an internalized strategy which appears to work for Leila.

In conclusion while we note the increasing bias and negative pressure placed on many Muslims in Dutch public discourse – a matter of concern all interviewees referred to – our chapter also reveals: that the interviewees in this study identify not only as Muslim, but also as female, Turkish and as entrepreneurial too – all at the same time! In seeking to highlight the potent voices of these potent and agentic women we aim to promote a 'climate in which difference can be lived as enriching and valuable rather than as the oppressive effect of hierarchical binary oppositions' (Narayan 1997, p. 80), and to foster critical entrepreneurship scholarship which acknowledges the creative heterogeneity of all entrepreneurial identities.

Note

1 The women interviewed had various businesses, such as clothing shops, hairdresser and beauty salons, driving schools, consultancies in employment issues and real estate agencies. The interviews formed part of a continuous research project on the identities of migrant businesswomen in the Netherlands, and took place between 2004 and 2009. Additional research (forthcoming) has since been conducted also by the authors on Turkish Muslim women's entrepreneurship in Australia.

References

Ahl, H.J. (2002) 'The construction of the female entrepreneur as the other'. In Czarniaweska, B. and Hopfl, H. (eds) *The Production and Maintenance of Inequalities in Work Organizations*. London: Routledge, pp. 1–19.

Ahl, H. (2004) *The Scientific Reproduction of Gender Inequality: A Discourse Analysis of Research Texts on Women's Entrepreneurship*. Malmö: Liber.

Ahl, H. and Marlow, S. (2012) 'Exploring the dynamics of gender, feminism and entrepreneurship, advancing debate to escape a dead end?', *Organization*, 19(5), pp. 543–562.

Alcoff, L. (2006) *Visible Identities: Race, Gender and the Self*. New York: Oxford University Press.

Alvesson, M., Lee Ashcraft, K. and Thomas, R. (2008) 'Identity matters: Reflections on the construction of identity scholarship in organization studies', *Organization*, 15(1), pp. 5–28.

Alvesson, M. (2010) 'Self-doubters, strugglers, storytellers, surfers and others: Images of self-identities in organization studies', *Human Relations*, 63(2), pp. 193–217.

Appadurai, A. (2006) *Modernity at Large, Cultural Dimensions of Globalization*. Minneapolis, MN: University of Minnesota Press.

Bhabha, H. (1994) *The Location of Culture*. London: Routledge.

Bhabha, H. (1997) 'Minority maneuvers and unsettled negotiations', *Critical Inquiry*, 23(3), pp. 431–459.

Boje, D. and Smith, R. (2010) 'Re-storying and visualizing the changing entrepreneurial identities of Bill Gates and Richard Branson', *Culture and Organization*, 16(2), pp. 307–331.

Bonacich, E. (1993) 'The other side of ethnic entrepreneurship: A dialogue with Waldinger, Aldrich, Ward and Associate', *International Migration Review*, 27(3), pp. 685–692.

Bruni, A., Gherardi, S. and Poggio, B. (2004) 'Doing gender, doing entrepreneurship: An ethnographic account of intertwined practices', *Gender, Work and Organization*, 11(4), pp. 406–429.

Bruni, A., Gherardi, S. and Poggio, B. (2005) *Gender and Entrepreneurship: An Ethnographic Approach*. London: Routledge.

Calas, M., Smircich, L. and Bourne, K. (2009) 'Extending the boundaries: Reframing "entrepreneurship as social change" through feminist perspectives', *Academy of Management Review*, 34(3), pp. 552–569.

CBS (2012) *Annual Report on Integration 2012*. The Hague: Statistics Netherlands.

Chan, K. and Ong, J. (1995) 'The many faces of immigrant entrepreneurship'. In Cohen, R. (ed.) *Cambridge Survey of World Migration*. Cambridge: Cambridge University Press, pp. 523–531.

Chasserio, S., Pailot, P. and Poroli, C. (2014) 'When entrepreneurial identity meets multiple social identities: Interplays and identity work of women entrepreneurs', *International Journal of Entrepreneurial Behaviour and Research*, 20(2), pp. 128–154.

Cohen, S. (1999) 'Moral panic and folk concepts', *Paedagogica Historica*, 35(3), pp. 585–591.

Crenshaw, K. (1995) *The Intersection of Race and Gender – Critical Race Theory: The Key Writings That Formed the Movement*. New York: New Press.

Crenshaw, K., Gotanda, N., Peller, G. and Thomas, K. (1995) *Critical Race Theory: The Key Writings That Formed the Movement*. New York: The New Press.

Czarniawska, B. (1999) *Writing Management: Organization Theory as a Literary Genre*. Oxford: Oxford University Press.

Dana, L.P. (2007) *Handbook of Research on Ethnic Minority Entrepreneurship: A Co-evolutionary View on Resource Management*. Cheltenham: Edward Elgar.

Donnellon, A., Ollila, S. and Middleton, K. (2014) 'Constructing entrepreneurial identity in entrepreneurship education', *International Journal of Management Education*, 12, pp. 490–499.

Douglas, H. and Grant, S. (2014) *Social Entrepreneurship and Enterprise: Concepts in Context*. Prahran: Tilde Publishing.

Down, S. and Warren, L. (2008) 'Constructing narratives of enterprise: Cliches and entrepreneurial self-identity', *International Journal of Entrepreneurial Behaviour and Research*, 14(1), pp. 4–23.

Essers, C. and Benschop, Y. (2007) 'Enterprising identities: Female entrepreneurs of Moroccan and Turkish origin in the Netherlands', *Organization Studies*, 28(1), pp. 49–69.

Essers, C. and Benschop, Y. (2009) 'Muslim businesswomen doing boundary work: The negotiation of Islam, gender and ethnicity within entrepreneurial contexts', *Human Relations*, 62(3), pp. 403–424.

Essers, C. and Tedmanson, D. (2014) 'Upsetting "others" in the Netherlands: Narratives of Muslim Turkish migrant businesswomen at the crossroads of ethnicity, gender and religion', *Gender, Work and Organization*, 21(4), pp. 353–367.

Fanon, F. (1986 [1952]) *Black Skin, White Masks*. London: Pluto.

Fine, M. (2006) 'Contesting research: Rearticulation and "thick democracy" as political projects of method'. In Weis, L., McCarthy, C. and Dimitriadis, G. (eds) *Ideology, Curriculum, and the New Sociology of Education: Revisiting the Work of Michael Apple*. New York: Routledge, pp. 145–166.

Frenkel, M. and Shenhav, Y. (2006) 'From binarism back to hybridity: A postcolonial reading of management and organization studies', *Organization Studies*, 27(6), pp. 855–876.

Ghandi, L. (1998) *Postcolonial Theory: A Critical Introduction*. St Leonards: Allen and Unwin.

Ghorashi, H. (2003) 'Ayaan Hirsi Ali: daring or dogmatic? Debates on multiculturalism and emancipation in the Netherlands', *Focaal, European Journal of Anthropology*, 42, pp. 163–169.

Ghorashi, H. (2006) *Paradoxen van culturele erkenning: Management van Diversiteit in Nieuw Nederland (inaugural lecture)*. Amsterdam: Vrij Universiteit.

Gijsberts, M. and Dagevos, J. (2004) 'Concentratie en wederzijdse beeldvorming tussen autochtonen en allochtonen', *Migrantenstudies*, 20(3), pp. 145–168.

Grassl, W. (2011) 'Hybrid forms of business: The logic of gift in the commercial world', *Journal of Business Ethics*, 100, pp. 109–123.

Halford, S. and Leonard, P. (2006) *Negotiating Gendered Identities at Work: Place, Space and Time*. Basingstoke: Palgrave Macmillan.

Harmeling, S. (2011) 'Re-storying an entrepreneurial identity: Education, experience and self-narrative', *Education+Training*, 53(8/9), pp. 741–749.

Hillman, F. (1999) 'A look at the "hidden side": Turkish women in Berlin's ethnic labour market', *International Journal of Urban and Regional Research*, 23(2), pp. 267–282.

Ho, C. (2007) 'Muslim women's new defenders: Women's rights, nationalism and Islamophobia in contemporary Australia', *Women's Studies International Forum*, 30, pp. 290–298.

Holvino, E. (2010) 'Intersections: The simultaneity of race, gender and class in organization studies', *Gender, Work and Organization*, 17(3), pp. 248–277.

Johansson, A.W. (2004) 'Narrating the entrepreneur', *International Small Business Journal*, 22(3), pp. 273–293.

Jones, C. and Spicer, A. (2009) *Unmasking the Entrepreneur*. London: Edward Elgar.

Ketz de Vries, M. (1977) 'The entrepreneurial personality: A person at the crossroads', *Journal of Management Studies*, 14, pp. 34–57.

Kloosterman, T. and Rath, J. (eds) (2003) *Immigrant Entrepreneurship: Venturing Abroad in the Age of Globalization*. Oxford: Berg.

Korteweg, A. and Yurdakul, G. (2009) 'Islam, gender and immigrant integration: Boundary drawing in discourses on honour killing in the Netherlands and Germany', *Ethnic and Racial Studies*, 32(2), pp. 218–238.

Kruks, S. (2000) *Retrieving Experience: Subjectivity and Recognition in Feminist Politics*. Ithaca, NY: Cornell University Press.

Lutz, H. (1991) *Migrant Women of 'Islamic Background': Images and Self-images*. Amsterdam: Stichting MERA.

Mahalingam, R. and Leu, J. (2005) 'Culture, essentialism, immigration and representations of gender', *Theory and Psychology*, 15(6), pp. 839–860.

Makadok, R. and Coff, R. (2009) 'Both market and hierarchy: An incentive-system theory of hybrid governance forms', *Academy of Management Review*, 34(2), pp. 297–319.

McAdams, D. (1997) 'The case for unity in the (post)modern self: A modest proposal'. In Ashmore, R. and Jussim, L. (eds) *Self and Identity: Fundamental Issues*. Oxford: Oxford University Press, pp. 46–78.

McCall, L. (2005) 'The complexity of intersectionality', *Journal of Women in Culture and Society*, 3(3), pp. 1771–1800.

McClelland, D. (1987) 'Characteristics of successful entrepreneurs', *Journal of Creative Behavior*, 21(3), pp. 219–233.

Merens, A. (2000) 'Allochtone vrouwen op de arbeidsmarkt', *Tijdschrift voor arbeidsvraagstukken*, 16(3), pp. 278–291.

Mirchandani, K. (1999) 'Feminist insights on gendered work: New directions in research on women and entrepreneurship', *Gender, Work and Organization*, 6(4), pp. 224–235.

Mohanty, C. (2003) *Feminism Without Borders*. Durham, NC: Duke University Press.

Narayan, U. (1997) *Dislocating Cultures. Identities, Traditions and Third World Feminism*. New York: Routledge.

Narayan, U. (1998) 'Essence of culture and a sense of history: A feminist critique of cultural essentialism', *Hypatia*, 13(2), pp. 86–106.

Narayan, U. and Harding, S. (1998) 'Introduction: Border crossings: Multicultural and postcolonial feminist challenges to philosophy (Part I)', *Hypatia*, 13(2), pp. 1–6.

Narayan, U. and Harding, S. (2000) *Decentering the Center: Philosophy for a Multicultural, Postcolonial, and Feminist World*. Bloomington, IN: Indiana University Press.

Ogbor, J. (2000) 'Mythicizing and reification in entrepreneurial discourse: Ideology-critique of entrepreneurial studies', *Journal of Management Studies*, 37(5), pp. 605–635.

Özbilgin, M. and Tatli, A. (2008) *Global Diversity Management*. Basingstoke: Palgrave Macmillan.

Percoud, A. (2002) '"Weltoffenheit schafft jobs": Turkish entrepreneurship and multiculturalism in Berlin', *International Journal of Urban and Regional Research*, 26(3), pp. 494–507.

Pio, E. (2007) 'Ethnic minority women entrepreneurs and the imperial imprimatur', *Women in Management Review*, 22(8), pp. 631–649.

Portes, A. (1995) *The Economic Sociology of Immigration: Essays on Networks, Ethnicity, and Entrepreneurship*. New York: Russell Sage Foundation.

Powell, G.N. and Greenhaus, J.H. (2010) 'Sex, gender, and the work-to-family interface: Exploring negative and positive interdependencies', *Academy of Management Journal*, 53(3), pp. 513–534.

Prasad, A. (2003) *Postcolonial Theory and Organizational Analysis: A Critical Engagement*. New York: Palgrave Macmillan.

Prasad, A. (2006) 'The jewel in the crown: Postcolonial theory and workplace diversity'. In Konrad, A.M., Prasad, P. and Pringle, J.K. (eds) *Handbook of Workplace Diversity*. Thousand Oaks, CA: Sage, pp. 121–144.

Ram, M. and Carter, S. (2003) 'Paving professional futures: Ethnic minority accountants in the United Kingdom', *International Small Business Journal*, 21(1), pp. 55–72.

Rhodes, C. and Brown, A. (2005) 'Writing responsibly: Narrative fiction and organization studies', *Organization*, 12(4), pp. 467–491.

Rigg, C. and O'Dwyer, B. (2012) 'Becoming an entrepreneur: Researching the role of mentors in identity construction', *Education +Training*, 54(4), pp. 319–329.

Root, M. (1999) 'Multiracial Asians: Models of ethnic identity'. In Torres, R.D., Miron, L.F. and Inda, J.X. (eds) *Race, Ethnicity, and Citizenship: A Reader*. Oxford: Blackwell.

Rozaldo, M. (1980) 'The use and abuse of anthropology: Reflections on feminism and cross-cultural understanding', *Signs*, 5(3), pp. 389–417.

Ryan, L. (2011) 'Muslim women negotiating collective stigmatization: We're just normal people', *Sociology*, 45(6), pp. 1045–1060.

Sardar, Z. (2005) *Desperately Seeking Paradise: Journeys of a Sceptical Muslim*. London: Granta.

Sheth, N. (2010) 'The social context of entrepreneurship', *Journal of Entrepreneurship*, 19(2), pp. 99–108.

Siebers, H. (2009) 'Struggles for recognition: The politics of racioethnic identity among Dutch national tax administrators', *Scandinavian Journal of Management*, 25, pp. 73–84.

Spivak, G. (2008) *Other Asias*. London: Blackwell.

Steyaert, C. (2007) 'Of course that is not the whole (toy) story: Entrepreneurship and the cat's cradle', *Journal of Business Venturing*, 22(5), pp. 733–751.

Tedmanson, D., Verduyn, K., Essers, C. and Gartner, W. (2012) 'Critical perspectives in entrepreneurship research', *Organization*, 19(5), pp. 543–562.

Tedmanson, D. and Essers, C. (2015) 'Entrepreneurship and diversity'. In Blendl, R., Bleijenbergh, I., Henttonen, E. and Mills, A. (eds) *The Oxford Handbook of Diversity in Organisations*. Oxford: Oxford University Press.

Thomas, A. and Mueller, S. (2000) 'A case for comparative entrepreneurship: Assessing the relevance of culture', *Journal of International Business Studies*, 31(2), pp. 287–301.

Trinh, T.M. (2001) *Woman, Native, Other: Writing Postcoloniality and Feminism*. Bloomington, IN: Indiana University Press.

Wallace, B. (2007) *Entrepreneurship as embodiment: Bangladeshi women setting up businesses in East London*. Paper presented at the 5th Critical Management Studies Conference, Manchester, 11th-13th July.

Westwood, R. (2006) 'International business and management studies as an orientalist discourse: A postcolonial critique', *Critical Perspectives on International Business*, 2(2), pp. 91–113.

Zhou, M. (2008) 'Revisiting ethnic entrepreneurship: Convergencies, controversies, and conceptual advancements'. In Portes, A. and DeWing, J. (eds) *Rethinking Migration: New Theoretical and Empirical Perspectives*. New York: Berghahn Books.

11 Towards an understanding of effectual learning

Exploring four innovations in entrepreneurship education

Caroline Verzat, Olivier Toutain, Noreen O'Shea, Fabienne Bornard, Chrystelle Gaujard and Philippe Silberzahn

11.1 Introduction

Critical voices are being raised among entrepreneurship researchers regarding entrepreneurship education. Questions such as if and how it can be taught (Fayolle 2013), to what extent it can be learned (Mueller and Anderson 2014; Neergaard *et al.* 2012) still remain open, due to a lack of conclusive evidence.

The quantitative review of the literature carried out by Martin, McNally and Kay (2013) does underline the positive link between entrepreneurship education and the acquisition of the human capital assets required for entrepreneurial practice. But these authors also highlight on the one hand, methodological weaknesses among the studies analysed and on the other hand, a direct impact of studies with lower methodological rigour on overstating effects of entrepreneurship education training.

These criticisms are echoed in the way in which entrepreneurship education is taught. From this perspective, Béchard and Grégoire (2005) show that researchers in entrepreneurship education still tend to privilege one specific view of education over others. Some choose an economic view (entrepreneurship contributes to economic growth); others adopt a technicist view (what kind of technology should we use?); some favour an academic view (what contents should we teach?); while others prefer an individualistic view (what are the students' individual needs?). Whatever the perspective adopted by researchers teaching entrepreneurship, the authors also point out that the psycho-cognitive, socio-cognitive and ethical dimensions of educational practices and learning processes, have been and continue to be underestimated in the design and implementation of entrepreneurship education.

From a research perspective, entrepreneurship as a discipline has been recently established and there is as yet no clear consensus about what entrepreneurship is and what entrepreneurs actually do. Even if entrepreneurship research has rich historical roots anchored in economics and economic history, there is a growing tendency to borrow theories from different disciplines to grasp the entrepreneurial phenomenon (Landström and Lohrke 2010). Given the monodisciplinary organization of education, this may explain the gap between what is taught in entrepreneurship as opposed to what entrepreneurs actually experience in their daily working lives (Edelman, Manolova and Brush 2008). Specialists in each field do not collaborate in the design of educational programmes. Therefore, programmes proposed are either inadequate or incomplete. This helps in understanding why entrepreneurship educators face a very arduous task when they have to design appropriate learning activities for their students.

This exercise is even harder if we consider the definition of the entrepreneur offered by Jones and Spicer (2009). Rather than continuing to uphold entrepreneurship as the result of individually based endeavours, these authors exhort researchers, policy-makers and entrepreneurs themselves to recognize that 'enterprise is a fundamentally collective enterprise, based on social cooperation' and that envisioning entrepreneurship 'without the other is unthinkable' (Jones and Spicer 2009, p. 110). If this definition were adopted, educational design based on a description of individual entrepreneurial tasks and knowledge appears to be inadequate, where programs are designed on the principle that students learn and are assessed individually, with little consideration given to the acquisition of collective competencies.

Recently developed theories about entrepreneurship, such as the effectual process advocated by Sarasvathy (2001, 2008), Sarasvathy and Venkataraman (2011) also encourage us to go beyond the traditional positivist approach to educational design. Effectuation as a theory to comprehend entrepreneurship posits that the decision-making processes employed by entrepreneurs when envisaging opportunities for the creation of new value are more effectual than causal. They occur in situations of uncertainty, where the future is unpredictable, leading entrepreneurs to determine goals as a function of the resources they have at their disposal, rather than causally fixing goals in advance and then looking for resources in order to attain them. The authors encourage researchers and educators to adopt this effectual logic when designing studies and programmes in this domain because it will enable them to isomorphically experience entrepreneurial reality as it evolves. We take up this challenge because we believe that this approach will contribute to a better understanding of the epistemological implications of their effectual model, making the research practices of effectual entrepreneurship educators clearer. Furthermore, it may contribute to consolidating the claim made by Sarasvathy and Venkataraman that entrepreneurship, like the scientific methods experimented with from the seventeenth century on, may be considered as a democratic means for human problem solving (Sarasvathy and Venkataraman 2011). This entrepreneurial method can be 'evidenced empirically, is teachable to anyone who cares to learn it and may be applied in practice to a wide variety of issues central to human well-being and social improvement' (Sarasvathy and Venkataraman 2011, p. 125).

The purpose of this chapter, therefore is to explore ways in which both as researchers and teachers, we can find new ways of researching and educating the entrepreneurial mindset. We define this mindset as a way of thinking, learning and behaving that manifests itself through a proactive attitude (Bateman and Crant 1993; Crant 1996), which is a cognitive, affective and behavioural disposition that can be learned, assessed and refined. Our proposition is based on the belief that by reinventing the way we carry out and exploit our research, we can enhance and improve the design, implementation and evaluation of teaching and learning entrepreneurial processes. To support the creation of this researching/ learning/teaching process, we propose the adoption of an effectually designed process. In the educational field, this implies designing, testing and iteratively improving learning objectives, activities and assessment methods. This is possible only if teachers adopt reflexive processes about their teaching practice, enabling them to take on an action–researcher posture when designing their programmes. In so doing, they behave exactly as entrepreneurs do: they contribute to discovering and implementing novel processes for teaching and researching. We relate this to the concept of isomorphism which is used in continuing education of teachers involved in problem-based learning (PBL) (Draime *et al.* 2000; Wouters, Parmentier and Lebrun 2003). Considering that PBL is a new approach to teaching, which encounters fierce resistance among teachers, the isomorphic principle for engaging them in this method is to 'Teach the teachers as you would like them to teach their students'. To illustrate our proposition, we explore four different case studies, which enact this innovative research-action approach in the entrepreneurial education field.

The chapter begins by highlighting the need to build on a new learning theory. We first explore a theoretical framework which links a constructivist approach in teaching and learning and effectual entrepreneurial practice in order to justify a new educational design in entrepreneurship education. We then study how we can harness an effectual action-based research approach to explore new ways in entrepreneurship education. In this way, we combine characteristics of effectual teaching design and effectual research design in order to define a new effectual educational design. In the third section, we illustrate our theoretical framework by exploring four case studies enacted in France and the Netherlands.

11.2 Current debate about entrepreneurship education: why do we need to build on a new learning theory?

A recurring question in entrepreneurship education literature concerns the debate about epistemological foundations for understanding and teaching entrepreneurship. Combining Merriam and Caffarella's model with their data,[1] Byrne, Fayolle and Toutain (2014) show that the principal learning theories utilized in entrepreneurship education literature are those associated with cognitivist and socio-cognitivist schools of thought. These learning theories favour a transmissive teaching model based on and aiming at knowledge acquisition (as will be shown in Section 11.3.1). But for many researchers, the principal aims of entrepreneurship education should focus on the development of soft skills and attitudes like initiative taking, creativity, coping with uncertainty, leadership, socializing within entrepreneurial networks (Gibb 2002, 2011; Honig 2004; Löbler 2006; Neck and Greene 2011; Sarasvathy 2010; Sarasvathy and Venkataraman 2011). These authors argue that a contingent, socio-constructivist approach to teaching and learning is needed because it is more coherent with the collective nature of entrepreneurial learning, given the strongly embedded socialized, inter-connected and collaborative relations underlying entrepreneurial activity (Jones and Spicer 2009).

But this kind of change is not easy because it involves a radical turn in teacher and learner roles, in conceptions about learning as well as in the organizational design of educational institutions. A brief overview of the educational history of educational practices will contribute to comprehending the nature of this global and difficult change.

11.2.1 From transmissive, to functionalist and socio-constructivist teaching and learning models: a historical but difficult change

According to several authors that have studied the history of education practices (Barbier 2003; Barr and Tagg 1995; Bourdoncle and Lessard 2002; De Ketele 2000; Ramsden 2003; Thousand, Villa and Nevin 1998), the constructivist approach is opposed to the traditional and functionalist conceptions of learning. These latter conceptions have influenced teaching practice as well as students' normative perceptions regarding learning expectations and organizational design in educational institutions. Their emergence and guiding values appear to be closely connected to specific historical contexts highlighting diverse socio-economic needs in society.

Traditional transmissive teaching practice is based on a cognitivist theory of learning. It highlights the central role of the teacher as the expert, controlling objective scientific knowledge that must be appropriated and memorized by students. After the trauma of the First World War, a new generation of teachers emerged all over Europe in alternative schools at basic education levels (Cousinet 2011; Decroly 2011; Neill and Fromm 1960; Freinet 1993; Montessori and Chattin-McNichols 1995). Their conception of learning was borrowed from constructivist theories (Dewey 1916; Piaget 1975) and put the learner's progressive construction of knowledge to the forefront. Students were deemed to be responsible for their own choices with regard to learning. This should, in turn, help them change on a personal level and ultimately produce desirable changes in society. The teacher was considered more as a facilitator, operating on the sidelines. However, those new educational practices remained marginal during the first half of the twentieth century because of corporatist and political resistance present in most countries.

Functionalist theories of learning (Pavlov 2012; Skinner 1965; Watson 1970) emerged in the 1930s with a close connection to the Taylorism that was being practised in organizations. This approach turned out to be more influential in education because followers (Mager 1997; Bloom 1984) introduced decisive tools for designing and assessing learning objectives after the Second World

War. From this perspective, the learner was seen as being actively involved in the learning process and contents were focused on the acquisition of skills. But the teacher continued to initiate and retain control of the learning process. After such a training period, students were supposed to be able to transfer the procedures and techniques into their personal contexts.

But from the 1970s on, university teachers in professional faculties (e.g. medicine, engineering and law) observed that the expected transfer did not automatically take place. Many students demonstrated a lack of motivation and dropped out of the learning process early. Complex soft skills such as critical thinking, problem interpretation and solving, opportunity recognition, ethical and responsible behaviour were difficult to appropriate outside real contexts. New educational thinkers emerged (Bandura 1985; Bruner 1976; Knowles 1975; Vygotsky 1934), highlighting the social aspects of the socio-constructivist process. They explained that learners' intrinsic motivation and emotional arousal were central to the learning process – self-efficacy perceptions could be fostered through a succession of mastery experiences but also through association with other co-learners, with the teacher and external stakeholders adopting a cognitive, conative and affective guiding role. From a cognitive viewpoint, teachers or external experts fulfil their role by providing useful declarative and procedural knowledge either through courses, exercises or conferences. From the conative viewpoint, teachers and external stakeholders (like business partners or professional coaches) try to engage students into action. This role is particularly important when pedagogy involves project activities, event organizing and opportunity making. On the affective side, teachers and coaches respond to motivational, role-modelling, relational skills and confidence-building needs of students. Those needs are always present whatever the learning activity consists of but they are often bypassed when teachers focus only on knowledge acquisition or skill production goals.

On the contrary, active pedagogies (especially problem and projects based learning [PBL]) that originated in Canada and developed in innovative and participative cultures notably in Scandinavia, take on board those new perspectives. In his review of problem-based practices within educational theory, Gijselaers (1996) highlights three main principles regarding learning: (1) learning is a constructive process, (2) knowing about knowing affects learning, and (3) social and contextual factors affect learning. More precisely, Kolmos, De Graaf and Du (2009) found three common learning principles that cut across the different forms of PBL: (1) learning is organized around problems and carried out in projects so as to enhance motivation of students, (2) the contents of the problem link practice to interdisciplinary theories and is exemplary of overall objectives of curriculum, and (3) learning takes place in teams where students learn from each other, share knowledge and are collectively responsible for the learning process, especially the formulation of the problem. In this perspective, teachers act as facilitating tutors rather than experts. Tutors' facilitating role is a major concern of PBL research (Albanese and Mitchell 1993). Their attitude is seen as a critical factor which impacts students' ability to raise relevant questions and critical learning issues (Bouvy *et al.* 2010; Gijselaers 1996). However this facilitating attitude of tutors is not taken for granted even in PBL environments. Different empirical researches show that the tutors' facilitating attitude depends on the tutors' personal style, more or less focusing on students or on the discipline (Vierset, Bédard and Foidart 2009), on their ability to show social and cognitive congruence with the students (Schmidt and Moust 1995, 2000) and on their capacity to analyse and adapt to different student team leadership configurations (O'Shea *et al.* 2013).

This contrasted reality of tutors' facilitation capacities indicates that this new teaching role ('guide on the side' rather than 'sage on the stage') is a major professional change. Verzat and Garant (2010) have analysed the different barriers to this paradigmatic turn in three institutions which have globally adopted PBL or project-based learning. They observe that the socio-constructivist philosophy in fact cohabits with the other two previously mentioned teaching and learning approaches – traditional and functional. This arises not only because of the autonomy granted to university teachers regarding their didactical methods and personal stances, but also as a result of organizational factors. Teaching and learning philosophies are directly connected to organizational processes overseeing the professional role and careers of teachers: recruitment criteria, the time and means dedicated to pedagogical training, evaluation and promotion measures. Up to now, with regard to all these organizational processes, most academic institutions favour disciplinary research excellence and production rather than pedagogical investment.

It is also due to the overall structure of the university, the curricula planning, the cost and quality assessment of the academic institution as well as its governance. Discipline-based faculties and scientific mainstream epistemology justify and guarantee a total autonomy to teachers in their class. The global curriculum is decomposed into one course – one-teacher units corresponding to the specialities of each member of the faculty, taking little account of potential overlaps. The traditional silo-organization of universities offers little space for trans-disciplinary pedagogical teamwork and negotiations on resources. It attributes teachers' resources (time and assistants) according to the quantity of courses rather than on their quality. Assurance of learning and accreditation processes tends to foster a more functionalist skill-based design and assessment approach. These managerial processes can force teachers to more explicitly align their teaching design with professional learning goals and objectives aimed at by the academic institution. But they remain based on an individual approach (one course one teacher). They also require a larger administrative techno-structure, the inclusion of quality teaching criteria and specific resources for pedagogical training, all of which increase educational costs. Thus these institutions need to find supplementary financial resources and to constantly balance administrative and scientific powers. This usually generates a lot of inertia in the decision processes. The third socio-constructivist logic remains largely marginal because it is not easy to promote at institutional level. It relies on the presence of activist groups of teachers who face complex uncertain situations, a struggle against disciplinary frontiers and believe in collective learning. Their logic becomes significant and visible at institutional level if they gain sufficient power in the organization to be able to reorganize the global curriculum and student assessment processes. This capacity is highly dependent on the existence of transformational leadership within the institution as well as investment in pedagogical research to gain legitimacy.

It is no wonder then that entrepreneurship educators do not share common views on teaching and learning theories. Entrepreneurship researchers promoting their own recent discipline logically defend a scientific knowledge-based view of entrepreneurship education. Business schools and faculty managers who have to decide on investing resources in educational programmes plead for assessment of clear pre-defined learning goals and objectives. New perspectives based on pragmatic socio-constructivist approaches to education come from practice-based entrepreneurial coaches, reflexive educational practitioners (Kearney 1998; Gibb 2002; Pelletier 2005; Jones 2011, 2013; Surlemont, Fayolle and Filion 2009) or researchers coming from the entrepreneurial world who claim that the current practices in entrepreneurial education are inadequate. These critiques based on socio-constructivist learning theories are presented in the following section.

11.2.2　Critical views of current practices in entrepreneurship education

The exponential increase of entrepreneurship education (EE) in schools (European Commission 2013) has been accompanied by a similar development in research publications (Fayolle 2013). However, this general trend carries in its wake three major critical axes. Firstly, EE is mainly studied as an external concept, focusing on pedagogies and experimentation which lack critical reflective approaches by EE educators (Fayolle 2013; Neck and Greene 2011). More generally, there is still a need for learning theories to be based on reflexive approaches to improving education (Carlile and Jordan 2005; Schön 1983). In other terms interplays between educators and curricula are not taken sufficiently into account. Secondly, and directly resulting from this, questions such as 'what', 'how' or 'for which results' dominate the field of EE but the question 'why' is understudied (Byrne *et al.* 2014; Naia *et al.* 2014). Thirdly, there is a need in EE to match learning goals and methods with targeted audiences (Blenker *et al.* 2011; Fayolle 2013). In education research, this generates the need for constructive alignment in education design between outcomes, activities and assessment (Biggs 1999; Biggs and Tang 2003).

These critical views of EE have led to highlighting new perspectives in educational principles, which can be summarized through five categories both represented in EE, and learning theories in education research.

First of all, the socio-constructivist approach is more conducive to the appropriation of entrepreneurial skills, as well as behavioural and emotional development within a life-long perspective (Cope 2005; Corbett 2005; Gibb 2002; Harrison and Leitch 2005; Löbler 2006; Messeghem and Verstraete 2009; Neck and Greene 2011; Politis 2005). In learning theories, the growing recognition of the socio-constructivist approach in higher education with a view to building global competences has drawn attention in education research (Barbier 2003; Barr and Tagg 1995; Bourdoncle and Lessard 2002; Ramsden 2003; Thousand *et al.* 1998). In the same way, the harnessing of transformative learning approaches to identify and analyse the role of self-efficacy perceptions, intrinsic motivations and self-identity illustrates how the socio-constructivist approach can be implemented to design new perspectives (Bandura and Cervone 1986; Deci and Ryan 2000; Mezirow 1997).

Secondly, efforts to train creativity and initiative-taking have shown how the innovative design of EE can be more closely linked to the development of an entrepreneurial mindset (Fillis and Rentschler 2010; Neck and Greene 2011; Nyström 1993; Sarasvathy 2010; Sarasvathy and Venkataraman 2011). In learning theories, creativity is considered as a competence that can be trained in simulated habitable environments (Amabile 2001; Csikszentmihalyi 1997).

Thirdly, the use of experimentation to educate effectual contingency-based processes is more effective when implementing new educational perspectives in EE. In learning theories, this approach refers to experiential learning including trial and error as a basis of problem and project-based learning (Kolb 1984).

Fourthly, to be efficient these new perspectives in educational principles need collaboration and connection to the entrepreneurial world (Fayolle 2013; Gibb 2002). In learning theories, collaborative learning is a condition for the generation of socio-cognitive conflicts in PBL (Johnson 1991; Thousand *et al.* 1998), for the encouragement of peer role-modelling and the stimulation of self-efficacy perceptions (Bandura 1985).

Finally, reflexive metacognitive abilities in entrepreneurial decision-making are closely linked with the exploration of new perspectives in EE. In learning education, it mostly refers to self-directed learning attitudes and processes in order to produce metacognitive abilities (Flavell 1979; Knowles 1975).

Thus, the current debate in entrepreneurship education (why, what and how we should teach entrepreneurship) happens to coincide with the more global debate about educational principles based on the historical development of new learning theories. However, the move from a traditional learning paradigm to a socio-constructivist perspective on learning in entrepreneurship education is not only due to the global evolution of educational views about learning. It is also rooted in ontological questions regarding the essence of entrepreneurial processes and phenomena, which invite us to open new epistemological perspectives. This argument will be developed in the following paragraph.

11.2.3 New perspectives in entrepreneurship inviting new epistemologies

The epistemological framework for entrepreneurship education has principally been based on the individual entrepreneur and the process of identifying and exploiting new opportunities. Paying attention to the collective transformation processes in entrepreneurship education implies moving beyond this approach.

For instance, Shane and Venkataraman pointed out that entrepreneurship 'cannot be explained solely by reference to a characteristic that certain people have, independent of the situations in which they find themselves' (Shane and Venkataraman 2000). But they designed their conceptual framework to examine the influence of individuals and opportunities, rather than environmental antecedents and consequences (Shane and Venkataraman 2000, p. 219). In the same way, a significant amount of research in the area of entrepreneurial intention has been designed based on Ajzen's model of the 'theory of planned behavior' (Ajzen 1991). Krueger and Carsud stressed that 'understanding and predicting new venture initiation requires research using theory-driven models that adequately reflect the complex perception-based processes underlying intentional, planned behaviours such as new venture initiation' (Krueger and Carsrud 1993). Such approaches illustrate scientific ways of thinking and acting based on hypothetico-deductive reasoning methods that continue today. In entrepreneurship education, the implementation of this traditional way of thinking and reasoning has led schools and educators to tacitly design learning objectives based on individual capabilities to further entrepreneurial intentions; to identify and exploit opportunities and, finally, to create new businesses. To take account of institutional constraints, the classical pedagogical approach based on planned learning methods and objectives, dominates entrepreneurship education.

For example, despite historical criticism (Meyer and Rowan 1977) the business plan still appears to be an indispensable ritual because research about its outcomes remains confused (Stone and Brush 1996) and contradictory. Researchers have attempted to show the causal nexus between the ability to design a business plan and the survival of the firm (Delmar and Shane 2003), while others have highlighted the absence of any causal relationship between business performance and the implementation of the business plan (Karlsson and Honig 2009). Despite this paradox, researchers have studied ways to improve the business plan in entrepreneurship courses (Lahm 2008) while others have attempted to assess outcomes of business creation processes (Kuehn, Grider and Sell 2009) or even 'to burn' the business plan (Ananou 2007; Cohen 2008; Honig 2004). Finally, research and courses in entrepreneurship are still implemented using a programmatic causal vision: teachers design their courses using a planning approach with predetermined phases and processes. Tools and methods are replicated, causality and the predetermination of outcomes whatever the context continue to be taken for granted.

But, as Jones and Spicer wrote, 'entrepreneurs are implicated with others and with governing the prospects for their freedom' (Jones and Spicer 2009, p. 114). Thereby, schools and educators should be distributing rewards for socialized productions (Jones and Spicer 2009) more than for mythological individual successes. For this purpose, both the content of entrepreneurship education and the pedagogical stance of the educator should be revisited. For instance, given that cooperation is the central axis in the workplace, educators, would-be entrepreneurs and students have to acquire the abilities to navigate, decode and connect with this socialization process inherent in economic and social life. Therefore, educators cannot be mere expert observers or even trainers alongside the students involved in the learning process (i.e., designing their own business plan by exploiting an opportunity). They must be learning stakeholders embarked on the same entrepreneurial 'adventure': they form a singular learning community.

We consider that the effectual approach to entrepreneurship education and to research on this subject could provide a lever with which to change mentalities. Sarasvathy and Venkataraman (2011) believe that the entrepreneurial effectual method can 'unleash the potential of human nature'. If we apply their indications for future research on the entrepreneurial method with regard to educational design (Sarasvathy and Venkataraman 2011, p. 125), new questions arise: (1) Can we use inter-subjectivity as a key unit of analysis in educational design, that is, to focus on transformation and co-creation processes rather than on assisting the individual learner to reach predesigned objectives? (2) How can we cope with, and even foster, the heterogeneity of entrepreneurial phenomena while the classroom context and assessment systems usually tend to produce homogenous collective norms? (3) What 'teachable mechanisms' could be used that are so 'internally consistent with each other that they "make sense" in terms of the overall purpose of the method, namely to unleash the potential of human nature to achieve desired ends and to generate viable and valuable new ends' (Sarasvathy and Venkataraman 2011, p. 129)? The following section explores these questions in order to propose new ways of researching and educating the entrepreneurial mindset.

11.3 Harnessing an effectual action-based research to entrepreneurship education approach

Observing the still significant gap that exists in the literature regarding the effective design and implementation of entrepreneurship education, we explore action-research epistemology and practice as a potential ally for providing both a research and educational lens. Our intuition is that action research informs the construction of effectual entrepreneurial learning processes. We will then pinpoint the coherence that we find in the literature on action-research principles in education and new entrepreneurship theories, leading us to propose a dual framework for the design of effectual entrepreneurial education.

11.3.1 Toward effectual educational design?

Very little evidence of what could be called 'an effectual educational design' or 'effectual teaching' exists in entrepreneurship literature. Sarasvathy (2008) suggests that students should be taught how to use both causal and effectual toolboxes by effectively experimenting with them. Although she uses case-studies, in-class exercises, interactive lectures, etc., in her own classes, she specifies that one difference is that all my course materials, pedagogical devices and in-class discussions revolve around the students' own new ventures rather than on general theories or best practices. This is the first and most important challenge of teaching effectuation. One pedagogical challenge here is to get the students' 'trust and buy-in' (Sarasvathy 2008). Effectual teaching implies helping students set up their own networks, starting with who they are, what they know and whom they could enrol in their project. She goes on by saying that starting with a live project on the first day is startling and uncomfortable for students. They have to 'make' rather than 'find' an opportunity. This implies trying rather than thinking first, accepting failure as a learning process, and dealing with their own fears.

Bonazzi (2014) indicates that very little research in entrepreneurship education associates effectual teaching with learning from failure, or indicating how to deal with failure in live projects. To fill this gap, he and his team experimented an effectual monitoring process of students' live entrepreneurial projects in their educational setting, called GILAP (Grow It Like A Plant). He observes that this monitoring model of students' effectual processes was inspired by and carried out by following an action-research process. Although their article does not provide many details, a long informal discussion with authors showed that the GILAP methodology itself emerged out of several cycles of trials and errors in the pedagogical and research design. Babson College Entrepreneurship Research Conference 2015 provides another example. BCERC director's welcome message associates the entrepreneurship research leadership of Babson College with their educational 'thought and action®' methodology:

> The 35th BCERC is sure to be energizing, informative, and social, with opportunities to discuss the latest research in entrepreneurship with leading and enthusiastic academics. … As the No. 1 leader in entrepreneurship for 21 consecutive years, Babson College is globally recognized for our one-of-a-kind Entrepreneurial Thought and Action® (ETandA) methodology that teaches undergraduates, graduates, and executives to balance action, experimentation, and creativity with a deep understanding of business fundamentals and rigorous analysis as the ideal approach to creating economic and social value.
>
> (Zacharakis 2015)

These two examples tend to verify Leitch, McMullan and Harrison's proposition that action-research learning processes are consistent with collaborative entrepreneurial learning (Leitch, McMullan and Harrison 2009). It is also consistent with our understanding of the key success factors of PBL educational innovating teams (Verzat and Garant 2010), namely cycles of innovative experimentations closely associated with research efforts provided by a learning community of passionate educators. This helped them to find sponsors and resources in the institution so as to gain power and legitimacy which is ultimately necessary to transform the global curriculum.

Considering the current stage of knowledge about entrepreneurship education – little is known, there is massive uncertainty about relevant teaching and learning processes – our intuition is that there is a parallel between (1) what teachers try and experiment as entrepreneurship educators; (2) what they want their students to learn, and (3) how they conceive their research process. All the three processes have something to do with trying, failing, learning and growing. Thus, the main idea is to examine the propositions that teachers have to behave effectually to teach effectuation and that effectuation learning has a great deal in common with action-research processes.

To further the study of effectual educational design more specifically, we now take a closer look at action-research processes.

11.3.2 Action-research epistemology and practice

Effectuation theory is explicitly associated with a pragmatist scientific approach. Pragmatism as opposed to positivism means that their scientific inquiry deals with experimental design, measurement and inference so as to discover feasible ways to solve actual problems rather than theorizing and validating natural laws that could help predict future events. Argyris *et al.* (Argyris, Putnam and McLain Smith 1985) recognize Lewin and Dewey as the founders of action-science. John Dewey applied the inductive scientific method of problem solving, notably in the field of education. He worked in close connection with early educational pioneers like Freinet and Montessori in the 1920s. The psychologist Kurt Lewin founded the Research Center for Group Dynamics at the MIT in 1945. He particularly studied the role of group atmosphere and leadership styles and their impact on social problem solving. He described action research as 'proceeding in a spiral of steps, each of which is composed of planning, action and the evaluation of the results of action' (Kemmis and McTaggart 1990, p. 8). Lewin argued that in order to 'understand and change certain social practices, social scientists have to include practitioners from the real social world in all phases of inquiry' (McKernan 1991, p. 10). Dewey and Lewin criticized the traditional separation of knowledge and action and articulated an experimental theory of inquiry. This theory was a model both for the scientific method and for social practice, with the aim of integrating both.

Action-research can be defined as a process of fundamental research in human sciences that comes from a desire for change and is based on a research intention. It pursues a dual objective of producing social change and creating fundamentally new knowledge (Liu 1997). Kemmis and McTaggart (1990, p. 5) propose this definition: 'a form of collective self-reflective inquiry undertaken by participants in social situations in order to improve the rationality and justice of their own social or educational practices, as well as their understanding of these practices and the situations in which these practices are carried out'. As reported by Zuber-Skerrit (1992, p. 2), cited by Masters (1995), four basic elements are found in all definitions of action-research: empowerment of participants, collaboration through participation, acquisition of knowledge and social goal.

Action-research is based on participative principles which require an agreed-on ethical framework between researchers and stakeholders engaged in the situation:

> The participatory nature of action-research makes it only possible with, for and by persons and communities, ideally involving all stakeholders both in the questioning and sense making that informs the research, and in the action which is its focus.
>
> (Reason and Bradbury-Huang 2007)

In its most advanced form, action-research is emancipatory (Masters 1995). Its goals are closely linked to humanist empowering values. Empowerment refers to the progression of individual perception of skills, self-esteem, initiative and control (Eisen 1994) through a process implying participation, competence, self-esteem and critical conscience at the individual but also collective level (Rapoport 1970). This process is centred on highlighting individual and community forces, rights and abilities rather than their weaknesses or needs. It also means helping actors to formulate their own critical reflection by extending their theoretical knowledge. Practitioners are therefore more able to assess technical as well as social factors and values that inform and underpin situations or projects. As a consequence, action-research can move power relationships between groups and individuals. It is a process of social change.

> A society beginning to move from one epoch to another requires the development of an especially flexible, critical spirit. Lacking such a spirit, men cannot perceive the marked contradictions which occur in society as emerging values in search of affirmation and fulfilment clash with earlier values seeking self-preservation.
>
> (Freire 1973)

Action-research is conducted through three typical phases (Liu 1997). The first phase is an exploratory phase so as to identify the problem and to examine possibilities for establishing common ground among researchers and concerned actors. This phase includes value sharing, goal setting and negotiation of sufficient time, human and material resources. The second phase is dedicated to action and reflection cycles. It consists of different activities, which are conducted either off site (for research design and evaluation) or on site (for observation and experimentation). In each cycle, activities are as follows: diagnosis, agreed-on problematics, hypotheses, choice of actions, implementation phases and evaluation of results. Several cycles can be observed at local levels leading to a global historical understanding of change process and roles evolution. The third, final phase is dedicated to the diffusion of results and to the gradual disengagement of researchers. Ideally, actors at that stage are so autonomous that they can take on further problems even in other situations, while researchers change their focus of analysis. They move away from participating in concrete situations where action research is construed as a method towards studying more fundamental questions about systemic social change conditions, harnessing action learning as an ethos (Pedler, Burgoyne and Brook 2005).

The activities of the different phases are conducted at different regulation levels with researchers and stakeholders. The first and third phases must be conducted at strategic levels with researchers and decision-makers making allowance for resources. The second phase needs a coordination team for global design and local design as well as experimentation teams involving both practitioners and researchers.

Since action-research deals with unpredictable social change, it is a risky business. It therefore needs an informal dynamic network of allies to cope with obstacles, negotiations and changes in representations. According to Liu (1997), the critical parameters for success are the following: (1) to identify relevant stakeholders; (2) to take great care of the quality of information used to minimize misunderstandings; (3) to establish spaces for dialogue and negotiation; (4) to develop a particular attitude that leads every actor to feel that s/he is considered as a potential author; and (5) to use the simplest possible language. It corresponds to an ecological style of thinking (Tsoukas and Dooley 2011) acknowledging connectivity, recursive patterns of communication and feedback, non-linearity, emergence, ineffability and becoming. Action-research is recommended only in situations where no previous expertise or scientific knowledge exists about the nature of the problem and about possible valid solutions. Action-research epistemology has been extensively developed in educational sciences, notably in management education (Revans 1980; Raelin and Raelin 2006).

11.3.3 Action-research in education

In his article about the origins of action-research in education (Adelman 1993) reports that Kurt Lewin developed 'methods and principles to enable the school to act as the agency of democratic change within its community'. He notes that in the 1930s, Lewin was already closely connected to Dewey's learning theories and to Tyler's work on assessment through service studies by groups of teachers reflecting on their own practices. After Lewin's early death in 1947, participative action-research in education developed in the UK, in the USA and in Australia where social policy provided extensive budgets for intervention programmes in education aimed at the empowerment and inclusion of the poorest populations. In the last decade Koshy (2009) mentions that there has been a growing interest in action-research methodology among educationists (teachers, policy makers and administrators) associated with specific international journals for publication such as *Educational Action Research* and active networks of educational practitioners.

Winter (1996) highlights the following distinguishing characteristics as central to the action-research process in education:

1   'Reflexive critique, which is the process of becoming aware of our own perceptual biases;
2   Dialectic critique, which is a way of understanding the relationships between the elements that make up various phenomena in our context;
3   Collaboration, which is intended to mean that everyone's view is taken as a contribution to understand the situation;
4   Risking disturbance, which is an understanding of our taken-for-granted processes and willingness to submit them to critique;
5   Creating plural structures, which involves developing various accounts and critiques, rather than a single authoritative interpretation;
6   Theory and practice internalized, which is seeing theory and practice as two interdependent yet complementary phases of the change process'.

Zeichner (2001) points out that most action-research in education involves university academics and teachers, who reject a standards or objective-based approach to curriculum development and favour a pedagogy-driven conception of curriculum development as a process dependent on teachers' capacities for reflection. Reflexivity implies a shift from applied research designed and controlled by expert teachers or researchers to the educational practitioners' perspective (Pineau 2013; Schön 1983). This is not an easy exercise because it associates critical capacities, individual self-reflection as well as shared collective goals and terminology. Referring to his own practice of educational action-research, Adelman (1993) explains that the most difficult stage is the preliminaries:

> To move from felt troubles and anxieties to a statement of an issue, teachers have to engage in persistent reflexive thought about their own and others' practices. ... Prior to the clarification, there is a period of between a week to 3–4 months of awkward talking around anecdotes and images trying to locate key actions and acceptable terminology.
>
> (Adelman 1993, p. 16)

Koshy (2009) offers an overview of the different models and definitions of action-research in education. They all follow spiral forms showing a succession of experimentation cycles. She proposes this simple definition:

> I consider action-research as a constructive enquiry during which the researcher constructs his or her knowledge of specific issues through planning, acting, evaluating, refining and learning from the experience. It is a continuing learning process in which the researcher learns and also shares the newly generated knowledge with those who may benefit from it.

Amstrong and Moore (2004) specifically insist on the inclusion issue present in educational action-research. Their model shows how the collaborative spiral leads to inclusion through deep transformation of learners and educators at the same time. Typical questions raised throughout the different activities highlight critical action-research success factors mentioned earlier: experiential learning, accessible language for all, shared values based on democracy and acceptance of difference, critical, creative and reflexive thinking, awareness about context and power relationships. We cannot help linking them to the sense-making mechanisms in the effectual method (Sarasvathy and Venkataraman 2011) which are based on experiential, deep transformative learning as well as to the social and critical approach taken by Jones and Spicer (2009).

Therefore, we propose that educational action-research informs us about effectual educational design. This argument is supported by the intriguing coherence found between research implications for new entrepreneurship theories (Jones and Spicer 2009; Sarasvathy and Venkataraman 2011) and action-research principles and features, as summed up in Figure 11.1.

This coherence leads us to propose a theoretical framework about effectual educational design. This framework will be exposed in the following section. In the last section of our chapter it will be illustrated by four cases of radical innovations in the field of entrepreneurship education. Since then, a certain number of radical pedagogical innovations aimed at developing entrepreneurial skills and attitudes have recently emerged in different places, situated outside traditional transmissive courses or even business planning competitions. Although they apparently adopt very different pedagogical methods according to the target groups and partners they work with, we found out that they have common features based on a socio-constructivist perspective of learning and teaching and that the educational team is itself involved in an entrepreneurial effectual process with regard to educational design. Building on these two arguments, we posit that they are engaging in a reflexive practice or explicit action-research that follows our proposed framework.

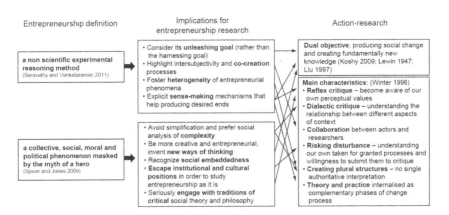

Figure 11.1 Action-research principles and features coherent with new entrepreneurship theories

Table 11.1 Framework part 1 – characteristics of effectual teaching design and framework part 2 – characteristics of effectual research design

Dimension of teaching design	Typical characteristic in effectual teaching design	Justification in entrepreneurship theories	Justification in educational action-research theories
Main learning goal	**1** Empowerment and social change	Unleashing goal (Sarasvathy and Venkataraman 2011) Escape institutional and cultural positions to study entrepreneurship as it is (Jones and Spicer 2009)	Produce social change (Koshy 2009; Lewin 1947; Liu, 1997) Let new beliefs emerge for future harmony and elevations of life courses (Koshy 2009)
Didactical design (activities, assessment, technology)	**2** Disruptive didactical design = risk and uncertainty involved	Be more creative and entrepreneurial, invent new ways (Jones and Spicer 2009) Starting with one's own real project is startling and uncomfortable (Sarasvathy 2008). Effectual reasoning used only in situations of true uncertainty (Sarrouy-Watkins 2014)	Create fundamental new knowledge (Koshy 2009; Lewin 1947; Liu 1997) Risking disturbance (Winter 1996) Action-research recommended only in situations where no previous expertise or scientific knowledge already exists (Liu 1997; Raelin and Raelin 2006; Revans 1980)
Duration	**3** Time for deep transformation	*(No explicit condition of duration)*	Collaborative planning allowing deep transformation (Amstrong and Moore 2004) Negotiate sufficient time, human and material resources when setting up action-research protocol (Liu 1997)
Target learners and number of participants	**4** Inclusion of heterogeneous participants	Foster heterogeneity in the classroom rather than produce homogenous norms (Sarasvathy and Venkataraman 2011)	Thinking about barriers to inclusion (Amstrong and Moore 2004)

Framework part 1 – characteristics of effectual teaching design

Framework part 2 – characteristics of effectual research design

Dimension of research design	Typical characteristic in effectual research design	Justification in entrepreneurship theories	Justification in educational action-research theories
Sense-making mechanisms about unleashing potential and generating desirable ends	**5** Systematic reflexivity for educators and learners	Get the students' 'trust and buy-in': starting with who they are, what they know and whom they could enrol in their project (Sarasvathy 2008)	Reflexive critique: become aware of our own perceptual values (Winter 1996) Crucial importance of teachers' capacity for self-reflection (Adelman 1993; Pineau 2013; Zeichner 2001) Development of all stakeholders as reflexive practitioners (Schön 1983) Deep transformation of learners and educators at the same time (Armstrong and Moore 2004)
	6 Dialectic critique	Seriously engage with traditions of critical theory and philosophy (Jones and Spicer 2009)	Dialectic critique: understanding the relationship between different aspects of the context (Winter 1996) Develop a flexible critical spirit to perceive contradictions when emerging values in search of affirmation and fulfilment clash with earlier values seeking self-preservation (Freire 1973)
	7 Collective action-research cycles and diffusion of results about educational process and results	Explicit sensemaking mechanisms that help produce desirable ends (Sarasvathy and Venkataraman 2011)	Action and reflection cycles (diagnosis, agreed-on problematics, hypothesis, choice of action, implementation and evaluation of results (Liu 1997) Continuing learning process where learners and researchers share the newly generated knowledge with all those who may benefit from it (Koshy 2009) Theory and practice internalized as complementary phases of change process (Winter 1996)

Dimension of research design	Typical characteristic in effectual research design	Justification in entrepreneurship theories	Justification in educational action-research theories
Inter-subjective key unit rather than individual unit	8 Systematic teamwork	Highlight intersubjectivity and co-creation processes (Sarasvathy and Venkataraman 2011) Entrepreneurs are implicated with others and with governing their prospects for their freedom (Jones and Spicer 2009)	Collaboration between actors and researchers (Winter 1996) Questions and discussions of research emerge in negotiated consensus (Koshy 2009; Liu 1997) Agreed-on ethical framework between researchers and stakeholders engaged in the situation (Reason and Bradbury-Huang 2007)
	9 Habitable workspaces for exploration and community building	Educational entrepreneurial ecosystems as places for creativity, networking and learning community building (Toutain, Gaujard, Mueller, Bornard 2014)	Critical parameters for success: presentation of all relevant stakeholders, quality of information, spaces for dialogue and negotiation, empowering attitude, simple language so that all stakeholders feel as responsible actors (Liu 1997)
Means favouring heterogeneity	10 Open multidisciplinary partnerships within complex environment	Avoid simplification, prefer social analysis of complexity, recognize social embeddedness (Jones and Spicer 2009)	Creating plural structures – no single interpretation (Winter 1996) Thinking about power relations and context (Amstrong and Moore 2004)

11.3.4 Proposed framework about effectual education design

Table 11.1 sums up the framework we propose with which to analyse effectual educational design. It is composed of two parts, which appear to be closely interconnected: the effectual teaching design (Part 1 composed of four elements) and the effectual research design (Part 2 composed of six elements). The ten elements of our model connect action-research theory to Sarasvathy and Venkataraman (2011) and Jones and Spicer (2009).

The teaching design model (part 1 of our framework) is inspired by different sources: Fayolle and Gailly's (2008) teaching model, but also by Biggs' theory of constructive alignment (Biggs and Tang 2003). The main idea of the teaching model is to enable teachers to determine, circumscribe and describe didactical choices, given that, in effectual education, they will call on situated knowledge and experience rather than mobilizing traditionally acquired knowledge and competences. They will in turn empower the heterogeneously constructed learner groups (**4**) to construct and shape their own learning trajectories, co-creating inputs, co-assessing outcomes and adapting future phases to ongoing changes in the learning environment (**1**). At the same time, they will consider the methods, tools, activities which they can use to coach learners to express and deal with the risks and uncertainty encountered during the process (**2**). They will also align goals, objectives and partially achieved outcomes with the necessary temporal dimension they believe is required to ensure deep transformative learning for all stakeholders (**3**).

As Fayolle and Gailly (2008) put it, any teaching model in entrepreneurship is inspired by ontological roots referring to implicit or explicit definitions of entrepreneurship but also to implicit conceptions about learning. We add an epistemological development to these roots by extending the isomorphic principle used to assess the quality of teachers' continuing education (Draime *et al.* 2000; Wouters *et al.* 2003): 'teach teachers as you want them to teach their students'. In other words: put teachers in a learning situation that is coherent with the learning situation you would like them to organize for their students. We go a little further by saying that learning theories, teaching practices and research practices should be coherent (or aligned) in the case of effectuation.

Then the main idea of the research model (framework part 2) is to deepen our understanding of the epistemological implications of the effectual method proposed by Sarasvathy and Venkataraman (2011) and to render explicit the research practices of effectual entrepreneurship educators. Sarasvathy and Venkataraman's argument (Sarasvathy and Venkataraman 2011) is based on the parallel they establish between entrepreneurship development and Bacon's analysis of the democratization of scientific methods from the seventeenth century onwards. At that time scientists realized that formal models, data gathering techniques, analytical techniques and experimental techniques to test correspondence with reality were not due to the special abilities of a few geniuses but could be codified and taught to many more people at schools. It implied struggling against the conception of evidence as testimony and authority and to articulate another source of evidence, namely empirical evidence. Then science could diffuse and expand as a general method making humanity able to understand universal natural laws and exploit nature's potential. Similarly with regard to entrepreneurship, Sarasvathy and Venkataraman (2011) suggest that the heroic conception of the entrepreneur can be overcome as researchers begin to codify and share with a larger community what entrepreneurs actually do. Empowering many more people with effectual reasoning and processes should therefore help humanity to behave more entrepreneurially, that is, to generate new desirable ends and new designs in their local contingent environments.

Although they never name action-research as their source of inspiration, they indicate very similar intuitions about back and forth inter-relations between research, education and practice: 'the movement here has the potential to go beyond a purely scholarly one of formulating and testing hypotheses to active interactions between research and pedagogy and practice that can inform and transform one another' (Sarasvathy and Venkataraman 2011, p. 116). At the end of their article, they put forward three areas for researching about this entrepreneurial method: '1) making the inter-subjective a key unit of analysis' (Sarasvathy and Venkataraman 2011, p. 126), that is, having a deeper sociological longitudinal understanding of exchanges between all stakeholders that produce commitment and relational cohesion as well as production in new ventures. '2) seeing heterogeneity as a basis for the design of human artefacts' (Sarasvathy and Venkataraman 2011, p. 127), which starts from the acknowledgement that human behaviour is hetero-geneous, labile and highly contextual. Thus taxonomies and coherent categories that are compelled by institutions appear in fact artificial, because patterned and path-dependent processes produce them. In that perspective risk-taking should not be attributed to innate traits but to learned experience and deliberate practice. And research should focus on those patterns that emerge through interactions and produce change in specific contexts. '3) specifying the role of the entrepreneurial method and the mechanisms that embody it' (Sarasvathy and Venkataraman 2011, p. 128), meaning that scholars should sit in with real entrepreneurs at micro-level to identify how they concretely specify an interesting social or economic change problem, and how their action and thinking mechanisms 'hang together' logically and 'make sense' so as to generate viable and desirable new ends.

We believe that these three orientations are articulated more precisely and 'hang together' logically in action-research processes. Therefore our framework clarifies six elements regarding effectual research design, which are inspired by action-research but also correspond to Jones and Spicer's recommendations for research (Jones and Spicer 2009). These six elements are numbered **5** to **10** in Table 11.1. In action-research, inter-subjective group and leadership pro-cesses are considered *the* key-unit of analysis that produces new perceptions and desires for social change. Since new knowledge has to be elicited, systematic collaborative teamwork between researchers and practitioners (**8**) is the way to articulate what makes sense for actors as well as lessons from experience and new evidence. It necessitates agreeing on the problem at stake but also on an ethical framework and roles between all stakeholders. This process takes place when workspace (and time) is 'habitable' for actors involved (**9**). Inhabiting means that creativity, networking and failure are allowed; all actors can play a role and express themselves. This is dependent on the quality of information, on the presence of all relevant stakeholders but also on the empowering attitude of researchers and decision-makers and on the use of the simplest possible language. Heterogeneity is fostered when open multi-disciplinary partnerships with stakeholders of complex environments are offered (**10**). As a consequence, social complexity and power relationships cannot be avoided. They have to be recognized and analysed. This can be done if plural structures (different regulation levels, different local teams) offer flexible spaces of negotiation, expression and interpretation. The great challenge is to elicit sense-making mechanisms. Action-research revolves around spiral action and reflection cycles (**7**) where actors and researchers continuously learn from what is undertaken. Researchers not only sit in with real entrepreneurs so as to observe them as suggested by Sarasvathy and Venkataraman (2011). They play a facilitating role by providing concepts enlightening tacit experiential knowledge of entrepreneurs but also by questioning evidence, not hesitating to engage in critical debates that arise in the context (**6**). This process starts with empowering actors by emphasizing forces and resources of all persons who are present (who they are, what they know, whom they know). This engages a progressive self-reflection for all actors (**5**), including researchers, about their potential, desires and realistic capabilities.

Action-research implies adhering to a socio-constructivist view of learning but also to new evidence about finalities and methods of scientific work. It is opposed to classical positivist traditions of natural sciences because of its methodological orientations and because of its finalities (Liu 1997). On the methodological side, action-research studies complex social situations and their evolution rather than one isolated phenomenon. It favours the subjective involvement of researchers and their sharing of knowledge production with practitioners while positivism advocates for objectivity. While positivist theories seek intelligibility so as to build universal predictive laws, action research aims at identifying one viable transformation path in a contingent unique situation where no universal law could be applied. As this epistemological model is not mainstream, it is a risky business for researchers. In that sense adopting this epistemological approach is akin to behaving like an entrepreneur in the academic world. We believe this is the unique way to produce creative knowledge about the unknown transformational social processes of effectuation teaching. This audacity is required according to Jones and Spicer: 'Entrepreneurship research could be a great deal more creative and inventive than it has been. ... Entrepreneurship research could, as some have been arguing in recent years, be something far more, well, entrepreneurial' (Jones and Spicer 2009, p. 112).

We will now apply this framework to analyse four cases of radical pedagogical innovation in the field of entrepreneurship education, which happen to propose a rather coherent effectual approach in their educational design.

11.4 Illustrations of four cases studies of effectual educational design

In this section, we first present the methodological approach used to collect the data and analyse the four cases under study. We then proceed to outline the results that were obtained following the application of our proposed framework and to discuss the effectual and isomorphic processes that were inherent in the design of both the teaching and research components.

11.4.1 Methodology to meet our theoretical framework

We collected qualitative data within four pedagogical contexts, two in France and two in the Netherlands. The reason for reporting on these cases is based on two criteria, which account for radically new educational practices:

1   The originality of their pedagogy: educators made out-of-the-box choices regarding entrepreneurship educational design (definition of learning goals, activities, assessment, teacher stances, workspace design and/or technology). In all four cases, little scientific knowledge or expertise existed in relation to their initiatives.
2   The inclusion of new target groups: all four experiences reach new populations compared to those usually found within their institutions, thus justifying a claim for inclusion.

The data collection methods used were devised according to what was deemed negotiable with the teams and participants involved:

• Semi-direct interviews with stakeholders, regularly written debriefings by all participants and film analysis in the first example (Alice-lab).[2]
• Semi-direct interviews of educators and pre-post questionnaires in the second example (MOOC).
• Semi-direct interviews with educators, films and documentary analysis in the third and fourth examples (Knowmads and Studio HVA).

We assumed a constructivist grounded approach in analysing the data (Glaser and Strauss 1999) as well as case study methodology (Yin 2013). As Charmaz indicates (Charmaz 2000), a grounded approach implies setting up an iterative process of regarding, listening to, reacting to and understanding the data, gradually appropriating the patterns and meanings that emerged. As the following section will show, this methodological approach, building on the ten-dimension framework proposed (see Table 11.1) enabled us to highlight the characteristics of both effectual research and teaching design which help to generate effectual educational design (see Tables 11.2 and 11.3). There was clear evidence of the establishment of an entrepreneurial-isomorphic configuration among the different stakeholders involved in the

Table 11.2 Effectual teaching design in the four cases

	Alice-Lab (FR-2014)	MOOC-Effectuation (FR-2013)	Knowmads (NL-2009)	Studio HVA (NL-2006)
1 Main learning goal = Empowerment and social change	Develop the entrepreneurial mindset at any age	Understand effectuation 'Entrepreneurship for all'	'Reeducate', develop one's own tools	Grow skills and develop potential in innovative interactive media
2 Disruptive didactical design (activities, assessment, technology) = risk and uncertainty involved	- Real entrepreneurial or intra-preneurial projects - No course, hands-on project to develop a prototype - Dual coaching for each team - Self-assessment tools - Flexible involvement (go/ no go procedure, 2 training speeds)	- Massive open online course - Self-assessment + formal assessment (MCQ) - Virtual lab (submit your own project)	- No formalized programme (self-emerging projects) - Only coaching, no course - Collective decision-making - Body movement, storytelling workshops	- Practice-based work with a touch of research to develop a working prototype in collaboration with the client - Multidisciplinary teams guided by experts from the industry and university
3 Duration = Time for deep transformation	13 weeks	5 weeks	12 to 24 months	20 weeks
4 Target learners = inclusion of heterogeneous participants	31 participants Mixed teams (design s tudents, entrepreneurship students + executives from partner firms)	3,500 participants French speakers all around the world	23 participants Drop-out students from 23 to 35 years old	300 students Final year students or recent graduates from Applied Universities in EU

Table 11.3 Effectual research design in the four cases

		Alice-Lab (FR-2014)	MOOC-Effectuation (FR-2013)	Knowmads (NL-2009)	Studio HVA (NL-2006)
Sensemaking mechanisms about unleashing potential and generating desirable ends	5 System reflexivity for educators and learners	Regular logbooks written by all participants (students, coaches, researchers) Self-assessing criteria and collective jury designed by each team	Regular forums to answer participants' questions Appeal to participants' testimonials on their own projects	Reflexivity tools for participants	Personal coaching of student
	6 Dialectic critique	Mixed teams of coaches (business + design) generating debates about projects Observations and debates thanks to external critical actors: doctoral students + education philosopher	Mixed team of coaches (business + design) generating debates about projects	'Invisible learning' project	Education team is a mix of designers, programmers, social/digital media experts, researchers, copywriters and storytellers
	7 Collective action-research cycles and diffusion of results about educational process and results	Action research protocol with partners (schools, incubator, students, partner-firms) Creative workshops with entrepreneurs and scientific community	Collaboration with external research team for evaluation of results and learning analytics Blogs and popular science books on effectuation for French speakers	'Open books' under creative commons license for sharing experience and results with readers	Close partnership with university

	Alice-Lab (FR-2014)	MOOC-Effectuation (FR-2013)	Knowmads (NL-2009)	Studio HVA (NL-2006)
8 Systematic teamwork Inter-subjective key unit rather than individual unit	Mixed student teams of different size (4 to 8) Coaching team regular informal discussions + supervision Choice of project based on mutual agreements Trial and error prototypes tested with stakeholders	Educating team informal meetings Open collective forums on the net	Educating team formal and informal meetings Create your own network with the help of other participants Systematic collective decisions on process negotiation	Educating team regular meeting Collective decisions with leaders Collaboration with clients on prototype working
9 Habitable workspaces for exploration and community building	Nomadic workplaces Unexpected demand of celebration by participants in the end	Virtual lab set up after unexpected participants' demand to explore mutualized learning	Community building in co-working spaces	Informal discussions in open space around cooking area
10 Open multidisciplinary partnerships within complex environment Means favouring heterogeneity	Mixed partners: start-ups and large firms, for profit and NGOs	Invited entrepreneurs from different origins and sectors in forums and blogs	Connections with several entrepreneurial networks	Partnership with external entrepreneurial networks

projects. This led to a stream of effectual learning and teaching processes that enabled all actors, on their different levels, to attain and achieve their objectives.

11.4.2 Characteristics of effectual teaching design in the four cases

The first case is an effectual teaching experimentation, carried out in France in 2014. It was elaborated by a team of action-researchers in entrepreneurship (the Alice-lab team) who had decided to 'act differently' in their job, in order to test new ways of educating the entrepreneurial mind-set. Instead of planning a long-term specifically defined project, they deliberately set up encounters with a wide range of people they thought would be interested in participating in the design and implementation of a novel way of teaching and learning entrepreneurship. Following a two-day creative seminar, ending with a final debate with two entrepreneurs, this led to a first version of the programme that was then presented to potential stakeholders, helping to progressively shape the proposition.

The programme tested was a 13-week training module (60 hours), which brought together teams of design and entrepreneurship students with executives from five firms (31 participants), around innovation projects commissioned by the firms. Each team was counselled by entrepreneurial coaches, design experts and researchers in educational studies. Using a participatory, collaborative approach, out of the box thinking and ethnographic exploration in the field were encouraged. An assessment contract was negotiated with each team for self-evaluation purposes. Each participant (students, coaches, teachers, researchers) had to write a logbook, in order to analyse events, and students were asked to highlight lessons that could be turned into skills for their future career. From a research point of view, this experimentation was also an innovative way of producing results through the testing of a new business model for entrepreneurship education.

The second case is a MOOC (Massive Open Online Course) experimentation, designed around the subject of effectuation theory. It was launched by a business school in France in 2013, and called 'Entrepreneurship for all'. It was one of the first MOOCs in the business field and also the first one designed to study entrepreneurship in a French context. This project emerged due to the initiative of a teacher and researcher, a former entrepreneur himself, who managed to convince his school's executive committee to support the project. At the time of conception, he had no idea of how to do this or what audience could be expected. But he was convinced that the only way to understand what a MOOC really is, was to produce one! The MOOC attracted 3,500 participants, and lasted for a period of 6 weeks. The program proposed quizzes and a peer-graded case study based on a real start-up, with both self-assessment and formal assessment processes. The aim was to promote the idea that everybody can become an entrepreneur, focusing on learning about how entrepreneurs think and act.

The third and fourth cases correspond to projects run by two innovative pedagogical schools situated in the Netherlands. The first one, called Knowmads, was launched in 2009. The second one run by Studio HVA, was proposed in 2006. The programmes targeted different learners: young entrepreneurial students from 23 to 35 years old were involved in the Knowmads project; final year students or recent graduates from Applied Universities were targeted by Studio HVA. This difference revealed the initial mind-set of the project leaders. Knowmads did not want to have anything to do with the University, preferring a separate space, with no formalized programme or teachers. Studio HVA tried to innovate within the system, gradually negotiating the means required. Knowmads sought to 're-educate' the students, helping them develop their own tools, whereas Studio HVA followed a formalized programme to experiment and try out entrepreneurship as a potential career path. Table 11.2 summarizes the characteristics of these four cases.

At first glance, these four cases appear to be significantly different: Alice, Knowmads and Studio HVA are face-to-face projects while Effectuation is an online programme (MOOC) with no physical contact. The MOOC is primarily based on a course (1-hour video) given every week with 3,500 participants while Knowmads is based on coaching only with 23 participants. Yet despite these differences, the cases verify the four elements of our framework:

1   Empowerment and social change: they all aim at changing mindsets and have practical impact; the shared finality is always to enable students to find their own way towards building a more desirable future for themselves, whatever perspective they choose (a network, an entrepreneurial project, a traineeship, a future career …).
2   Disruptive didactical design: they all represent a novel approach in designing a programme.
3   Time for deep transformation: they last long enough to enable a real impact. With regard to this third characteristic, the MOOC appears significantly shorter than the other programmes. A deep transformation can take place, however, because the programme increases involvement by mixing video viewing and multiple choice questionnaires with three additional activities: participation in discussion forums, work on case studies of real start-ups, and optional participation in a virtual lab where learners can present their own projects and receive feedback and advice from other participants. Involvement in these activities is optional and decided by the participants. A research programme conducted by the authors on the Mooc's learning analytics shows that there is a significant correlation between the self-directedness exhibited by participants and the progression of their entrepreneurial self-efficacy. This explains why even if the duration may seem short, an open space for self-transformation can take place.
4   Inclusion of heterogeneous participants: they either mix participants from diverse origins within teams or allow open enrolment (in the case of the MOOC).

As explicitly developed in the case of the MOOC, the educational design appears closely connected to a research process undertaken by educators in all four cases. This is the second part of the framework.

11.4.3 Characteristics of effectual research design

Among these four case studies, the French examples offer a more explicit understanding of their research design process than the two Dutch examples. Both French examples call on an effectual action-based research approach, which creates pedagogical experiments whereas the two Dutch examples are anchored in an effectual educational design approach, in which we carried out a research study. This is why we offer a more comprehensive view of the two French examples from the research design point of view. This is illustrated in two stories (see Appendix to Chapter 11), which take the form of interviews with the founders of the experimentations. These stories highlight the innovative features of both modules as well as their effectual process mixing educational and research design.

What struck us most in all four examples is the range of means that are displayed by the educating teams to continually adjust their educational methods and tools to effectively correspond to and reflect on the learning journeys experienced by learners. The experiences were designed as quasi-experimentations, in the sense that there was a lot of uncertainty in the beginning about results and also about the process. The pedagogical methods were very diverse. Some of them were agreed on from the beginning (e-learning sessions, films or logbooks, for example) but many of them emerged during the educators' experiential learning process which enabled them to take learners' or coaches' suggestions or demands into account (setting up of a forum, prototyping, emergent jury criteria, request for celebrations, meetings with other teams …). From that perspective, we can speak about a co-creation process that was established between educators and learners but also between learners as well as with researchers. The frontier between research and co-construction is very tenuous. To achieve constant adaptation, all dimensions of our research design framework are observed.

1   Systematic reflexivity for educators and learners: all experimentations included various creative tools for enabling reflexive processes by all stakeholders: logbooks, forums, personal coaching and self-assessment methods. Since the experience was negotiated and accepted in the first place as an experimentation by all stakeholders, the different reflexive tools provided data material for collective research about the process and the results. The MOOC founder makes it very clear: We set out to create the MOOC by inventing what needed to be invented and acting as reflective practitioners. We capitalized our knowledge by writing about lessons learned in blogs

and by developing academic research on how a MOOC helps learn entrepreneurial skills.

Dialectic critique: there is a constant stream of debates, discussions and constructive criticism thanks to the multidisciplinary composition of teams at all levels and authorization of free speech. Usually hidden critiques are made possible because there are spaces for doing so and people are allowed to express themselves either spontaneously or during feedback sessions. Because researchers familiar with these concepts were involved in the local teams, effectuation processes were explicitly brought into the conversations. They could be observed and commented on by participants, as the Alice founder puts it:

> "Many issues and questions in entrepreneurship education were at stake. Consequently, I carried out this action research by doing, by using conceptual notions and reflection during the experiment." The same kind of statement is made by the MOOC founder: "If you want to understand what MOOCS are about, the only way is to produce one. The field is so new, that classic research through interviews or literature review would have yielded nothing. By doing so, we were consistent with effectuation, which is my field of specialization. ... Every person involved in the project had to learn something new."

Collective action-research cycles and the diffusion of results about educational processes have very clearly shown that the MOOC example as well as the Alice example have founders who followed action-research cycles. They had to negotiate the right to conduct this experimentation in their institution in the first place. They then discovered new resources on the way while providing evaluation and results about the experimentations. Their research process is considered 'organic' by the Alice founder:

> We participated at conferences writing papers on what we were currently experiencing, what we progressively learnt thanks to the different tests.

1 Systematic teamwork: All students work in teams even in the MOOC experience. Moreover educators also work in teams and consider themselves to be part of a learning community along with the students.
2 Habitable workspaces for exploration and community building: the four cases experiment different forms of workspace (nomadic, virtual or open space mixing living and working arrangements such as cooking). This workspace is designed in such a way that people are attracted to it because it enables them to feel they belong to it. And at the same time, it moves them away from their usual routines. Open warm spaces encourage a move to encounter new ideas and new people.

3   Open multidisciplinary partnerships within complex environments: All cases invite partners from different sectors and origins. Diversity of participants was a condition of both experimentations: 'Having such a diverse range of people in the same educational module had never been tried out, observed or analyzed in literature' (Alice founder).

> Entrepreneurship for everybody ... promotes the idea that everybody can be an entrepreneur, regardless of age, gender, education, country of origin and approach to entrepreneurship. ... Unlike traditional research projects, the production of knowledge is not aimed only at an academic audience, but also at professionals and the general public so that all can learn and contribute, which is typical of action research.
>
> (MOOC founder)

On the whole, the educational processes displayed in these four contexts appear to apply effectual principles to themselves as a new way to make research:

> So does the Alice founder: "We carried it out as an effectual research. We are now conscious of the fact that we are not in the mainstream and that's a totally new way to carry out research."

Action-research is challenging for those who embrace it because they are personally committed to changing and learning and because they are opposed to mainstream positivist research stances. Adopting this 'effectual educational design process' in entrepreneurship education represents a real challenge to the classical pedagogical approach that is practised in business schools or universities. Indeed the four radical innovators appeared to a certain degree as dissidents in their own institutions: 'Please break the rule. We did' proclaims Moravec[3] (Hart *et al.* 2013) in his latest book. The efforts made to render this research process explicit, and to disseminate the results seemed to compensate for the tremendous personal investment that was required: through research collaboration, educating teams developed their understanding of the process. This understanding helped them to cope with the complexity resulting from uncertain, unpredictable situations, notably with new university partners, to gain more confidence in their own intuitions and to accept the cost of lower investment in reputation-making traditional publications. The dissemination of their original research process played a strategic role in gaining more academic recognition and in institutionalizing those innovative programmes within the curriculum. Just like entrepreneurs who follow a dialogical process of project and identity build-up (Bruyat and Julien 2001) and who calculate acceptable losses, this constitutes another facet of the parallel between learners and educators in terms of effectuation (Sarasvathy 2001) and transformative learning processes (Mezirow 1997).

11.5 Conclusion

This chapter aimed to explore new ways in which both researchers and teachers experiment learning models more based on a socio-constructivist approach than on the positivist view. In the first part, we pointed out the actual debate about current limitations of EE and the necessity, even if it is a complex process, to change and to move away from the classical guiding philosophy of education in order to imagine new horizons and new epistemologies. In the second part, we showed how an effectual action-based research approach offers new pragmatic perspectives to innovate in entrepreneurship education. In the third part, we illustrated this proposition by presenting four case studies based on an effectual design. Despite within case differences, these examples show how educators engaged in effectual thinking (1) do not hesitate to adapt their teaching design in the face of uncertainty and unpredictability; and (2) break with the linearity of teaching plans that are built in order to be reproduced without taking account of the complexity of the learning process, the learning community and the learning context.

Therefore, the main challenge is to be effectual by staying as close as possible to the entrepreneurial way of doing, acting and thinking, both from an individual and collective perspective. For this purpose, we recommend following the principle of isomorphism. While our intention was not to show that entrepreneurs would be the most effective in educating others into their mindset, we believe that our results demonstrate how it is possible to act as an 'academic entrepreneur' (Landström, Harirchi and Åström 2012) when designing educational frameworks or researching in entrepreneurial education (Geenhuizen and Nijkamp 2012). The framework proposed for this entrepreneurship education research based on effectual educational design is closely related to action-research epistemology. By applying it to four cases of radical pedagogical innovations, we highlighted that future challenges in entrepreneurship education will depend on our capacity to change the relationship between researchers, educators and would-be entrepreneurs in order to further co-learning processes. As Jones and Spicer said 'Entrepreneurship is not about entrepreneurs. It is about relations with others ... What we find when we unmask the entrepreneur is the face of the other' (Jones and Spicer 2009).

In this way, the myth of the individual hero disappears behind the entrepreneurial learning community that is both at the origin and a result of the creation of an entrepreneurial educational ecosystem. The different examples show that each ecosystem is singular. It is made up of its own living species interacting with environmental components in an interdependent, systemic way. Through interactive processes, researchers, educators, students and all stakeholders co-produce a sustainable entrepreneurial ecosystem. This generates a fruitful space to motivate and speed up the dissemination of an entrepreneurial culture and mindset. Like beavers who build their dams in wetlands, contributing to the maintenance of the dynamic equilibrium of the environment, the adoption of the 'effectual educational design process' has the same effect. It maintains biodiversity levels, enabling all stakeholders (the diverse species of the entrepreneurial ecosystem) to learn how to develop their own learning strategies and to make new ideas.

Educational designers (like beavers) can create the conditions for learning, teaching and researching in a collaborative way (Taddei 2009), generating desirable yet unpredictable social change within the ecosystem. In enacting these collaborative processes, they produce 'antibodies' along the way by acquiring meta-competences that lead them to be more sustainable or 'antifragile' (Taleb 2013). These processes include the key parameters inherent in the implementation of action-research: ensuring diversity of participants through inclusion, systematically encouraging experiential, collaborative processes (learning in teams at all levels like all stakeholders), coping with failure, social complexity and power relations, adopting a critically constructive posture and using a comprehensive language.

Enacting this collaborative action-research approach entails many practical implications from educator perspectives. By building on the cooperative dimension present in the reflective practitioner stance that educators adopt (Schön 1983), we propose activating this approach by transforming the five effectual principles into pedagogical practices. Posture is of crucial importance here, beholding entrepreneurial educators to behave like 'academic entrepreneurs':

- Taking risks in designing and implementing pedagogy.
- Experimenting via trial and error.
- Coping with failure and dealing with diversity.
- Converting these experimentations into new teaching knowledge.
- Transferring this new knowledge into other fields and learning contexts.

More specifically, following the 'Pilot-in-the-Plane principle', educators recognize that the future is made or created rather than built on predictions. Consequently, they adopt a back seat approach, relinquishing control over the process to further learning empowerment for all learners. In so doing, they replace their role as 'guide' with that of 'reflexive coach' (Vial, Caparros-Mencacci and Ketele 2007), navigating permanently between causation and effectuation in order to analyse situations and facilitate learners in progressing through their various learning trajectories.

This posture is all the more important given that the literature in entrepreneurship education emphasizes the difficulties in establishing clearly determined learning outcomes. By acknowledging the 'Co-Creation Partnership principle', educators focus on providing the sense-making tools that enable learning to emerge gradually throughout the process. Due to the sense-making filter, they enable learning objectives to be co-created and permanently revised, taking account of learner expectations.

The 'Lemonade principle' is respected when educators invite the surprise factor into the process, recognizing and working with learner characteristics as potential catalysts for moving forward. As they navigate through the process, educators constantly weigh up the risks, thinking about the 'Affordable Loss principle', while favouring the most satisfactory goals. Above all, educators work with the skills, know-how and networks they have at their disposal (the 'Bird-in-Hand principle'), creatively imagining the possibilities that can be enacted with available means.

But more importantly, applying an effectual education design needs time. In other words, entrepreneurial courses are a starting point; educators plant seeds encouraging learners to regularly water their crop, by leaving the control of the learning process to the learner.

Notes

1 Data from the period 1991–2011 in the EE literature in five leading entrepreneurship journals (*Journal of Business Venturing, Entrepreneurship Theory and Practice, Journal of Small Business Management, Entrepreneurship and Regional Development* and *International Small Business Journal*) and in two high-impact factor education journals (*Academy of Management Learning* and *Education and Journal of Management Education*).
2 Alice-Lab (Action Learning for Innovation Creativity and Entrepreneurship) is a research centre (www.alice-lab.com).
3 Founder of Knowmads.

References

Adelman, C. (1993) 'Kurt Lewin and the origins of action research', *Educational Action Research*, 1(1), pp. 7–24.

Ajzen, I. (1991) 'The theory of planned behavior', *Organizational Behavior and Human Decision Processes*, 50(2), pp. 179–211.

Albanese, M.A. and Mitchell, S. (1993) 'Problem-based learning: A review of literature on its outcome', *Academic Medicine*, 68(1), pp. 52–81.

Amabile, T.M. (2001) 'Beyond talent: John Irving and the passionate craft of creativity', *American Psychologist*, 56(4), pp. 333–336.

Amstrong, F. and Moore, M. (2004) 'Action research: Developing inclusive practice and transforming cultures'. In Amstrong, F. and Moore, M. (eds) *Action Research for Inclusive Education*. Falmer: Routledge, pp. 1–16.

Ananou, C. (2007) *Faut-il brûler les plans d'affaires?* Paper at the Vème Congrès International de l'Académie de l'Entrepreneuriat, Sherbrooke, Quebec.

Argyris, C., Putnam, R. and McLain Smith, D. (1985) *Action Science*. San Francisco, CA: Jossey-Bass.

Bandura, A. (1985) *Social Foundations of Thought and Action: A Social Cognitive Theory*. Englewood Cliffs, NJ: Prentice Hall.

Bandura, A. and Cervone, D. (1986) 'Differential engagement of self-reactive influences in cognitive motivation', *Organizational Behavior and Human Decision Processes*, 38(1), pp. 92–113.

Barbier, J.M. (2003) *Conférence Introductive*. Brest: ENSIETA.

Barr, R.B. and Tagg, J. (1995) 'From teaching to learning. A new paradigm for undergraduate education', *Change: The Magazine of Higher Learning*, 27(6), pp. 12–26.

Bateman, T.S. and Crant, J.M. (1993) 'The proactive component of organizational behavior: A measure and correlates', *Journal of Organizational Behavior*, 14(2), pp. 103–118.

Béchard, J.-P. and Grégoire, D. (2005) 'Entrepreneurship education research revisited: The case of higher education', *Academy of Management Learning and Education*, 4(1), pp. 22–43.

Biggs, J. (1999) 'What the student does: Teaching for enhanced learning', *Higher Education Research and Development*, 18(1), pp. 57–75.

Biggs, J. and Tang, C. (2003) *Teaching for Quality Learning at University*. Milton Keynes: Open University Press.

Blenker, P., Korsgaard, S., Neergaard, H. and Thrane, C. (2011) 'The questions we care about: Paradigms and progression in entrepreneurship education', *Industry and Higher Education*, 25(6), pp. 417–427.

Bloom, B.S. (1984) *Taxonomy of Educational Objectives Book 1: Cognitive Domain*. New York: Addison Wesley.

Bonazzi, R. (2014) *Grow it like a plant: une étude de cas sur la formation en entrepreneuriat* Paper at the 5émes Journées Georges Doriot Conference, Rabat, Maroc.

Bourdoncle, R. and Lessard, C. (2002) 'Note de synthèse [Qu'est-ce qu'une formation professionnelle universitaire ? Conceptions de l'université et formation professionnelle]', *Revue Française de Pédagogie*, 139(1), pp. 131–153.

Bouvy, T., de Theux, M.-N., Raucent, B., Smidts, D., Sobieski, P. and Wouters, P. (2010) 'Compétences et rôles du tuteur en pédagogies actives'. In Raucent, B. and Villeneuve, L. (eds) *Accompagner des étudiants*. Bruxelles: De Boeck Supérieur, p. 371.

Bruner, J. (1976) *The Process of Education*. Cambridge, MA: Harvard University Press.

Bruyat, C. and Julien, P.-A. (2001) 'Defining the field of research in entrepreneurship', *Journal of Business Venturing*, 16(2), pp. 165–180.

Byrne, J., Fayolle, A. and Toutain, O. (2014) 'Entrepreneurship education: What we know and what we need to know'. In Chell, E. and Karataş-Özkan, M. (eds) *Handbook of Research on Small Business and Entrepreneurship*. Cheltenham: Edward Elgar, pp. 261–288.

Carlile, O. and Jordan, A. (2005) 'It works in practice but will it work in theory? The theoretical underpinnings of pedagogy'. In O'Neill, G., Moore, S. and McMullan, B. (eds) *Emerging Issues in the Practice of University Learning and Teaching*. Dublin: Aishe Readings, pp. 11–26.

Charmaz, K. (2000) 'Grounded theory: Objectivist and constructivist methods'. In Denzin, N.K. and Lincoln, Y.S. (eds) *Handbook of Qualitative Research*. Thousand Oaks, CA: Sage, pp. 509–535.

Cohen, R. (2008) 'Faut-il brûler les plans d'affaires?', *L'Expansion Management Review*, 128(1), pp. 22–30.

Cope, J. (2005) 'Toward a dynamic learning perspective of entrepreneurship', *Entrepreneurship, Theory and Practice*, 29(4), pp. 373–397.

Corbett, A.C. (2005) 'Experiential learning within the process of opportunity identification and exploitation', *Entrepreneurship Theory and Practice*, 29(4), pp. 473–491.

Cousinet, R. (2011) *Une méthode de travail libre par groupes*. Paris: Editions Fabert.

Crant, J.M. (1996) 'The Proactive Personality Scale as a Predictor of Entrepreneurial Intentions', *Journal of Small Business Management*, 34(3), pp. 42–49.

Csikszentmihalyi, M. (1997) *Creativity: Flow and the Psychology of Discovery and Invention*. New York: Harper Perennial.

Deci, E.L. and Ryan, R.M. (2000) 'The "what" and "why" of goal pursuits: Human needs and the self-determination of behavior', *Psychological Inquiry*, 11(4), pp. 227–268.

Decroly, O. (2011) *Le Développement du Langage Parlé Chez L'enfant: Imitation, Comprehension, expression*. Toronto: University of Toronto Libraries.

Delmar, F. and Shane, S. (2003) 'Does business planning facilitate the development of new ventures?', *Strategic Management Journal*, 24(12), pp. 1165–1185.

Dewey, J. (1916) *Democracy and Education*. London: Macmillan Press.

Draime, J., Laloux, A., Lebrun, M., Parmentier, P. and Wouters, P. (2000) *Repenser la formation pédagogique des nouveaux enseignants universitaires*. Paper at the AIPU Conference, 10–13 April, Paris.

Edelman, L.F., Manolova, T.S. and Brush, C.G. (2008) 'Entrepreneurship education: Correspondence between practices of nascent entrepreneurs and textbook prescriptions for success', *Academy of Management Learning and Education*, 7(1), pp. 56–70.

Eisen, A. (1994) 'Survey of neighborhood-based, comprehensive community empowerment initiatives', *Health Education and Behavior*, 21(2), pp. 235–252.

European Commission (2013) *Entrepreneurship Education: A Guide for Educators*. Brussels: EU.

Fayolle, A. (2013) 'Personal views on the future of entrepreneurship education', *Entrepreneurship and Regional Development*, 25(7–8), pp. 692–701.

Fayolle, A. and Gailly, B. (2008) 'From craft to science: Teaching models and learning processes in entrepreneurship education', *Journal of European Industrial Training*, 32(7), pp. 569–593.

Fillis, I. and Rentschler, R. (2010) 'The role of creativity in entrepreneurship', *Journal of Enterprising Culture*, 18(1), pp. 49–81.

Flavell, J.H. (1979) 'Metacognition and cognitive monitoring: A new area of cognitive–developmental inquiry', *American Psychologist*, 34(10), pp. 906–911.

Freinet, C. (1993) *Education Through Work: A Model for Child-Centered Learning*. Lewiston, NY: Edwin Mellen.

Freire, P. (1973) *Education: The Practice of Freedom*. London: Writers' and Readers' Publishing Co-operative.

Geenhuizen, M.V. and Nijkamp, P. (2012) *Creative Knowledge Cities: Myths, Visions and Realities*. Cheltenham: Edward Elgar.

Gibb, A. (2011) 'Concepts into practice: Meeting the challenge of development of entrepreneurship educators around an innovative paradigm', *International Journal of Entrepreneurial Behaviour and Research*, 17(2), pp. 146–165.

Gibb, A. (2002) 'In pursuit of a new "enterprise" and "entrepreneurship" paradigm for learning: Creative destruction, new values, new ways of doing things and new combinations of knowledge', *International Journal of Management Reviews*, 4(3), pp. 233–269.

Gijselaers, W.H. (1996) 'Connecting problem-based practices with educational theory', *New Directions for Teaching and Learning*, 68, pp. 13–21.

Glaser, B. and Strauss, A. (1999) *The Discovery of Grounded Theory: Strategies for Qualitative Research*. Chicago, IL: Aldine Transaction.

Harrison, R.T. and Leitch, C.M. (2005) 'Entrepreneurial learning: Researching the interface between learning and the entrepreneurial context', *Entrepreneurship Theory and Practice*, 29(4), pp. 351–371.

Hart, G., Moravec, J.W., Spinder, P., Stokman, B., Besselink, T., Bree, E., Cobo, C., Hartkamp, C., Hoff, R. and Renaud, C. (2013) *Knowmad Society*. Minneapolis, MN: Education Futures LLC.

Honig, B. (2004) 'Entrepreneurship education: Toward a model of contingency-based business planning', *Academy of Management Learning and Education*, 3(3), pp. 258–273.

Johnson, D.W. (1991) *Cooperative Learning: Increasing College Faculty Instructional Productivity.* ASHE-ERIC Higher Education Report No. 4, Washington, DC: George Washington University.

Jones, A. (2013) *The Fifth Age of Work: How Companies Can Redesign Work to Become More Innovative in a Cloud Economy.* New York: Night Owls Press.

Jones, C. (2011) *Teaching Entrepreneurship to Undergraduates.* Cheltenham: Edward Elgar.

Jones, C. and Spicer, A. (2009) *Unmasking the Entrepreneur.* Cheltenham: Edward Elgar.

Karlsson, T. and Honig, B. (2009) 'Judging a business by its cover: An institutional perspective on new ventures and the business plan', *Journal of Business Venturing*, 24(1), pp. 27–45.

Kearney, P. (1998) *Enterprising Ways to Teach and Learn.* New York: Enterprise Design.

Kemmis, S. and McTaggart, R. (1990) *The Action Research Planner.* Geelong: Deakin University Press.

De Ketele, J.M. (2000) 'Approche socio-historique des compétences dans l'enseignement'. In Bosman, C., Gerard, F.M. and Roegiers, X. (eds) *Quel Avenir Pour les Compétences? Pédagogies en Dévelopement.* Bruxelles: De Boeck, pp. 83–92.

Knowles, M.S. (1975) *Self-directed Learning: A Guide for Learners and Teachers.* Chicago, IL: Association Press.

Kolb, D.A. (1984) *Organizational Psychology: Readings on Human Behaviour in Organisations.* Englewood Cliffs, NJ: Prentice-Hall.

Kolmos, A., De Graaf, E. and Du, X. (2009) 'Diversity of PBL-PBL learning principles and models'. In Du, X., de Graaff, E. and Kolos, A. (eds) *Research on PBL Practice in Engineering Education.* Aalborg: Sense, pp. 9–21.

Koshy, V. (2009) *Action Research for Improving Educational Practice.* Thousand Oaks, CA: Sage.

Krueger, N.F. and Carsrud, A.L. (1993) 'Entrepreneurial intentions: Applying the theory of planned behaviour', *Entrepreneurship and Regional Development*, 5(4), pp. 315–330.

Kuehn, K.W., Grider, D. and Sell, R. (2009) 'New venture assessment: Moving beyond business plans in introductory entrepreneurship courses', *Journal of Entrepreneurship Education*, 12, pp. 1267–1278.

Lahm, R.J. (2008) 'More trouble than it is worth? Detecting and prosecuting plagiarism in business plans', *Journal of Academic Administration in Higher Education*, 4(1), pp. 113–117.

Landström, H., Harirchi, G. and Åström, F. (2012) 'Entrepreneurship: Exploring the knowledge base', *Research Policy*, 41(7), pp. 1154–1181.

Landström, H. and Lohrke, F. (2010) *Historical Foundations of Entrepreneurial Research.* Cheltenham: Edward Elgar.

Leitch, C.M., McMullan, C. and Harrison, R.T. (2009) 'Leadership development in SMEs: An action learning approach', *Action Learning: Research and Practice*, 6(3), pp. 243–263.

Lewin, K. (1946) 'Action research and minority problems', *Journal of Social Issues*, 2(4), pp. 34–46.

Liu, M. (1997) *Fondements et Pratiques de la Recherche-Action.* Paris: Editions L'Harmattan.

Löbler, H. (2006) 'Learning entrepreneurship from a constructivist perspective', *Technology Analysis and Strategic Management*, 18(1), pp. 19–38.

Mager, R.F. (1997) *Preparing Instructional Objectives: A Critical Tool in the Development of Effective Instruction.* Atlanta, GA: Center for Effective Performance.

Martin, B.C., McNally, J.J. and Kay, M.J. (2013) 'Examining the formation of human capital in entrepreneurship: A meta-analysis of entrepreneurship education outcomes', *Journal of Business Venturing*, 28(2), pp. 211–224.

Masters, J. (1995) 'The history of action research'. In Hughes, I. (ed.) *Action Research Electronic Reader*. Sydney: University of Sydney. Available at: www.scu.edu.au/ schools/gcm/ar/arr/arow/rmasters.html.

McKernan, J. (1991) *Curriculum Action Research: A Handbook of Methods and Resources for the Reflective Practitioner*. London: Kogan.

Messeghem, K. and Verstraete, T. (2009) 'La recherche en entrepreneuriat: état des thèses soutenues entre 2004 et 2007', *Revue de l'Entrepreneuriat*, 8(1), pp. 91–105.

Meyer, J.W. and Rowan, B. (1977) 'Institutionalized organization: Formal structure as myth and ceremony', *American Journal of Sociology*, 83, pp. 340–363.

Mezirow, J. (1997) 'Transformative learning: Theory to practice', *New Directions for Adult and Continuing Education*, 74, pp. 5–12.

Montessori, M. and Chattin-McNichols, J. (1995) *The Absorbent Mind*. New York: Holt Paperbacks.

Mueller, S. and Anderson, A.R. (2014) 'Understanding the entrepreneurial learning process and its impact on students' personal development: A European perspective', *International Journal of Management Education*, 12(3), pp. 500–511.

Naia, A., Baptista, R., Januario, C. and Trigo, V. (2014) 'A systematization of the literature on entrepreneurship education. Challenges and emerging solutions in the entrepreneurial classroom', *Industry and Higher Education*, 28(2), pp. 79–96.

Neck, H.M. and Greene, P.G. (2011) 'Entrepreneurship education: Known worlds and new frontiers', *Journal of Small Business Management*, 49(1), pp. 55–70.

Neergaard, H., Tanggaard, L., Krueger, N.F. and Robinson, S. (2012) *Pedagogical interventions in entrepreneurship from behaviourism to existential learning*. Paper presented at the ISBE 2012 Conference, Dublin.

Neill, A.S. and Fromm, E. (1960) *Summerhill: A Radical Approach to Child Rearing*. Boston, MA: Hart Publishing.

Nyström, H. (1993) 'Creativity and entrepreneurship', *Creativity and Innovation Management*, 2(4), pp. 237–242.

O'Shea, N., Verzat, C., Raucent, B., Ducarme, D., *et al.* (2013) 'Coaching tutors to observe and regulate leadership in PBL student teams or you can lead a horse to water but you can't make it drink …', *Journal of Problem Based Learning in Higher Education*, 1(1), pp. 84–113.

Pavlov, I.P. (2012) *Conditioned Reflexes*. London: Dover Publications.

Pedler, M., Burgoyne, J. and Brook, C. (2005) 'What has action learning learned to become', *Action Learning: Research and Practice*, 2(1), pp. 49–68.

Pelletier, D. (2005) *Invitation à la Culture Entrepreneuriale*. Paris: Septembre éditeur.

Piaget, J. (1975) *L'équilibration des Structures Cognitives: Problème Central du Développement*. Paris: Presses univ. de France.

Pineau, G. (2013) 'Les réflexions sur les pratiques au cœur du tournant réflexif', *Education Permanente*, 196, pp. 9–24.

Politis, D. (2005) 'The process of entrepreneurial learning: A conceptual framework', *Entrepreneurship, Theory and Practice*, 29(4), 399–424.

Raelin, J.A. and Raelin, J.D. (2006) 'Developmental action learning: Toward collaborative change', *Action Learning: Research and Practice*, 3(1), pp. 45–67.

Ramsden, P. (2003) *Learning to Teach in Higher Education*. London and New York: Routledge.

Rapoport, R.N. (1970) 'Three dilemmas in action research with special reference to the Tavistock experience', *Human Relations*, 23(6), pp. 499–513.

Reason, P. and Bradbury-Huang, H. (2007) *The Sage Handbook of Action Research: Participative Inquiry and Practice*. Thousand Oaks, CA: Sage.

Revans, R.W. (1980) *Action Learning: New Techniques for Management*. London: Blond and Briggs.

Sarasvathy, S. (2010) *Entrepreneurship as economics with imagination*. Ruffin Series of the Society for Business Ethics, Ethics and Entrepreneurship 395, Ruffin, NC, p. 112.

Sarasvathy, S.D. (2001) 'Causation and effectuation: Toward a theoretical shift from economic inevitability to entrepreneurial contingency', *Academy of Management Review*, 26(2), pp. 243–263.

Sarasvathy, S.D. (2008) *Effectuation: Elements of Entrepreneurial Expertise*. Cheltenham: Edward Elgar.

Sarasvathy, S.D. and Venkataraman, S. (2011) 'Entrepreneurship as method: Open questions for an entrepreneurial future', *Entrepreneurship Theory and Practice*, 35(1), pp. 113–135.

Sarrouy-Watkins, N. (2014) *La théorie de l'effectuation et l'incertitude du couple produit-marché dans le processus de création d'entreprise*. Université de Reims Champagne-Ardenne.

Schmidt, H.G. and Moust, J.H.C. (1995) *What makes a tutor effective? A structural equations modelling approach to learning in problem-based curricula*. Paper presented at the *Annual Meeting of American Educational Research Association*, San Francisco, CA.

Schmidt, H. and Moust, J.H.C. (2000) 'Factors affecting small-group tutorial learning: A review of research'. In Evensen, D.H. and Hmelo-Silver, C.E. (eds) *Problem-based Learning: A Research Perspective on Learning Interactions*. Mahwah, NJ: Lawrence Erlbaum Associates, pp. 1–21.

Schön, D.A. (1983) *The Reflective Practitioner: How Professionals Think in Action*. New York: Basic Books.

Shane, S. and Venkataraman, S. (2000) 'The promise of entrepreneurship as a field of research', *Academy of Management Review*, 25(1), pp. 217–226.

Skinner, B.F. (1965) *Science and Human Behavior*. New York: Free Press.

Stone, M.M. and Brush, C.G. (1996) 'Planning in ambiguous contexts: The dilemma of meeting needs for commitment and demands for legitimacy', *Strategic Management Journal*, 17(8), pp. 633–652.

Surlemont, B., Fayolle, A. and Filion, L.J. (2009) *Pédagogie et Esprit d'Entreprendre*. Bruxelles: De Boeck.

Taddei, F. (2009) *Training Creative and Collaborative Knowledge-builders: A Major Challenge for 21st Century Education*. Paris: OECD.

Taleb, N.N. (2013) *Antifragile: Things That Gain from Disorder*. New York: Random House.

Thousand, J.S., Villa, R.A. and Nevin, A.I. (1998) *La Créativité et l'Apprentissage Coopératif*. Paris: Les Éditions Logiques.

Toutain, O., Mueller, S., Gaujard, C. and Bornard, F. (2014) 'Dans quel Ecosystème Educatif Entrepreneurial vous retrouvez-vous?', *Entreprendre & Innover*, 23.

Tsoukas, H. and Dooley, K.J. (2011) 'Introduction to the Special Issue: Towards the ecological style', *Organization Studies*, 32(6), pp. 729–735.

Verzat, C. and Garant, M. (2010) 'L'accompagnement des étudiants dans les institutions d'enseignement supérieur'. In Raucent, B., Verzat, C. and Villeneuve, L. (eds) *Accompagner des Étudiants: Quels Rôles Pour l'Enseignant? Quels Dispositifs? Quelles Mises en Œuvre?* Bruxelles: De Boeck, p. 563.

Vial, M., Caparros-Mencacci, N. and Ketele, J.-M.D. (2007) *L'Accompagnement Professionnel? Méthode à l'Usage des Praticiens Exerçant une Fonction Éducative*. Bruxelles: De Boeck.

Vierset, V., Bédard, D. and Foidart, J.M. (2009) 'La psychosociologie: Un cadre inter-prétatif de la fonction de tuteur dans un dispositif d'apprentissage par problèmes', *Pédagogie Médicale*, 10(3), pp. 211–228.

Vygotsky, L.S. (1934) *Language and Thought*. Cambridge, MA: MIT University Press.

Watson, J.B. (1970) *Behaviorism*. New York: Norton.

Winter, R. (1996) 'Some principles and procedures for the conduct of action research'. In Zuber-Skrerritt, O. (ed.) *New Directions of Action Research*. Bristol: Falmer Press, pp. 9–22.

Wouters, P., Parmentier, P. and Lebrun, M. (2003) *Formation pédagogique et développement professionnel des professeurs d'université*. Communication présentée au colloque de l'AECSE (Association des Enseignants et Chercheurs en Sciences de l'Education), Toulouse.

Yin, R.K. (2013) *Case Study Research: Design and Methods*. Los Angeles, CA: Sage.

Zacharakis, Z. (2015) *Welcome foreword to the Babson College Entrepreneurship Research Conference*. Presentation at the Babson Conference.

Zeichner, K. (2001) 'Educational action research'. In Reason, P. and Bradbury, H. (eds) *Handbook of Action Research: Participative Enquiry and Practice*. Thousand Oaks, CA: Sage, pp. 273–283.

Zuber-Skerrit, O. (1992) 'Improving learning and teaching through action learning and action research', *Higher Education Research and Development*, 12(1), pp. 45–58.

Appendix to Chapter 7

Table A.1 Articles using the terms 'critical' or 'critique' and 'entrepreneurship' in title

No	Date	Topic	Theories used/ emphasis	Author	Country context/ Theory	Journal
Critical review of a theme/topic/sub domain						
1	2003	Graduate entrepreneurship	Critical review of problems	McLarty	UK	Inter. J. of Entrepreneurship and Innovation Management
2	2003	Entrepreneurial learning	Critical reflection on learning from discontinuous events	Cope	Theory	Management Learning
3	2006	Education and training	Critical assessment	Ibrahim & Soufani	Canada	Education and Training
4	2007	Critique of network concept in entrepreneurship	Discusses two strands of network research	O'Donnell, Gilmore & Cummins	Review	Management Decision
5	2005	Entrepreneurship, innovation and marketing (EIM)	Develop conceptualization of critical linkages between (EIM)	Swami & Porwal	Theory	Journal of Advances in Management
6	2008	Social entrepreneurship in a transitional economy	How rural Chinese enterprises act as social entrepreneurial institutions	Poon, Zhou & Chan	China	Journal of Management Development
7	2007	SME internationalization	Critique and policy implications	Wright, Westhead & Ucbasaran	Review/ theory	Regional Studies
8	2009	Research methods in the leading small business-entrepreneurship journals	Critical review of use of research methods	Mullen, Budeva & Doney	Review	Journal of Small Business Management
9	2009	Transnationalizing entre-preneurship	Spatially informed synthesis of transnational entrepreneurship for economic geography	Yeung	Theory/ review	Progress in Human Geography

No	Date	Topic	Theories used/ emphasis	Author	Country context/ Theory	Journal
10	2010	E-entrepreneurship	E-entrepreneurship as a method of recruitment	Lewis, Daunton, Thomas & Sanders	UK	Inter. Journal of E-Entrepreneurship and Innovation
11	2011	Social entrepreneurship	Critical review of social entrepreneurship as a new discipline	Dacin, Dacin & Tracey	Review	Organization Science
12	2011	Social entrepreneurship	Critical discourse analysis	Mason	Theory	Social Enterprise Journal
13	2012	Social entrepreneurship	Habermas/ critical theory	Teasdale & Mason	Theory	Social Enterprise Journal
14	2012	International entrepreneurship	Critical review and research agenda	Kiss, Danis, & Tamer Cavusgil	Review/ Emergent economies	Journal of Business Venturing
15	2012	International entrepreneurship	Critical analysis over 20 years	Peiris, Akoorie & Sinha	Review	J. of International Entrepreneurship
16	2012	The role of trust in entrepreneurship	Review of relationship between trust and entrepreneurship	Welter & Smallbone	Theory	Inter. Journal of Small Business Management
17	2013	Sustainability entrepreneurship	Sustainability/ critical management studies	Levinson	Theory	Inter. Journal of Entrepreneurship and Innovation
18	2013	E-recruitment	E-recruitment in e-entrepreneurship	Lewis, Daunton & Sanders	UK	Inter. Journal of E-Entrepreneurship and Innovation
19	2013	Off the books' entrepreneurship	Compares competing theories about the informal economy	William, Nadin, Newton, Rodgers & Windebank	Theory	Inter. Entrepreneurship and Management Journal
20	2013	Challenges political ideals; argues for sustainable development and social justice as bases for entrepreneurship	Presents alternative narratives used in education by 15–16-year-old pupils	Komulainen, Korhonen & Raty	Finland	International Journal of Qualitative Studies in Education
21	2014	Informal entrepreneurship	Critical evaluation of the neo-liberal approach	Williams & Youseff	Latin America	J. Entrepreneurial Organizational Management
22	2014	The use of global entrepreneurship monitor data in academic research: a critical inventory and future potentials	Critical review and inventory of journal articles using Global Entrepreneurship Monitor data	Bergmann, Mueller & Schrettle	Multiple countries	International Journal of Entrepreneurial Venturing

No	Date	Topic	Theories used / emphasis	Author	Country context / Theory	Journal
23	2014	Human capital and entrepreneurship research	Critical review	Theory	Review	Entrepreneurship Theory and Practice

Critical study of a 'standpoint' issue to overcome marginalized experiences/contexts

No	Date	Topic	Theories used / emphasis	Author	Country context / Theory	Journal
24	2000	Immigrant entrepreneurship	A critical review of outsiders	Rath & Kloosterman	The Netherlands	International Migration Review
25	2001	Ethnic entrepreneurship	The role of black entrepreneurs in the hip hop industry	Basu & Werbner	US	Ethnic and Racial Studies
26	2008	African entrepreneurship	Impediments to entrepreneurship	Onuoha	Nigeria	African Journal of Entrepreneurship
27	2010	Entrepreneurship: a critical outlook on housing developers	Characteristics of indigenous/ non-indigenous housing developers	Jaafar & Aziz	Malaysia	International Journal of Construction Management
28	2011	Women entrepreneurs	Critical issues and challenges	Sarbapriya & Ray	India	J. of Contemporary Business Studies
29	2012	Entrepreneurship development among women	Need for a holistic view of entrepreneurship development	Singh	India	Journal of Business Diversity
30	2012	Entrepreneurship development amongst academic women		Lau, Haug & Wright	US	Journal of Business Diversity
31	2012	Black African transnational entrepreneurs	Transition from ethnic enclave to disaspora	Ojo	London, UK	Journal of African Business
32	2012	Gender, entrepreneurship and firm performance	An epistemological critique	Marlow & McAdam	Theory	Inter. J. of Entrepreneurial Behaviour and Research
33	2013	Critical issues for women	Challenges faced by women entrepreneurs	Kumbhar	India	European Academic Research

Critical research practices

No	Date	Topic	Theories used / emphasis	Author	Country context / Theory	Journal
34	2006	Critical realist approach to institutional entrepreneurship	How to consider actors' actions and structures without conflating them	Leca & Naccache	Theory	Organization
35	2010	Structuration of individual and opportunity	Critical realist comment	Mole & Mole	Theory	Journal of Business Venturing
36	2013	Structural antecedents of institutional entrepreneurship in industrial networks: a critical realist explanation	How a critical realist epistemology can facilitate a more multi-layered explanation of collective change	Matthyssens, Vanden-bempt & Bockhaven	Theory	Industrial Marketing Management

No	Date	Topic	Theories used/ emphasis	Author	Country context/ Theory	Journal
Critical entrepreneurship						
37	2000	The effects of ideological control	Entrepreneurship as discriminatory, gender-biased and ethno-centric	Ogbor	Theory	Journal of Management Studies
38	2005	Critique of entrepreneurship	Ideological critique	Armstrong	Theory	Book
39	2012	Social entrepreneurship	Radical enactment of the social through five types of critical research	Dey & Steyaert	Theory	Social Enterprise Journal
40	2012	Challenging assumptions/ ideologies/ methodologies	Challenges functionalist nature of entrepreneurship	Tedmanson, Verduyn, Essers & Gartner	Theory	Organization
41	2011	Critical theories of entrepreneurship	Connects entrepreneurship to patterns of power and domination	Spicer	Theory	Book
42	2014	Conceptualise criticality	Four interpretations of emancipation	Verduijn, Dey, Tedmanson & Essers	Theory	Inter. J. of Entrepreneurial Behaviour and Research

Appendix to Chapter 11

Box A.1 The ALICE-lab experimentation

1. What does this module consist of?

It's a 13-week training module (60h), which brings together interdisciplinary students and executives in a team around an innovation project commissioned by the firms. Five firms participated in the programme. Each team was counselled by entrepreneurial coaches and experts with various academic and professional profiles. Using a participatory, collaborative approach, the teams had to get to know each other and then get to grips with the project by trying to understand the initial problem area identified. They were encouraged to avoid preconceived solutions. The assessment contract was negotiated with each team: they had to develop their own specific grid based on the four educational objectives of the entrepreneurial mindset development which resulted from my post-doctoral research work: identify an opportunity, design a realistic innovative project, marshall and manage resources, and demonstrate value creation. In the end, they evaluated themselves and each student had to reflect individually on the experience by analysing events and highlighting lessons that could be turned into skills for their future career.

2. To what degree is this module innovative?

I think it's a radical innovation for several reasons. Firstly, there isn't any unanimity in academic literature on what the entrepreneurial mindset really means or what the learning outcomes should be. They emerged during the process, which is an unfamiliar approach. Secondly, having such a diverse range of people in the same educational module had never been tried out, observed or analysed in literature. Thirdly, for each stakeholder, for example, my institution or for the firms involved, the disruption caused by this experiment has been clearly perceived. Finally, from a research point of view, we tried out a new way of producing results by testing our new business model for Entrepreneurship Education.

3. How did this innovation develop? Are there different phases? With whom? What were the results?

According to me there are three phases. Firstly, we focused on stimulating imagination and designing our new business model with the Alice-lab community of researchers. We organized a final workshop to test our concept with two entrepreneurs. Then, we explored our environment, trying to propose our programme to potential stakeholders (partner firms, schools and incubator). As a result, it helped us to progressively shape our proposal and to enrol support from a big firm that wanted to experiment this programme. Finally, we launched the programme and during its implementation, I had to continuously negotiate the means and objectives, balance with resources and manage conflicts.

4. What is the research process associated with this pedagogical innovation?

I wanted to exploit the opportunity offered by the Paris Chamber of Commerce that organizes funding for research projects. That's why I built an action-research project, which brought together several researchers from different schools. I aimed at experimenting and testing a new educative business model. Many issues and questions in entrepreneurship education were at stake. Consequently, I carried out this action research by using conceptual notions and reflection during the experiment. We participated at conferences writing papers on what we were currently experiencing, what we progressively learnt – thanks to the different tests. This is a sort of organic research approach where we revealed what happened.

5. To what degree can this research process be considered different from those usually performed in entrepreneurship research?

The first time we presented our research, they asked: 'sorry, but where is the research?' because we didn't undertake it traditionally using hypothesis, or predictive protocol. But how do you analyse something that is marching on? It's so innovative that we couldn't have forecast anything. We carried it out as an effectual research. We are now conscious of the fact that we are not in the mainstream and that's a totally new way to carry out research. However, some international researchers demonstrated a high level of interest in our project and think that we dared do something very differently that could highlight new perspectives. I am convinced that it is the right way despite the concrete evidence we still have to provide.

6. In what sense can educational designers of this pedagogical innovation be considered as entrepreneurs?

Up to now I was not personally an entrepreneur even if I was in an entrepreneurial environment. For this original experiment I was surrounded by incubators, entrepreneurs, coaches and experts. Due to the fact that I knew about effectuation theory, I definitely practised it by reasoning with many effectual cycles! For instance when problems appeared, I was looking for resources around me, identifying what I can control or not, who are the relevant stakeholders, how to manage the euphoric and depressive phases of any entrepreneurial project. In addition it was impossible to forecast details for each class-run. We can finally draw practical lessons from this experience such as how to sell the project, how to plan and how to provide sufficient results for companies.

Box A.2 The MOOC experimentation

1. What does this module consist of?

The second case is the creation of a MOOC (massive open online course) to teach Effectuation. It is an introduction to entrepreneurship, and more specifically to Effectuation (Sarasvathy 2001). It was a six-week course (1 hour per week) with quizzes and a peer-graded case study based on a real start-up. There was no prerequisite so the audience was broad. In terms of learning objectives, we wanted participants to understand how entrepreneurs think and act, realize that this can be done by anybody, and therefore gain the confidence to do it themselves.

2. To which degree is this module innovative?

The module was innovative in the sense that it was one of the first business MOOCs, and the first on entrepreneurship in French. It was subtitled 'Entrepreneurship for everybody' and based on effectuation to promote the idea that everybody can be an entrepreneur, regardless of age, gender, education, country of origin and approach to entrepreneurship. It was also the first to feature a real start-up as a case study with the active involvement of the founder.

3. How did this innovation develop? Are there different phases? With whom? What were the results?

I became interested in MOOCs in the summer of 2012 after the success of Stanford's MOOC. I trained as a software scientist, I love technology and I have always been interested in innovation (which I also teach and research). I joined academia late, after a long career as an entrepreneur, and I grew disappointed by academia's focus on abstract research and the corresponding lack of interest in pedagogy. As a result, it immediately seemed very clear to me that MOOCs were a unique opportunity for those who were interested in pedagogy. Given my knowledge of IT, I also thought that MOOCs would impact business schools through their disruptive effects and I felt confident I could handle such a project. I started to forward articles on MOOCs to a few colleagues, and lobbied them to join me in trying to have the school do a MOOC. We met to discuss this several times. Two of them were part of the school's executive committee and, in November 2012, they managed to convince the committee to give it a try and launch a MOOC. We had no idea how one did a MOOC nor did we know what to expect in terms of participation.

4. What is the research process associated with this pedagogical innovation?

Launching the MOOC was a step into the unknown but my reasoning was simple: if we want to understand what MOOCs are about, the only way is to produce one. The field is so new that classic research through interviews or literature review would have yielded nothing. By doing so, we were consistent with effectuation, which is my field of specialization, in that action is the root cause of novelty in the world (Sarasvathy). Initially we tried to sign an agreement to develop the course with Coursera, a pioneering MOOC provider. When that failed, we decided to produce the course ourselves and we found a platform and an operator. So we had to learn how to manage the technical side in addition to the pedagogical side. So the research covered what to teach, how to teach it (you cannot just film a normal lecture) and how to organize the course. Every person involved in the project (including communication) had to learn something new.

5. To which degree can this research process be considered different from those usually performed in entrepreneurship research?

The particularity of this research project is that it is based on action. It mixes academics and non-academics (the platform provider, the support staff). We set out to create the MOOC by inventing what needed to be invented and acting as reflective practitioners. We capitalized our knowledge by writing about lessons learned in blogs and by developing academic research on how a MOOC helps learn entrepreneurial skills. Unlike traditional research projects, the production of knowledge is not aimed only at an academic audience, but also at professionals and the general public so that all can learn and contribute, which is typical of action research. In addition, and in line with effectuation, the process is also aimed at creating a new education market with innovative business models.

6. In what sense can educational designers of this pedagogical innovation be considered as entrepreneurs?

The MOOC certainly was an entrepreneurial process in the sense of the creation of a new social artefact (Simon, Sarasvathy). The social artefact is not only the MOOC, that is, a set of new resources (videos, quizzes, exercises, etc.) but also a network of stakeholders: the participants, the online community (forums, Facebook, LinkedIn) and associations created around the MOOC. Because it was disruptive, the school found it difficult to define the institutional setting for the MOOC once past the experimental stage, and fundamental questions were raised such as who should be in charge of MOOC within the organization? Who should pay? What business model should we have, etc.?

Index

Page numbers in *italics* denote tables, those in **bold** denote figures.

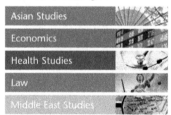